Pa[illegible]her Geography

National Qualification Revision Notes

written by
Mike Townsend
Principal Teacher of Social Subjects
Sgoil Lionacleit, Benbecula
Western Isles

edited by
Ritchie Cunningham
Headteacher
Inverness High School,
Inverness, Highland

designed by
Eddie Broadley
Headteacher
Glen Urquhart High School,
Inverness-shire, Highland

CB PUBLISHING Ltd
Inverness

Acknowledgements

The publishers and the author wish to acknowledge and thank the following sources which were used as a basis for research, for figures or text.. Every effort has been made to trace and acknowledge all copyright holders, but if any have been inadvertently overlooked, the publishers will be pleased to make any necessary arrangements.

Corel Gallery for Macintosh Clip Art Libraries : Digital Vision "Views of the Earth': CB Publishing Ltd for a wide variety of sources taken from various texts and copymasters sets including the following - Credit Geography 1999, Core Topics Copymaster sets (Atmosphere / Hydrosphere, Lithosphere / Biosphere, Rural / Urban Geography, Population / Rural Geography, Development & Health), People and Place Textbook and Copymaster Sets D/D/E+ : Gemini Graphics for various artworks used throughout the text : Bob McAllister (for inspiration and excellence) : Yorkshire Dales National Park Authority (for various sources) ; Lake District National Park (for various sources) : Culbin Forest (Forest Enterprise) - various sources : Population Concern ; Christian Aid ; Oxfam : Comic Relief Organisation : David Waugh (The British Isles, The World, Integrated Approach, etc) : Broadley & Cunningham (Core Themes Geography - both 'Physical' and 'Human' texts - Longman UK) : Broadley & Goring (Studies in Geography - Books 1 & 2 - Oliver & Boyd) : Meadowhall Shopping Centre, Sheffield : 'Lakeland View' - periodical : Earthwatch issue 9 : Third World Guide 1999 : Gaia Atlas of Planet Management, Gaia Peace Atlas, Gaia First Peoples, Gaia Atlas of Future Worlds (N.Meyers et al. Pan Books) : Highlands & Islands Enterprise (Inverness) : Alan Doherty (various inspirational ideas and sources) : Landshapes (Goudie, Brunsden et al.) : Themes in Human geography (Mel Rockett, Arnold-Wheaton) : N.Thomson & K.MacLean, Landscapes and people of Western Europe, Oxford; The Geographical Magazine (various issues) : B.Knapp, Systematic Geography, Unwin-Hyman : Lines & Bolwell, Revise GCSE Geography, Letts : Baterman & Rowles, Examining GCSE Geography , Stanley Thornes : J.Seager (ed), The State of the Earth Atlas, Unwin; G.N.Minshull, The New Europe, Hodder & Stoughton; Seymour & Girardet, Blueprint for a Green Planet, Dorling Kindersley : P.Knox, Urban Social Geography, Longman: R.Collard, The Physical Geography of Landscape, Unwin-Hyman; Galbraith & Weigand, Landforms, Oxford : C.Clarke, Themes in Geography (Physical, Human Environment, International Issues), Hodder & Stoughton : The New Oxford School Atlas, Oxford : The Guardian Newspaper, London : The Observer Newspaper, London : A.Goudie, Nature of the Environment, Blackwell Scientific; BBC2 Horizon programme "China's Child" 1984 : Oxfam and Save the Children, U.K. : UNCTAD, 1995; ICO, 1996; ICCO, 1997 : New Scientist (various issues): E.Broadley would also like to thank J.Smith and B.Njoku (Gemini) for their advice and help.

The publishers wish to apologise in advance should there be any omissions.

The publishers and the author wish to thank the following for permission to reproduce photographs :
M.Townsend (Cover photo, 63, 111, 167-168, 195, 225), Gemini Newscan International (217, 222), J.Swinton (183, 184), J.Spence (141l + r)
E.Broadley (figs. 43, 50, 117, 118, 136-138, 196), Aerofilms (120), S.Paul (69a, 157), J.Hocking (223), A.Bendick (159)
A special thanks to Jessie Anne MacDonald for her patience and efficiency in typing the original manuscript.

Dedicated to Maighread and Iain.

Cover and book design by CB Publishing Ltd, Inverness 1999. Front cover photograph by Mike Townsend. Back cover of the UK by satellite from Digital Vision 'Views of the Earth' CD of stock photography - well worth investigating.

Illustrated by Eddie Broadley and Ritchie Cunningham.

Published by **CB Publishing Ltd**
18 Lochlann Terrace
Culloden
Inverness IV2 7PZ

First edition 2000

ISBN 0 -872985-39-4

Typeset in Helvetica Narrow, Charcoal Bold and Nadianne on the Apple Macintosh by Eddie Broadley.
Produced in Drumnadrochit, Inverness-shire, Scotland.
Printed in Forres, Morayshire, Scotland by Ainster Press Ltd.

Cover photograph by Mike Townsend

Contents

Introduction

What this book covers

Key Points of Knowledge
These Higher Geography Revision Notes cover all aspects of the course, providing students with a simplified skeleton of the key points covered by the course.

Summaries for each Core/Application
Each section contains a useful summary of what you need to know for your revision and preparation.

Sample assessments and/or exam questions
In addition, at the end of each section of these notes there are sample exam questions and / or assessments which you can attempt against the clock to judge your own progress through your revision and preparation.

Glossary of key words and ideas
At the end of these notes there is a glossary of the key words used within the Geography course.

At the end of each page
Shade in the white page circle to show you have read and understood everything. *(Look below, beside the page number)*

The Higher Geography course

The course - sometimes referred to as ***Higher Still Higher Geography*** or the **National Qualification in Geography at Higher Level** - is made up of two compulsory units :

Geography : Core (H)	**2 credits (80 hours)**
Geography : Applications (H)	**1 credit (40 hours)**

In addition to the 120 hours the Higher Geography course is planned to take in school, there are an extra 40 hours built in so that teachers and pupils can revise, go over more difficult sections, sit unit assessments and prepare for the final, external examination.

A successful award in Higher Geography

To successfully gain an award in Higher Geography students must be organised in **two ways** -

- Revise, prepare and sit unit assessments for the three credits during the Geography course - the Physical Core, the Human Core and the Applications unit
- Revise, prepare and sit the external examination at the end of the Geography course.

To do so successfully, students should -

- know the structure of the Higher Geography course
- read, learn and thoroughly know the various parts of each of the Core and Application units chosen
- Revise and thoroughly prepare for each of the unit/credit assessments and go on to use their revision preparations for a thorough revision in the build up to their final, external examination.

The Higher Geography course is structured as follows -

Core Geography
2 units based on the main theories developed and used within Geography, and the course aims to build on what you learned in Standard Grade. The two units studied are -

Physical Core	*Atmosphere*
	Hydrosphere
	Lithosphere
	Biosphere
Human Core	*Population Geography*
	Rural Geography
	Industrial geography
	Urban Geography

Students must sit internal (school-based) assessments, - for the Physical Core and for the Human Core units, as listed above. Success in both unit assessments will give the student the opportunity to sit the final, external examination at the end of the Higher Geography course.

Applications Geography
There is a choice within the Applications unit as the applications are divided into two groups of three. Students will be required to study three Applications; one from each of the two groups and a third from either group. This part of the course aims to give students the opportunity to develop aspects of the physical and human cores in real-life situations in various parts of the world. The two groups are -

Group One
Application (a) - Rural Land Resources
Application (b) - Rural Land Degradation
Application (c) - River Basin Management

Group Two
Application (d) - Urban Change and its management
Application (e) - European Regional Inequalities
Application (f) - Development and Health

In order to gain a credit (pass) in the Application Unit, students must attain all three outcomes (parts of the assessment). Students must do so in relation to **one** of the applications from Group One, and **one** of the applications from Group Two plus a **third** application from either Group One or Group Two. Success in the unit assessment will give the student the opportunity to sit the external examination at the end of the Higher Geography course.

Geographical Methods and Techniques (GMT)
Candidates must also pass one Physical and one Human GMT assessment within the Higher Geography course. These are labelled in this book as **GMT** in the assessment sections.

***Preparation and thorough revision are essential for success at Higher Geography** - read page 4 for a simple but essential guide to preparing yourself properly*

1 Plan Ahead

- Work out a Revision Timetable - start planning well before your exams begin
- Make your books, notes, jotters and essays more user-friendly - add summary notes, sub-headings, highlight words and make revision cards. Use key words lists or spider charts. Make large know-it-all sheets (A3 size) - do what works for you
- Everyone revises differently - find out what routine works best for you - working alone or with someone else; mornings or nights, always work in short sharp bursts of 25-30 minutes at a time & take short breaks in between
- Take notes of important (or key) points when revising - do this in a jotter for each subject or in headed folder sections - this will help for future revision. Try previous exam questions - set against the clock - try explaining answers to difficult questions to someone else
- Ask for help if there are things you don't understand.
- If you are feeling stressed out, talk to someone.

2 Don'ts

- Don't leave revision to the last minute
- Don't avoid revising subjects you find difficult or don't like
- Don't forget that there is life beyond revision and exams
- Don't cram ALL night before an exam
- Don't revise all the time - a good revision plan means planning leisure time and breaks for things you like to do
- Don't PANIC !

3 Prepare for the big day

- Have a good breakfast if you can
- Give yourself plenty of time to get to the exam room
- Make sure you know which exams are on which days in which rooms
- Take everything you will need with you - extra pens, pencils, calculators, tissues, etc
- Visit the loo before going in to the exam
- Read over your examination instructions sheet
- If really feel anxious breathe slowly and deeply while waiting for the exam to start

4 Pace yourself

- Read the instructions for each exam - ask the invigilator if anything is unclear
- Read all of the questions, twice if necessary, give your self time to think before diving in to each question
- If you are stuck with a question, go on to the next one - you can always come back to the unfinished one later
- If you are really stuck, try to have an intelligent guess!
- Leave time to read through and check your answers before the exam finishes

Don't drown in a sea of work - follow these simple steps and survive !

Do your best 5

- YOU'RE YOU - you can only do your best on the day of each exam
- Knowing that you have done your best can help overcome feelings of letting anyone down
- Don't go through the answers afterwards with friends - it only helps make you more worried
- Look ahead to the next exam - you can't go back and change things - always try to be positive

6 Parents

- Give encouragement, not pressure
- Give your support not criticism
- Make it easy for your child to study
- Keep things in perspective
- Get advice from the school if you are worried
- Exams are important - but they are not the only key to a successful future

Revision tips and suggestions

Make a revision plan

Prepare yourself for revision. Sort out all your Geography notes into sections - Core and Applications.

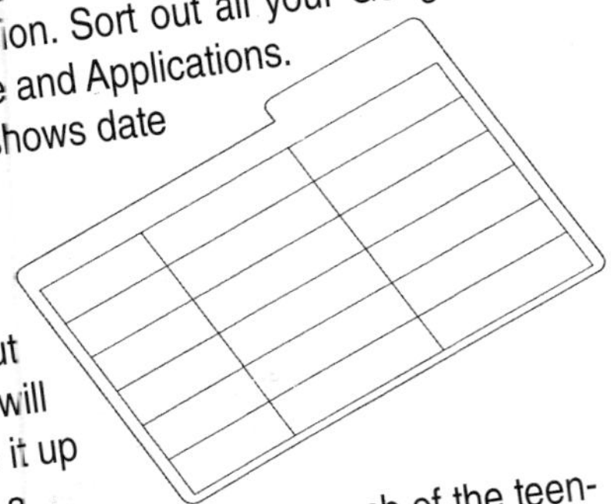

Draw up a table which shows date times, sections to be revised, when you will try practice exam questions. Do this about two weeks before you will start your revision. Pin it up in your room. Sort out a desk or table to sit at and clear away as much of the teen-age clutter as you can. What looks organised helps you to clearer thinking in the long run!

Revising sections of the course 2

Make yourself a whole lot of **'revision cards'** about postcard size or a little larger. For each section of the Higher Geography course, for example **Lithosphere,** use lots of cards and on each one choose a sub-section, say glaciation, carboniferous limestone scenery, weathering, slopes, etc. Neatly write (and high-light) all the Key Words & Ideas for each sub-section. Use these in your final preparations before the big day. **See pages 129 to 132 for examples of revision cards.**

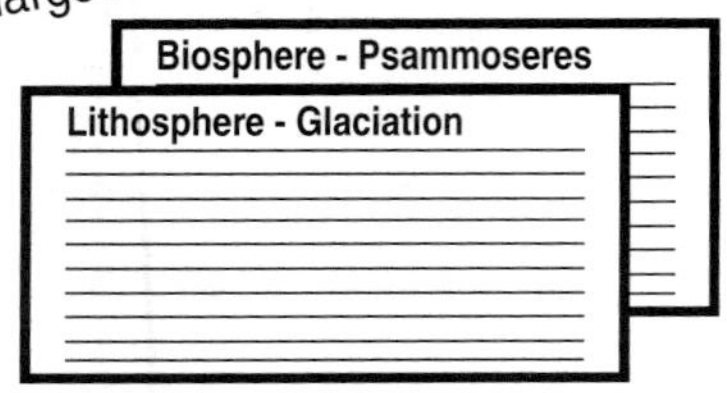

Revising sections of the course 1

Obtain some large white sheets of A3 size paper (or even the back of unused wallpaper). Have enough sheets, one for each section of the Higher Geography course. Call them your **"All I need to know"** or master sheets. Take each section of your notes (and the corresponding section of these revision notes and pick out then write and illustrate each of the **Key Points** or important **Ideas** associated with the section of work.

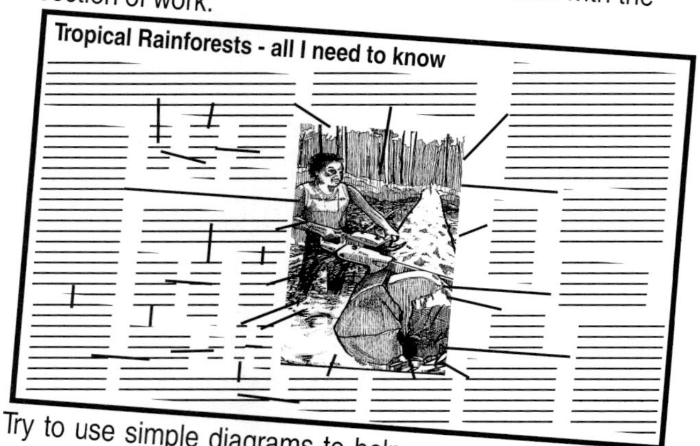

Try to use simple diagrams to help you revise. See if you can interlink or connect the Key Words or Ideas. Work out what **relationships exist** as you go along. This will help you with the assessment and/or exam questions. Use **colour** to highlight important points and shade in the diagrams so that you end up with a colourful master sheet.

Revision know how

Putting these ideas for good and thorough revision together would see you as the **learner at the centre of a planned programme**. Whatever you do make sure that you plan it well, include lots of short, intense learning sessions broken up by short breaks - these help keep your concentration levels high for longer. Include leisure and social time in your plan. **Vary your revision** so that you avoid boredom as much as possible. The best theories of learning tell us that learners must return to what they have learned frequently and that active revision (writing, drawing, etc) is always the best way.....

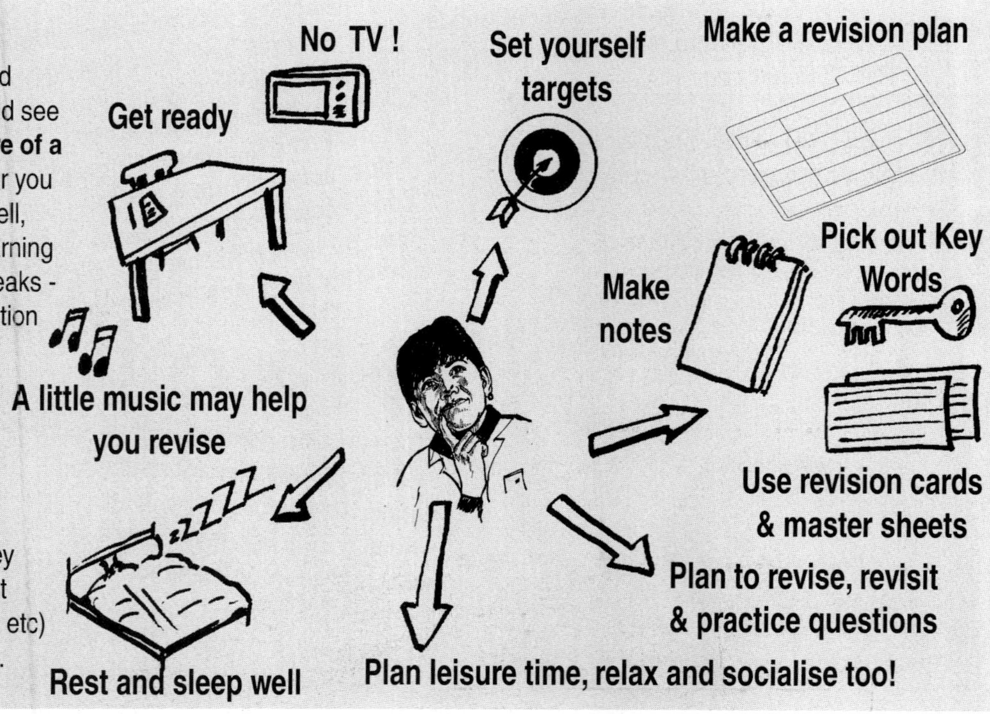

Before the Unit assessments.....

Before the unit assessments, find out more about -

what to expect in the way of likely questions

- look at the end of each section of these notes for some ideas.

which learning outcomes are being assessed

- these are described below and can be checked against the sample assessments at the end of each section of these notes - it's well worth spending a little while reading these and looking at the sample questions. Try to get a feel for what to expect.

the conditions under which you will sit the assessments

- ask about when you will be asked to sit them, how long you can expect to be given to answer them fully, and remember you will not be able to have access to your books or these notes when you sit the assessments !

You are on your own - so be as well prepared as possible....

Learning Outcomes (what you are expected to be able to show evidence of) for..................the..

Can you follow instructions ?

Try this three minute test of your ability to follow instructions. Set yourself 3 minutes...ready ? **START....**

1. Read everything before you do anything.
2. Put your name in the top right corner of this page.
3. Circle the word 'name' in the second sentence above.
4. Draw five small squares in the top left corner of this page.
5. Put an X is each square mentioned in sentence 4 above.
6. Put a circle around each square.
7. Sign your name at the foot of this page.
8. After the signature write "Yes, Yes, Yes".
9. Draw a circle around sentences 3 and 7.
10. Draw a triangle in this space......
11. Write down the answer to 17 x 11 - here.....
12. Draw a circle around the word 'circle' in sentence 6.
13. Loudly call your name now and then check the clock.
14. If you think you can follow instructions well call out... "I can follow instructions well !"
15. Add 107 and 458 - write the answer here -
16. Put a circle around your answer to sentence 11.
17. Count out in your normal speaking voice from one to ten.
18. What is the capital of Chile ? - write answer here -
19. Repeat sentence 14. Hurry time is running out!!
20. Now that you have finished reading carefully, do only sentences one and two.

What did you learn from this exercise ?

Physical and Human Core

Learning Outcome 1

Explain the major systems of physical geography with reference to different scales and change over time.

Learning Outcome 2

Explain the major systems of human geography with reference to different scales and change over time.

For both Learning Outcomes 1 and 2, show this through

a. The identification and description of the geographical phenomena which are accurate and clear

b. The explanation of the geographical phenomena is accurate and clearly expressed.

Learning Outcome 3

Demonstrate a knowledge, understanding and application of geographical methods and techniques.

Show this through.....

a. The application of the method and technique is appropriate, clear and accurate

b. The interpretation, explanation and conclusions reached are clear and valid

Applications Geography

Learning Outcome 1

Describe the physical environment and human activity and explain the ways in which they interact.

Show this through.....

a. The description of the physical environment or its formation is accurate and clear.
b. The description of the human environment or activity which is accurate and clear.
c. The detailed explanation of the interaction which is accurate and clear.
d. The explanation of the environmental consequences or issues arising from the interaction is accurate and clear.

Learning Outcome 2

Interpret and analyse complex geographical information.

Show this through.....

a. The interpretation of information is accurate.
b. The analysis is accurate, takes account of the information which may include differing points of view and indicate relationships.

Learning Outcome 3

Describe and evaluate possible strategies for environmental management or solutions to the issues arising from the interaction.

Show this through.....

a. The descriptions, strategies or solutions are accurate & detailed
b. The evaluation of strategies or solutions is valid.

Before the final Exam........

Before the final exam, check the length of each paper and the **number of questions** you have to answer in a **set time** i.e.

Length of exams

Suggested time allocation -

Paper 1 (Core) 1 hr 25 mins = 8 questions - approx 10 mins each question.

Paper 2 (Applications) 1 hr 20 mins = 2 questions - approx 40 mins each question.

Note that **time** must be allowed for **reading the questions** and **checking over the answers** at the end.

Is time running out for you ?

In the Exam.......

- Check the **instructions** on the front of the paper i.e. exactly how many **questions** to be answered and from which section.
- Look for and highlight **key words** in each question. i.e. for a **named case study** area, describe and explain **social** and **economic** consequences and **comment** on **effectiveness** of **solutions**.
  Don't forget that marks will be given for following **each instruction**. (If you fail to answer the whole question, you will lose vital marks).
- Check the number of **marks** for each question/section and adjust your answer length accordingly. Make sure that the points you make are relevant and write in **sentences**. Unless specified, avoid using lists (i.e. your points should be able to stand on their own and be clearly understood).
- You may leave **gaps** between your answers. This allows you to add extra points later on.
- Use **named examples** to back up your answers. It is also important to **quote** values from graphs, tables etc. presented in the question. (Don't forget that one aspect of the exam is testing your ability to use information).
- Try to use simple but well labelled **diagrams** and/or **sketches** as part of your answers. Markers always give credit for the use of such illustrations. Always **refer** to your diagrams in your written answer.
- Use real **named examples** at every opportunity in your answers. State clearly what areas, examples, places, problems you have studied as part of an answer.
- With **map questions** it is helpful to mark in **pencil** key points / squares/lines of cross-sections etc. This will save time and avoid confusion when answering the questions.
- Give 6 figure grid references for evidence to support your answers.
- Read over and **always check your answers** before the end of the exam paper. Add in anything you left space for earlier. If you have failed to complete a question in the time try a **quick attempt** at it by writing its number, its main heading and a quick list of **bullet points** which may gain you a couple of marks. These may be vital to your success!

SUMMARY OF FINAL EXAM TIPS

Check front of paper for key instructions

Check marks available for each question/section

Highlight key words in each question

Study and quote evidence from sources (maps, diagrams, graphs, etc.)

Write in sentences. Leave a gap after each section

Use simple diagrams, sketches or other relevant illustrations

Always try to give named examples

Read answers carefully. Add extra points if time allows

Success !

UNDERSTANDING THE QUESTION

Many marks are lost in exams through candidates not understanding or answering the question. Below are lists of **instructions** and **key words** commonly used in **Geography** papers:-

INSTRUCTION	*MEANING - what to do*
Account for	Give reasons and explain
Analyse	Examine in detail and comment on
Annotate the sketch	Label the key features
Assess	Consider the importance of
Comment on	Identify the key points, give brief explanation
Compare	Examine similarities and differences
Contrast	Point out the main differences
Describe	Write down the main characteristics
Discuss	Provide different opinions on a subject
Examine	Look carefully and closely at
Explain	Given reasons for, why, how etc.
Identify	To point out and name
Locate	State where a place or feature is
Outline	Note the main points
Rank	Place in order of size
Select	Choose
Suggest	Provide an idea or reason

Stress busters - a ten point checklist for students facing the final exams

Deep anxiety will really stop you performing to your best in the final exam. The only real answer is to be as well prepared as you possibly can be. Don't be put off by a little nervousness - this may actually help you by generating adrenaline and boosting your thinking and energy in the exam. Use this 10 point checklist to help dispense with anxiety and exam stress.....

1. **Work** through these revision notes and be in control
2. **Be positive** say nice things to yourself, tell yourself you can succeed, congratulate yourself on your successes, treat any failures as a chance to learn and do better next time..
3. **Plan well** do other things as well as revising - plan leisure time, exercise and socialising and time to relax. All work and no play make students very boring robots...
4. **Face up** to those things that are making you anxious. Change yourself, your routine break the exam into different sections and tackle each part. Manage your work in small pieces.
5. **Sleep** get enough and don't study just before lights out. Allow some time to turn off.
6. **Talk to others** your friends who are also facing the same stress are not a good outlet. Find someone else who can take your mind off the exams. Talk to yourself, sing an Ally MacBeal song (imagine your own backing singers if you really have to...)
7. **List** make lists as they can help organise your life and tasks in hand.
8. **Concentrate** think, base your work around key points, focus in on them not your worries.
9. **Keep a sense of proportion** you will survive all of this.
10. **Smile, sing and laugh** these will make you feel better, try them now !

Now read on to page 9 for the first revision section of these notes

2. Atmosphere

The main idea of the Atmosphere section of the Physical Core is....***The characteristics of the atmosphere vary spatially and provide climate and weather conditions which interlink with other systems.***

What do you need to know ?

Students should have a knowledge and understanding of -

A Global scale.......

- effects of the atmosphere on the receipt of radiation at the Earth's surface - causes of latitudinal variation of radiation receipt
- patterns of atmospheric and oceanic circulation and their influence on the redistribution of energy over the globe - principal circulation cells, pressure and wind belts, influence of ocean currents
- global climate change - physical and human causes of global warming
- *interpretation of climatic maps, diagrams & graphs*

B Regional scale.......

- nature, origin and movement of air masses, including convergence and divergence
- weather types associated with different air masses
- role of continental tropical and maritime air masses on West African climate - particularly rainfall amounts & distribution
- *construction and analysis of climate graphs.*

This section focuses firstly on the major global climatic influences and then considers, in more detail, factors which produce climatic variation on a regional scale.

Energy exchange in the Earth-Atmosphere system

Energy comes into the system from the **Sun**, while the system energy is exchanged between Earth and its atmosphere.
99% of the atmosphere is made up of just two gases - **Nitrogen** and **Oxygen.** A futher 0.93% is made up of **Argon**. The remainder includes a significant number of other gases including **Carbon Dioxide** and **Ozone**.
The composition of the atmosphere **varies with altitude** and also close to industrial areas where various pollutants seriously affect air quality. Close to oceans and seas, **Water Vapour** makes up a significant proportion of the atmosphere.

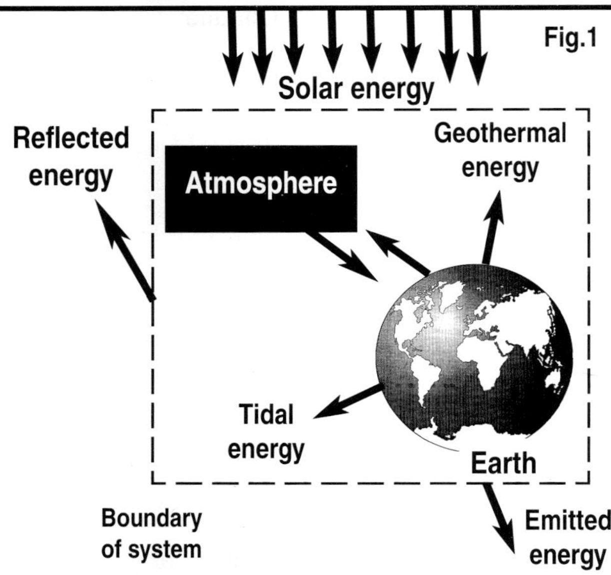

Fig.1

Factors which influence climate on a global scale

Solar Radiation

The Earth receives **radiation** from the Sun. However, of all the radiation that arrives at the **edge** of the **atmosphere**, only a proportion reaches the Earth's **surface.** Also, not all regions on the surface receive the same amount of **radiation (sunlight)** (fig.3) The factors, which have an important influence on **climate**, are considered in the following sections -

(i) Solar Energy Distribution in the Earth-Atmosphere System

Radiation from the sun produces **energy** in the form of **heat** and **light**. However, as already mentioned, not all of this energy is **absorbed** by the **Earth's surface**.

Figure **2** summarises this information:-
From an initial 100% of **Solar Energy** - 17% is **reflected** by **clouds** and 8% is reflected by **dust** and **gases**; 23% is **absorbed** by the **Atmosphere** (4% by **clouds** and 19% by **Water Vapour, Gases** etc); only 52% reaches the **Earth's surface** (6% is **reflected** and the remaining 46% is **absorbed** by the **surface**).

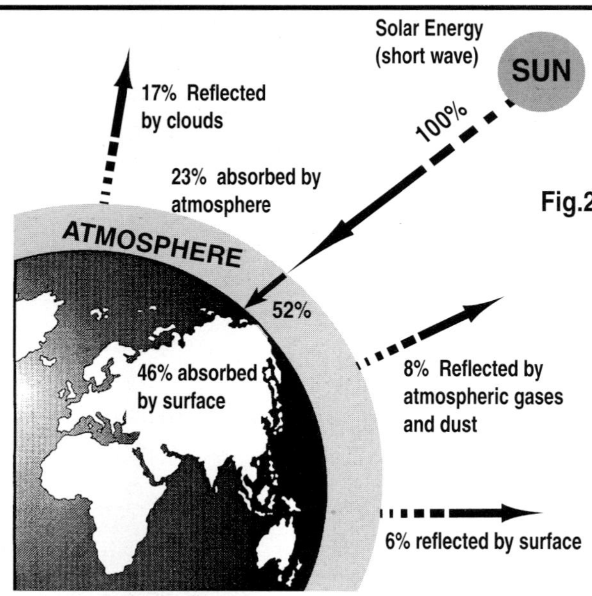

Fig.2

Total absorbed = 23% (by the atmosphere)
= 46% (by the earth's surface) = 69%
Earth's albedo = 17% + 8% + 6% (or 100 -69) = 31%
Total energy = 100%

(ii) **Differences in Insolation received in Tropical and Polar Latitudes**

Note ***Insolation*** *means the sun's (**Solar**) **radiation** which is received by the Earth's surface.*

Tropical Latitudes receive **more** solar radiation than **Polar latitudes** for **2** main reasons:-

- In **Polar** regions the radiation has to penetrate a **greater depth** of **atmosphere** (absorbs more heat) i.e. **XZ > AC**(See figure **3**).
- The same amount of solar energy is received over a much **greater area** in **Polar** regions (less heating) i.e. **XY > AB**(see figure **3**).

Fig.3

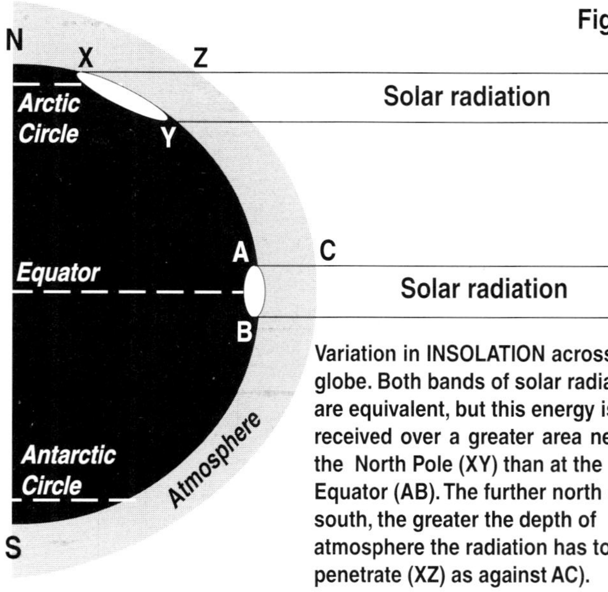

Variation in INSOLATION across the globe. Both bands of solar radiation are equivalent, but this energy is received over a greater area nearer the North Pole (XY) than at the Equator (AB). The further north or south, the greater the depth of atmosphere the radiation has to penetrate (XZ) as against AC).

(iii) **Variations of Radiation with Latitude**

The previous section showed why **Tropical** regions (**Low** latitudes) receive **more** solar radiation (**insolation**) than **Polar** regions (**High** latitudes).

The amount of energy actually **absorbed** by the surface depends on the **Albedo effect** i.e. the proportion of radiation which is **reflected** by different surfaces.

i.e. ICE and SNOW - **high** reflection
WATER - **high** reflection
FOREST - **low** reflection

There is a net **gain** (surplus) of **energy** in **Tropical** areas caused by various factors -

- the **high** angle of the sun's rays
- the **thin** layer of atmosphere for solar radiation to penetrate -
  - **forests** (**low** albedo) absorb more energy
  - **12 months** with sun at a high angle

However, in **Polar** areas there is a net **loss** (**deficit**) of **energy**. This relates to -

- the **low** angle of the sun's rays
- the **thicker** layer of atmosphere
  - **ice/snow** (**high** albedo) absorb less energy
  - sun at a **low** angle for **most** of the year.

Insolation received by the **surface** is shown in various ways in figure **4**.

Fig.4

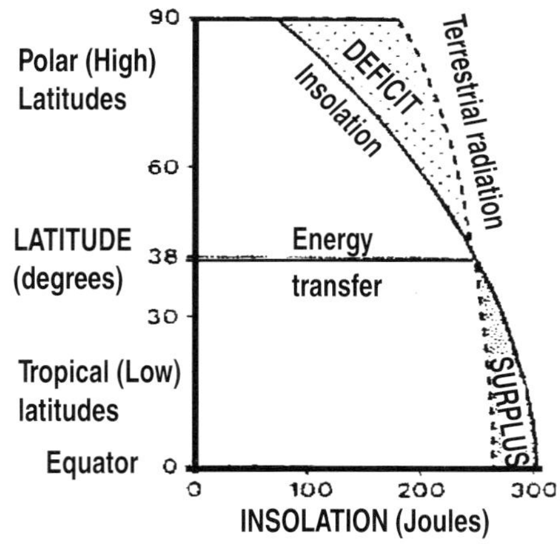

Insolation at the North Pole

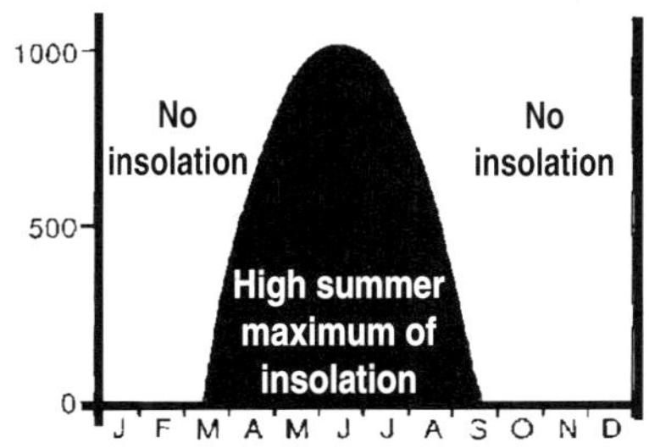

Insolation at the Equator

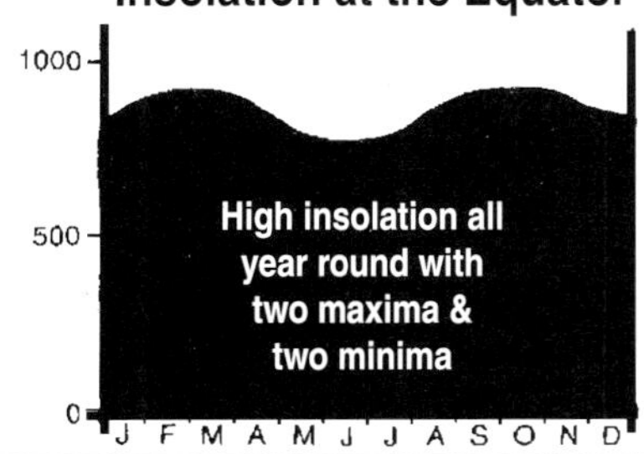

In summary

In **Tropical Latitudes - more** energy is **absorbed** than is **reflected** i.e. creating an **energy surplus**.
In **Polar Latitudes** more energy is **reflected** than is **absorbed** i.e. creating an **energy deficit**.
The **net result** is a **transfer of energy** from the **Tropics** to the **high latitudes**.

Patterns of Atmospheric and Oceanic circulation

Large-scale movements of air in the atmosphere and water in the oceans have an important influence on climate and the transfer of energy over the globe.

(i) **Atmospheric Circulation** - see figures **5** and **6**.

This is mainly caused by differences in **air pressure** i.e.

(a) winds blow from **high** to **low** pressure
(b) winds blow **away** from **Polar** and **Sub-tropical highs**
(c) winds blow **towards** the **Equatorial Low** and **Temperate Lows**

Global wind patterns

Fig.5

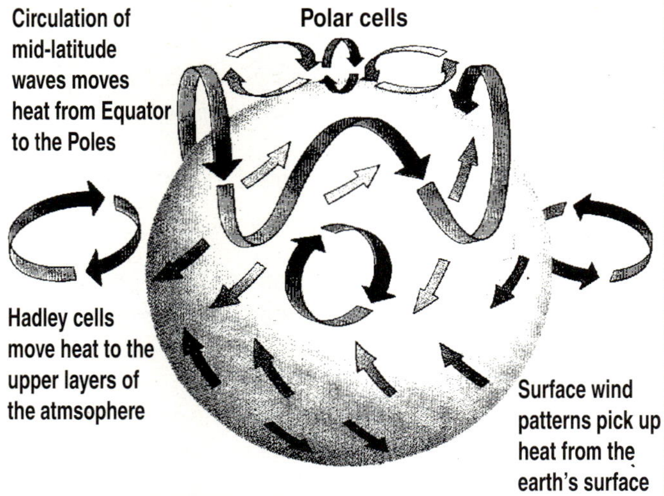

(ii) **Atmospheric Circulation 2** - see figure **6**

Three **Circulation Cells** - the tropical **Hadley Cell** (**A**), the **Ferrel Cell** (**B**) and the **Polar Cell** (**C**) are found in each **hemisphere** - see figure **6**.

- **Heating** over the **Equator** drives the cells and winds i.e. heating causes **air** to **rise** at the **Equator** creating **low pressure**.
  Air at **ground** level moves in from **Sub-tropical areas** to replace the rising Equatorial air.
- **Cold, dense** air **subsides** (sinks) in **Polar** regions creating **high pressure**. Cold air then moves **outwards** from this **Polar High** pressure region to **Temperate Low** pressure areas.
- Finally, **warm** air moves from the **Sub-tropical highs** to the **Temperate** lows.

Atmospheric circulation and winds

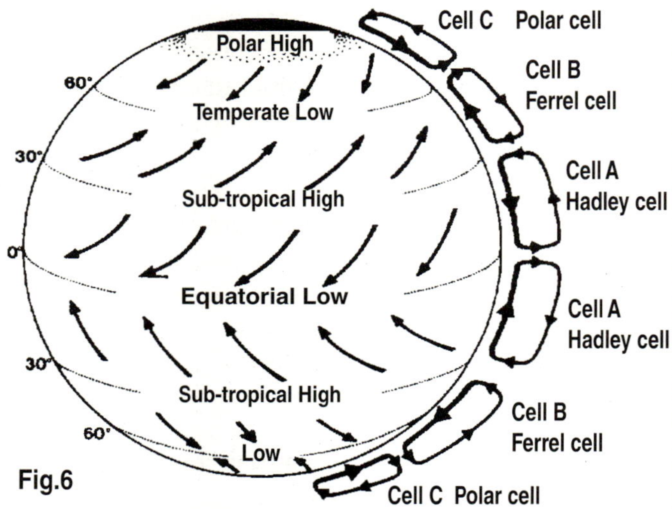

Fig.6

(iii) ***Atmospheric circulation** is **modified** by the **Coriolis Force** created by the Earth's **rotation** (see fig. 7),*
*i.e. Winds are deflected to the **right** in the **Northern** Hemsiphere and to the **left** in the **Southern** Hemisphere.*

There are two main wind belts in each hemisphere - see figures **7** and **8**. The **Trade Wind Belt** covers nearly half the earth's surface and is found between latitudes 30 N and 30 S. These are fairly constant and predictable winds because of the relative permanence of the subtropical high-pressure zones from where they originate.

The **Mid-Latitude Westerlies** which develop from the poleward sides of the subtropical high-pressure zone. The trade winds from both hemispheres meet near the Equator in what is called the **Inter-Tropical Convergence Zone (ITCZ)**. The **ITCZ** moves between the tropics with the seasonal shift of the equatorial low pressure. This is an area of **convection** (uplift of air) and the winds are weak and are called the **Doldrums**. There are two other zones of convergence - the polar fronts in both hemispheres, where the westerlies meet the polar easterlies. There are also two important **zones of divergence**, the subtropical high-pressure zones, which are areas of relatively light winds usually called the **horse latitudes**.

Global wind belts & the coriolis effect

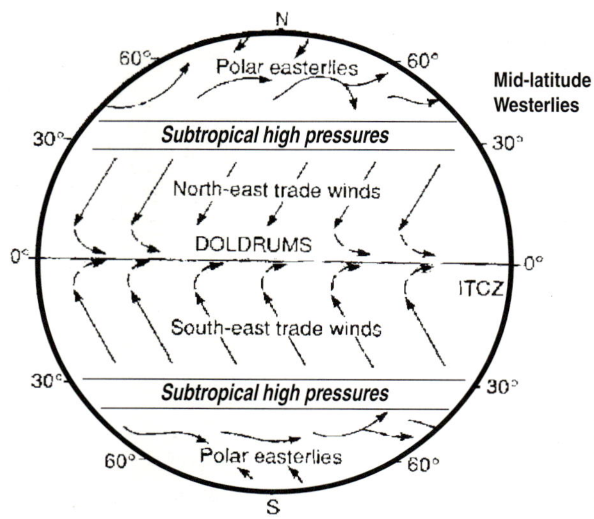

Fig.7

Fig.8 **Atmospheric Circulation - July**

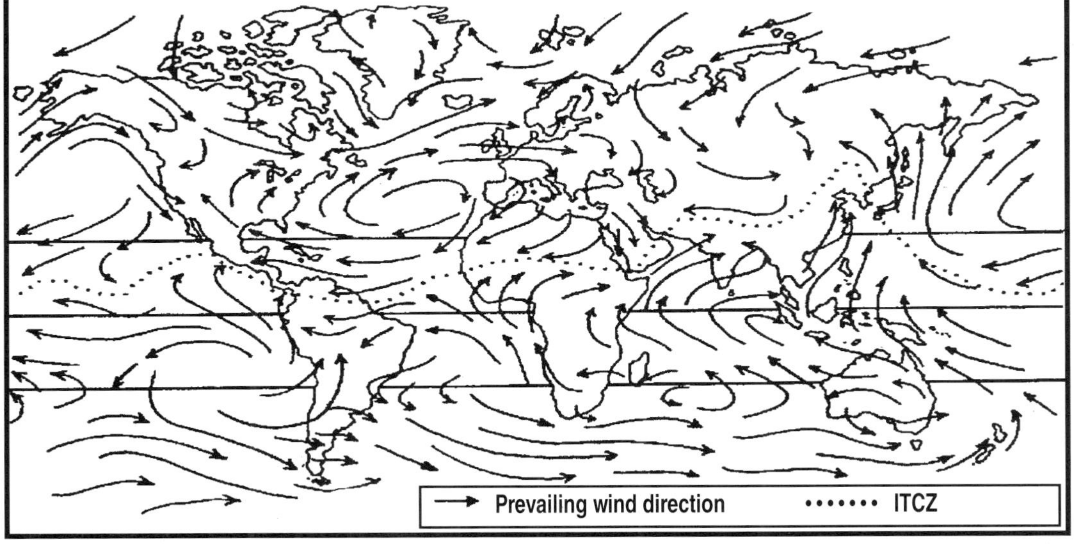

(iv) **Oceanic Circulation**

Energy is **redistributed** in the oceans by **ocean currents**. The movement of water can result in **warm** water being transferred to **high latitudes**, e.g. the **North Atlantic Drift** and **cool** water being transferred to **Low latitudes**, e.g. the **Canaries Current** - see figure **10**.

A range of factors influence ocean currents:-

- **Uneven heating** of surface water in **high** and **low** latitudes (see figure **9**) sets up **convection currents** which transfer energy.
- **Winds** cause a **frictional drag** on large water surfaces i.e. **ocean currents** tend to follow the **prevailing wind directions**.
- The **Coriolis Force** means that currents are deflected to the **right** in the **northern hemisphere** and to the **left** in the **southern hemisphere**.
- Ocean current **direction** is modified by the **shape** of the **continents**.

Land and ocean heating Fig.9

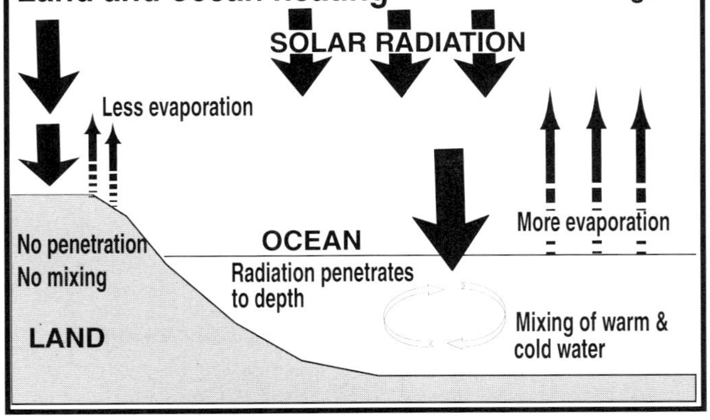

Note *In the **Atlantic Ocean** the principal **warm** currents are the **Gulf Stream**, the **North Atlantic Drift** and the **Brazil Current**.*
***Cold** currents include the **Labrador**, **Canaries** and the **Benguela** currents - see figure **10**.*

Fig.10 **Ocean Circulation model - simplified version**

The ocean currents, in the same way as the atmosphere, transfer energy from the Tropics towards the poles.

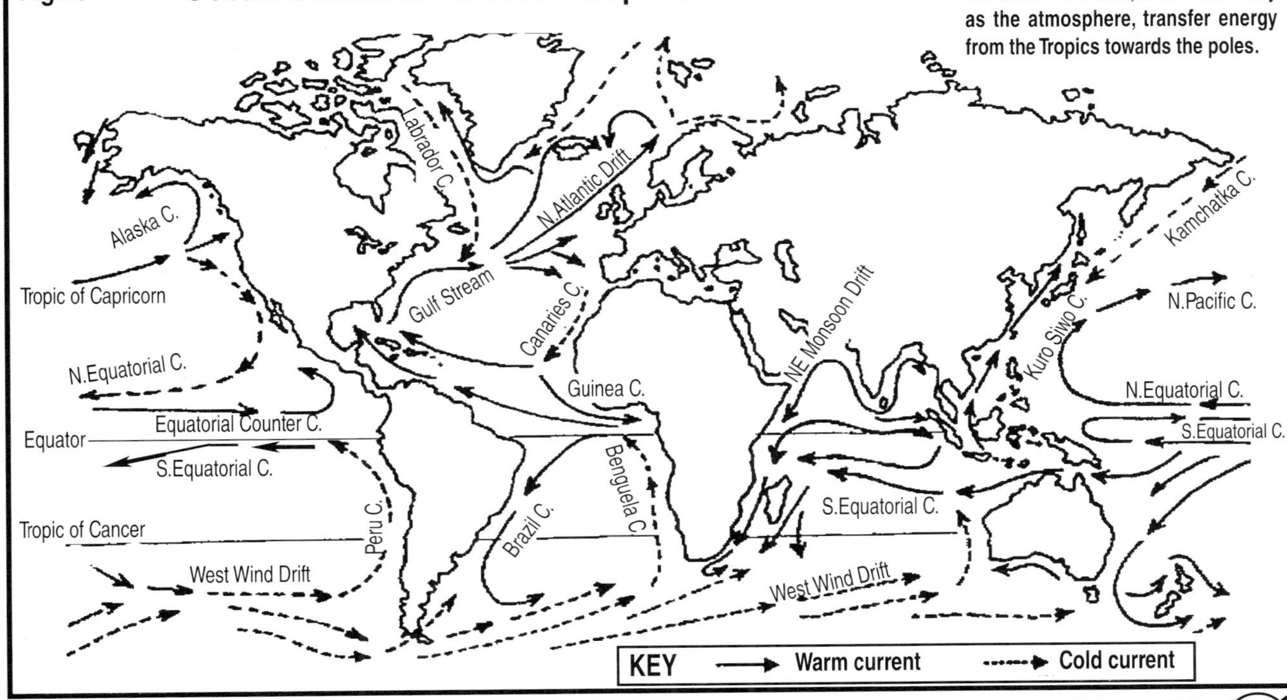

Fig.11

Changing temperature of the Planet

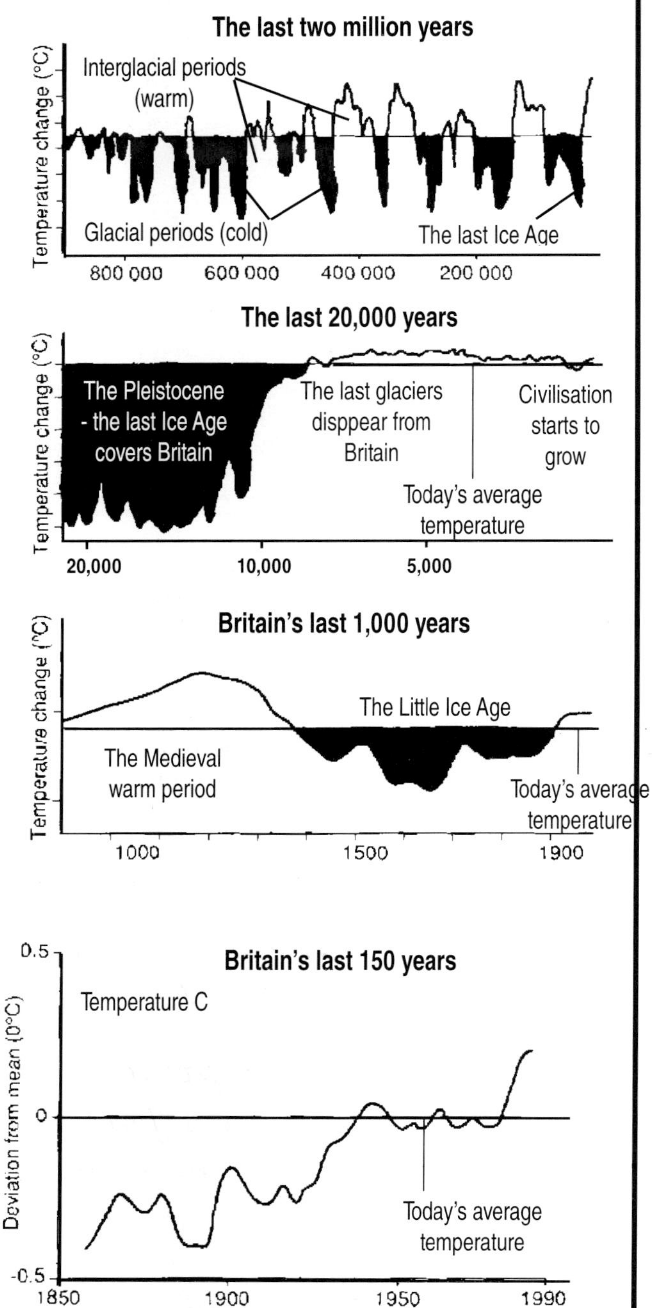

Global climate changes

Figure **11** shows that over the last few million years there have been significant fluctuations in global temperature.

These may be caused by a variety of **physical** and **human** factors.

Physical Factors for fluctuations in global temperature

- Variations in **Solar Energy**
- Astronomical factors i.e. **tilt** of the Earth's **axis**
- Changes in the Earth's **orbit**
- **Volcanic Eruptions** i.e. **dust** may scatter **Solar Radiation** - giving a **reduction** in temperature
- Over a long period **oceanic alteration** and / or **continental drift**.

Human Factors for fluctuations in global temperature

- The **Greenhouse Effect** i.e. Greenhouse gases (**Methane**, **CFCs**, **Carbon Dioxide** released from **forest burning, use of fossil fuels** etc.) trap heat in the Earth's atmosphere causing a **rise** in temperature.
- **War** e.g. bombing of Dresden, Iraq, etc. may release **smoke** into the atmosphere (**Atomic testing** releases **dust**) - may cause **slight fall** in temperature.

Note There is a **natural greenhouse effect** which keeps the planet 33^{0}C warmer than it would otherwise be. Since the average temperature on Earth is around 15^{0}C, Earth would freeze without this natural greenhouse effect and most forms of life would die out. The reason why the greenhouse effect is reported so often is that the natural process is being enhanced by human activities. It is this enhanced greenhouse effect and the consequent **global warming** which is considered a threat to life on the Earth.

The hole in the Ozone layer

Ozone is very important to the planet. It is concentrated in the stratospheric layer towards the top of the atmosphere. Here it blocks ultra-violet light and the removal of ozone allows harmful UV radiation to reach the Earth's surface. This poses a threat to humans and other life forms as it can cause skin cancers. It has been proved that human activity is directly responsible for the depletion of the ozone layer. Holes in the ozone layer above the Poles have been discovered. They result from the production of **CFCs** which destroy ozone. Scientists now agree that ozone depletion will cause an enhancement of the Greenhouse Effect and therefore ever increasing of global temperatures (by 3^{0}C by 2100AD), rising sea-levels (by 65cm in 2100AD), more planetary water vapour, significant changes in climate patterns across the globe, more skin cancer deaths, destruction of ecosystems in some areas and long-term atmospheric effects.

Climate on a regional scale - Equatorial and Savanna Regions of Africa

Air masses and the West African climate

(seasonal movement of the **ITCZ**)

The climate of **West Africa** (in countries such as **Nigeria** and **Ghana**) has marked seasonal **variations**. Annual **rainfall** is high near the coast, producing **Equatorial Rainforest** vegetation.

However, as one moves **north** away from the coast, rainfall diminishes with distinct **seasonal** contrasts, and Rainforest gives way to **Savanna** Tropical Grassland). The seasonal changes are related to movement of **air masses**.

An **air mass** is a very large volume of air with particular **temperature** and **humidity** characteristics (i.e. the air mass may be warm or cold; dry or moist) - see figure **12**.

The air masses which affect the West African climate are the **MT** (**Maritime Tropical**) - warm, moist air bringing **wet** weather) and the **CT** (**Continental Tropical**) - warm, dry air bringing **dry** weather). The **MT** air mass originates over the **Atlantic Ocean** and the **CT** air mass originates over the **Sahara** Desert.

The **ITCZ** (Inter-Tropical Convergence Zone) is where the **Trade Winds** converge resulting in a **low** pressure area which brings **rainfall** to West Africa. In **July** the ITCZ migrates **North** over the Southern Sahara and the region is affected by the **Tropical Maritime** air mass - this brings rainfall to the region. The ITCZ is not fixed, but moves north or south with the seasonal movement of the area of most intense heating (sometimes called the **Thermal Equator**).

In January the ITCZ migrates **south** and only the coastal areas near the Gulf of Guinea are affected by **Tropical Maritime** air. The Southern Sahara is mostly dominated by **dry Tropical Continental** air with conditions of **drought**. Places close to the coast e.g. **Lagos** which receive the **MT** air mass for longer periods have higher rainfall than the places **inland** further north e.g. **Kano** (or Agades), where the **CT** air mass is prevalent.

The ITCZ - Inter-Tropical Convergence Zone

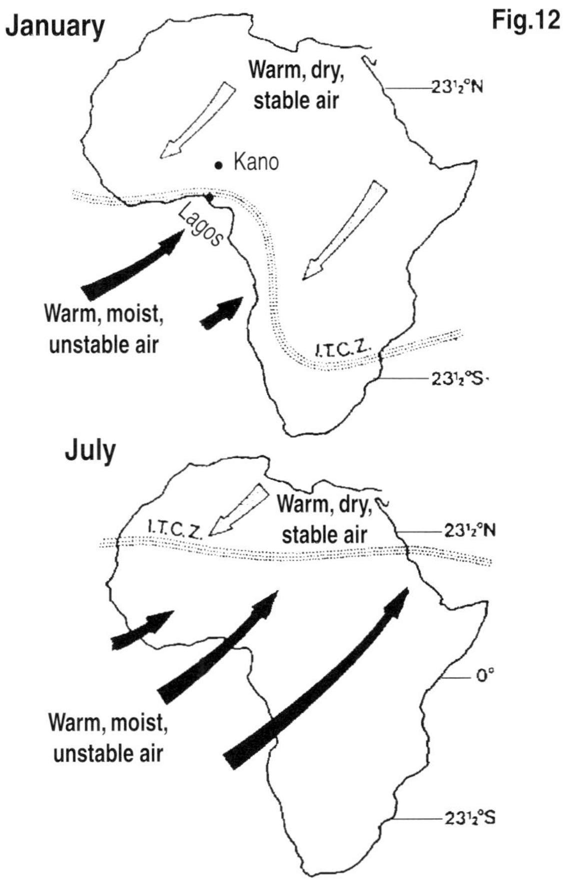

Fig.12

El Nino years, as figure 13 shows, trigger a series of climatic changes on a global scale......

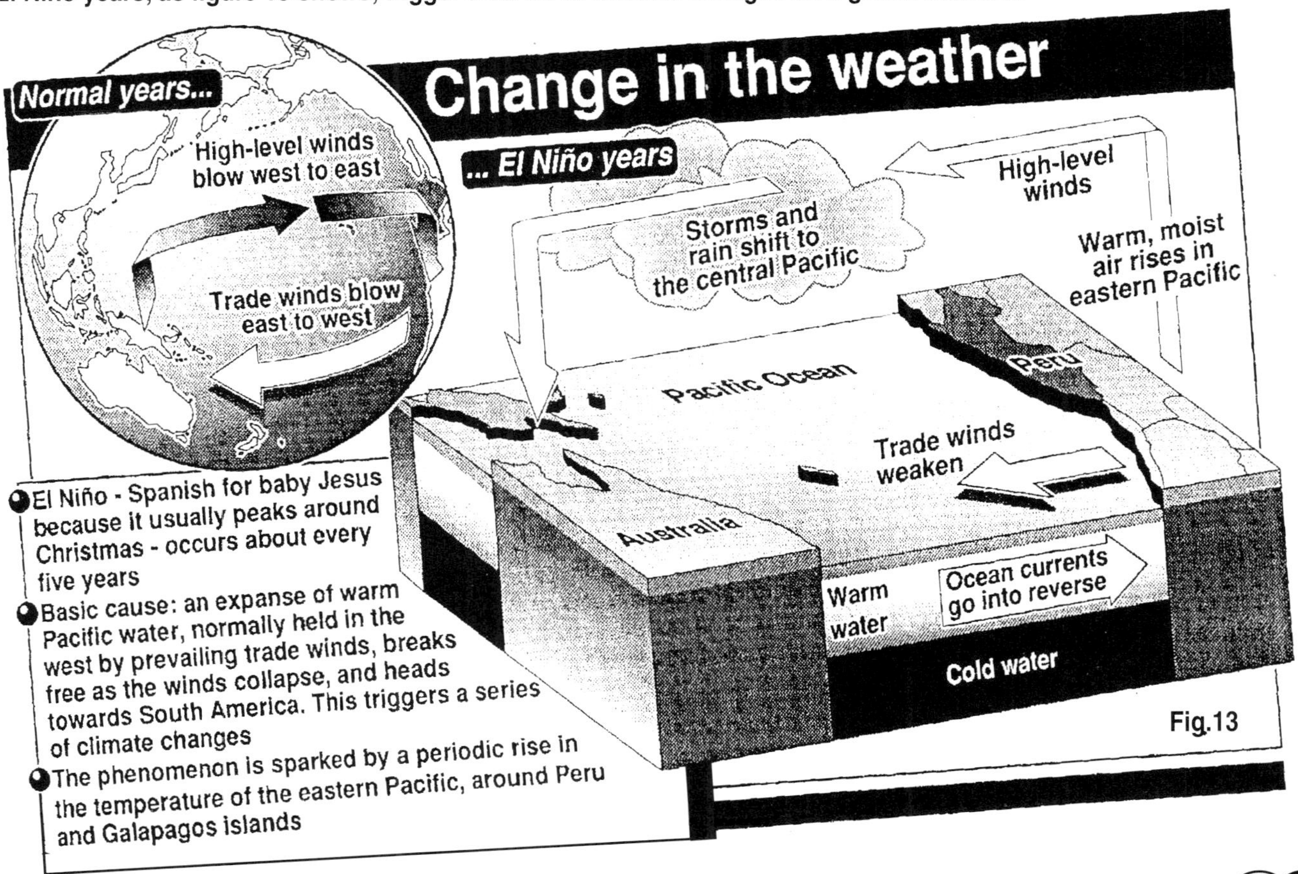

Fig.13

Atmosphere Revision : Summary Notes

The main Idea........
The characteristics of the atmosphere vary spatially and provide climate and weather conditions which interlink with other physical systems.

The Atmospheric System

1..The Earth-Atmosphere system is dependant on inputs of **energy** from the sun.
2..25% of the sun's energy is reflected back into space, 23% transformed into heat, **46% reaches the Earth's surface** and 6% is reflected by the Earth's surface.
3..Trace gases play an important part in absorbing long-wave radiation and return much of this energy to the surface. This is the **Greenhouse Effect**.
4..Inputs of energy in the Earth-Atmosphere system equal outputs.
5..The atmosphere receives most of its energy from the Earth's surface.

Atmospheric Circulation

1..The **sun's radiation** only strikes the earth at the vertical between the Tropic of Cancer and the Tropic of Capricorn.
2..Areas equatorward of 38^0 receive more heat than they lose areas poleward of 38^0 lose more heat than they receive.
3..Unequal distribution of heat drives the atmospheric circulation.
4..Air moves from areas of high pressure to areas of low pressure. This is the **Pressure Gradient Force**.
5..The **Coriolis Force** is produced by the earth's rotation and it deflects moving air to the **right** in the northern hemisphere.
6..At high altitudes the **geostrophic wind** flows parallel to the isobars.
7..**Friction** partly counteracts the Coriolis Force.
8..**Rossby Waves** are generated by temperature differences and are important mechanisms for mixing air masses.

Winds and Ocean Currents

1..**The Trade-wind Belt** covers nearly half the earth's surface between 30^0S and 30^0N.
2..The trade winds meet near the Equator in the Inter-Tropical Convergence Zone or **ITCZ**.
3..The two important zones of divergence are the **Sub-tropical high pressure** zones.
4..**Land** surfaces heat faster and cool faster than water surfaces.
5..**Oceans** act as a store of energy.
6..**Temperature ranges** are greater over land areas than over the oceans.
7..**Ocean currents** are a mechanism for exchanging energy.
8..At latitudes greater than 30^0 the **west** coasts of continents receive contact with **cold currents** while the **east** coasts are in contact with **warm currents**.

Climatic change / Greenhouse Effect

1..A variety of methods are used to investigate past climates including; **pollen analysis**, **dendrochronology** and **isotope analysis**.
2..**Milankovitch** suggested that three astronomical cycles combine to determine the onset of the glaciations.
3..**Volcanic activity** and shifts in the Rossby waves are also blamed for **climatic change**.
4..The rise in levels of greenhouse gases through human activity has given rise to fears of an enhanced Greenhouse Effect.
5..**Greenhouse gases** have increased through burning of fossil fuels, deforestation, increases in domesticated herds, extension of rice growing and release of CFC'S.
6..The **six warmest years** on record have occurred since1980.
7..An **enhanced greenhouse effect** would raise sea levels and alter climatic patterns worldwide, with many developing countries coming off worst.

Ozone layer / Acid rain

1..The **ozone layer** is an ozone rich layer in the stratosphere which shields the earth from much of the sun's ultraviolet radiation.
2..**CFC**'s are considered to break down the ozone layer faster than it is being created.
3..The first **hole** in the ozone layer was discovered in 1982 over the Antarctic continent in winter.
4..**Volcanic eruptions** are also believed to cause depletion of ozone.
5..**Decreases in ozone** concentration in the stratosphere will cause more skin cancers, a decrease in crop yields and possibly widespread environmental damage.
6..**Acid rain** has a pH lower than 5.6. Sulphur dioxide and oxides of nitrogen are the main culprits.
7..Acidity in **Europe's lakes** has soared since the Industrial Revolution.

Air Masses / Rainfall variability

1..**Air Masses** influence the weather because the air retains its characteristics of heat and humidity for some time.
2..Air heated in its lowest layers is made more **unstable** while air cooled in its lowest layers is made more **stable**.
3..The **ITCZ migrates** further over land than over ocean.
4..Clouds in the ITCZ form cloud clusters.
5..**Saharan droughts** in the 1970's and 1980's were characterised by strong air subsidence (sinking) over the region.
6..Failure of the rains in areas of **West Africa** has led to **desertification** and widespread **migration**.
7.. **Precipitation** of individual years varies from the average. **Arid areas** have the highest variability.

Atmosphere Revision : Unit style assessments

Marks

1a. Describe the factors which affect the amount of **solar radiation** reflected from the Earth's surface. (5)

1b. Explain why there is a **net loss** (deficit) of solar energy towards the Poles and a **net gain** in Tropical areas. (5)

2 GMT The table provides rainfall statistics for climate stations at **Agades** and Lagos in **West Africa** (see fig.**14**).

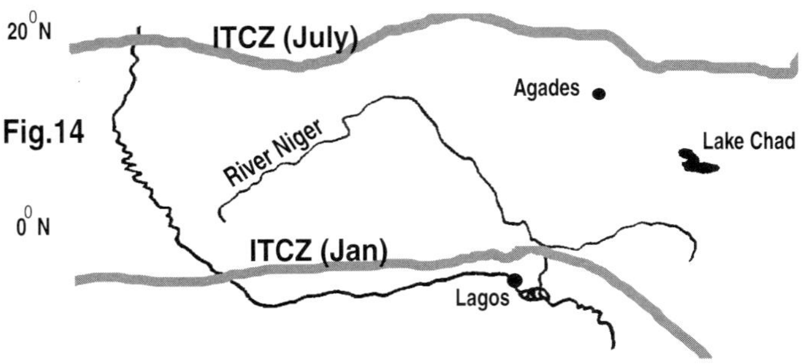

Fig.14

Monthly Rainfall (mm)	Agades	Lagos
Jan	-	25
Feb	-	33
Mar	-	67
Apr	-	145
May	12	268
Jun	21	390
Jul	56	262
Aug	75	82
Sept	24	173
Oct	-	201
Nov	-	75
Dec	-	23

a. Construct **graphs** to compare the two rainfall patterns. (4)

b. Describe and explain differences between the two graphs with reference to the ITCZ and movement of air masses. (6)

Atmosphere Revision : Exam style assessments

1. Study the two graphs figures **15** and **16**.

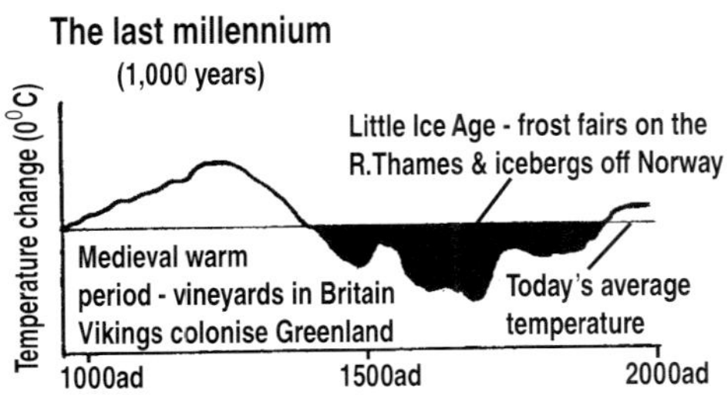

Fig.15

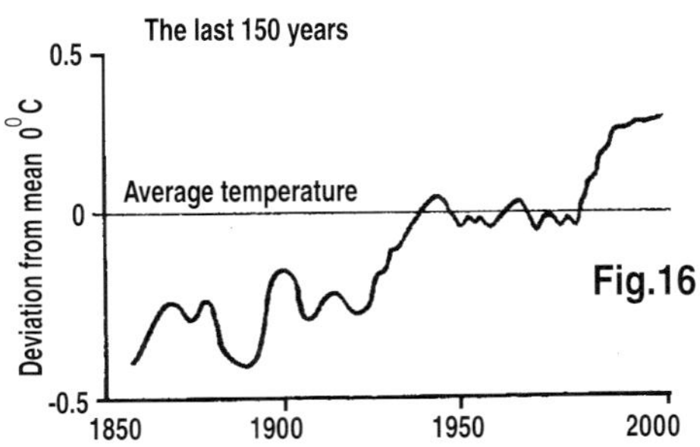

Fig.16

Describe in detail variations in global temperature (i) over the last **millennium** (ii) over the last **150 years** (4)

2. Explain possible reasons, both physical and human, for the **variations in global temperature** shown by the two graphs. (6)

3. Look at figure **17** - atmospheric circulation and surface winds.

Explain the global atmospheric circulation pattern shown in figure **17**. (5)

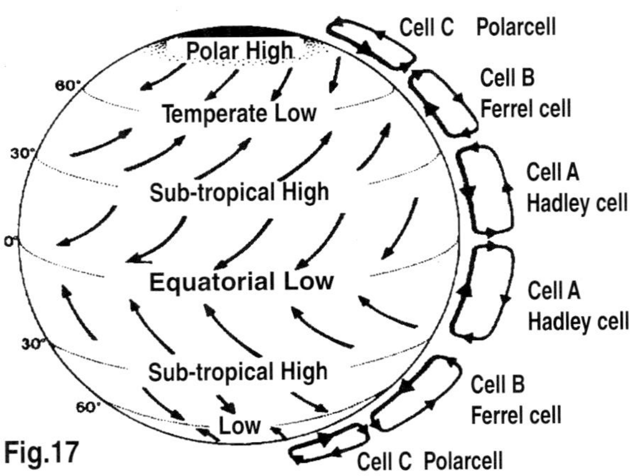

Fig.17

4. Describe the role of either atmospheric circulation or oceanic circulation in the redistribution of energy over the planet. (Look at figs **8 / 10** on page **12** of this book) (5)

3. Hydrosphere

The main idea of the Hydrosphere section is....
The water cycle, which constitutes a major physical system, operates on a variety of scales. On the Earth's surface, the movement of water is a major agent in the formation of landforms and landscapes.

What do you need to know ?

Students should have a knowledge and understanding of -

A The Hydrological Cycle

- components of the global hydrological cycle
- areas of sufficiency and deficiency and effects of climatic variability with reference to the Savanna regions of Africa north of the Equator

B Fluvial landforms and landscapes

- movement of water within drainage basins - inputs, storage, outputs
- *construction and analysis of hydrographs*
- effects of flowing water in terms of erosion, transportation and deposition and the resultant landforms - upper, middle and lower sections of river basins
- *methods of collecting and presenting river flow data*
- characteristic landscape features within a drainage basin; explanation of formation of such features and identification of river features from Ordnance Survey (OS) maps.

This section relates to the movement of water and its impact on the formation of landforms and landscapes.

Water, water everywhere.......

Water is a vital component of the Earth's atmosphere and surface. It is essential for life on the planet and even in its gaseous form it plays an important role in absorbing radiation and transferring energy between the Earth and its atmosphere.

Despite the fact that only 3% of the water on the planet is fresh water and that only a third of that is available for use by humans, the usable **hydrosphere** holds more than enough water for all current needs. However, water like other resources is not evenly distributed across the globe. Some parts suffer regular droughts while others experience floods.

In **developed** countries such as the USA or the UK, each person consumes over 100 litres of water each day (for all uses, washing, cooking etc.). People tend to take water for granted. But in **developing** countries such as Tanzania or India, less than 25 litres per person each day is not unusual (see figure 18).

Of all water use, **irrigation** uses 73%, **industry** uses 21% and **domestic** use is only 6%. The water used in industry and in homes is often returned to rivers and can be re-used. 70% of all water used for irrigation however is lost to the atmosphere or into the ground - but irrigated land produces 20% of world food supplies.

The landscapes of the Earth are sculpted in an environment in which water plays a major role. The continuing cycle of water in the **global hydrological cycle** has created a range of landscapes produced by erosional, transportational and depositional work of water.

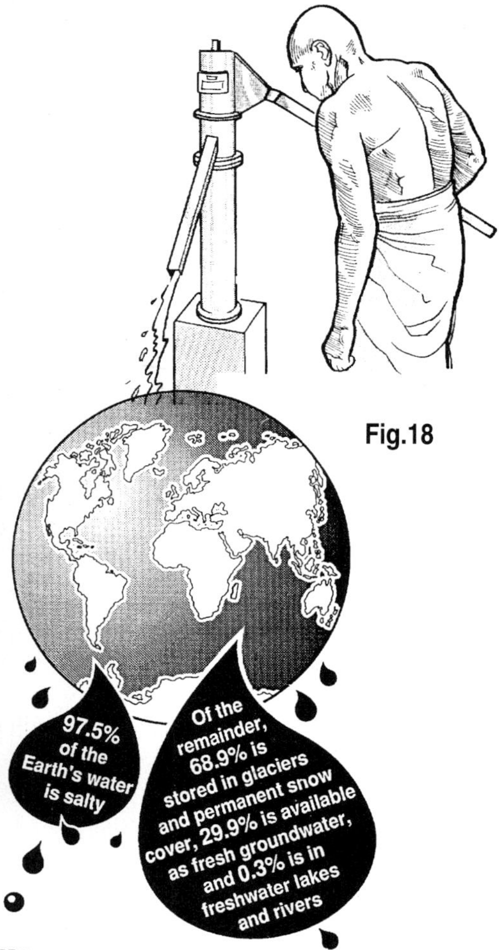

Fig.18

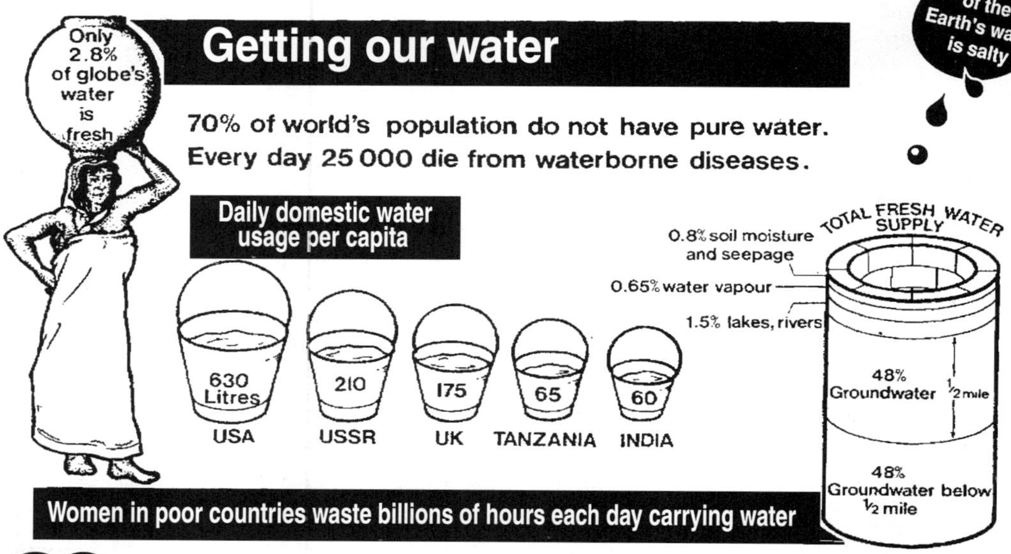

The Hydrological Cycle

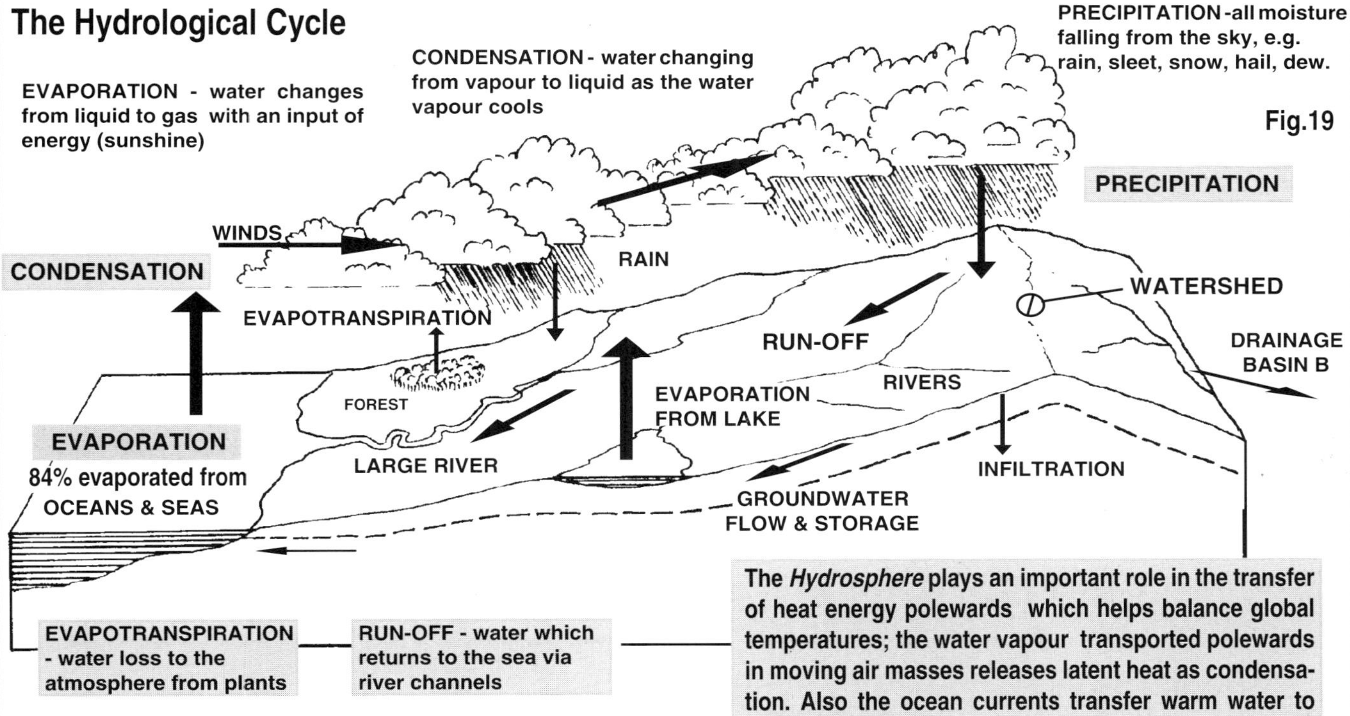

The *Hydrosphere* plays an important role in the transfer of heat energy polewards which helps balance global temperatures; the water vapour transported polewards in moving air masses releases latent heat as condensation. Also the ocean currents transfer warm water to higher latitudes.

The Hydrological Cycle

(This is the **system** which describes the **distribution and movement of water** between the earth and its atmosphere).

Heat energy from the sun causes **evaporation** from water surfaces (rivers, lakes and oceans) and **transpiration** from **plants**. The warm, moist air (containing **water vapour**) rises and, as it cools, **condensation** takes place to form **clouds**. Wind energy may move clouds over land surfaces where **precipitation** occurs. The rainwater flows, either, over the ground (**run-off / surface flow**) into rivers and back to the ocean, or downwards through the soil and rocks (**groundwater**). Water is stored mainly in the oceans (97.5%) with **ice caps holding** about 2% and the remaining 1% as lakes, rivers and groundwater.

Climatic Variability and Water Supply

In West Africa (**Savanna Regions**) the migration southward of the **ITCZ** results in an annual period of **drought** from December through to February (see figure **20**).

When the ITCZ migrates north in July, **rainfall** occurs.

Water must, if possible, be collected in **reservoirs / tanks** in the **wet** season to be stored for use in the **dry** season.
The **water table** moves up and down depending on **seasonal** rainfall. **Wells** alternatively provide water or dry up.
Irrigation is commonly used for crop production.

Variations in the annual rainfall patterns in the **Sahel** are shown in figure **21**. The shaded area on the map shows the Sahel region. The graph shows that rainfall in the Sahel is highly variable, with wet years (above the 'average' line) and dry years (below the 'average' line).

The Sahel droughts of the last thirty years were the result of several years of poor rainfall, not just one bad year. Scientists continue the research into the variability of rainfall across the area, including linking **sea surface temperatures** with droughts on land and into the influence of high-altitude **jet streams** on rainfall .

West Africa : ITCZ movement

Fig.20

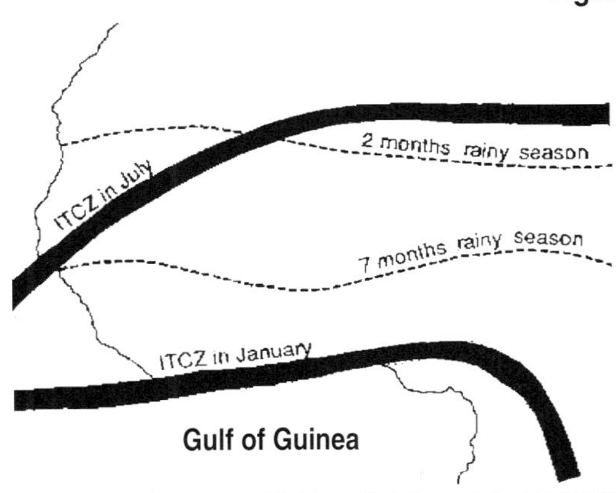

Meteorological drought (period of abnormally low rainfall).
Agricultural drought (reduction in soil moisture hence a reduction in agricultural output)

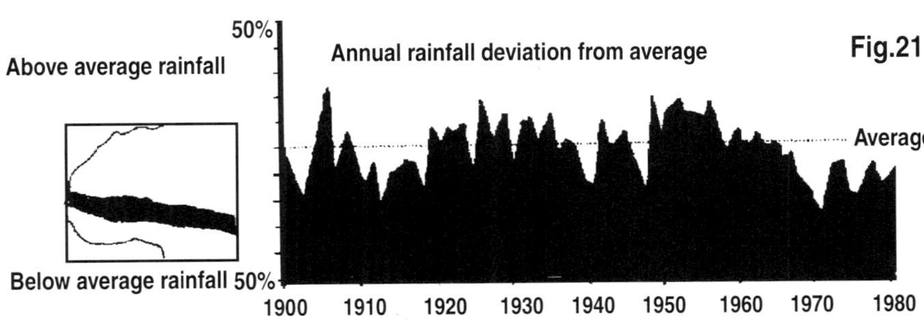

Fluvial landforms and landscapes

(i.e. relating to running water)

Drainage Basins

A **drainage basin** is part of the hydrological cycle (fig.**22**) and may be viewed as an individual **system** with

INPUTS — i.e. **precipitation** (rain, snow etc.) enters the basin

STORAGE — i.e. some water is **stored** in lakes or in the **soil**

OUTPUTS — i.e. Water is **lost as** it flows away to the sea or through **evapotranspiration** to the atmosphere.

A drainage basin is the catchment area of a stream bounded by a watershed. Streams however join together forming tributaries of longer rivers and the river system has a much larger catchment incorporating the drainage basins of all its tributaries.

Drainage patterns

Although drainage systems make many varied patterns it is possible to group many of them into a classification such as that shown in figure **23**.

Rectangular drainage is a very regular pattern found in areas where there are well-defined lines of weakness such as faults or joints in the rocks.

Deranged drainage is an 'immature' network found on landscapes covered by glacial deposits.

Parallel drainage develops on uniformly dipping rocks.

Trellis drainage develops on older and folded rocks.

Dendritic drainage is found in areas of low relief or very gently dipping rocks.

Radial drainage forms where streams flow out from a central high point - usually domes linked with volcanic cones.

Note: *The movement of water in a basin relates to the **permeability** of the **underlying rock**.*

If a rock is **impermeable** (or **impervious**) it does not allow water to pass through it e.g. **granite** or **clay**. Water in impermeable areas flows **across** the ground **surface**.

A **permeable** rock allows water to **pass through it** and may be of **two types**:-

- Pervious rocks e.g. **carboniferous limestone** contains **joints** (cracks) which allow water to flow downwards.
- Porous rocks e.g. **chalk** have small **pores** (air spaces) which allow water to **pass through** the rock itself.

A **porous** rock can also **store** water in its pores and can be used as a reservoir (known as an **aquifer**).

Drainage basin and watershed

Fig.22

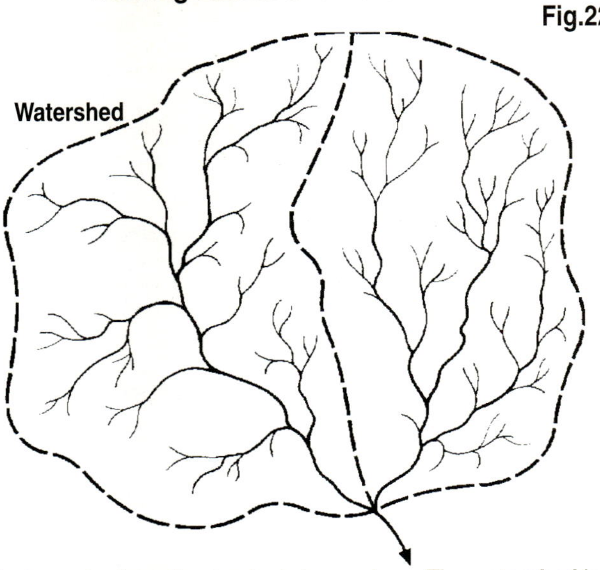

Drainage basin and watershed shown above. The **watershed** is the high ground which separates different drainage systems. Within any river system each tributary will have its own watershed.

Drainage patterns or systems classification

Fig.23

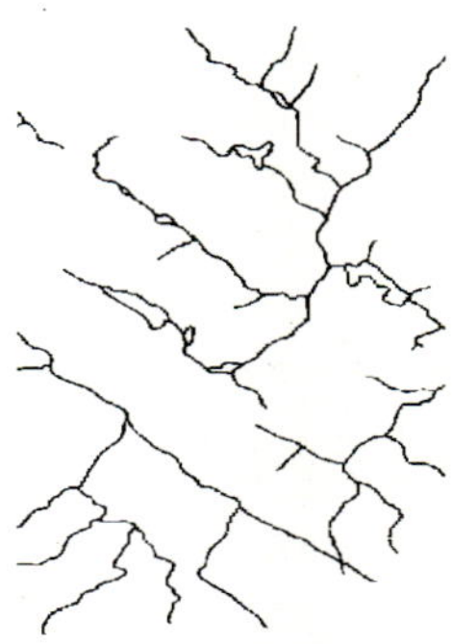

Rectangular drainage

Deranged drainage pattern

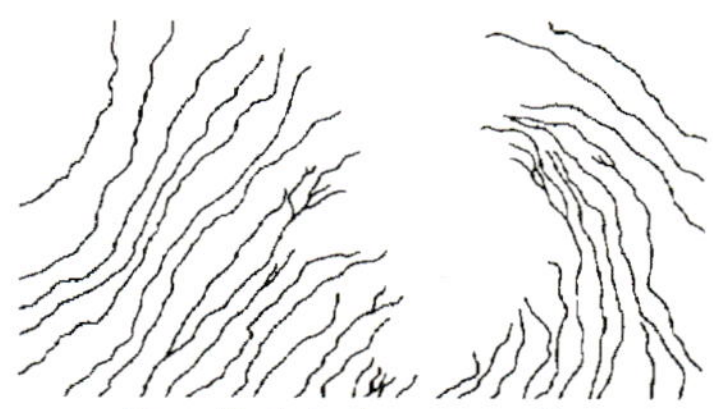

Parallel drainage pattern

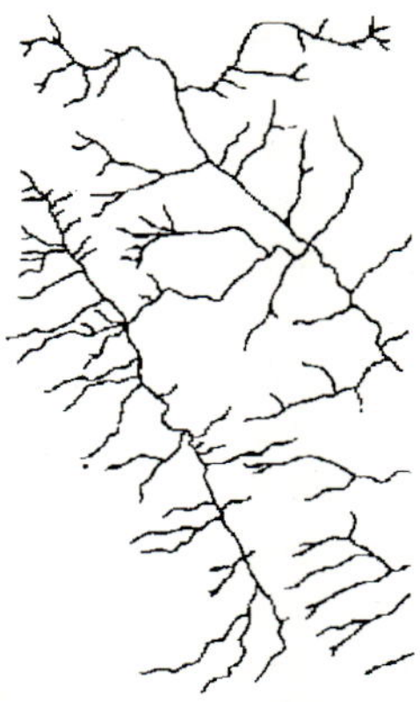

Trellis drainage pattern

Dendritic drainage pattern

Radial drainage pattern

Analysis of Hydrographs

A **hydrograph** shows the relationship between **rainfall** and **river flow** (**discharge**) - see figure **24**. Normally, after a period of heavy rain there is a time lag (the **basin lag**) before the **floodwater** flows down the river **course**. The basin lag will normally be longer if the region is highly vegetated i.e. the water takes longer to flow across the ground. In areas where there is little vegetation (or **urban** areas), the basin lag will be shorter and **flooding** is more likely. **Deforestation** will reduce the basin lag and increase the risk of flooding.

(See **revision cards** on page **129**).

Fig.24

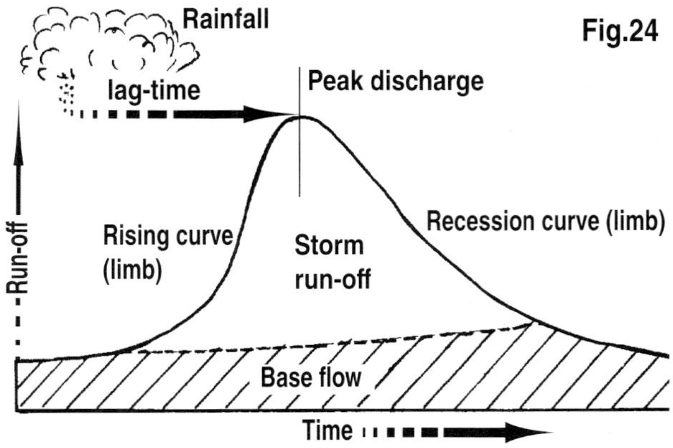

The Effects of Flowing Water

Processes along a river's course or river valley -

Erosion - consists of four main processes **- Hydraulic action** (where water **drags** poorly consolidated material from the river banks/bed; **Corrasion** (where sediment in the water is used to **scour the river bed**); **Attrition** (rock fragments in the water collide with each other - gradually becoming more rounded) and **Solution** (where rocks e.g. limestone are slowly **dissolved** by the water) - see figure **25**.

Transportation - occurs in **4** ways:- **Bed Load** (generally particles which bounce along the river (**Saltation**) and particles which roll along the river bed (**Traction**)); **Suspension** (finer materials are carried within the water - helped by the water's turbulence) and **Solution** (consists of dissolved material e.g. from limestone) - see figure **26**.

Deposition - this takes place when the water no longer has sufficient velocity/energy to transport material - the material may be deposited in layers of different size i.e. **sorted** e.g. **fluvioglacial deposits.**

Note : *There is an important relationship between* ***water velocity*** *in a river and* ***particle size*** *e.g. clay, sand, gravel etc. (This can be shown on a* ***graph*** *- fig.***40** *on page* ***25****). River velocity is illustrated in figure* ***27****.*

For a given particle size, a **particular velocity**, is required for **erosion** to occur (i.e. to pick up particles).

The water velocity needed to **transport** particles in **suspension** is less than the velocity required to pick them up.

As water velocity **decreases**, then deposition of larger particles takes place first.

Very **fine particles** e.g. clay are carried by the river in **suspension** over long distances and are only deposited in very slow-moving water.

Sand can be eroded / transported at a **lower velocity** than either coarser particles e.g. gravel or finer materials e.g. clay.

River processes

Fig.25

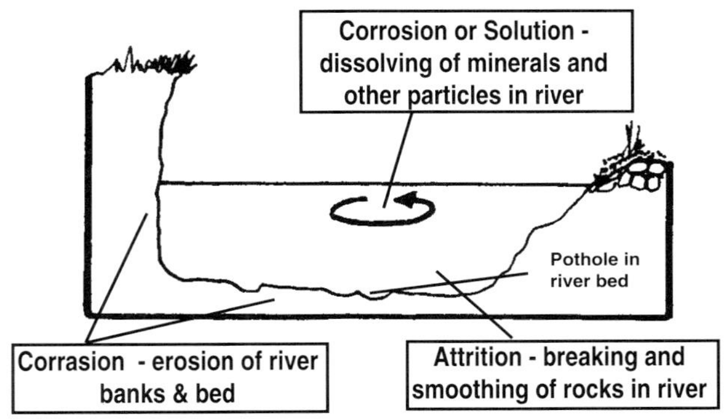

Transportation processes in a river

Fig.26

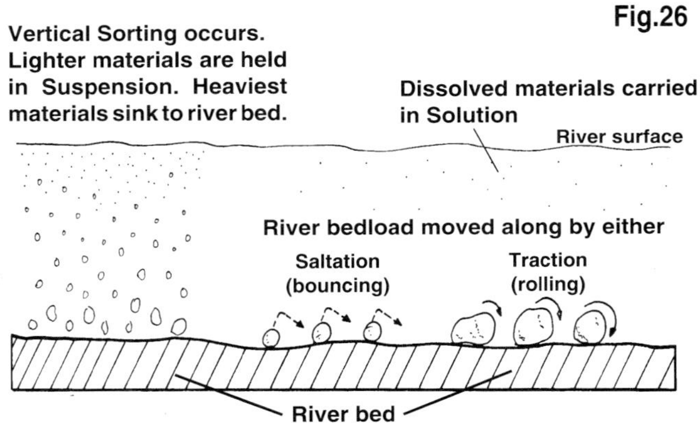

River velocity

Fig.27

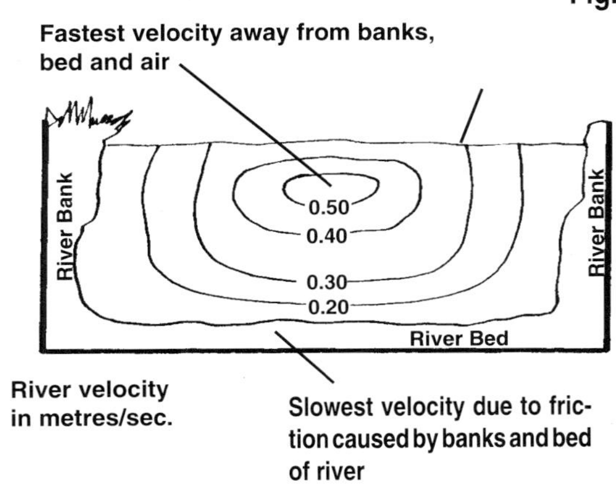

Fig.28

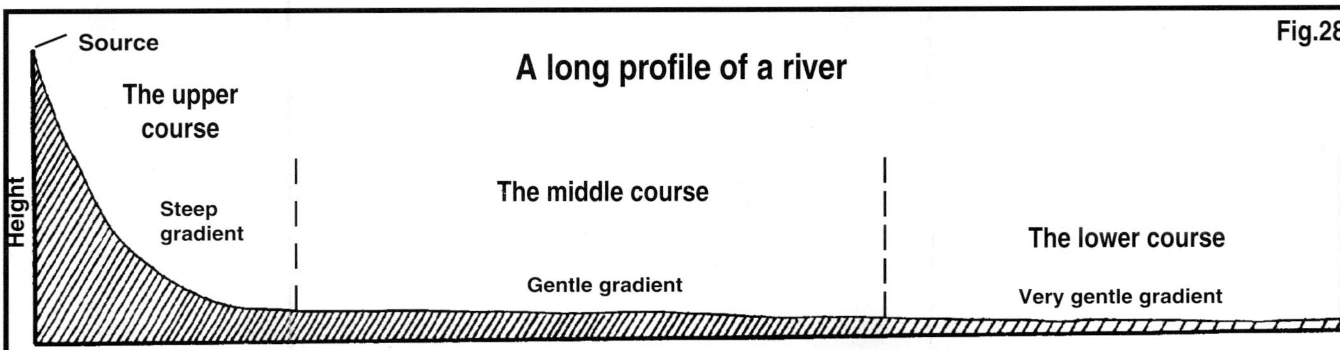

Changes along a River valley (basin)

A typical (**model**) river valley may be divided into **3 stages**:- **upper**, **middle** and **lower** see figure **28**.

In the **upper course** or valley the **gradient** is **steep** and the valley, is narrow and deep (**V-shaped**) with the main process being **vertical erosion** (**downwards**). The river itself is narrow but relatively deep with high energy (**fast flowing**) and it transports a **bedload** of coarse, angular rock fragments. Important features in the upper course are **waterfalls**, **gorges**, **interlocking spurs**, **potholes** in the river bed, etc. - see figure **29**.

In the **middle course** or valley the gradient is **less steep** and the valley is **broader** and **shallower**. The river is **wider** but appears to flow more slowly - there is some vertical erosion accompanied by **lateral** erosion (**sideways**) - as the **velocity** of the water **decreases** the bedload transported by the river consists of **finer** material, but **rounded** by **attrition**. The slower water flow encourages **deposition**, particularly on the **convex** bends of **meanders**. (The most important features of the middle course) - see figure **30**.

In the **lower course** or valley the land is almost **flat** with a very **broad valley** (or **flood plain**). The river is **wide** with a major process being **deposition**. Erosion is less significant (except during **floods** when the river is said to be in **spate**) and the river transports large volumes of mainly **fine material** (well rounded by attrition) in its bedload and also in **solution / suspension**. The river channel displays great variability, with migration of channels common and river **braiding** (separation of the river channel into several interlocking smaller ones).
Features of the lower course include a **flood plain**, **levees**, **meanders** and **ox-bow lakes** - see figure **31**.

The upper course

Fig.29

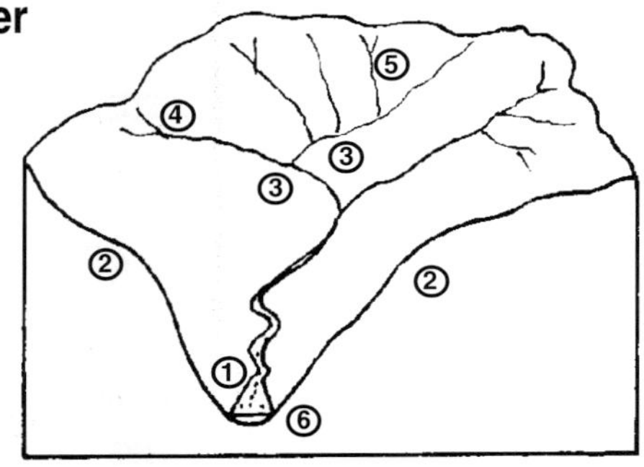

Many small tributaries or hillside 'burns' cut straight down into the landscape.
Key features of a river in its upper course are ..

1. **Narrow river flowing like a torrent, through boulders.**
2. **Steep, V-shaped valley sides right down to the riverside.**
3. **Interlocking spurs.**
4. **Many tributaries feeding into the main river.**
5. **Waterfalls and rapids common.**
6. **There is no flood plain.**

The middle course

Fig.30

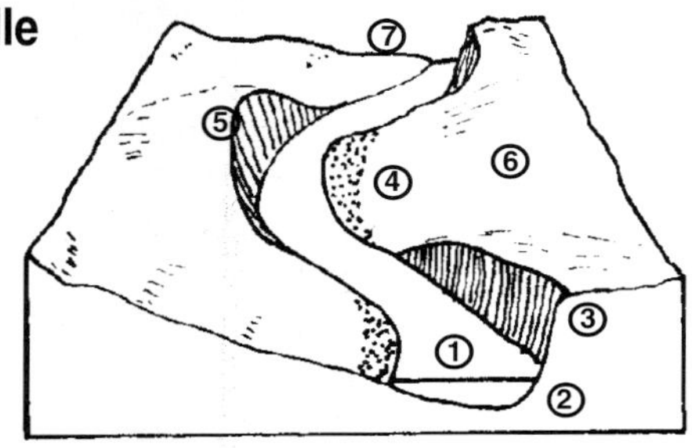

As the volume of water increases in the river, lateral (sideways) erosion becomes more noticeable. **Key features** of a middle course are ..

1. **The river flows fastest on the outside of a meander.**
2. **The river is deepest on the outside of the bend.**
3. **The riverbank is undercut by a strong current creating river cliffs.**
4. **Mud, silt and sand are deposited by slower water on the inside of the bend.**
5. **Steep valley slope (river cliff).**
6. **Gentle slope of valley (point bar).**
7. **The river has a floodplain on one side:**

The lower course

Fig.31

The river meanders across a wide floodplain formed from silts, mud, gravels and sands deposited by the river.
Key features of the river in the lower course.........

1. **A wide river flowing down a very gentle gradient.**
2. **Wide flood plain on both sides of main river.**
3. **River bluffs indicate edge of floodplain.**
4. **Large meanders common in the lower course.**
5. **Ox-bow lake in abandoned river channel.**
6. **Eyots (silty islands in the river), show that river braiding is taking place.**
7. **Levees (raised river embankments) form during floods.**
8. **Point bar opposite a river cliff in large meander.**
9. **Backswamp**

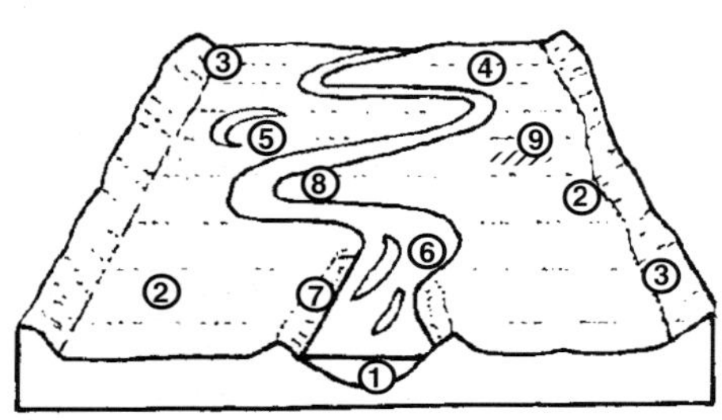

Fig.32

Stages in Meander formation

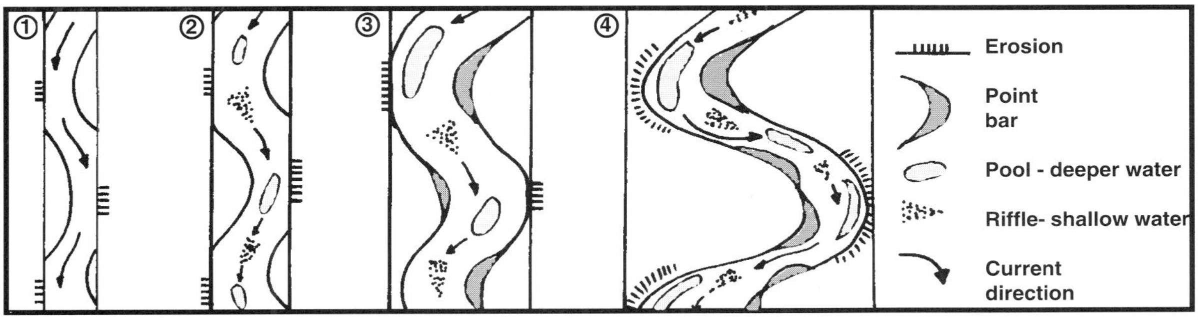

Fluvial Geomorphology

The study of processes and landforms associated with rivers is know as **Fluvial Geomorphology**. Up until the 1950's the emphasis in fluvial geomorphology was on the qualitative description of processes of erosion, transportation and deposition. Little attempt was made to measure or quantify and understand these processes in detail. Since the 1950's the emphasis has now changed to a more detailed study of fluvial processes, examining precise measurements and observations made in the field. This study of processes gives a truer understanding of fluvial landforms and is particularly valuable in helping to solve the problems that rivers pose for people. This **applied fluvial geomorphology** demands an understanding not only of river landscapes but also of the factors such as discharge variations in rivers, the nature and amount of bedload and forms of river channels and the changes they undergo. Fluvial geomorphologists use fieldwork to establish greater understanding of the above. Maps and diagrams can be made of meander formation (figure **32**), ox-bow lake formation (figure **33**) showing actual and predicted stages, channel switching and geomophological diagrams showing landforms (figure **34**).

Fig.33

Stages 1 & 2 of the formation of an Ox-bow lake

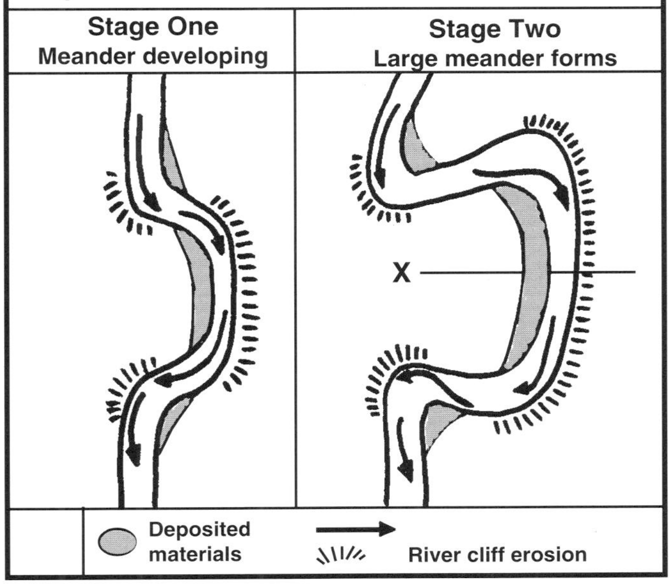

Mapping - recognition and interpretation of the river / valley features

- When describing rivers / river valleys mention the **stage** (**upper, middle or lower course**), **gradient**, **width** of **river valley**, **depth** and **shape** of valley (**V** or **U-shaped** - narrow / broad, flat flood plain, etc).
- Describe the **river course** - twisty / straight and **direction** of flow / changes of direction - is the river **tidal** ? Mention specific **features** e.g. waterfalls, meanders, ox-bow lakes, embankments (flood prevention ?).
- Look for evidence of **artificial drainage** (unusually straight).
- Finally, is there any sign of **underground drainage** i.e. dry valleys or streams, disappearing / re-appearing streams (**springs**), and swallow / potholes / caves suggest a permeable rock, e.g. carboniferous limestone. **(See revision cards on pages 130 -131).**

Floodplain landforms and depositional environments

Fig.34

The location and deposits mapped then illustrated on a block diagram of a typical floodplain

① **Point bars** and **channel bars** - these occur where active deposition is found at the inside bends of meanders or where braiding takes place mid-channel and at the junction of channels (**confluences**)

② **Cut-off** and **abandoned channels** - low gradients and large meanders result in whole bends or parts of bends being cut-off producing **ox-bow lakes**.

③ **Meander scrolls** - over time point bars are commonly deposited on the inside of meanders, each separated by intervening swales. These are known collectively as meander scrolls.

④ **Levees** - along the edge of the river channel flooding can lead to greater deposition and can result in raised banks called levees.

⑤ **Splays** - occur where a river breaks through a levee and the rapid flow of water leads to a spread of channel deposits onto the flood plain.

⑥ **Backswamps** and **lakes** - because of deposition of floodplain materials, damming of water flow frequently occurs forming backswamps and lakes especially where tributaries are blocked.

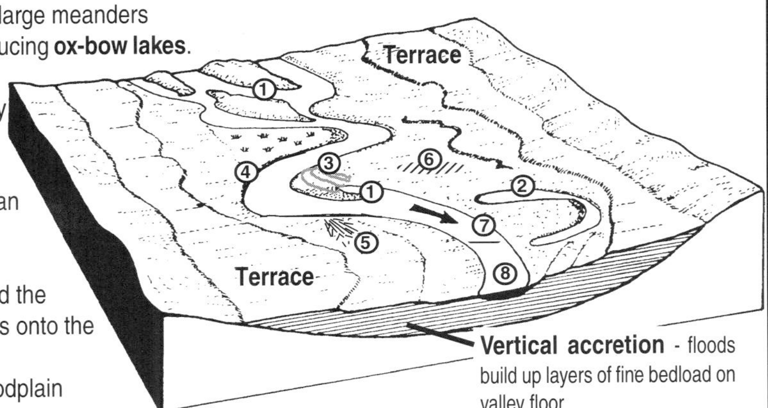

Vertical accretion - floods build up layers of fine bedload on valley floor

Alluvium
Bedrock

⑦ **Riffle** - shallow water shoal
⑧ **Pool** - deeper water

Hydrosphere Revision : Summary Notes

The main Idea........

The water cycle, which constitutes a major physical system, operates on a variety of scales. On the Earth's surface, the movement of water is a major agent in the formation of landforms and landscapes.

The Global Hydrological Cycle or Water Cycle

1..The global **hydrological cycle** involves the continuous transfer of water between ocean, atmosphere and land.
2..97.5% of water is **sea water.**
3..The flow of water in the hydrological cycle is linked with the **transfer of energy**.
4..**Evaporation** is greatest over the Tropical portions of the oceans.
5..There is a **net transfer** of water in the hydrological cycle from **land to sea**, equivalent to 7% of the water moving in the cycle.
6..The **water budget** is the difference between **precipitation** and **potential evapotranspiration**. In the UK precipitation exceeds **evapotranspiration** in winter and the reverse is true in the summer.

Drainage Basins

1..Drainage basins are bounded by **watersheds**.
2..Precipitation over land may be : **intercepted** by vegetation; **evaporated**; **transpired** by plants; flow overland or **infiltrate** into the soil.
3..**Run-off** is water which doesn't infiltrate the ground flowing over the surface.
4..**Permeable** soils let water pass through.
5..**Infiltration** decreases with time.
6..More water can infiltrate sand than can infiltrate silt.
7. Water moves in the ground as **throughflow**, **interflow** and **groundwater flow** (some passes out of the river basin system as **deep basin outflow**)
8..**Aquifers** are rocks which are permeable and can hold a great deal of water.
9..The **aeration zone** lies between the **water table** and the **soil-water zone.**

Streams and Stream hydrographs

1..Water reaching stream channels can arrive as **quickflow**, which is fairly rapid (as overland flow and soil throughflow).
2..**Groundwater** takes some time to arrive at streams from the time of precipitation and therefore tends to arrive continuously at stream channels. **Baseflow** is supplied by groundwater.
3..A **hydrograph** is a record of channel flow made up of quickflow and baseflow.
4..**Basin lag** is the time delay between the peak of a rainfall episode and the peak discharge.
5..**Stream hydrographs** are influenced by : basin shape; gradient of long profile; drainage density; vegetation coverage and rock/soil type.
6..The average annual flow pattern for a river is its **regime**.
7. **Floods** may occur when : rainfall is exceptional; rainfall is combined with snow melt; land drainage is improved; land is deforested.
8..**Flood control** may be expensive and action will depend on the cost of damage a flood causes and of the likelihood of a flood.

Rivers processes

1..Rivers are agents of **erosion, transport and deposition**.
2..River **processes** alter slope, width, depth, sediment and river load.
3..**Hydraulic action** is the effect of a river, removing unconsolidated material from the river bed and banks.
4..**Corrasion** is the main method of river erosion, dragging sediment across the surface, deepening channels.
5..**Headward erosion** occurs at the source, where undercutting extends the river channel.
6..Eroded material is **transported** in three ways : **suspension, bed load (saltation** and **traction**) and **solution**.
7. **Bed load** is moved by **saltation** (a bouncing motion) or **traction** (a sliding motion).
8..The load carried by a river increases with increased discharge and velocity.
9..The lowest velocity at which grains of a given size can be picked up is said to be the **critical erosion velocity**.
10..Varying load capacities in rivers will produce **sorted sediments**.

River Landscapes

1..**'V' shaped valleys** are usually associated with the upper course of a river.
2..**Valley shapes** depend on the geology, efficiency of weathering/slope processes and the capacity of the river.
3..**Floodplains** are built up by channel deposits and overbank deposits.
4..**Straight river channels** are rarely found in nature.
5..**Meander** formation is linked to the development of **riffles** and **pools**.
6..The flow of water in meanders is **helicoidal** (corkscrew), transferring eroded material from **river cliffs** to **point bars**.
7. Erosion at the neck of a meander can change the river's course and produce an **ox-bow lake**. **Meander scrolls** are indicators of former river courses.
8..**Braiding** occurs when rivers become overloaded with sediment.
9..A drop in relative sea level increases erosion ; at first in the lower reaches of the river. This is called **rejuvenation**.
10.The headward limit of rejuvenation is marked by a **knick point** in the river's long profile. Where relative sea levels have changed a number of times, a number of knick points may be present.
11.**Terraces** are often the remnants of former floodplains. Several changes in relative sea level can produce **stepped terraces**.
12.Rivers discharging into the sea may divide into a number of smaller channels, called **distributaries**, as **alluvium** builds up in the main channel.
13.**Deltas** are commonly composed of topset beds, fore-set beds and bottom-set beds.
14.**Fine sediment** may be carried considerable distances out to sea by **turbidity currents**.

Hydrosphere Revision : Unit style assessments

1a. With the aid of figure **35** explain what is meant by the term **hydrological cycle**. (5)

1b. Describe and explain the ways in which **human activity** might modify the natural hydrological cycle (5)

Fig.35

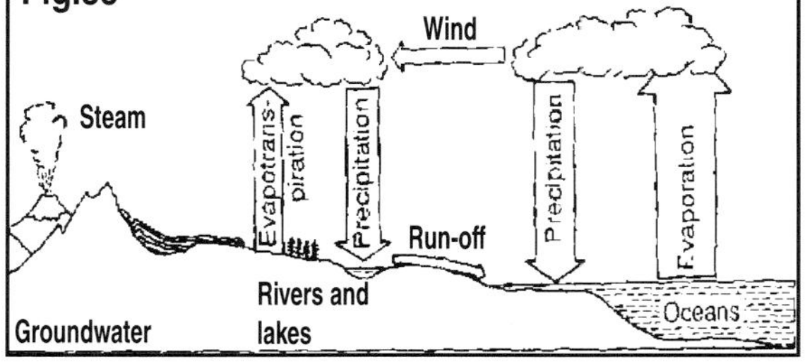

2a. With the aid of an annotated diagram or diagrams, explain the formation of a **meander** and show how it develops over time into an **ox-bow lake**. (5)

2b. Examine figure **36** which illustrates the variations in stream channel characteristics from the source to the mouth of a typical river. Describe the relationships illustrated. (5)

Fig.36

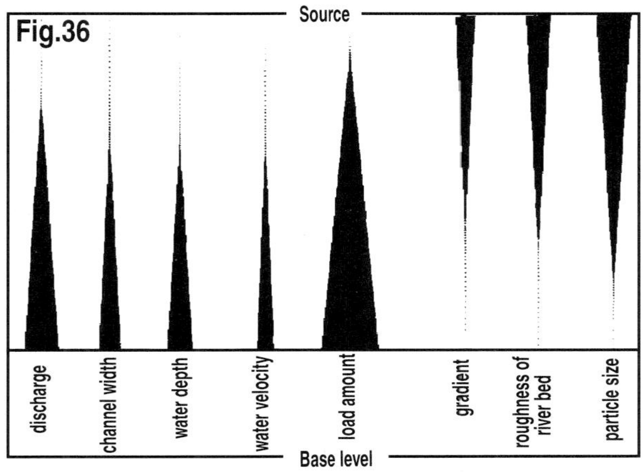

3a. GMT Describe the main components of a stream **hydrograph**. (4)

3b. Examine figure **37** which shows a hydrograph for the River Carron (1988).

(i) Describe the hydrograph shown in figure 37.
(ii) Give possible explanation for variations in the flow of the River Carron in 1988.
(iii) Explain how the hydrograph may be of value to people living along the banks of the River Carron. (6)

Fig.37

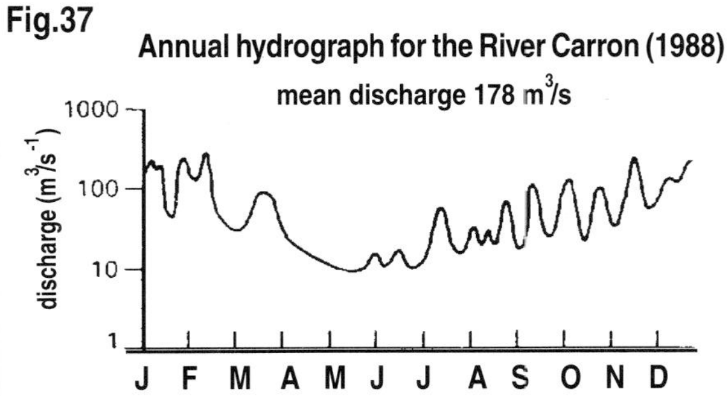

4a. **Either**
Explain the factors which influence the shape of different **V-shaped** valleys **or**
Explain the relative contributions of **slope processes** and **river erosion** in forming a **V-shaped valley.**
You may illustrate your answer. (4)

4b. Examine figure **38** which shows a simple **fieldsketch** of part of the middle course of the River Carron. Draw a rough copy of the fieldsketch and clearly identify the main river landforms and indicate the associated processes responsible for the formation of the landscape shown. (6)

Fieldsketch of part of the River Carron

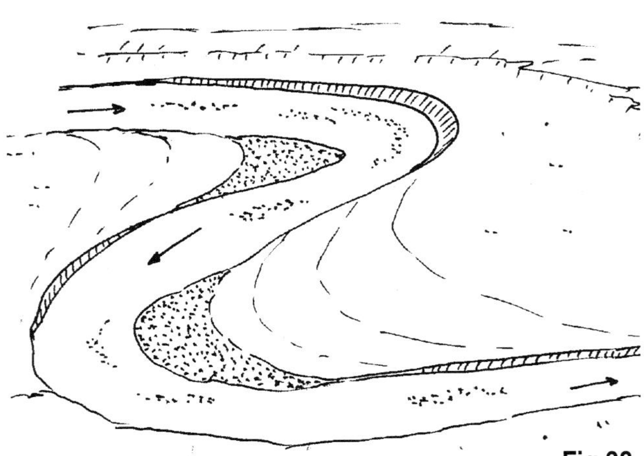

Fig.38

Hydrosphere Revision : Unit style assessments

5. GMT Figure **39** shows figures for precipitation and channel flow (discharge) in a river basin over a 48 hour period.

Fig.39

Time (hours)	Precipitation (mm)	Time (hours)	Channel Flow (m^3 / sec)
0 - 3	1	0	1.00
3 - 6	3	6	0.75
6 - 9	5	12	1.25
9 - 12	2	18	2.00
12-48	-	24	2.50
		30	3.00
		36	2.50
		42	2.00
		48	1.25

a. Construct a **hydrograph** for channel flow and **bar graph** for precipitation and use this information to estimate the **basin lag** during this period. (5)

b. Land use in the area is currently under review. Explain how the above hydrograph would be affected by -
(i) Building a large industrial estate and motor way on the flood plain
(ii) Developing forests in the river basin (5)

Hydrosphere Revision : Exam style assessments

1. GMT Examine figure **40** which shows a graph relating particle movement to velocity in a river channel.

Describe and explain the relationship between river processes (erosion, transportation and deposition) and water velocity for material of particle (grain) size 0.1 mm. (5)

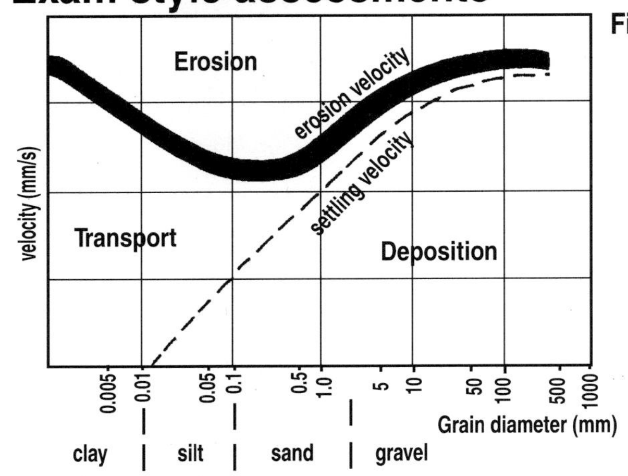

Fig.40

2. **Fieldwork** examining a river **meander** provided the information as shown in figure **41**. Comment on the results obtained, explaining any differences in river bedload and water depth. (5)

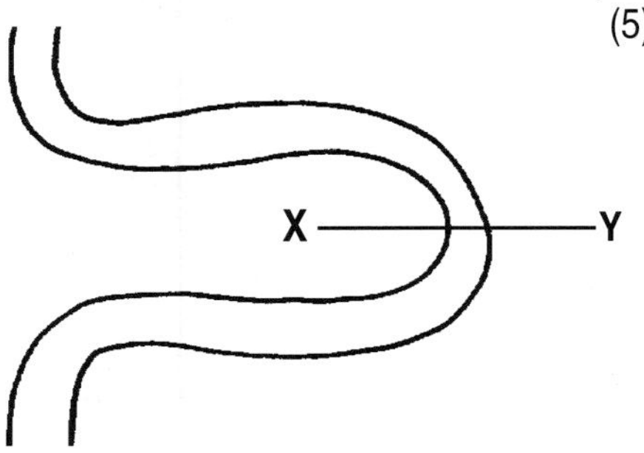

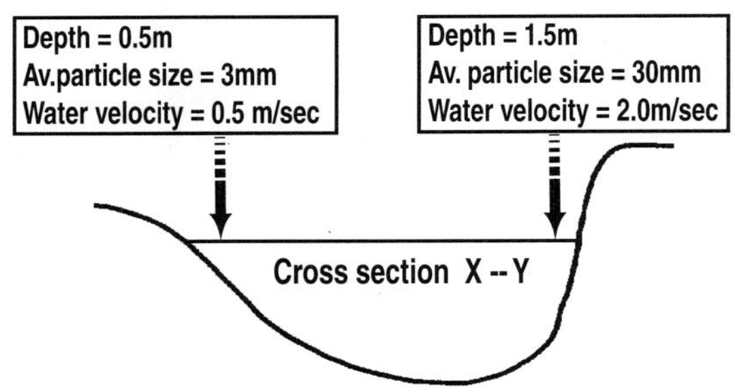

Fig.41

3. Figure **42** below shows samples of the **bedload** found at different points along a river course.

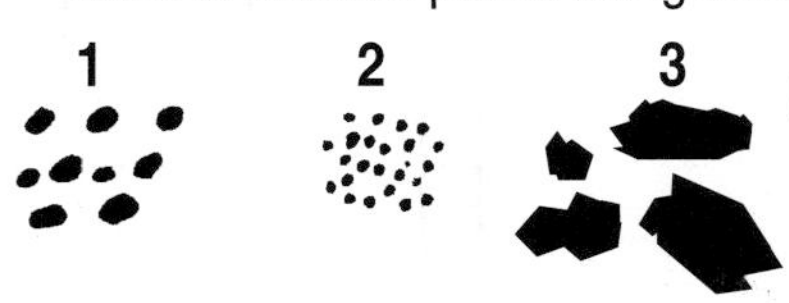

Fig.42

a. Match the sample to the appropriate stage of the river, i.e. **upper, middle, lower course**. (4)

b. Justify your choices commenting on the nature of the bedload and how it was formed. (6)

Fig.43

4. GMT

a. Draw an **annotated fieldsketch** of figure **43**. (5)

b. Choose **one** of the features shown in the photograph and explain its how it was formed. (5)

4. Lithosphere

The main idea of the Lithosphere section is....
The Lithosphere displays a range of landforms and patterns which can be explained by reference to a variety of processes on different scales

What do you need to know ?

Students should have a knowledge and understanding of -

A Process of slope formation

- the modification of relief forms by active geomorphological processes, including the nature and effects of weathering and mass movement on slope forms - soil creep, slopewash, mudflows, scree slopes, rockfalls, landslips and landslides
- analysis of data on listed mass movements

B The development of regional landscapes; the influence of structure, rock type, erosion and deposition upon relief forms and patterns on the regional scale. This is illustrated by study of the following landscape types in the United Kingdom - glaciated upland; upland limestone ; scarp and vale scenery (Jurassic limestone and chalk) ; and should include the following -

- detailed descriptions of the formation of the characteristic features of these landscapes
- the identification of landscape features from these landscapes on OS maps
- the identification and labelling of main landscape features on maps, aerial photographs and sketches
- construction and interpretation of cross-sections and transects

Lithosphere and Rural Land Resources

Both the **Lithosphere** (**core**) and **Rural Land Resources** (**application**) require an understanding of three different landscape types :- Glaciated Upland, Upland Limestone and Scarp & Vale Scenery. The Lithosphere also requires knowledge of **weathering** and **slope formation.** Rural Land Resources includes detailed understanding of **Rural Land Management** i.e. conservation bodies and methods, conflicts over land use, rural management schemes, National Parks etc. There is some overlap between these two sections and we look at Lithosphere in this chapter and Rural Land Resources in chapter 10.

Landscapes

Landscapes are a complex mixture of landforms of varying ages and origins. The landscape is the result of **agents of erosion** working on the **rocks** of the earth's surface over very long periods of time, at different scales - see figure **44**. The different rates of erosion depend upon the resistance of the rocks being acted on - this variation is known as **differential erosion.**

Landscape processes → **Fig.44**

Creating →	Readjustment →	Modification →	Shaping
Orogenies, intrusions faulting	Ice Ages, development of deserts	by glaciers, rivers, sea	Weathering slope processes human activity
Tens of millions →	1-2 million years →	Thousands of years →	Hundreds of years

The Cycle of Erosion or Rock Cycle

Landscapes are the result of two major sets of processes at work on the surface of the Earth. **Mountain Building** - includes all new material which is added to the surface or cause its uplifting, e.g. volcanic eruptions, folding, etc. **Denudation** - the combination of processes which attack, destroy, erode rocks and landforms on the surface. Denudation processes can best be viewed as a series of distinct operations which form an interacting system known as the **Cycle of Erosion** - see figure **45**. All the processes are dominated by **gravity** since all debris or rock fragments are removed, carried downstream to be deposited in valleys, lakes or the sea by agents of erosion -ice, water, wind, humans.

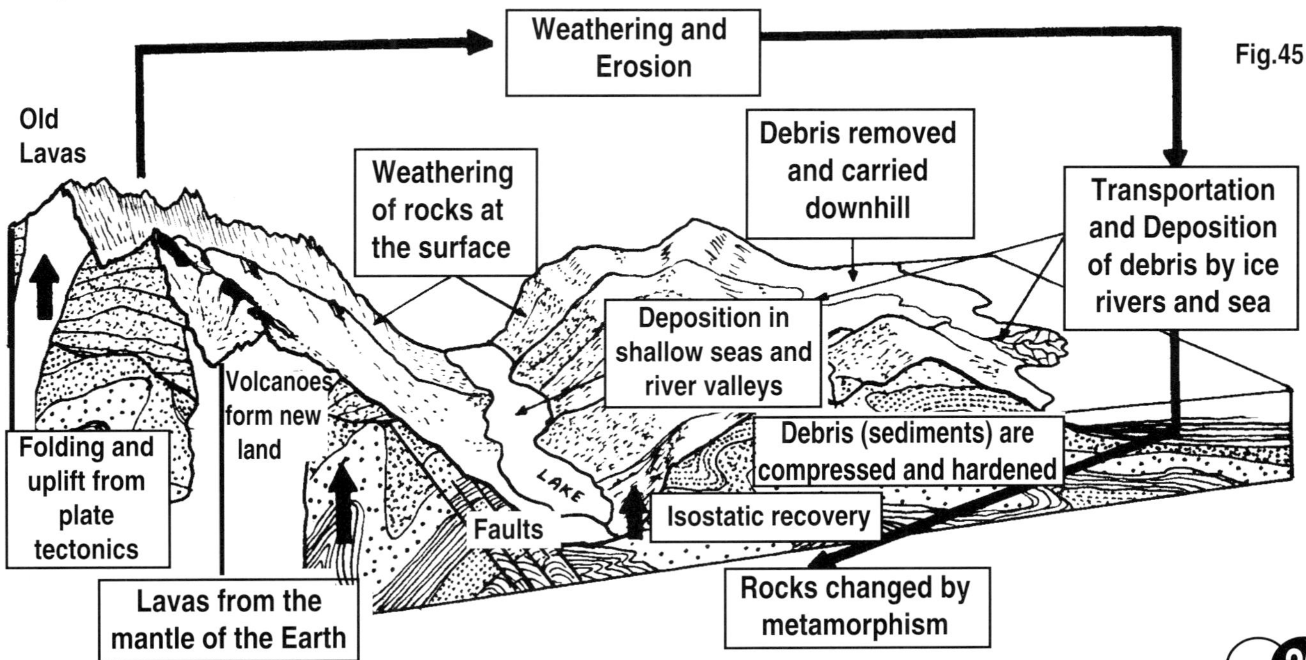

Fig.45

Rocks and Scenery

Fig.46

Landscapes and landforms are influenced by the type and structure of rock. The Highlands of Scotland are mainly composed of granite, schist and gneiss - they are harder than the sedimentary rocks which make up most of the Lowlands. Many hills in the Central Lowlands of Scotland (e.g. Ochils, Pentlands) are composed of lavas and are harder and more resistant than surrounding rocks. Older rocks tend to be harder than young sedimentary rocks which tend to be soft and easily eroded.

IGNEOUS ROCKS

An **Igneous** rock is made up of material which was once molten. Igneous rocks can be classified into two main types: **Extrusive rocks** - lavas & ashes which cool on the surface developing smaller crystal structures. Hard and resistant rocks which include Basalts, Andesites, Obsidian, Pumice and Tuffs (ash).
Intrusive rocks - molten magmas which cool below the surface and develop large-medium crystals. Very hard and resistant rocks which include Granites, Dolerites, Pegmatites, Porphyry (giant crystals).

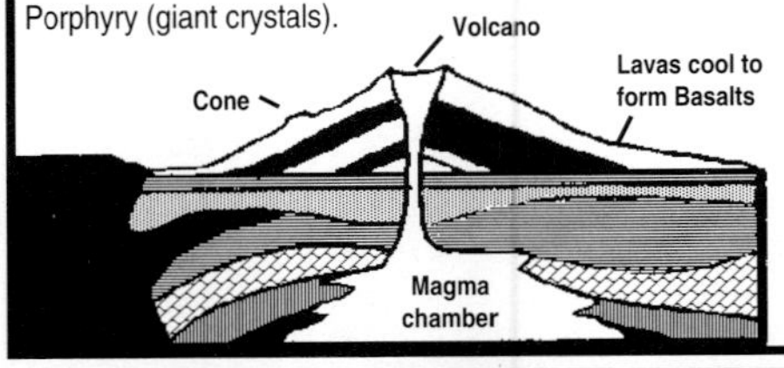

SEDIMENTARY ROCKS

Sedimentary rocks are formed from tiny particles (sediments) which are carried by rivers and are eventually deposited in lakes, seas and oceans. Examples of sedimentary rocks include Limestones(including Chalks), Sandstone, Shales, Coals & Rock Salts. Sedimentary rocks often form low lying areas, valleys and low hills which have been subject to erosion. Sedimentary rocks however, erode at different rates and in different ways and whole areas, such as that of SE England display differential erosion patterns due to these differences in speed of erosion.

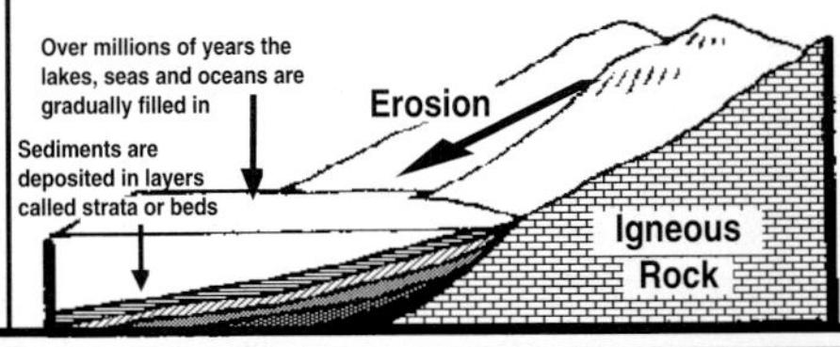

METAMORPHIC ROCKS

A **Metamorphic** rock is an existing rock - an igneous, sedimentary or other metamorphic rock - which has been changed either by heat or pressure or both. Often very hard and known as recrystalline, metamorphic rocks include Marble, Quartzite, Schist and Gneiss. Metamorphic areas often form the last remnants of very old mountainous areas and display a characteristic 'knobbly landscape' pattern of hills and mountains such as that of NW Scotland or the Outer Hebrides.

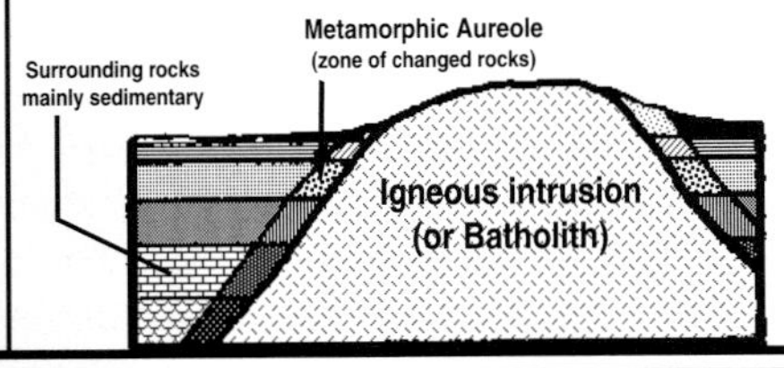

Processes of slope formation

Slope formation relates closely to **2 processes:-**
Weathering loosens rock/soil material which then becomes vulnerable to the **Mass Movement** processes outlined below.

Weathering is defined as all processes, **physical, chemical and biological,** by which rocks are **loosened** and **fragmented** by exposure to the elements (principally by **weather**). It is small-scale natural breakdown of rock. The weathered material forms a layer which lies on top of unaltered rock and is known as the **regolith**.
The main types of weathering are described below and shown on figure **47**.

Fig.47

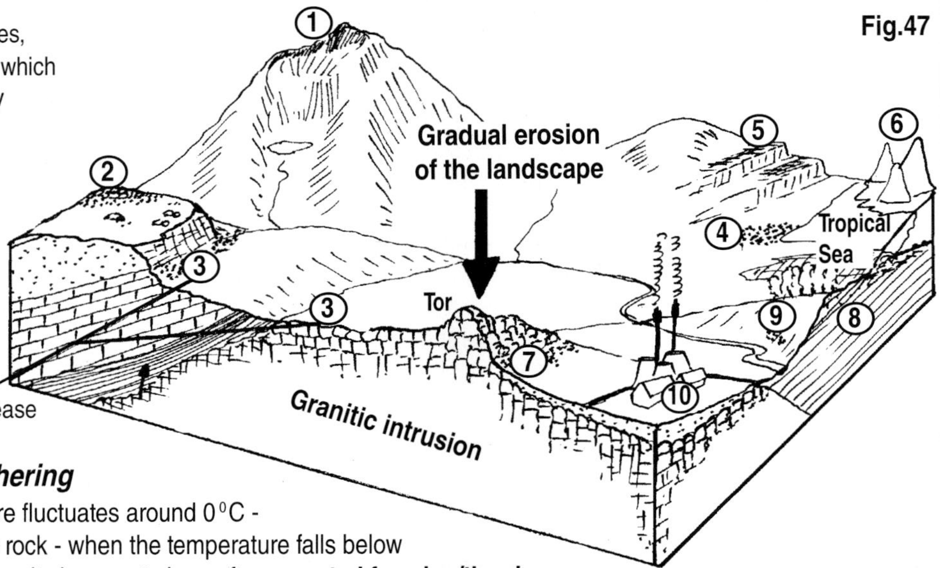

Physical (or Mechanical) Weathering

① **Frost Shattering** - where temperature fluctuates around 0 °C - water enters joints and cracks in the rock - when the temperature falls below 0 °C the water freezes and **expands** as it changes to ice - after **repeated freezing/thawing** the cracks widen and the rock shatters - rock **fragments** accumulate beneath crags or cliffs as **scree** (or **talus**).

② **Exfoliation** (**Onion Weathering**) - common in desert regions - rock surfaces **expand** in the heat of the day and **contract** at night as the temperature falls - the surface is weakened and eventually breaks or peels off (like layers of onion).

③ **Pressure Release** or unloading occurs as the surface rocks are eroded, the pressure is gradually released on underlying rocks which can expand and crack at the surface.

④ **Granular disintegration** is the result of grain-by-grain break up of porous rock e.g. sandstone being overstressed by the growth of salt crystals. This occurs in hot areas when groundwater is continuously evaporated leaving salt deposits behind.

Chemical Weathering

⑤ **Solution or carbonation** is the weathering process performed by rainwater on limestones. Rainwater contains a weak carbonic acid which slowly dissolves calcium carbonate (limestones). Where there is soil cover the process of solution is more effective.

⑥ **Tower Karst** scenery occurs where there is rapid chemical weathering in tropical areas as carbonation is accelerated by heat.

⑦ **Granite Tors** indicate that subsurface chemical weathering has occurred before the rocks are exposed at the surface by erosion.

Biotic Weathering - by plants, animals and humans

⑧ **Vegetation cover** shades soil surfaces. Plant roots expand as plants grow and can force rocks apart. This sets off weathering.

⑨ **Animals** - burrowing animals can expose rocks to weathering. Limpets release acids attacking coastal rocks.

⑩ **Industrialisation** by humans has increased the acidity of rainwater accelerating chemical weathering. Humans quarry and mine on a large scale exposing rocks to weathering.

Weathered material builds up where it is formed: no movement is involved except where the effects of gravity cause it to slip or fall downwards. This often involves Mass Movement of debris (see figure 48).

Mass Movement (or mass wasting)

Mass movement occurs when weathered material moves downhill under the force of **gravity** (often lubricated by rainwater). Mass movement (or **mass wasting**) includes **soil creep, mudflows, landslides, rockfalls, slumping** and **slope wash -** see figure 48**.**

Slopes represent the basic unit of every landscape. They are the ideal method for classifying any landscape since each comprises a series of slopes of different sizes and shapes.

Mass movement on any slope depends upon a variety of factors including **geology, climate**, **vegetation**, **type of regolith**, **human activities** and **time**. Human beings influence mass movements by deforesting slopes, removing grass, by quarrying, road building and walking in large numbers on steep slopes.

(**Solifluction** is the slow downhill movement of soil (or scree) cover after repeated freeze-thaw processes).

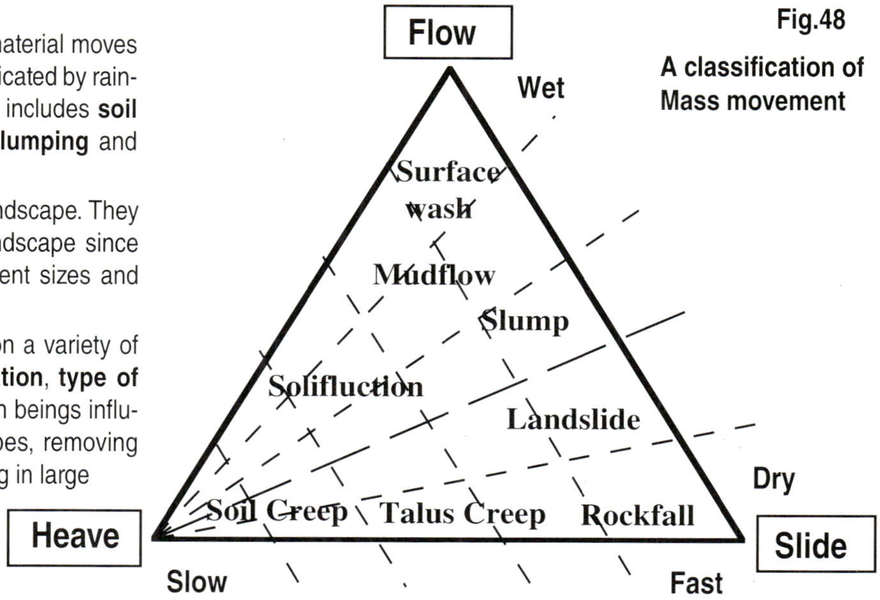

Fig.48

A classification of Mass movement

Rockfall

+ p 103

Fig.49

Broken rock falling downslope usually very suddenly and quickly. The material collects at the foot of the slope and is known as a **talus** (e.g. a **scree slope**).

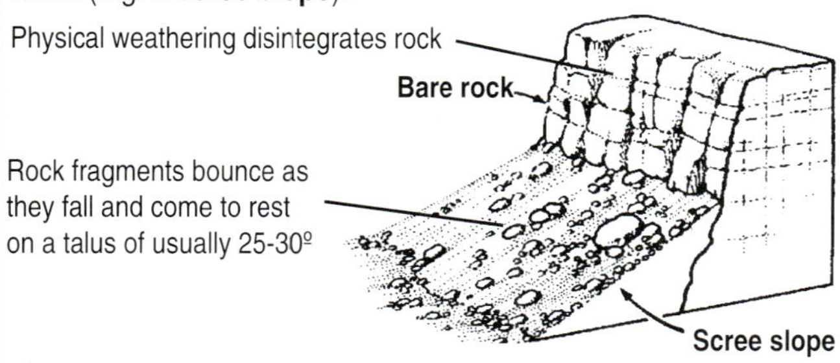

Rockfall involves rapid movement but in relatively dry material.

Mudflow

Fig.50

A flow of saturated materials downslope usually after torrential rainfall and in areas of sparse vegetation. They are deeper than slides and resemble the flow of a stream.

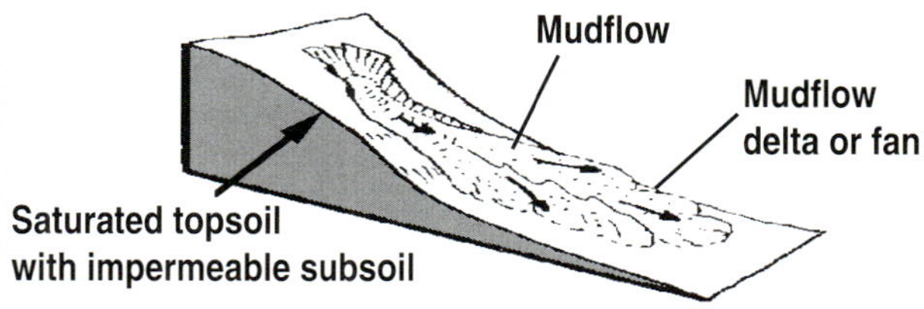

Mudflow on steep farmland shown opposite.

The flow occurred after heavy rainfall over a two week period.

The flow is in danger of destroying a power line.

Landslide

Fig.51

Rapid movements of soil or rock on less steep slopes.
Slides usually occur after heavy rain or snowmelt. The increase in the overlying weight causes rock or soil to slide downhill.

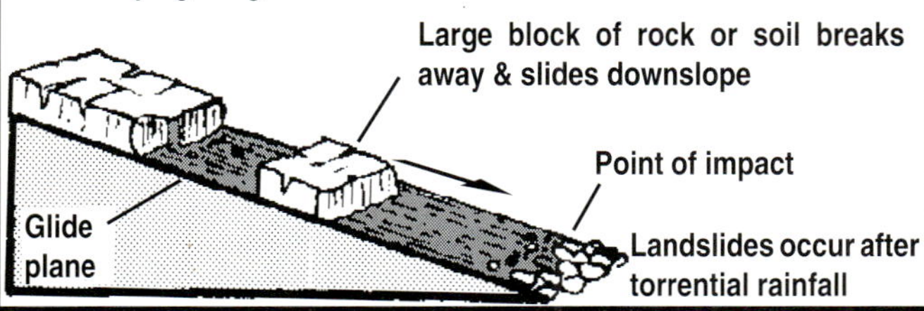

Slumping

Fig.52

Slumps occur in weaker rocks and involve some rotational movement. For example, where clay underlies sandstone, slumping can occur after heavy rainfall or earthquakes.

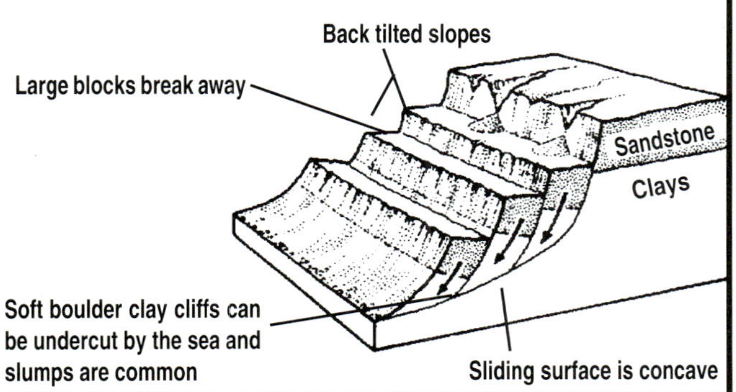

Soil Creep

+ P101

Fig.53

A very slow process in which saturated soil expands at right angles to the slope. As the soil dries out it contracts in a vertical direction - the result is a creeping, downward movement. Where soil cover or vegetation is removed the rate of creep is greatly increased.

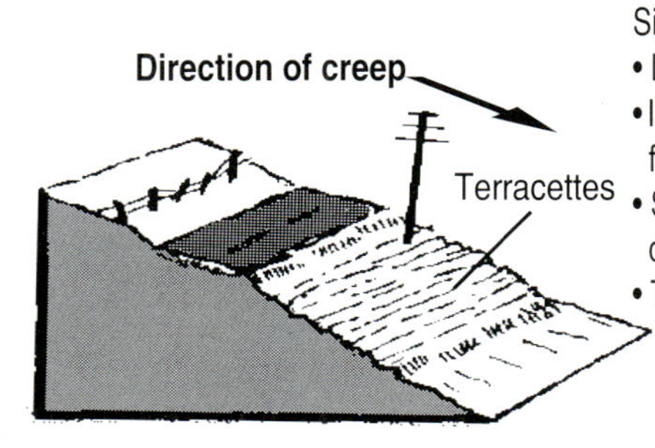

Signs of Soil Creep :
- Listing telegraph pole
- Increasing soil depth at foot of slope
- Stones can pile up downhill behind walls
- Trees bent downhill

Glaciated Upland Landscapes

Fig.54

Typical major areas of the British Isles which are classified as glaciated upland landscapes are shown on figure **54** - they include the **Scottish Highlands** (Grampian Mountains, NW Highlands); the **Southern Uplands**; **The Lake District** and **The Pennines** ; **Snowdonia** (and the Cambrian Mts of Wales).

Glaciated Upland Landscapes are characterised by high relief displaying jagged mountains dissected by deep, sculpted valleys; by huge corries and lochans; by long narrow lochs, etc. These landscapes form some of the most spectacular and sensitive scenery in the British Isles. Some areas are National Parks - e.g. The Lake District, Snowdonia, etc.

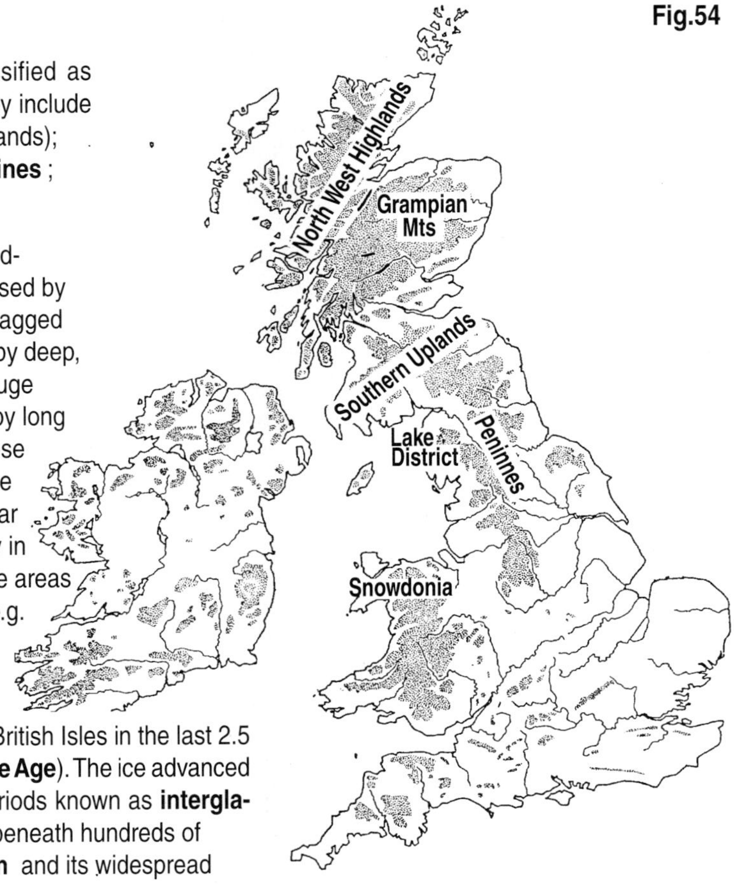

As many as 20 different glacial periods have affected the British Isles in the last 2.5 million years (the **Pleistocene** period which includes the **Ice Age**). The ice advanced in periods known as **glacials** and retreated in warmer periods known as **interglacials**. Until 18,000 years ago most of the British Isles lay beneath hundreds of metres of ice. Geomorphologists talk of the **glacial system** and its widespread effects on the landscape.

The Glacial System

A **glacier** behaves as a system with inputs, processes and outputs (see figure **55**). Glacial activity is a balance between the **accumulation** of snow and ice and **ablation** or loss by evaporation and meltwater to river systems.

Inputs to the glacial system include snow (falling as precipitation or from avalanches above). The glacier is water, as ice, in **storage**.

Outputs from the glacial system include **water**, either as meltwater or as water vapour as a result of evaporation; also **rock debris** and **ice** trapped in hollows.

Where inputs exceed outputs, there is a zone of accumulation - usually found in high areas.

In lower areas where outputs exceed inputs, the zone of ablation exists.

The **zone of equilibrium** normally corresponds to the snow-line and is where rates of accumulation and ablation are equal. Glaciers flow by **basal sliding** and **internal deformation**. Seeping meltwater accumulates at the base of the glacier and the weight of the upper layers of the glacier causes the lower layers to behave as a fluid. The rate of flow varies with the nature of the bedrock, amount of ice and slope.

The Glacial system

Fig.55

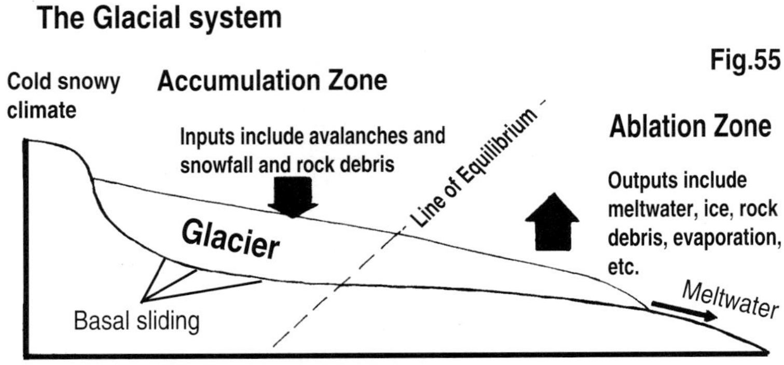

Glacial flow

Fig.56

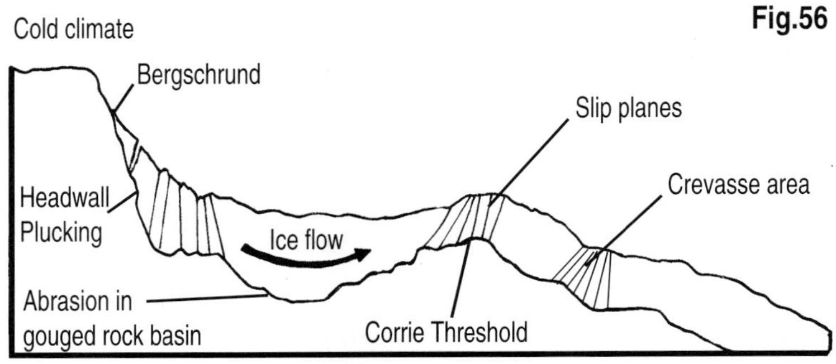

Glacial erosion occurs through **abrasion** (sandpapering effect) and **plucking** (tearing). Erosion is influenced by rock type and structure and the relief of the area. Abrasion occurs when rock under a glacier is worn away by the grinding action of rock fragments embedded in the ice. Plucking is the removal of rock fragments which have become frozen into the base and sides of a glacier, for example on the back wall of a corrie. Generally abrasion produces smoothed surfaces whilst plucking tends to produce jagged features. Where pressures from the ice above produce extending and compressing flows (see figure **56**) **differential erosion** creates a varied landscape. In the ablation zone, deposition occurs beneath the ice, by dumping at its margins and through meltwater or **fluvioglacial** processes.

Relief features of Glaciated Upland Landscapes

The upland or mountain areas of the British Isles display many characteristic features of glaciated areas such as those illustrated in the figure below. These features of upland glaciation may be classified according to their **formation** - the table below provides the key to figure **57** and describes the formation classification for features of upland glaciation.

Glacial Erosion	Glacial Deposition	Fluvioglacial (Meltwater)	Post-Glacial
Pyramidal Peak	(9) Moraine (terminal, lateral and/or medial)	(11) Outwash Plain	(13) Scree
(1) Arete	(10) Erratics	(12) Lochan (Tarn)	(14) Alluvial Fan
(2) Corrie (Cwm/cirque)			(15) Misfit stream
(3) Roche Moutonnee			(16) Gullies
(4) Hanging Valley			
(5) U-shaped valley			
(6) Ribbon (or Finger) Lakes			
(7) Abraded summits			
(8) Truncated spurs			

Fig.57

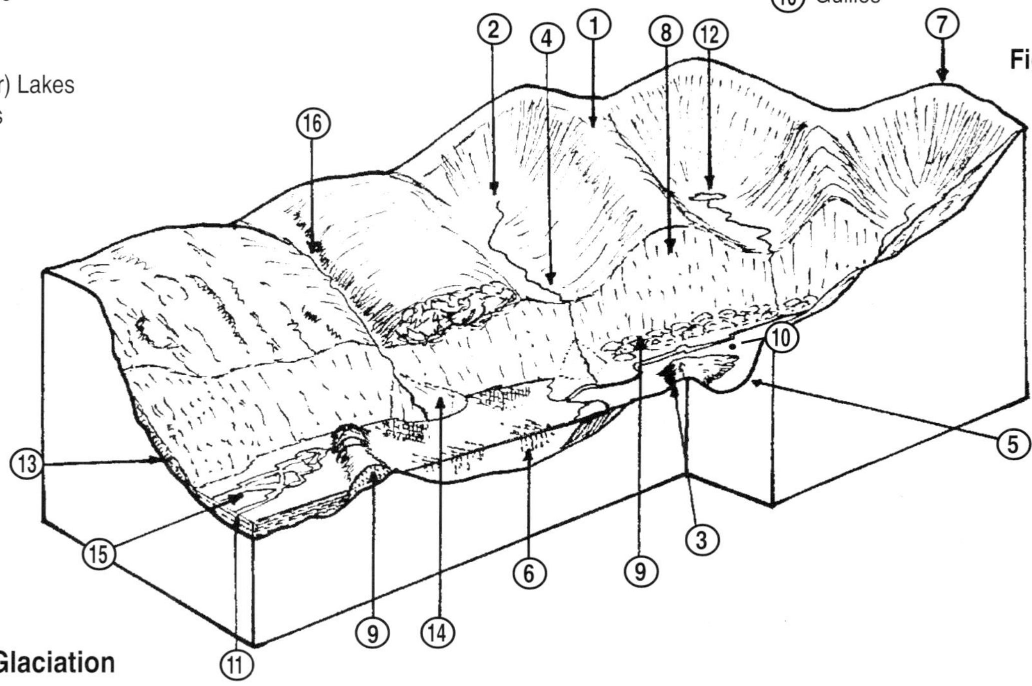

Stages in Upland Glaciation

Fig.58

During the Ice Age

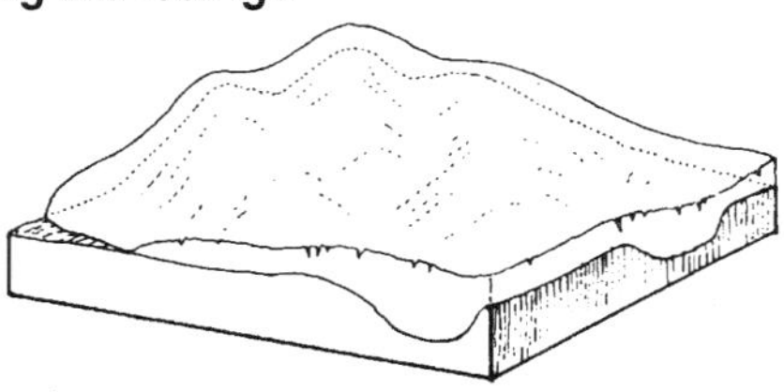

End of the Ice Age

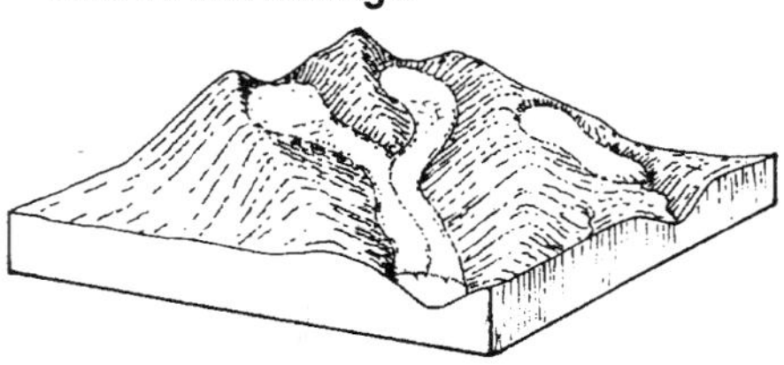

Glacial Erosion processes include

- **Abrasion** when rock under a glacier is worn away by the grinding action of of rock fragments embedded in the ice
- **Plucking** - the removal of rock fragments which have become frozen into the base and sides of the glacier
- **Frost shattering** - loosens rock, making it more easily eroded by abrasion and plucking (called the **freeze-thaw** process)

The results of glacial erosion processes are illustrated in figure **58**.

Present day

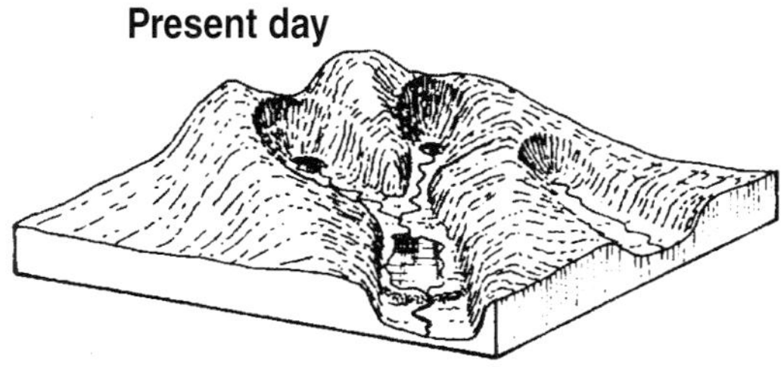

It is important when revising glacial erosion that candidates can explain the formation of various features of upland erosion. For more detailed information please refer to **pages 131 -132 (Revision Cards on Glacial features and processes).**

The formation of Corries

Fig.59

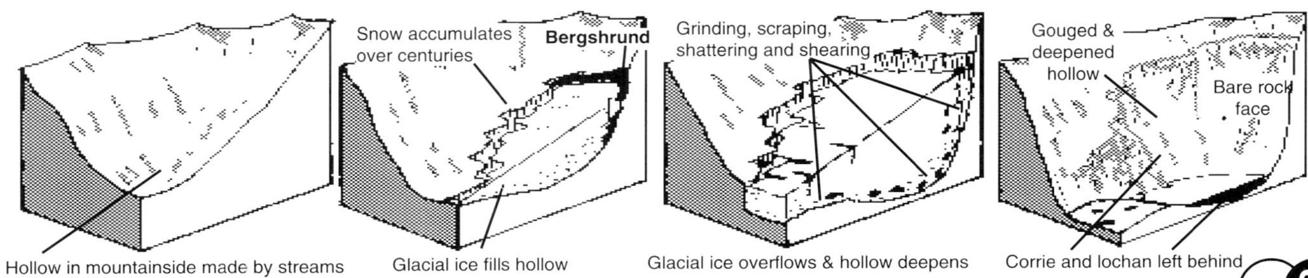

Glacial deposition

Glaciation affected not only the major mountain or upland areas, their summits and slopes, but also the great valleys and lowland plains around their fringes. These areas also display many characteristic deposition features such as those illustrated in figure **60**.

Features of glacial deposition

Fig.60

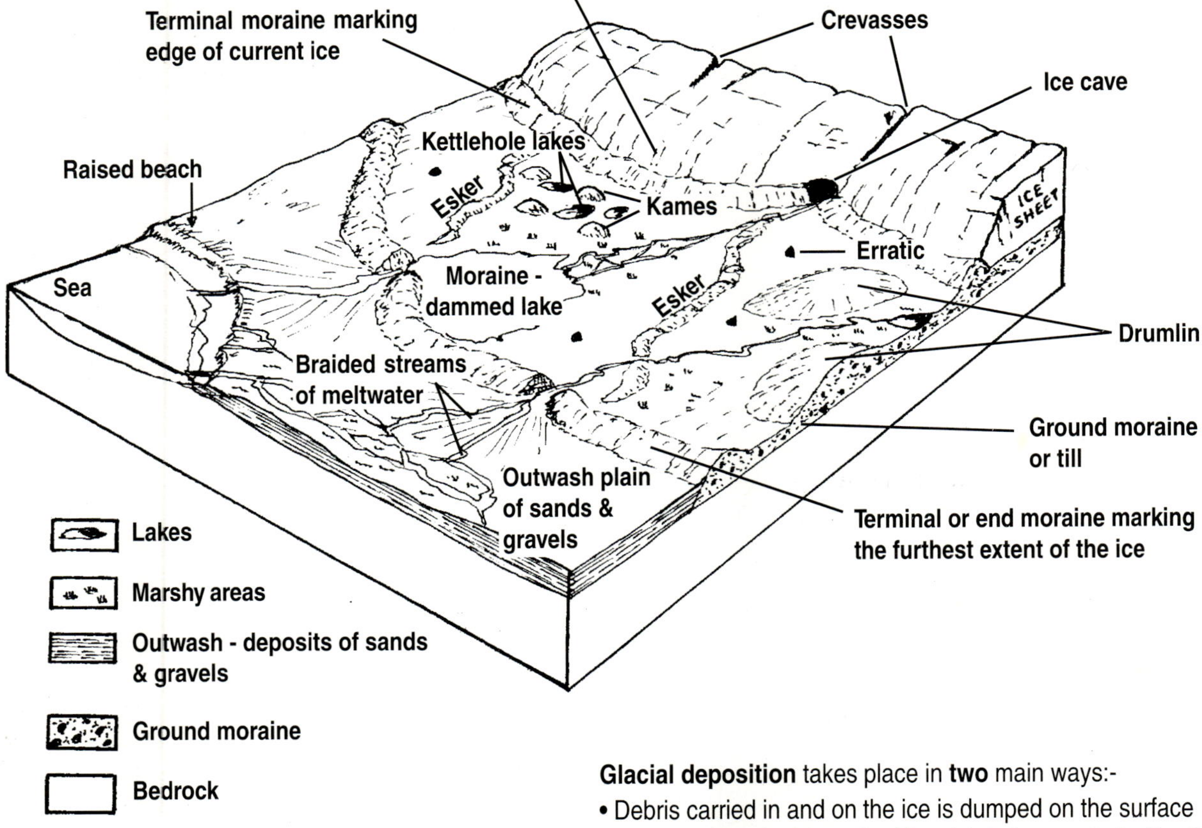

Glaciers are able to transport huge quantities of materials (rock debris). The debris can be carried in three ways:-

- **Subglacial debris** - moved along the floor of the valley either by ice (as ground moraine) or by meltwater streams under the glacier.
- **Englacial debris** - carried within the glacier itself.
- **Supraglacial debris** - carried on the surface of the glacier.

The collective name for all the materials (boulders, sands, gravels, clays, etc) deposited by glaciers is **drift.**

Drift deposits can be classified into:-

- **Ground moraine** (or **till**) including **unsorted** materials directly deposited by ice.
- **Fluvioglacial materials** (or **outwash**) - including **sorted** materials deposited by meltwater streams.
  Fluvioglacial deposits also include materials originally deposited by the ice and later picked up and redeposited by meltwater. Materials deposited by water are **sorted into layers** as deposition occurs - the heaviest debris being deposited first (at the bottom) and the lightest debris deposited last (at the top).

Landscapes produced by glacial deposition are very complex. Melting ice deposits moraine mainly at the ends and edges of retreating glaciers. The later advances of ice (remember there have been as many as 20 Ice Ages affecting the British Isles) steamroller and bulldoze the earlier glacial deposits, reshaping and redepositing them in new areas.

Glacial deposition takes place in **two** main ways:-

- Debris carried in and on the ice is dumped on the surface of the land as the ice melts. The debris is unsorted with all sizes of rocks, stones and fine fragments mixed up and left on the surface. This material is known as **ground moraine** (or till) and it often contains evidence to indicate the main direction of ice flow. Elongated boulders are often left with their long-axes pointing in the ice movement direction.

- As the ice melts, outflowing streams of meltwater flowing from the snout of the glacier carry away rock debris. The streams deposit this material, mainly sands and gravels, across the floor of U-shaped valleys. This **fluvioglacial** material is sorted - arranged in layers - as it is deposited.

Landforms characteristic of glacial deposition can therefore be classified as either those deposited by ice (**glacial**) or those deposited by meltwater (**fluvioglacial**) - see figure **60**. Examples of each classification are listed below

Features of glacial deposition *include* - **erratics, moraines (terminal, lateral** (side) and **medial), drumlins.**

Features of fluvioglacial deposition *include* - **outwash plains, eskers, kames** and **kettleholes.**

Glacial features on OS Maps

Look for corries (**coire** in Scottish Highlands, **Cwm** in Snowdonia) with close, semi-circular contours, cliffs and scree - often contain a small lake (**tarn**), **Aretes** (sharp ridges) often separate adjacent corries. Pyramidal Peaks will have corries and aretes radiating outwards. U-shaped valleys (steep sides and flat valley floor may be occupied by long, narrow ribbon lakes or misfit streams). Hanging Valleys are tributary valleys which drop steeply often via waterfalls, to the main U-shaped valley (or Glacial trough).

Upland Limestone or Karst Landscapes

All rocks influence the landscape of which they are the base but none form such distinctive landscapes as Carboniferous or Mountain Limestone. The most extensive areas of Carboniferous Limestone in the British Isles are shown in figure **61**. Many of these form well-known landscapes such as the Yorkshire Dales, Peak District and the Cheddar Gorge. The scenery that has developed in such areas is known as **Karst** (named after an area of limestone in former Yugoslavia).

Carboniferous Limestone is a hard, grey sedimentary rock. It is made entirely of calcium carbonate ($CaCO_3$) and contains many fossilised remains. Limestone is both **permeable** (allows water to pass through it) and **pervious** (allows water through its rock structure) rock. It is the only common rock which is physically strong (hard) and yet will also dissolve slowly in rainwater. Consequently the joints (vertical cracks) and bedding planes (horizontal layers) within the limestone are gradually enlarged by underground water into wide channels and gaping chambers which can absorb surface drainage. The result is a 'Gruyere' landscape - one full of holes !

The geological history of Karst areas such as that of the Yorkshire Dales begins in the Carboniferous Period between 345 and 280 million years before present. Shallow tropical seas covered the area. Corals formed on the sea floor where skeletal remains of sea creatures were also deposited. Over a period of 60 million years these were compressed into limestones as other sediments were overlain. Massive crustal movements then uplifted the entire area forming a giant anticline (upfold) known as the Pennines. As the younger sedimentary rocks have been eroded, the limestone has been exposed, forming rugged uplands reaching 600 metres in parts of the North Pennines.

Carboniferous Limestone Areas

Fig.61

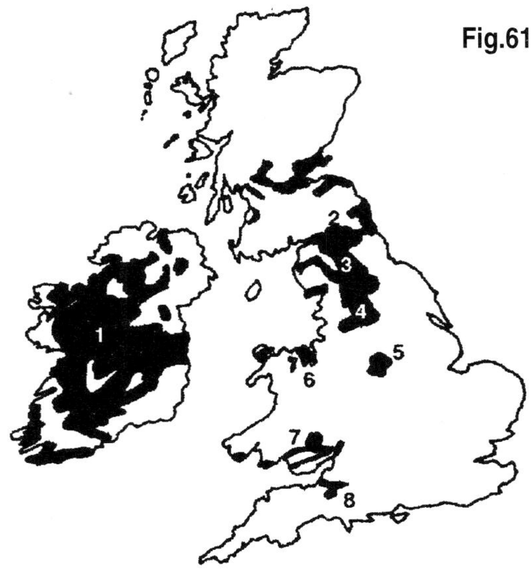

1. Central Plain
2. Cheviot Hills
3. Pennines
4. Yorkshire Dales
5. Peak District
6. North Wales
7. Brecon Beacons
8. Mendip Hills

The main outcrops of Carboniferous Limestone in the Yorkshire Dales were first exposed two million years ago. Since then, alternating climates of the Ice Ages have shaped the limestone by contrasting erosional processes. The process of **solution** has been of major importance in shaping the limestone landscape. The rate at which limestone dissolves depends upon the amount of carbon dioxide present in the water acting upon it. The availability of this gas depends on the richness of the vegetation which in turn is determined by the climate. During interglacial periods water rich in CO_2 dissolved the limestone and eroded cave systems. This process continues in the present day climate.

GlacioKarst Scenery

Fig.62

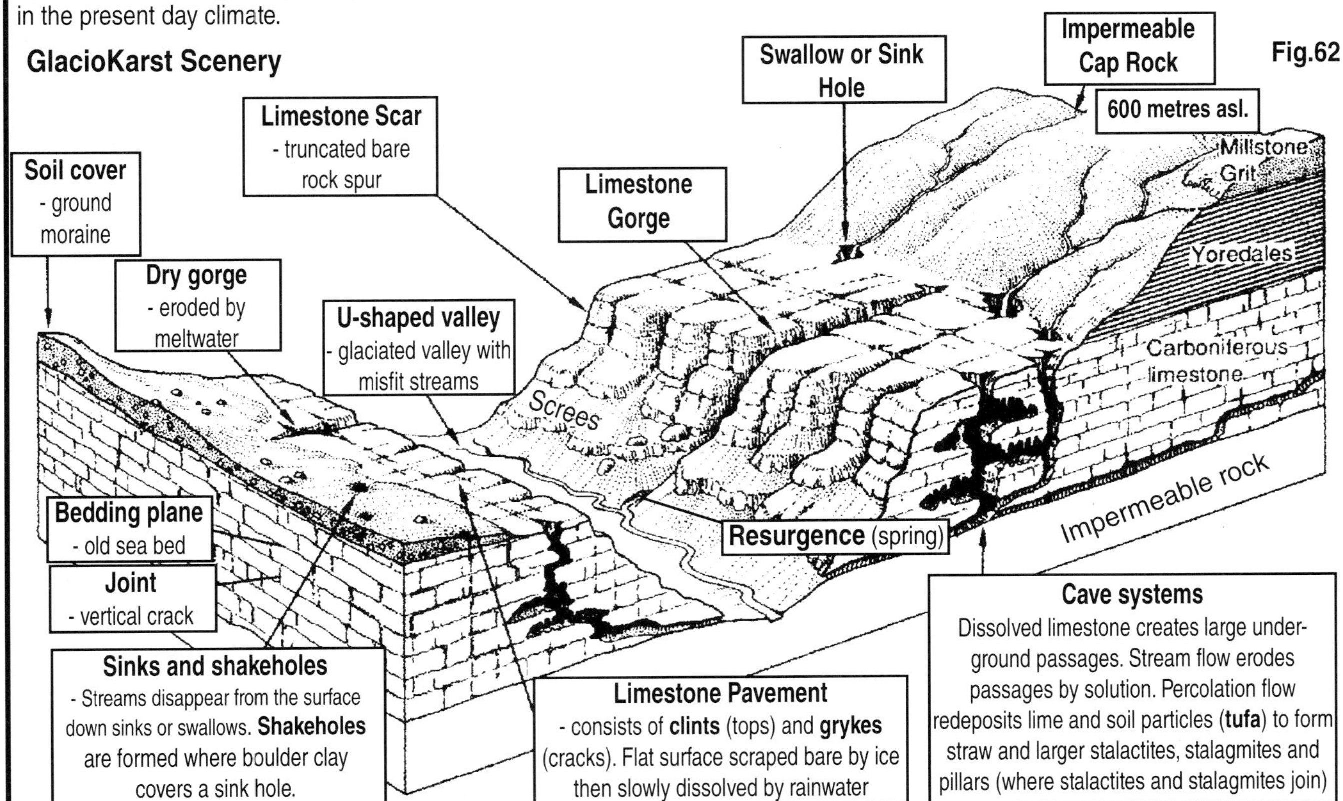

During glacial periods sub-surface systems were frozen. Ice became the main agent of erosion but on the surface only. Large glaciers scoured the landscape. They deepened the valleys (Dales), truncated many of the scars, and sculpted bare the plateau areas. In warmer periods meltwater carved deep gorges and enlarged the main dales. Geologists refer to the landscape which is the product of these alternations as **Glaciokarst** - see figure **62** for the main landscape features. (See page **129** - Revision cards),

Limestone Pavement overlooking Ingleborough Hill, Yorkshire Dales **Fig.63**

Formation of a Limestone Pavement **Fig.64**

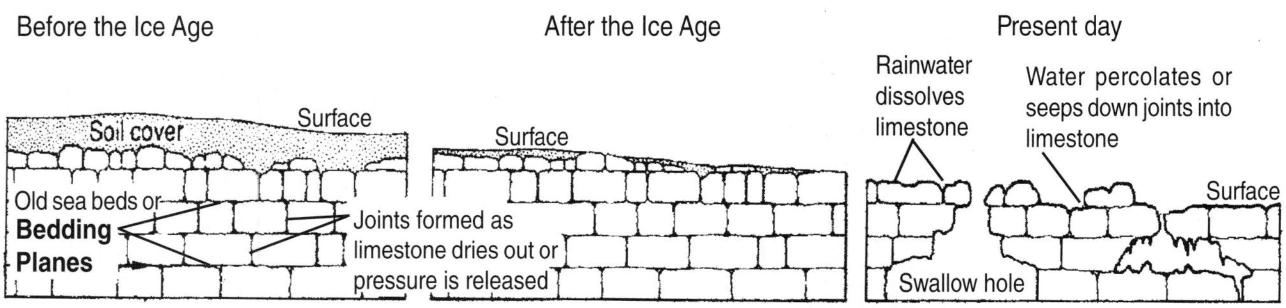

Classification of Limestone landforms

- **Surface features caused by solution** are flat areas of exposed limestone - for example limestone pavements with clints and grykes.
- **Drainage features of Karst areas** - rivers which have their source on surrounding impermeable rocks may disappear down swallow holes or sinks, enlarged joints (or pot holes) and into cave systems, caverns and underground galleries. A resurgence or spring is where a stream reappears at the surface where the permeable limestone meets the impermeable underlying rocks, such as slate.
- **Surface features resulting from underground drainage** - where meltwater streams surged through underground cave systems as the last glaciers melted, the resultant enlarged caverns became too large to support the rock above them and they collapsed, creating limestone gorges. Where the area above a cave system collapses, then a small surface depression forms - called a **doline**. Steep sided dry valleys also occur where gorges have been further eroded by winter streams or small glaciers.
- **Underground depositional features** - these are the classic cave features including straw stalactites (young & wafer thin), stalactites (from the ceiling) and stalagmites (from the ground), pillars and flowstones.

O.S. Maps of Carboniferous Limestone Areas

- Look for **upland areas up to 600 metres** above sea-level
- Look for **frequent rock features** for example - scars, bare rock surfaces, gorges, limestone pavements, shakeholes and sink holes.
- Look for **rivers disappearing down swallowholes and re-appearing as springs** with dry valleys - evidence of pervious rock. Look for **pot holes, caves,** etc.

Scarp and Vale scenery - Chalk and Clay Landscapes

These include areas with **Chalk** and **Jurassic limestone** (both are softer forms of limestone which are less resistant to erosion than Upland or Carboniferous (older & harder) limestone. They form lower, more rounded hills beside relatively flat vales often composed of soft **Clay**.

Typical areas of Scarp and Vale scenery are shown in figure **65** and include the Chilterns, the North and South Downs (Chalk & Clay) and the Cotswolds (Jurassic Limestone).

Structure of Scarp and Vale areas

In the North and South Downs, the rocks have been **folded** to form an **anticline**. Subsequent erosion has exposed underlying clay. The chalk layer has a gentle **dip slope** and a steep **scarp** slope - as shown in figure **66**.

Limestones in the UK

Fig.65

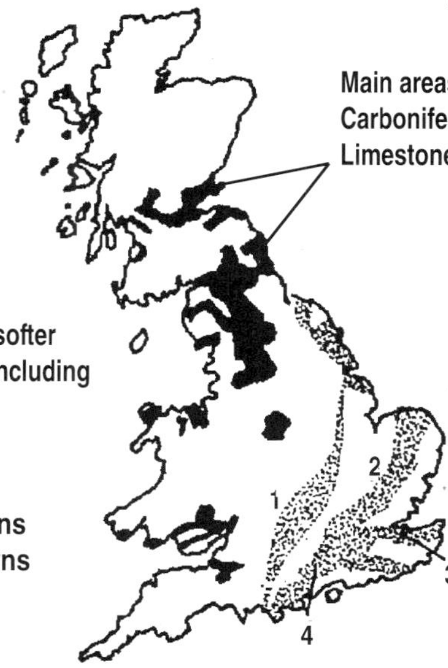

Scarp and Vale scenery

Fig.66

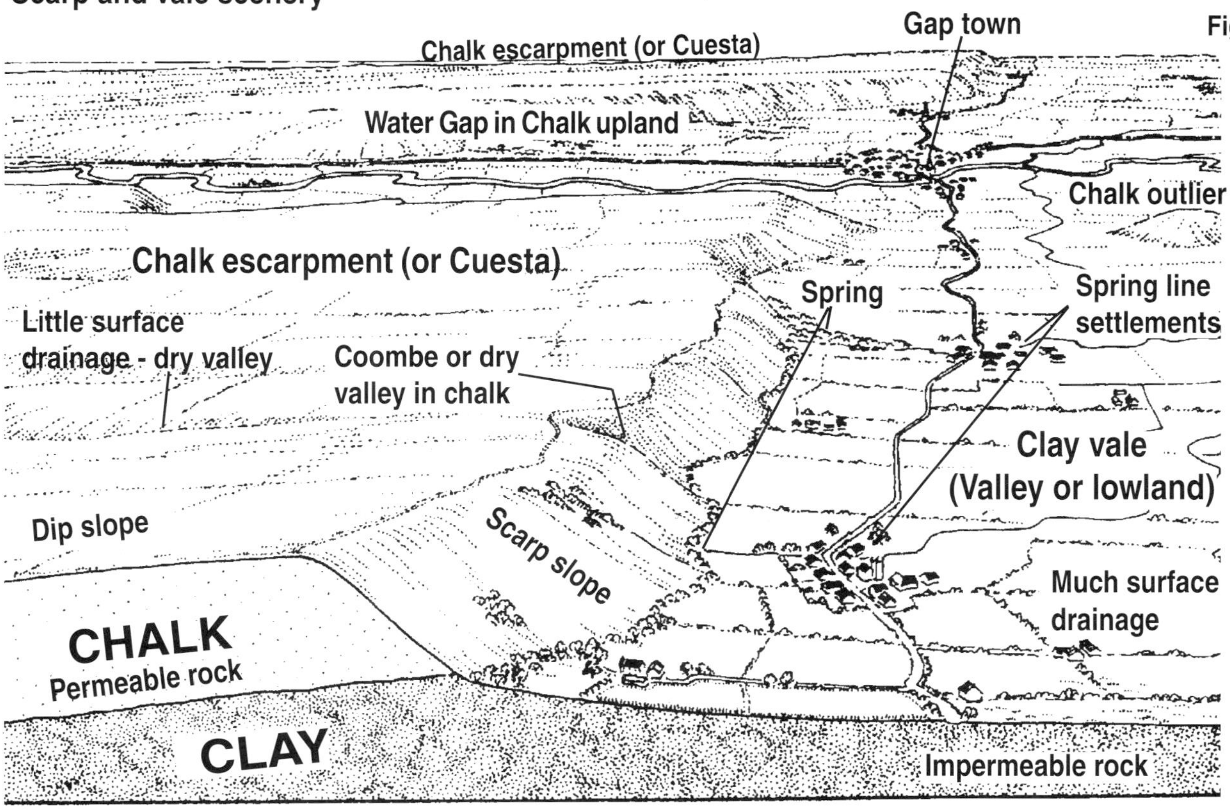

Relief and drainage of Scarp and Vale areas

(**On O.S. Maps look for - rounded hills** about 200m with a steep scarp slope and a gentle dip slope. **Springs** may be present at the foot of the scarp slope and there may be **dry valleys** on the dip slope).

The relief consists of a **cuesta** (or **escarpment**) i.e. a gentle dip slope and steep scarp slope in the chalk with a flat, low lying clay vale at the foot of the scarp slope. The chalk Downs rise to about 250 metres. The **permeable chalk** overlies the **impermeable clay** which forms a valley (vale). Rainwater flows down through the chalk and accumulates above the clay. The chalk **aquifer** (rock which can hold water) becomes saturated with water up to a level known as the **water table**)- where the water table meets the ground surface e.g. at the foot of the scarp, springs are formed. Dry valleys are found on the dip slope (formed when the water table was higher). The clay vale has surface drainage (impermeable).

Settlement, Communications and Farming

Ancient settlement at the top of scarp (for good defence, drainage and supplies of flint from the chalk). **Modern settlement** at the foot of the scarp along the **springline** (good water supply, on clay vale with fertile soils). **Gap towns** are found where rivers have eroded through the escarpment. Communications follow gaps and dry valleys and run parallel with the foot of the scarp slope. Sheep farming and cereals (with fertiliser) are the main land use on chalk and mixed farming (arable and dairy) on the clay vale.

Recent farming changes in Chalk landscapes

In the chalk downlands of the Hampshire Basin in Southern England, farming has been experiencing changes in recent years.

Changes
Agribusiness - farms commercially run by large companies.
Amalgamation of smaller farms to form more efficient units with larger fields and more extensive use of farm machinery, fertiliser, etc.

Benefits
Greater output as larger fields allow more efficient use of machinery.
Widespread use of fertiliser means that the same crops can be grown year after year with less need for crop rotation.

Concerns
Larger fields have resulted in the destruction of hedges, woodlands etc. Loss of wildlife habitat with less shelter and more risk of soil erosion.

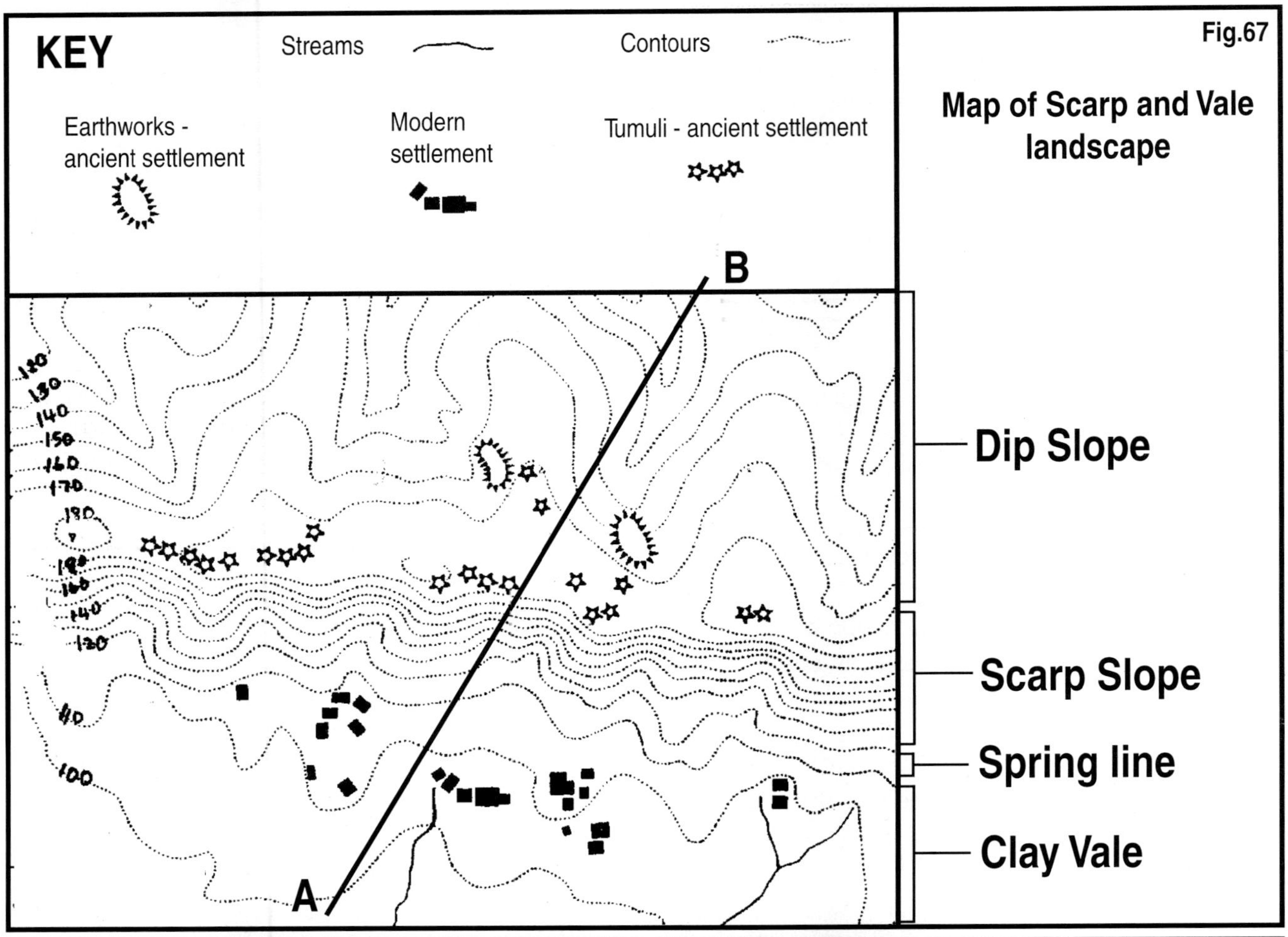

Fig.67 Map of Scarp and Vale landscape

Transect across Scarp and Vale landscape (A --- B) Fig.68

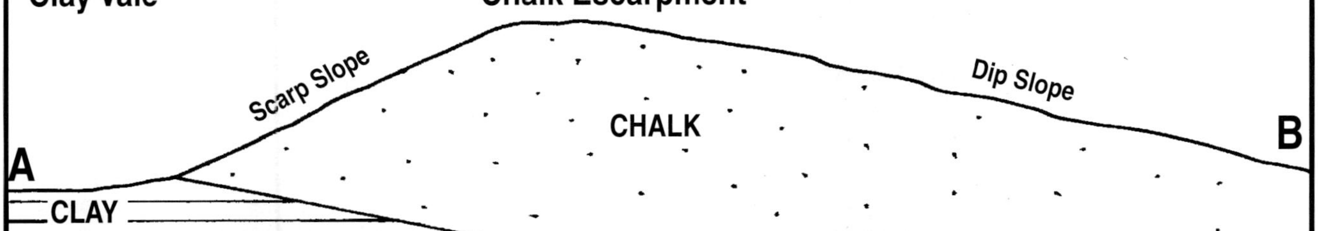

Relief & Geology	Clay Vale - low lying with undulating wide valley (below 100 metres). Clay forms impermeable zone .	Chalk escarpment (or cuesta) rising to over 200 metres above sea-level. Escarpment forms major area of map extract and dwarfs clay vale. Chalk forms a relatively more resistant upland with a scarp slope, dip slope and several small dry valleys (or coombes) located along its edge and longer dry valleys on the dip slope.
Drainage	Excess surface drainage on impermeable clays. Streams and springs common. Waterlogging common in periods of heavy rainfall. Aquifer at surface.	Lack of surface drainage on permeable chalk escarpment. Aquifer located well below surface even in periods of heavy rainfall. Dry valleys common. Some filled with bournes (winter streams).

Lithosphere Revision : Summary Notes

The main Idea........

The Lithosphere displays a range of landforms and patterns which can be explained by reference to a variety of processes on different scales

British Isles Geology

1. Major **tectonic** movements together with long periods of intense **mountain building** and **erosion** have been common features of Britain's geological development.
2. Britain's **complex geology** is the product of its varied past and consists of a combination of **igneous**, **sedimentary** and **metamorphic** rock types of varying ages and structures.
3. All rocks influence the development of the landscapes of which they form the base.
4. **Landscapes** are a complex mixture of **landforms** of varying ages and origins.
5. Landscapes are the result of **agents of erosion** working on the rocks of the earth's surface over very long periods of **time** at different **scales**.

Weathering

1. **Weathering** is the small-scale natural breakdown of rocks on the surface and can be classified into **3** main types :- **Physical Chemical** and **Biotic** weathering.
2. **Physical weathering** leads to rock disintegration, producing large rock fragments, for example **frost shattering** (or **freeze-thaw**)
3. **Chemical weathering** leads to rock decomposition, producing smaller rock fragments, for example, **solution** of limestone.
4. **Biotic** or biological weathering is a combination of both physical and chemical weathering caused by plants and animal action.
5. The unconsolidated weathered rock layer is called **regolith**.

Mass Movements

1. The movement of unconsolidated regolith or debris down a slope by gravity is known as **mass movement** or **wasting**.
2. **Gravity, rock type** and **structure, slope angle** and **water content** are important in determining the nature of mass movements.
3. **Steep slopes** produce **rapid** mass movements including rockfalls, landslides, mudflows and slumping.
4. **Gentle slopes** produce **slower** mass movements including slope wash and soil creep.
5. **Humans** influence mass movements through deforestation, road building and quarrying.

Slopes

1. The relationships between inputs, processes and outputs determine the **angle of any slope**.
2. The angle of a slope is measured with reference to the horizontal and is determined by the **horizontal length of the slope** and its **vertical height**.
3. **Slopes in plan** consist of slope segments, which have constant angles and are straight, and **slope elements** which are curved. They are either **concave** or **convex**.
4. Slopes change in time by **declining**, **retreating** or **replacing** the original slope. These processes often work in combination on a slope.
5. Perfect balance between the inputs and outputs results in a **graded slope** developing.
6. The majority of slopes are **less than 45 degrees**.

Glaciated Upland Scenery

1. Glaciers and ice-sheets occurred in Britain during the **Pleistocene** period which consisted of a number of **glacial** and **interglacial** periods, reflecting climatic fluctuations.
2. Glacial activity is a balance between **accumulation** of snow and **ablation** of melting of ice.
3. Evidence of previous glaciations has been partly obliterated by subsequent glaciations.
4. Glaciers follow and erode existing valleys.
5. Most of Britain has been modified by glaciation, especially the uplands, many of which have suffered intense glaciation.
6. **Abrasion** and **plucking** are the two most important processes of glacial erosion.
7. Glaciated uplands display features of glacial **deposition** especially in glacial **troughs**.
8. The main **erosional** features of glaciated uplands include - corries, aretes, hanging valleys, truncated spurs, U-shaped valleys, abraded summits, roche moutonnees, ribbon lakes
9. The main **depositional** features of glaciated uplands include moraines (unsorted deposits), drumlins, erratics together with fluvioglacial deposits (sorted deposits) eskers, kames, outwash plains.

Upland Limestone or Karst Scenery

1. Upland, Mountain or Carboniferous Limestone forms **Karst** scenery in the British Isles.
2. Karst landscapes are composed of eroded and weathered carboniferous limestone which produces an **angular** landscape, devoid of surface drainage.
3. **Solution** is of major importance in shaping karst scenery producing characteristic **limestone pavement** features such as **clints** and **grykes**, and dissolving sub-surface strata.
4. The **rate of solution** of limestone depends in part upon the amount of Carbon Dioxide present in water acting upon it.
5. **Glaciokarst** is the name given to areas of upland limestone displaying features of glacial erosion.
6. **Features** of Karst scenery include - limestone pavements, scars, gorges, dry valleys, swallow holes, shakeholes, cave systems with stalactites, stalagmites and pillars, resurgences.

Scarp and Vale Scenery

1. Several sedimentary rocks form a topography of **scarps** and **vales** in SE.England.
2. **Scarpland** is a young landscape of steep chalk or Jurassic Limestone slopes (scarps) separated by clay valleys (vales).
3. The structure and scenery of the landscape of SE.England has evolved as a result of a combination of natural processes including tectonic movements, differential erosion and deposition.
4. Humans have influenced the scenery of scarp and vale areas through draining vales and interrupting the **longshore drift** in the English Channel.
5. Features of Scarpland (Scarp & Vale) scenery include - escarpments, scarp/dip slopes, coombes and bournes, vales, outliers, springs, water gaps.

Lithosphere Revision : Unit style assessments

Fig.69a

1a. Make a simple **fieldsketch** of the landscape shown in figure **69a.** Label your fieldsketch to show the main features of **glacial erosion**. (5)

1b. Explain how the landscape shown in figure **69a** has been formed. (5)

2a. Describe and explain the processes which created the scree slope in figure **69b.** (4)

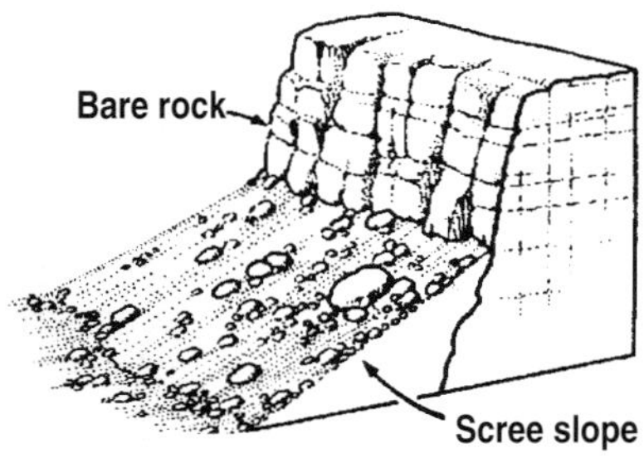

Fig.69b

2b. Explain how any two of the following processes cause landscape change

Mudflow **Landslip** **Soil Creep** (6)

3. GMT Use figure **70** (sketch map of an upland limestone area in Northern England).

Fig.70

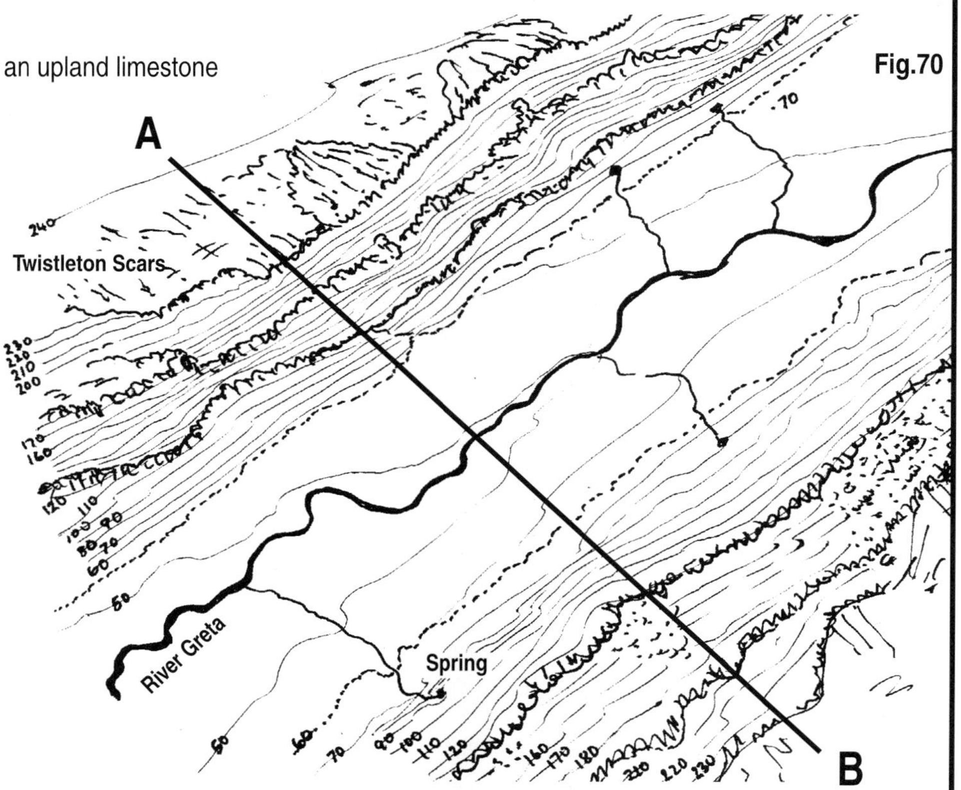

a. Draw an **accurate section** of the physical landscape between **A** and **B** on figure **70**. **Annotate** your cross section to show the main physical features. (5)

b. Explain the **pattern of drainage** across the section in terms of geology and slope. (5)

Lithosphere Revision : Exam style assessments

1. **GMT** Figure **71** shows a block diagram of an area of Chalk Downland in South East England.

Chalk Downland

Fig.71

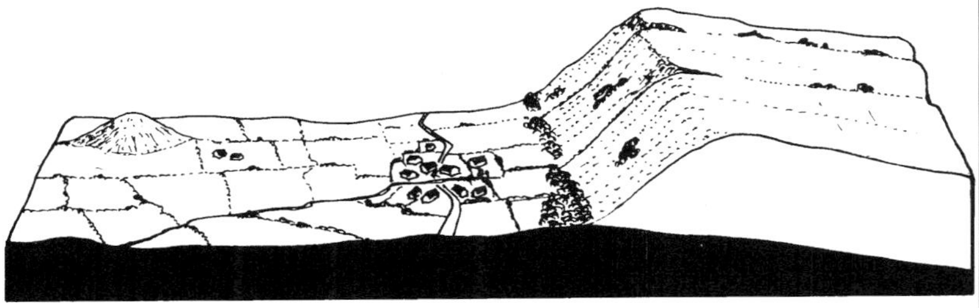

a. Identify, by using your own simple copy of figure **71**, the main features of structure, rock type and landscape of the area of Chalk Downland shown. (5)

b. In which way is Chalk Downland a good example of a landscape produced by **differential erosion** ? (4)

2a. Classify the following examples of weathering by type according to figure **72** - solution, exfoliation, burrowing, hydrolysis, pressure release, carbonation, frost shattering, root growth, granular disintegration, hydration (5)

Fig.72

A Classification of types of Weathering

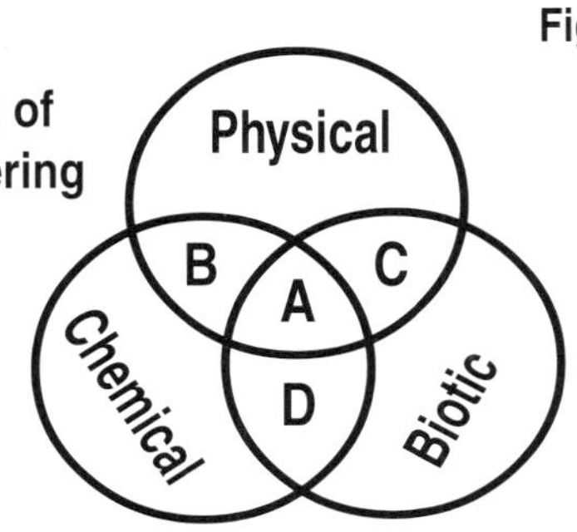

2b. Describe the processes operating on a free face which cause failure and rockfalls. (5)

For this question use either Map extract 928/90 (Helvellyn) or Map extract 973/115 (Snowdon)

3. **GMT** The diagrams below show grid squares of upland areas from the **Helvellyn** and **Snowdon** extracts.

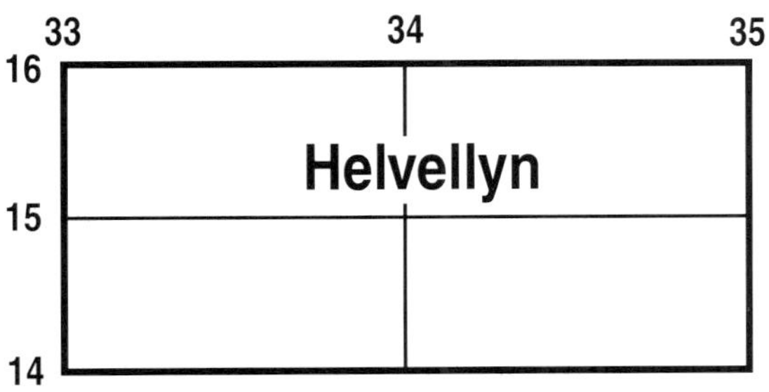

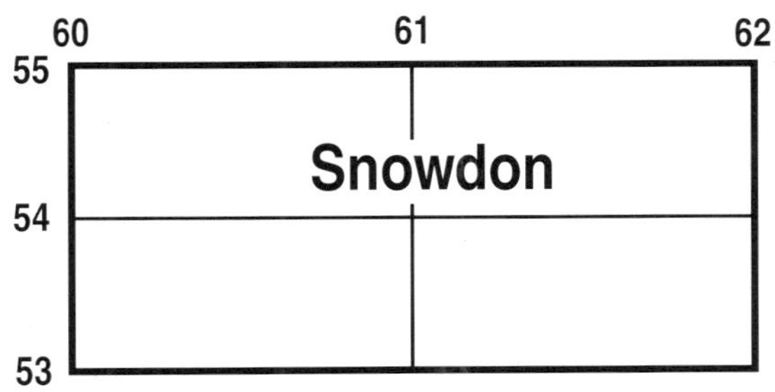

a. Draw a **sketch map** (relating to your chosen map extract) of the area covered by the grid squares and label features associated with **upland glaciation**. (4)

b. Describe and explain in detail the formation of **two** of your labelled features. (6)

4. **a.** Study figure **69a** which shows an area of upland glaciation. Describe with the aid of a sketch the **postglacial** processes of **weathering** and **mass movement** which have modified this landscape. (5)

b. For either point **238121** (**Helvellyn** map) or point **665535** (**Snowdon** map) - Make a simple **sketch** of the view **looking west** from the point on your chosen map extract and identify the main types of **glaciated valley**. Explain the formation of **one** of these valleys in detail. (5)

5. Study figure **63** on page **33** of the textbook.

a. Describe the features observed in the landscape shown in the photograph. (4)

b. With the aid of diagrams or sketches explain how the feature in the **foreground** has been formed. (4)

5. Biosphere

The main idea of the Biosphere section is....
Soils and vegetation can be viewed as ecosystems which are a set of interacting components.

What do you need to know ?

Students should have a knowledge and understanding of -

A Soils - properties and formation processes

- properties of podzols, brown earths and gleys - horizons, colour, texture, drainage
- the influence of soil-forming processes on profiles as demonstrated by podzolisation, gleying, organic and nutrient movement.
- analysis of soil profiles and data from soil surveys

B Vegetation

- evolution of vegetation communities as ecosystems to climax stages as demonstrated by vegetation succession on coastal dune belts and derelict or abandoned land, i.e. colonisation, the role of pioneer species and a knowledge of plant names at various stages in the succession
- interpretation and explanation of data from vegetation surveys and distributions with reference to the successions listed
- major alterations caused by human interference to temperate deciduous and coniferous forests

Soils and vegetation

This core section concentrates on the nature and formation of **soils** and processes which influence **vegetation** successions.

Soils - general properties and formation processes

a. Classification - 3 main types of soils

- **Zonal soils** - these relate to specific climates/vegetation zones e.g. **Podzols** - normally related to the Coniferous Forest or Taiga zone
- **Intrazonal soils** - these occur in more than one climatic zone e.g. **Rendzina** soils (shallow and containing calcium carbonate)
- **Azonal soils** - recently developed e.g. **alluvial** soils from rivers or **volcanic** soils.

b. World soils - zonal soil groups

Figure **73** is a diagram showing the major soil profiles to be found between the Equator and the North Pole. It also shows soil forming processes associated with the zonal soil types. The diagram also shows that there are no natural boundaries between the different soil groups that exist. There are **two** major groups of soils within this classification -

- **Pedocals** those with calcium carbonate present
- **Pedalfers** those with iron and aluminium present (no $CaCO_3$)

Zonal soils from North Pole to Equator Fig.73

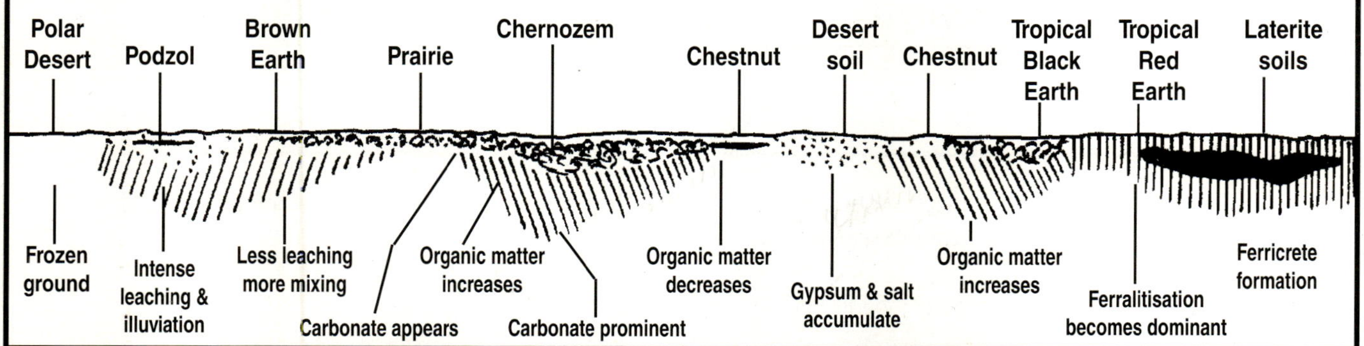

Soil formation - 5 main factors Fig.74

[1] **Climate** - important balance between precipitation and evaporation-

- Where **Precipitation > Evaporation**
  Pedalfer soils develop - rainwater leaches (dissolves and carries away downwards) minerals rich in **Al** (Aluminium) and **Fe** (Iron) from the topsoil (common in Tropical Forests)
- Where **Evaporation > Precipitation**
  Pedocal soils develop and are rich in calcium. These soils develop by upward movement of minerals - called **capillary action**
- Climate also affects the **rate of weathering** of the underlying rocks or **parent material**.

Soil

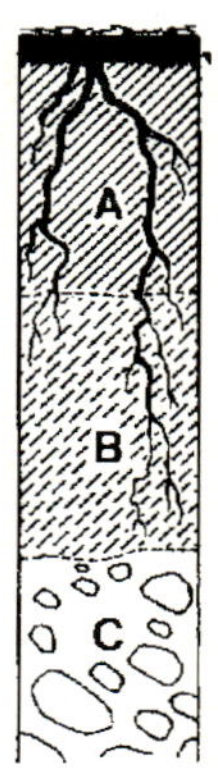

[2] **Parent Material** - rock etc., affects the colour and mineral content of the soil

[3] **Organisms** - soil **bacteria** absorb nitrogen from the air
- **creatures** such as worms mix & aerate the soil
- decaying **plants** provide **humus** for the topsoil
- **roots** bind the soil and help reduce erosion

[4] **Relief and Drainage** - gentle slopes (well drained) but steep slopes are prone to erosion and soil creep. Flat areas suffer poor drainage and are susceptible to waterlogging (gleying)

[5] **Time** - some soils take thousands of years to form; others, e.g. alluvial soils are deposited quickly.

Soil processes - soil formation is a system with inputs and outputs

Fig.75

Soil inputs

- **Water** from the atmosphere
- **Organic matter** from decaying plants and organisms
- **Nutrients & minerals** from weathered rocks
- **Respiration** from burrowing animals
- **Solar energy & gases** from the atmosphere

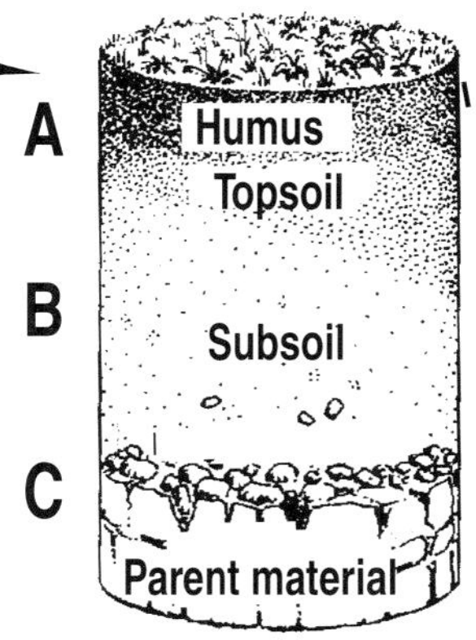

Soil outputs

- **Evaporation** or water loss in topsoil and from the soil surface
- **Water & nutrient loss** by capillary uplift in areas where evaporation exceeds precipitation
- **Nutrients** taken up by plants
- **Leaching** removes minerals from the topsoil
- **Soil erosion** removal of soil material by soil creep and slopewash

Describing soils - the **soil profile** above is used to describe a soil in detail. The profile is a cross-section of the soil.

The profile consists of three main layers known as soil **horizons** - there are 3 horizons - the **A, B** and **C** horizons -

Horizon	**A**	**Topsoil** (contains humus - plant litter-leaves)
Horizon	**B**	**Subsoil**
Horizon	**C**	**Parent material** (usually weathered rock)

Soil definitions - a brief glossary of soil related terms used in geography

- **Soil** *A mixture of mineral and organic fragments produced by a combination of physical, chemical and biological processes*
- **Texture** *Determined by the content percentages of sand, silt and clay present in a soil*
- **Structure** *Very important to the soil's fertility since structure affects aeration (air content) and workability - described as crumby, blocky, platy, structureless, etc.*
- **Leaching** *The dissolving and washing down of calcium and other bases through the soil as a result of percolating rainwater.*
- **Eluviation** *The process of washing down material such as organic matter or minerals through the soil*
- **Illuviation** *The deposition in a soil horizon of minerals, humus and other materials*
- **Gleying** *Waterlogging of soil*
- **Soil catena** *A soil sequence found on a slope*
- **Podzolisation** *Occurs where leaching is dominant removing oxides of iron and aluminium and clay minerals from the upper soil horizons*

Three soil case studies - sequence of soils commonly found in western Britain

Fig.76

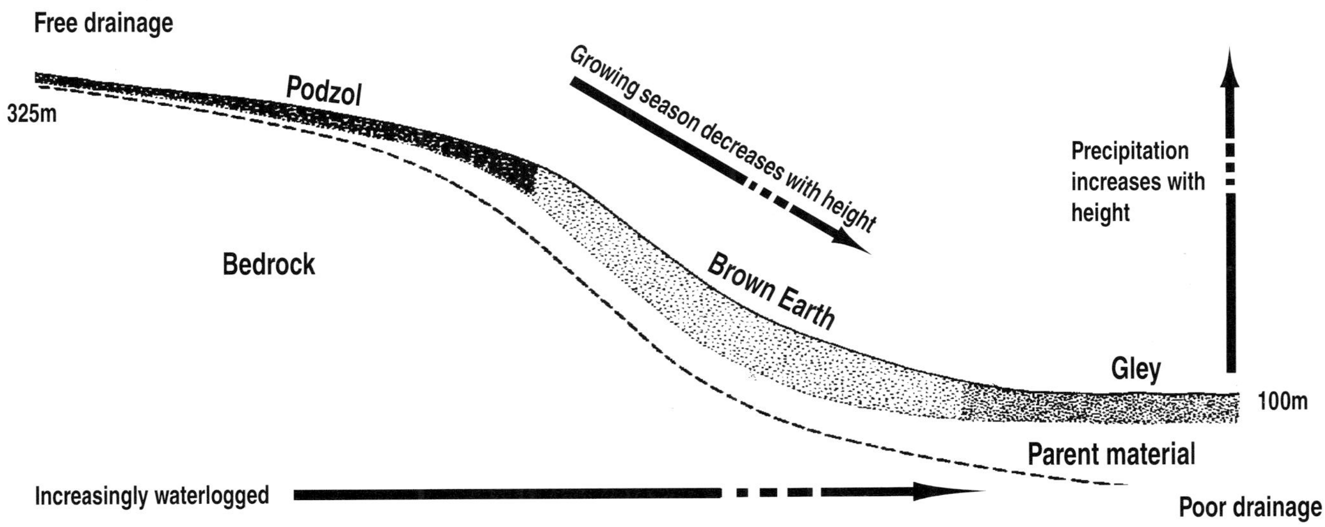

Podzol

A **zonal soil** found in Northern Europe associated with Coniferous forests (**Taiga**) where winter temperatures are low - water from spring snow melt causes extensive leaching. The Taiga contains a variety of trees (Pines, etc.) which release cones and needles to form a **very acid humus**. **Distinct horizons**.

Brown Earths

A **zonal soil** found further south in central Europe, associated with **Temperate Deciduous** forests - more fertile than podzols (thick leafy material from deciduous trees returns nutrients to the soil. The milder climate causes leaves to decompose quickly producing a **mild (less acidic) humus**. Earthworms, etc. help to mix the soil - horizons less distinct.

Gley soils

Formed where the ground is **waterlogged**. Common in Polar areas where the subsoil is frozen (**permafrost**). Also formed in flat poorly drained areas with impermeable rocks. A lack of oxygen and bacterial action. Very slow decay produces a thick layer of **acid humus** (**Peat**).

Three soil case studies - summary table for Podzols, Brown Earths and Gley soils

Fig.77

Soil: A horizon, B horizon, C horizon

Podzol

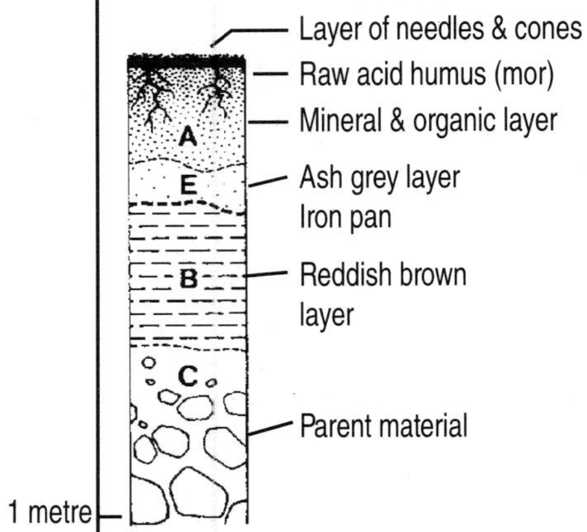

Brown Earth

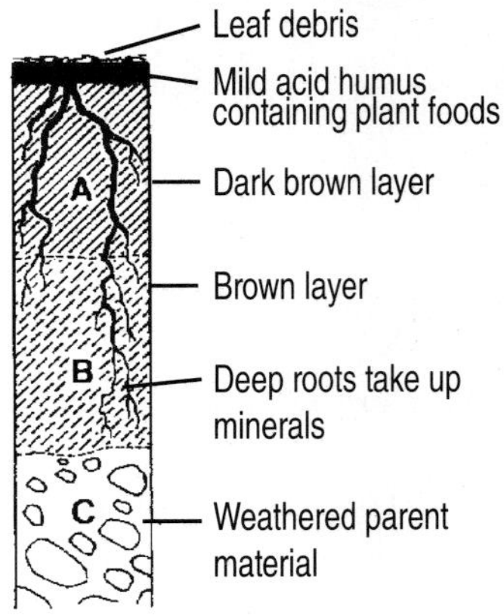

Gley

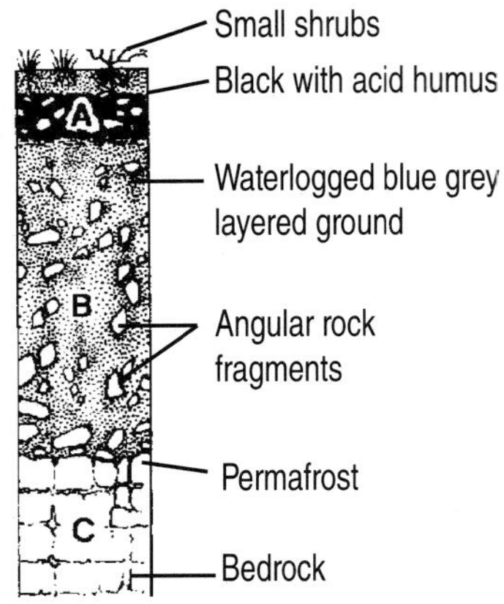

Soil	Podzol	Brown Earth	Gley
Main areas	Coniferous Forest or **Taiga** areas in Northern Europe, Siberia, etc	**Temperate Deciduous Forest** of Central Europe.	Areas with **poor drainage** or **permafrost**.
Relief & Drainage	Variable relief but often **poorly drained**.	Gently **undulating** land allowing **good drainage**.	**Hollows** and **flat** areas - poor drainage.
Climate	High rainfall/precipitation. Large snowmelt. Low temperatures.	Lower rainfall/precipitation. Higher temperatures. More rapid decomposition.	High rainfall/precipitation. Waterlogging.
Natural vegetation	**Coniferous trees** - pines, spruce **Cones** and **needles**.	**Deciduous trees**, e.g. Oak, Ash, Beech. Plentiful **leafy material**.	**Lichens, mosses, marshy** vegetation.
Type	**Pedalfer** soil - acidic	**Pedalfer** soil - less acidic.	**Pedalfer** soils.-
Processes	Heavy **leaching** dominant soil process. Formation of hard **iron pan** which can impede drainage.	Slight **leaching** (lower rainfall). Iron pans develop where leaching is more active.	**Gleying** - oxygen deficiency. Very slow decomposition.
Human Activities (Alterations to regions caused by human interference)	Long cold winter and short summer. Limited growing season. Little agricultural development - drainage and liming required. Limited cultivation of oats, potatoes and hay. Main land use is coniferous forest trees for softwood timber; uses include building, paper, matches. Little of this forest is cleared because cold climate and infertile soils limit agriculture.	Milder climate - longer warmer summers with adequate precipitation plus more fertile soils, better for agriculture - Cereals e.g. wheat and barley. Cattle grazing. Variety of major land uses including large scale urban and industrial complexes. Most of the original forest has been cleared for agriculture and settlement (climate more favourable and more accessible).	**Peat** for fuel - limited agricultural use - mainly **sheep** grazing. May be improved by **drainage** and **liming** (to reduce acidity).

Soils - problems and possible conservation methods

• **Soil erosion problems**	*Add vegetation through **Afforestation** (tree planting) and planting **cover crops** to reduce surface run-off.*
• **Shortage of water**	***Irrigation** through construction of dams and channels. Rebuild **groundwater** schemes.*
• **Excess of water**	*Build **dams** to control floods. **Field drainage** to improve waterlogged soils. Sand and lime, clay soils, to improve structure, drainage and workability.*
• **Acidity, infertility**	*Add **lime** to acidic soils. Add nitrogen-based **fertiliser** to improve soil fertility.*
• **Evaporation exceeds Precipitation**	*Use **dry farming** techniques - cover soils with a **mulch** (water retaining organic materials) to reduce water loss. **Irrigation** schemes can reduce difference in effective moisture available to the soil.*

Vegetation

Ecosystems or **biomes** are ecological communities of plants and animals extending over large natural areas associated with particular physical habitats. Ten major biomes are shown on figure **78**. Each biome is the natural result of change over time. Plant succession occurs as environmental conditions alter and favour certain species of plants. These species compete more successfully for available nutrients, light and space. Well-adapted species then replace earlier ones which become less-well equipped to compete.

World major biomes **Fig.78**

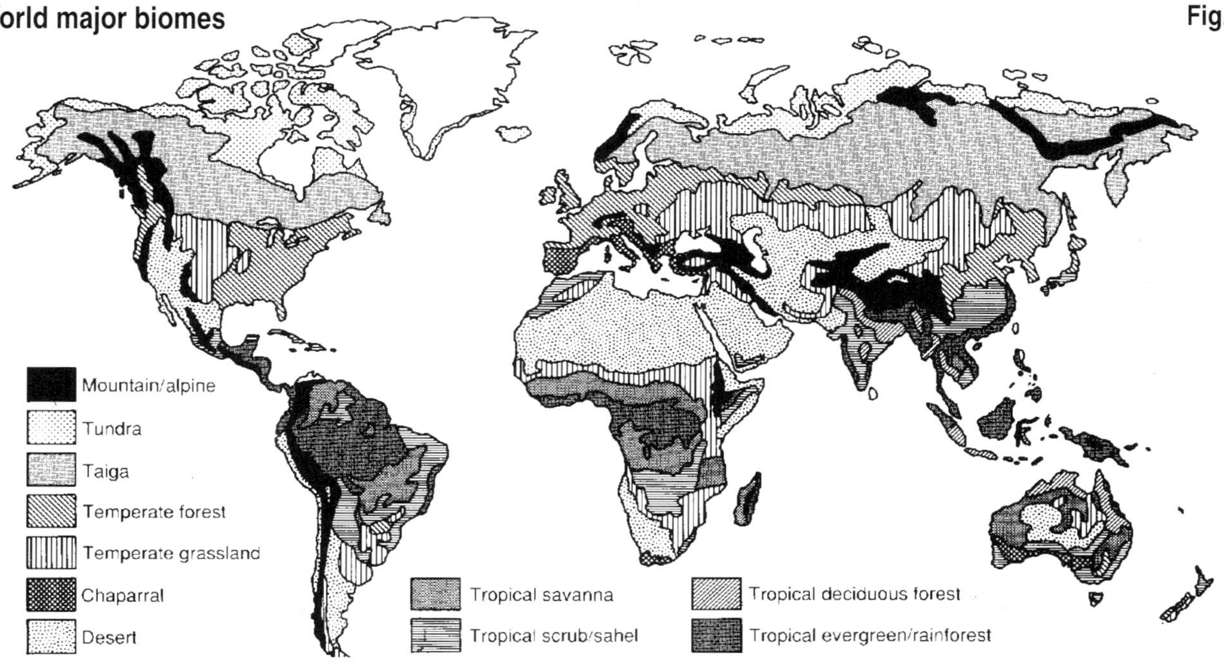

Sometimes over millions of years plant succession reaches a mature stage in the succession process. The ecosystem or biome becomes stable and relatively unchanging. This stage is called the **climax**. The climax community is said to be in a state of dynamic equilibrium, that is, it maintains overall stability despite continuous small environmental changes. When the climax lasts for hundreds or thousands of years and is seen to be dependent upon the climate, it becomes the **climatic climax** or **natural vegetation** of the area. Sometimes the climax can be determined by factors other than climate, such as soil (referred to as the **edaphic climax**) or human activity (referred to as the **plagioclimax**).
Main types of **seres** (plant communities) are shown in figure **79**.

Fig.79

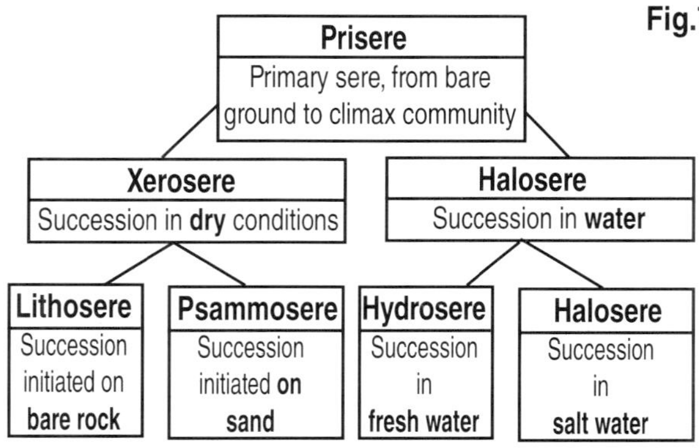

Definitions used in vegetation studies

Ecosystems or biomes - plant and animal communities living together in association with their **physical habitat (environment)**
Succession - this occurs when altered environmental conditions begin to favour certain plant species. These species can compete more effectively for available nutrients, space and light. Well adapted species will **succeed** (replace) earlier species which are now less well equipped to compete.
Pioneer stage - (the beginning of **colonization**) - may start with bare ground e.g. derelict land. The first plants to colonize are known as **pioneers** e.g. grasses, lichens. The plants slowly weather the surface, and decay to form a richer, deeper soil suitable for other plant species to move in.
Climax vegetation - the final stage in succession when the plant community remains relatively stable and unchanging. At the climax, the vegetation is in equilibrium (balance) with existing environmental conditions, i.e. climate and soil. The climax vegetation is the most complex group of plants in an area and develops over a long period of time.

Case studies of plant succession

Succession on derelict land e.g. **rubbish tips, slag heaps and building sites**. These sites are only **temporary** therefore plants must colonise **quickly** - however succession rarely develops beyond the **pioneer** stage.

Plants must be able to:-
- survive **adverse soil conditions**
- survive **the lack of moisture**
- **reproduce themselves quickly**

Common pioneer species include **groundsel** and **couch grass**. In some conditions succession might occur e.g. **nettles** and **rosebay willow herb,** which can survive the adverse conditions.

Case studies of plant succession

Psammoseres - succession in **sand dune vegetation** (coastal dune belts)

Plants in coastal dune belts face major difficulties. Near the shore the sand is often rich in shell material, increasing **alkalinity**. The environment is exposed to strong winds with blown sand frequently burying new plants. However, further inland, as more fertile soil develops, a greater variety of plants is found. The principal stages of succession (moving inland from the shore) are as follows - - see figure **80**.

Psammosere - succession on sand **Fig.80**

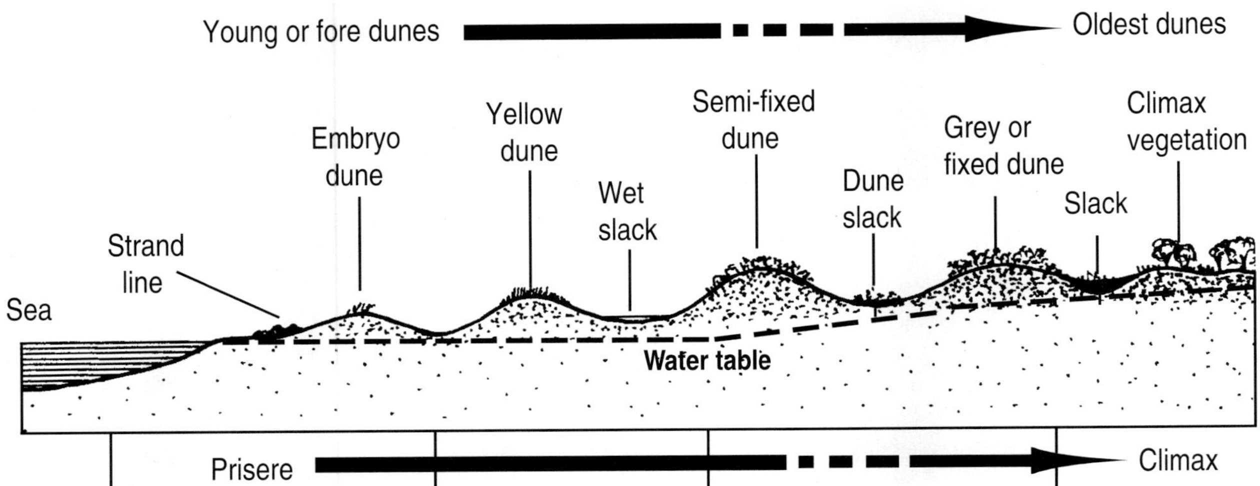

Zone	Zone 1 embryo & fore dunes	Zone 2 yellow dunes	Zone 3 grey (fixed dunes) & slacks	Zone 4 dune heath & grassland/woods
Changes inland	**pH declines** **salinity declines** **age of dunes increases** **available nutrients increases** **available fresh water increases** **humus content of the soil increases** **shelter increases**			
Main species of plants	Main species - Orache Saltwort Sandwort Sea Rocket Sand Couch Lyme Grass Marram (on fore dunes only)	Main species - Marram Grass Dune Fescue Sand Sedge Sea Holly Ragwort Thistles	Main species (dunes) - Marram Grass (limited) Red Fescue Annual meadow grass Wavy Hair grass Lichens & Mosses Herbs - Dandelion, Clover Chickweed, Bedstraw Shrubs - Sea Buckthorn Heather	Main species - Heather Gorse Fescues Cowslip Bird's Foot Trefoil Sea Buckthorn Oak Birch Pine
Adaptation to environment	Foreshore and strand line plants such as Sea Rocket and Couch Grass can withstand adverse conditions i.e. very windy, salty and sandy. Alkaline with no humus. Foredune plants such as Marram Grass (succeeds Couch Grass) thrive on supply of sand.	Yellow Dune plants such as Marram Grass like abundant fresh sand. Their long tap roots can reach water table. Their roots help bind the sand forming a fixed dune.	Fixed Grey Dune plants such as Dandelions, Mosses etc succeed Marram Grasses as it dies out further inland. Increasing shelter restricts the supply of sand. Decay of roots produces humus and a more fertile neutral soil. Greater variety of plants develop. Damp hollows (**slacks**) between dunes are colonized by willow and cotton grasses. The water table is near the surface encouraging plants such as these which prefer damp conditions.	Climax vegetation inland with **grassland** (machair in Western Scotland) common where soil is alkaline (rich in shell sand) *or* **Heathland** with **heather & gorse & woodland areas** found where soil is acidic (abundance of quartz sand).

Biosphere Revision : Summary Notes

The main Idea........
Soils and vegetation can be viewed as ecosystems which are a set of interacting components.

Soils

1. A **soil** is a mixture of mineral and organic fragments produced by a combination of physical, chemical and biological processes.
2. **Major soil groups** can be recognised on a global scale and include zonal, intrazonal and azonal soils.
3. **Zonal soils** are associated with zones of climate and vegetation, e.g. Podzols are normally related to the Coniferous Forests or Taiga areas.
4. **Intrazonal soils** are not confined to particular bio-climatic zones. They owe their characteristics to conditions common to different parts of the world, e.g. aridity, water-logging, parent material or relief, e.g. Rendzina soils (shallow and containing calcium carbonate).
5. **Azonal soils** lack well defined profiles as they have developed recently, independently of climate or vegetation. They include outwash, alluvium and clays.
6. A **Pedocal** is a major soil group in which the soils have calcium carbonate present due to capillary uplift within the soil. They are usually found in areas where evaporation exceeds precipitation, e.g. Chernozem soils.
7. A **Pedalfer** is a major soil group in which the soils have iron and aluminium present and no calcium carbonate within the soil. They are usually found in areas where precipitation exceeds evaporation, e.g. Podzol soils.
8. A soil is the product of the interaction of **5 major elements** including climate, organisms, relief, parent material and time.
9. Soils can be viewed as **Systems** with **inputs** (such as water, organic matter, nutrients, solar energy, etc.) and **outputs** (such as evaporation or water loss, nutrient loss, leaching and soil erosion etc.).
10. A **soil profile** consists of **3 main horizons** :
    the **A**-horizon or topsoil/ organic layer
    the **B**-horizon or subsoil/altered mineral layer
    the **C**-horizon or parent material.
11. The decay of dead organic matter by soil micro-organisms (bacteria and fungi) forms **humus**.
12. **Podzol soils** are zonal soils which form in Cool Temperate humid climates through illuviation of nutrients. They are characterised by a Bf layer and limited fertility.
13. **Brown Earths** are zonal soils associated with Deciduous Forests. They have a higher nutrient level and agricultural potential than podzols.

13.**Gley soils** are those soils which are water-logged either due to poor surface drainage (surface water gley) or high water table (ground water gley) Gleying can affect all soils and is characterised by blue-grey staining.

14. A **soil catena** is a soil sequence found on a slope.
15. **Leaching** is the dissolving & washing down of calcium and other minerals through the soil as a result of percolating rainwater.

Vegetation

1. **Ecosystems** or **biomes** are visually distinct units at different scales within the environment.
2. There are inputs, processes and outputs within an ecosystem.
3. **Solar energy** is the main driving force for all ecosystems.
4. Various elements of the environment act as **control mechanisms** on ecosystems, including climatic conditions, soils, drainage and human interference.
5. Vegetation within any ecosystem gradually becomes more complex through the process of plant **succession** which in turn influences soil development.
6. **Plant succession** occurs when altered environmental conditions begin to favour certain plant species. These species can compete more effectively for available nutrients, space and light. Well adapted species will **succeed** (replace) earlier species which are now less well equipped to compete.
7. **Pioneer stage** is the beginning of colonization and may start with bare ground, e.g. derelict land. The first plants to colonize are known as **pioneers**, e.g. lichens, mosses. The plants slowly weather the surface and decay to form a richer, deeper soil suitable for other plants to move in.
8. **Climax vegetation** is the final stage in succession when the plant community remains relatively stable and unchanging. The climax vegetation is the most complex group of plants in an area and develops over long periods of time.
9. **Edaphic climax** is the climax vegetation determined and influenced by soil factors.
10. **Plagioclimax** is the climax vegetation influenced by human activity.
11. A **sere** is a community of plants.
12. A **Prisere** develops from bare ground.
13. A **Halosere** develops in salt water.
14. A **Xerosere** develops in dry conditions, e.g. desert.
15. A **Hydrosere** develops in fresh water.
16. A **habitat** is a physical environment.
17. A **succession on derelict land** is characterised by quick growing pioneer plants which can withstand adverse soil conditions, a lack of moisture and must be able to reproduce themselves quickly, e.g. groundsel and couch grass. In some conditions succession may occur with nettles and rosebay willow herb flourishing.
18. A **Psammosere** develops on sand dune belts. A succession develops from the strand line inland via embryo and yellow dunes through grey or fixed dunes and slacks (wet hollows) to the oldest dunes where the climax vegetation can be found. Each dune zone is characterised by plant species.

Biosphere Revision : Unit style assessments

1a. Explain the difference between soil profile and soil horizon. (3)

1b. GMT For profiles **A** and **B** identify each of the soil types and the climatic zone or biome characterised by each. (3)

1c. Account for their development in each climatic zone. (4)

Fig.81

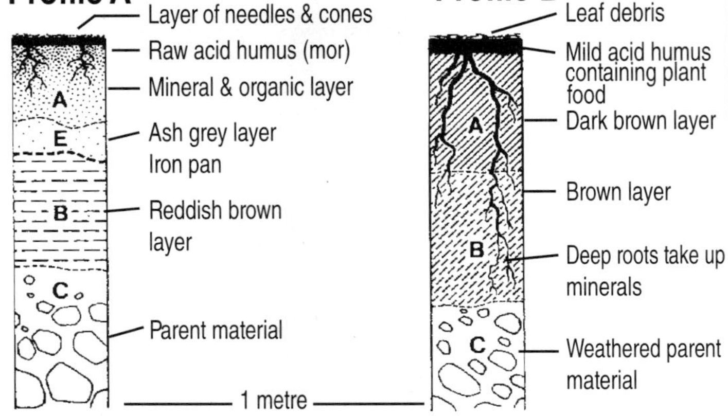

2a. Describe in detail what is meant by the term **climax vegetation**. (3)

2b. With reference to figure **82** explain why vegetation finds it difficult to grow on **derelict land** (4)

2c. Explain the ways in which **one** named plant species is adapted to survive these conditions. (3)

Fig.82

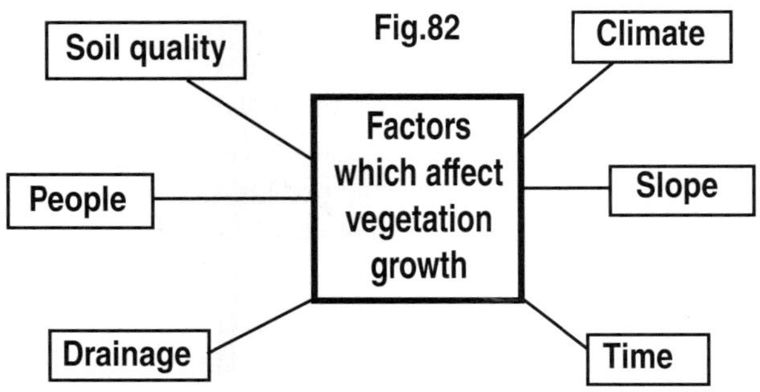

Biosphere Revision : Exam style assessments

1. Explain the meaning of **two** of the following terms - **succession** **pioneer species** **psammosere** (4)

2. GMT The following plants were noted on a field excursion across an area of sand dunes -
Marram grass **ragwort** **sea couch grass** **small willow trees**
i. Match these plants to the appropriate places on the sand dune cross-section (figure **83**) either point **A, B** or **C**.
ii. Briefly state how each plant would adapt to conditions in that particular location. (6)

Fig.83

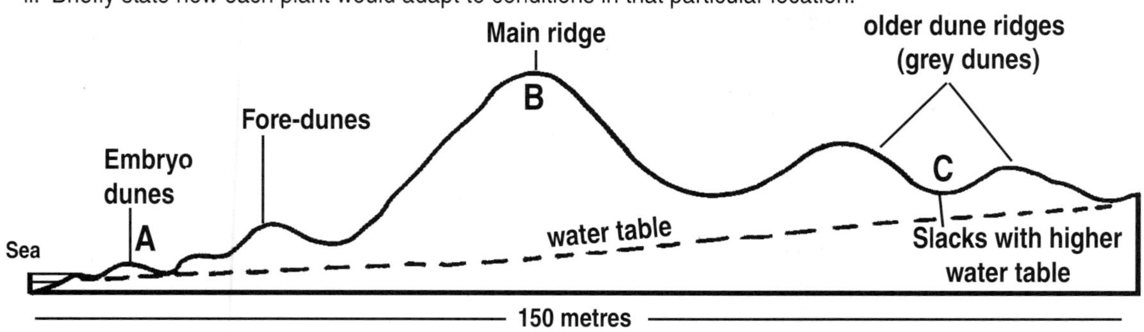

3. GMT Study the area descriptions which relate to the three soil types - **podzols, brown earths** and **gleys**.

Fig.84

	Western Isles	*Scottish Highland*	*Sherwood Forest*
Relief & Drainage	Flat moorland with poor drainage.	Variable relief sometimes with poor drainage.	Undulating land. Well drained.
Aspects of climate	Mild with high precipitation.	Cold winter with snow, Spring snowmelt. High precipitation.	Warm summer, mild winter. Moderate ppt.
Natural vegetation	Rushes, cotton grass, etc.	Scots Pine trees. (Coniferous Forest).	Oak trees. Temperate Deciduous Forest.

4. List the three soil types and match them to the appropriate area. For any **two** of the soils, explain how the natural environment contributes to soil formation. (6)

5. Explain why areas of Temperate Deciduous Forest such as the English Midlands have been subjected to much greater human interference than Coniferous Forest areas such as the Scottish Highlands. (4)

Terminology – test yourself on the Physical Core !

Try this test - and don't look back at any of the Physical Core sections - do this exercise to judge for yourself how well your revision is going for Higher Geography !

What to do This is a **terminology test.** Complete the **definitions** of each of these important/**key terms**. A few have been completed for you. Good luck !

Atmosphere

Atmosphere
Water vapour - Water as a gas.
Solar radiation
Albedo effect
Insolation - Sun's rays received by the Earth's surface.
Energy deficit
Energy surplus
Hadley Cell
Ferrel Cell - Temperate cell.
Coriolis force
ITCZ
Doldrums - Area of weak winds caused by convection.
Trade Wind Belt
El Nino
Milankovitch
Greenhouse Effect
CFCs
Ozone layer
Acid rain
Air masses

Hydrosphere

Hydrological cycle
Irrigation - Watering of dry or desert areas.
Condensation
Evapotranspiration
Run-off
Watershed - High land between river basins.
Groundwater
Aquifer - Water table.
Jet stream
Drainage basin
Precipitation - All forms of moisture falling from the sky.
Hydrograph
Discharge
Corrasion
Attrition
Solution
Saltation & siltation
Vertical sorting
River stages - Include upper, middle & lower.
Spate
Braiding
Levees - Natural embankments along a river.
Meanders
Ox-bows - Cut-off meanders.
Eyots
Pools & riffles

Lithosphere

Lithosphere
Agents of erosion
Differential erosion
Rock cycle
Orogeny - period of mountain building
Denudation - Weathering and erosion.
Igneous
Sedimentary
Metamorphic -Rocks that have been changed due to heat and / or pressure.
Weathering
Regolith
Biotic
Freeze-Thaw - Frost shattering process
Exfoliation
Carbonation
Concave & convex slopes
Mass movement
Solifluction - Gradual movement of soil/scree after repeated freeze-thaw processes.
Talus - a scree or debris slope.
Slumping
Landslides
Mudflow
Soil creep
Glacial system
Ablation - melting of ice/glacier.
Accumulation
Abrasion
Plucking - tearing action of glacier/ice sheet.
Fluvioglacial
Features of Glacial
- **erosion**
- **deposition** eg. drumlins, eskers, erratics, etc.
- **fluvioglacial features**
- **post glacial features**

Karst landscapes - upland limestone areas.
Permeable
Impermeable
Pervious
Porous
Glaciokarst scenery
Features of Karst scenery
Scarpland
Cuesta - escarpment in chalk landscape.
Scarps & dips
Coombes & bournes
Vale
Outlier

Biosphere

Soil
Vegetation
Zonal soils - soils specific to **climatic areas**
Intrazonal soils
Azonal soils
Pedocals
Pedalfers
Parent material
Humus - decomposed organic material
Topsoil
Subsoil
Podzol
Brown Earth
Gley soils - waterlogged soils
Soil inputs
Soil outputs
Texture
Structure
Leaching
Eluviation
Illuviation
Catena - soil development on a slope.
Podzolisation
Mor
Peat
Taiga - Coniferous Forest biome.
Temperate Deciduous
Afforestation - tree planting in large areas.
Mulch
Ecosystem
Biome
Succession
Pioneer stage
Sere
Hydrosere
Psammosere
Halosere - plant succession in salt water.
Prisere
Climax vegetation
Habitat - a local physical environment.
Groundsel
Couch grass
Nettles
Rosebay willow herb
Embryo dune
Yellow dune
Grey dune - fixed or semi-fixed dunes.
Slack
Machair
Marram grass
Sea Rocket - found in embryo dune areas.

6. Population

The main idea of the Population section is....
Population change and structure vary spatially and over time. Reasons for change are complex and involve human and environmental factors.

What do you need to know ?

Students should have a knowledge and understanding of -

A Demographic systems

- population structures vary with different levels of birth rates, death rates and migration
- population data is gathered using a census: variations in data quality result from a variety of factors which include variations in levels of wealth and literacy
- fertility and mortality vary over time : Demographic Transition Model - reasons for differences of fertility and mortality in the four stages of the model
- interpretation of population data in map, diagrammatic or tabular form

B Population change

- the role of fertility, mortality and migration as components within the demographic system
- the reasons for, and the general implications of population change including factors affecting birth rates and death rates, e.g. wealth and access to safe water and nutrition; population pyramids in developed and developing countries and problems caused by ageing population and long-life expectancy in developed countries

C Migration

- classification of types of circulation and migration on a space-time sequence including voluntary and forced migrations, long and short term ; seasonal migrations ; rural-urban and urban-rural migrations
- analysis of and reasons for contemporary migration streams and counter streams with reference to an example of each type of international migration (e.g. between and into European Union countries), rural-urban and urban-rural migration (e.g. within Nigeria or the UK) and forced migration (e.g. refugee movements in the Sahel)
- interpretation of flow diagrams showing migration streams

Demographic systems - demography is the study of population

The **structure of a population** depends on the balance between the **birth rate, death rate** and **migration**.
Population structures may be shown in a **population pyramid** which gives the **age** and **sex** breakdown of a population. Pyramids are important for identifying **trends** and **comparisons**. **Migration** (immigration & emigration) can have a dramatic effect on population structure (often influences males of working age)

Typical Pyramid Patterns - see figure 85

Developed Country, **e.g. France, USA, Switzerland**
The pyramid displays the following features

- **Narrow base** - low birth rate (due to small family culture, wide spread birth control, high standard of living, pension systems, career women, D.I.N.K.Y. (double income no kids yet) couples, low infant mortality, high literacy rates, etc.)
- **Almost constant width** - low infant mortality rates and few young deaths (balanced diets, natal care, widespread medical care, doctors & hospitals, good living conditions (sanitation, clean drinking water), absence of fatal endemic diseases)
- **Does not narrow until age 70** - high life expectancy (reasons as above & geriatric care, advanced medical treatments, drugs)

Developing Country, **e.g. India, Bangladesh, Ethiopia**
The pyramid displays the following features

- **Broad base** - high birth rate (due to desire to have large families (children can work and help adults, provide security in old age) oppression of women, high infant mortality rates, lack of effective birth control and availability of advice
- **Narrows quickly** - high infant mortality rates and many young deaths (lack of natal care, malnutrition & undernutrition, lack of health education, poor sanitation, endemic and epidemic disease, poverty, lack of medical care & supplies)
- **Narrow above age 50** - low life expectancy (reasons as above & poor living conditions (shanty towns, civil war, droughts, famines, lack of vaccination, etc.)

Population structure **Fig.85**

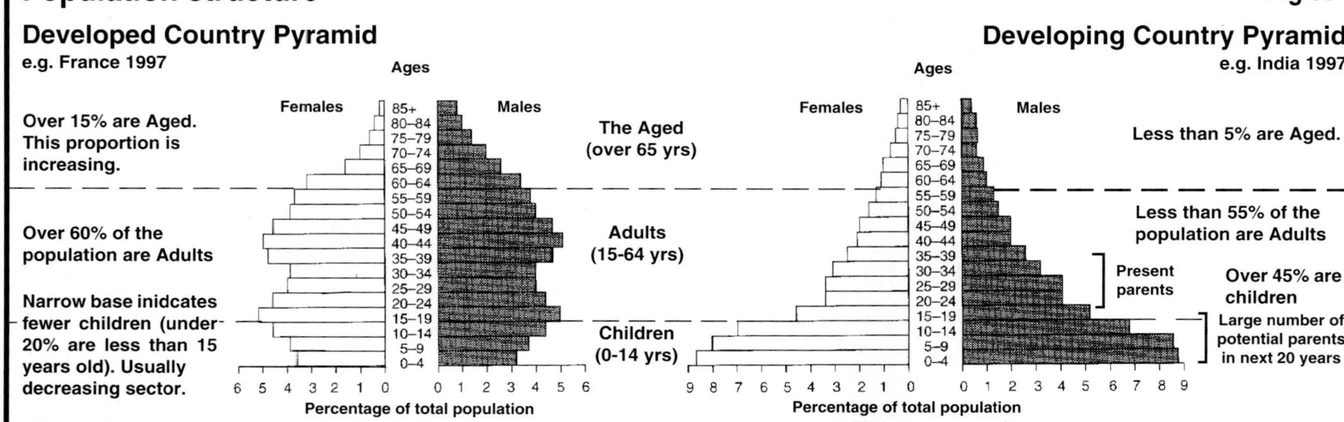

Gathering Population Statistics

Fig.86

Why is this information important ?

- To allow governments to **plan** ahead for provision of public services e.g. hospitals, schools, etc.
- Governments need statistics to set appropriate **tax rates** to finance services
- To allow governments to calculate dependency ratios and to examine the social and cultural distribution of populations

Methods of gathering population statistics

- **Census** (people count)
  - most important method - held every ten years in the UK (since 1801) next one is due in 2001
  - Census Forms are distributed by an **Enumerator** to every household
  - Census forms ask questions about age, sex, languages, occupation, number in household, etc.
  - Legal requirement on all to complete the forms and **interpreters** are available for those with language problems
  - Forms are collated and information is processed and collated using computer technology - CD roms used to store data

Registration
- used to update statistics, i.e. recording of births, deaths, migration, etc. provides new information between census years

Sampling
- **surveys** may be used to establish trends between censuses

Problems with gathering statistics
(especially in Developing Countries)

- High cost of conducting a census
- Lack of literacy (e.g. Gambia has 15% adult literacy)
- Size of the country (area and population e.g. China)
- Remoteness & lack of communications infrastructure (e.g. Brazil & the Amazon Basin)
- Migration (e.g. nomads in North African countries)
- Suspicion amongst people
- Internal strife and conflict (e.g. Kosovo, Algeria)

The Demographic Transition Model (or the Population Cycle)

The graph shown opposite details the model of **Demographic Transition**.
Demographers believe that all countries pass through the stages of this model over time. However, different countries are at different stages and may take different lengths of time to pass through each stage.

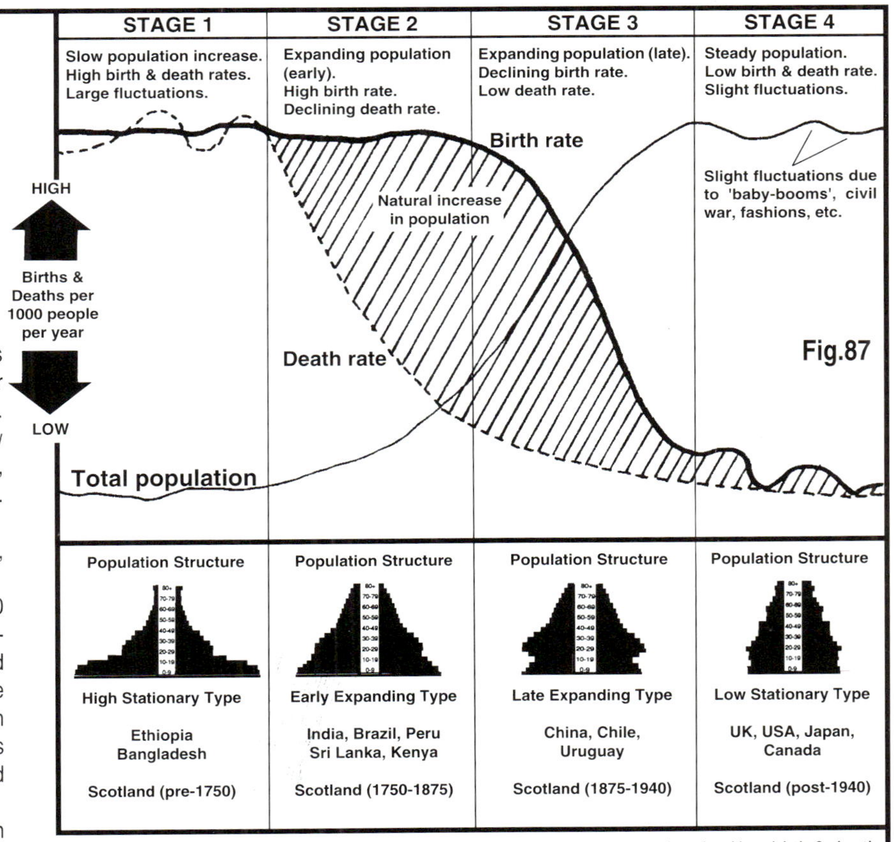

Fig.87

For example, before 1750, both birth and death rates were high in Scotland. The average family had 8 or more children but only half grew to become parents. Medical knowledge was limited and infant mortality was high. Few people lived to their 60's and famines, war and diseases reduced the population regularly. Scotland's population remained stable (**Stage 1**). Today, countries such as **Ethiopia** remain in Stage 1, for similar reasons.
Scotland's population increased rapidly between 1750 & 1875 (**Stage 2**). Advances in medical science (antiseptics, medicines, etc.), improved diets, clean piped water and decent housing combined to reduce the death rate and increased life expectancy, whilst birth rates remained high. A similar, large natural increase is experienced today in countries such as **India** and **Brazil**.
Between 1875 & 1940 (**Stage 3**) Scotland's population growth rate decreased. Improvements in public health and better drugs further reduced the death rate and increased life expectancy. A rapid decrease in birth rates, due to greater awareness of and efficiency of methods of contraception and the emancipation of women (greater choice in marriage, the 'vote') combined to reduce the natural rate of population increase.

Countries such as **China** & **Thailand** are thought to be in Stage 3 today. Indeed both nations are currently attempting to improve public health and introduce public contraception programmes to reduce their birth & death rates.

Scotland since 1940 has had low birth & death rates (**Stage 4**); the population growth is very low. Other developed countries such as the USA and Japan also have stable or stationary population growth rates. In some developed countries, e.g. **Sweden** the pyramid is very narrow at the base (shows very low birth rate) and may result in population **decline**.

Population change

Fertility, mortality and migration

Fertility relates to **birth rate** and **mortality** relates to **death rate**.

Population change depends upon the balance between the above **inputs / outputs** - as shown in figure **88**.

Population change is also illustrated on a global scale in figures **89** and **90**.

Reasons for and implications of population change

Developed countries

As a country develops the birth rate tends to fall and the death rate and infant mortality rate also tend to fall. The combination of these trends may result in a more **stable** or possibly **falling population** with less young people but a higher proportion of **old** people.

- **Falling birth rate in a developed country**
  As the birth rate falls and fewer babies are born, less maternity hospitals are needed (closures occur),and, as time passes, fewer school children leads to school closures and teacher redundancies. In the future fewer school leavers should help the unemployment situation, but there may be shortages of skilled labour and a smaller workforce will earn a lower tax revenue for the government. Less money will be available for public services and at the same time more hospitals and geriatric homes will be required. The total population will decline.
- **Increasing life expectancy in a developed country** leads to an ageing population. As life expectancy increases there will be more old, retired people who are classed as non-productive i.e. not working or paying income tax (needed to finance public services). The government will need extra finance to support these people i.e. for pensions, hospitals, geriatric care, etc.

NB A combination of lower birth rate and increased life expectancy may mean there is insufficient finance for required services.

Developing countries

- **Falling birth rate**
  As the birth rate falls (due to the introduction of birth control schemes) and the number of children falls it will enable the government to provide more effective education and medical services (vaccinations, etc.). Teacher/pupil ratios will reduce and this should improve literacy rates. Less mouths to feed should reduce malnutrition and undernutrition problems. In the future unemployment should fall together with housing shortages etc.
- **Falling death rate**
  As the death rate falls, life expectancy will increase with the population able to work more productively. The falling death rate together with a healthier population should reduce the need for spending on medical services, hospitals, doctors, etc. This should release money to finance other needs. The infant mortality rate (related to the death rate) will also fall resulting in a more stable population structure.

Fig.88

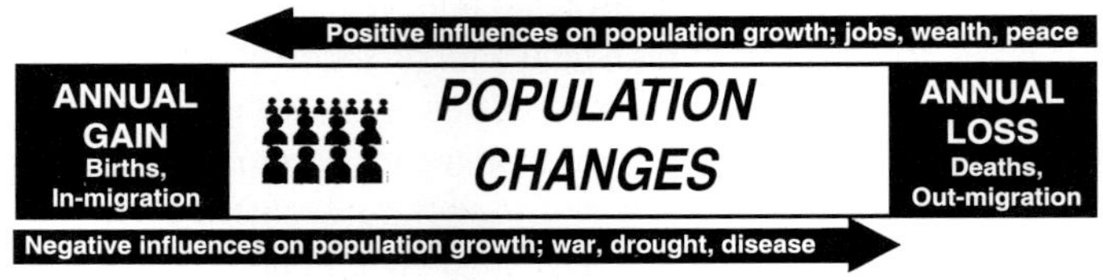

Fig.89

World Population Growth 1750 - 2001

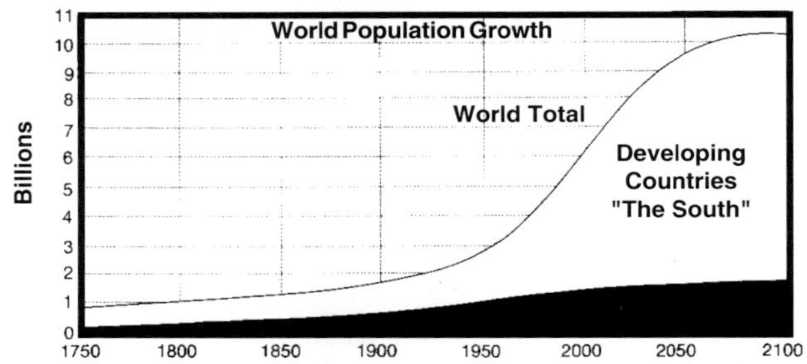

Projections of population for different regions **Fig.90**

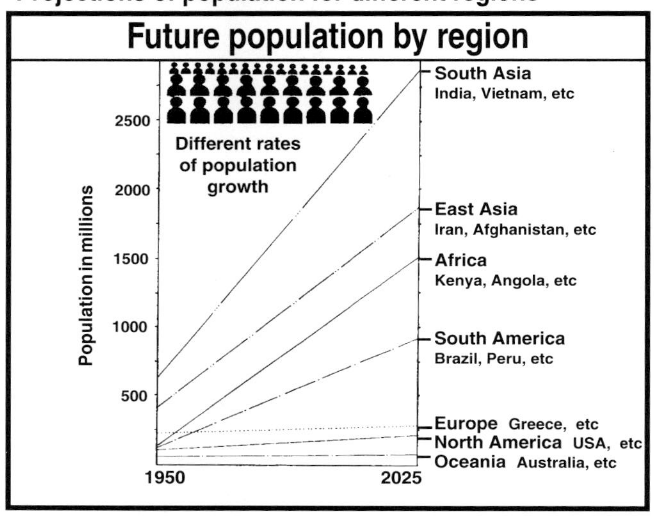

Population information

Fig.91

Population Census	A count of the total number of people living within a country's boundaries.
Birth Rate	The number of babies born in a year for every 1000 people in the population.
Death Rate	The number of deaths in a year for every 1000 people in the population.
Infant Mortality	The number of infants under 1 year old who die each year out of every 1000 babies born alive.
Life Expectancy	The average life span of the population of the country.
Dependency Ratio	The %age of the population not earning an income and are dependent on others. The Ratio is calculated thus: $\text{Dep.Ratio} = \left(\frac{\text{Children (0-14) + Aged (65+)}}{\text{Adults (15-64)}}\right) \times 100$

Migration

Migration is usually defined as being a movement of population involving a change of residence of a substantial duration. The diversity of migrations in terms of duration, distance and organisation has resulted in a wide range of types (figure **92**). Migration may be **temporary** or **permanent movement** away from the place of origin. Temporary movement (circulation) may be short-term (e.g. commuting) or longer term (e.g. employment contract in Saudi Arabia) or seasonal (e.g. transhumance in the Alps).

The two main types of migration are -

- **international migration** - involving the crossing of national boundaries
- **internal migration** - which is within a nation.

Emigration means the departure from and **immigration** means the entry into a country to change permanent residence.

Migration patterns can be selective in terms of age, gender and purpose and include the following -

- **Rural - Urban migration** e.g. Highlands to Glasgow
- **Urban - Rural migration** e.g. London to Hampshire
- **Urban - Urban migration** e.g. London to Inverness
- **Short distance internal migrations** in developed countries are often predominantly female
- **Long distance internal migration** in developed countries are often predominantly male
- **In developing countries internal & international migrations** are predominantly male
- **Professional classes** in developed countries are more migratory than are skilled or unskilled workers.

Migration and its causes **Fig.92**

Types of Migration

TEMPORARY MIGRATION
- Seasonal (e.g. nomads)
- Daily (e.g. Commuters)
- Long Term (eg. foreign workers)

PERMANENT MIGRATION
- Rural to Urban (e.g. Deccan Plateau to Calcutta, India)
- Urban to Rural (e.g. London to a Sussex commuter village)
- Urban to Urban (e.g. Glasgow to London)
- Between Countries (e.g. Hong Kong to UK)

Out of the 50 million displaced people, nearly half are refugees in their own country.

Causes of Migration

Lack of basic amenities, overcrowding, civil war, shortage of labour, poverty, polluted environment, better life with paid work, high infant mortality rate, medical services provided for all, lack of land, safer environment, radioactivity in environment, markets, desertification, poor health care, high population growth rate, entertainments, long-term drought, television & media, famine, better housing, earthquakes & floods, noise pollution, schools open to all, vandalism & crime, higher living standards, religious bigotry, ethnic cleansing, deforestation.

Migration may be **voluntary** e.g. from Turkey to former West Germany or **forced** e.g. from Bosnia to Germany - see figures **93** and **94**.

Analysis of migration - case study 1 - Turkish workers to former West Germany (Voluntary migration) **Fig.93**

Migraton usually involves **push factors** (those which drive people from their place of origin) and **pull factors** (attraction of the destination)

Push Factors
- Poverty in Turkey
- Unemployment
- Low wages
- Low standard of living
- Lack of training
- High inflation
- Housing shortages
- Natural disasters

Pull Factors
- High wages
- Higher standard of living
- Job prospects
- Education & training
- Low inflation
- Political stability

Former West Germany was regarded as a wealthy country and one in which there were well paid employment opportunities for migrant workers, predominantly male, from all over Europe.

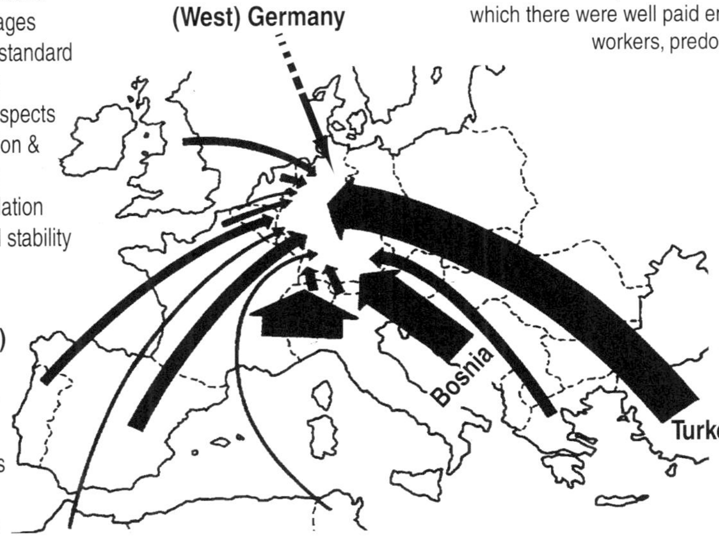

Host Country (W.Germany) Benefits
- 'Gastarbeiter' (Guestworkers) did menial jobs
- Solved employment shortages in less desirable jobs
- Enriched the country's culture
- A temporary workforce which could be repatriated (sent home)

Problems
- Language difficulties
- Discrimination & riots
- Housing shortages
- Local unemployment

Country of Origin (Turkey) Benefits
- Relieved local unemployment
- Returning workers brought back 'hard currency'
- Workers learnt new skills
- Workers sent money home to families (relieved poverty)
- Less crowding on land, etc.

Problems
- 'Brain drain' of more enterprising workers
- Lack of male workers at home
- Damaged Turkish economy
- Caused social problems due to lack of Turkish males

NB. *In recent years after the unification of East & West Germany unemployment increased & jobs were needed by native Germans. Germany has now restricted the issue of new work permits. Germany has given incentives to encourage repatriation of Turkish workers.*

Analysis of migration - case study 2 - Bosnian refugees to Germany (forced migration) **Fig.94**

Push factors

Civil War - Homelessness - Religious persecution - Ethnic Cleansing (of Muslims) - Breakdown of society - poverty - Food shortages - unemployment - injury - lack of Medical care

Pull factors

Political asylum - stability - Refuge from War - Housing - Employment prospects - Medical treatment available - Relatives in 'host' country - safety

Problems
- Discrimination
- Resentment by Germans
- Riots
- Language difficulties
- Recent restrictions on numbers

Analysis of migration - case study 3 - Rural - Urban migration - Indian countryside to Calcutta

Fig.95

Push factors

Poverty
Unemployment
Climatic problems - drought & floods
Famine
Malnutrition
Lack of land
Disease
Lack of services - shops, schools, hospitals
Caste system
Debt
Local disputes/civil war

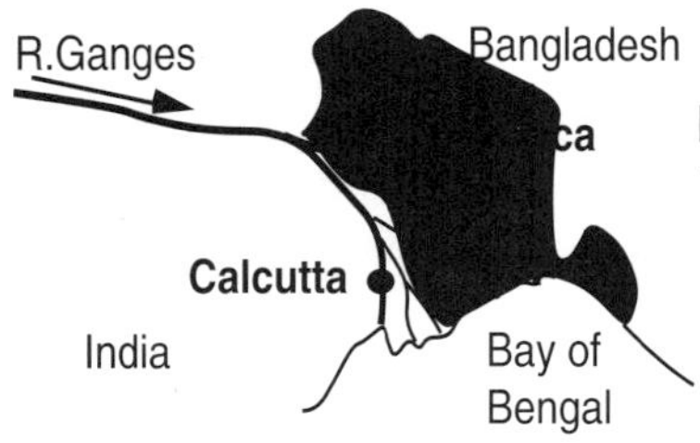

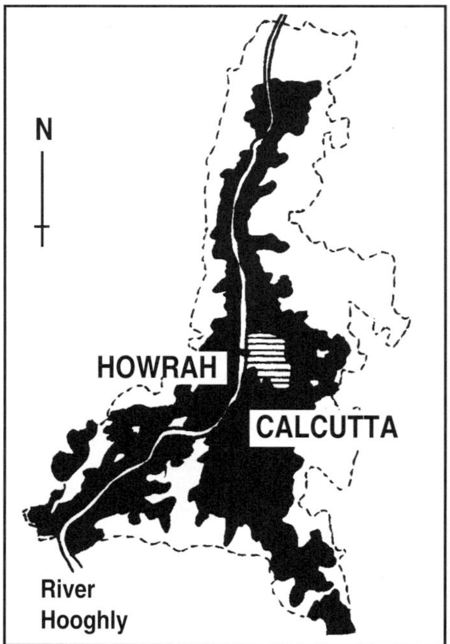

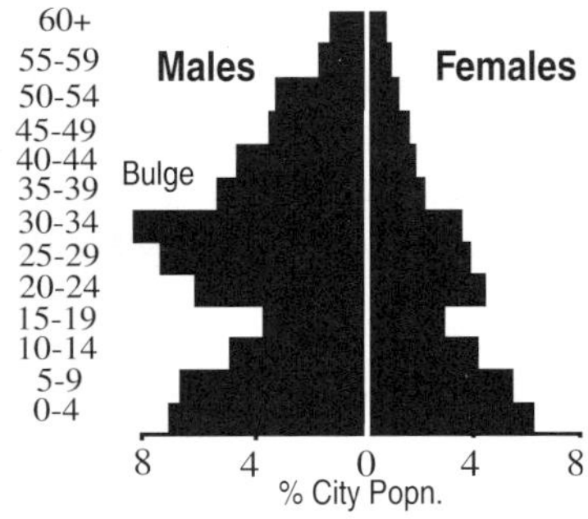

350 migrants per day are estimated to move into Calcutta in search of a better way of life, employment or to escape debt, famine or religious intolerance. Most migrants are young working age males (see population pyramid above). Most are homeless.

Pull factors

Employment prospects
Higher wages
Housing
More & better services (schools, shops, medical, entertainment)
Protection from natural disasters
Urban improvement schemes
Perception of improved living conditions and higher standards of living compared with rural areas

Problems associated with migration

Overcrowding
Shanty towns and poor living conditions
Lack of infrastructure
Lack of services for number of migrants including transport, water supplies, education, food, schools, etc
Unemployment
Calcutta described as a '**Miseropolis**'

Quality control ?

Fig.96

At the end of the 20th. century there are other 'developments' which are very likely to influence population changes, some of which have been around for over 100 years.......e.g.

- **Eugenics** is the theory of improving the human stock by selective breeding
- **Restricted marriage** between mentally deficient people in many US states in the early 1900s
- **Racial purity** - the concept was discredited by German fascist dictator Adolf Hitler's misuse of sterilisation on the grounds of racial purity and the killing of those considered unfit - Jews, blacks
- **Abortions** - many countries allow abortions to prevent the birth of disabled children
- **Sperm banks** have been developed in many countries, in some to improve the human stock
- **Genetic modification** is currently exercising governments in their approach to population developments, e.g. in UK and USA.

Forced to flee from home

Fig.97

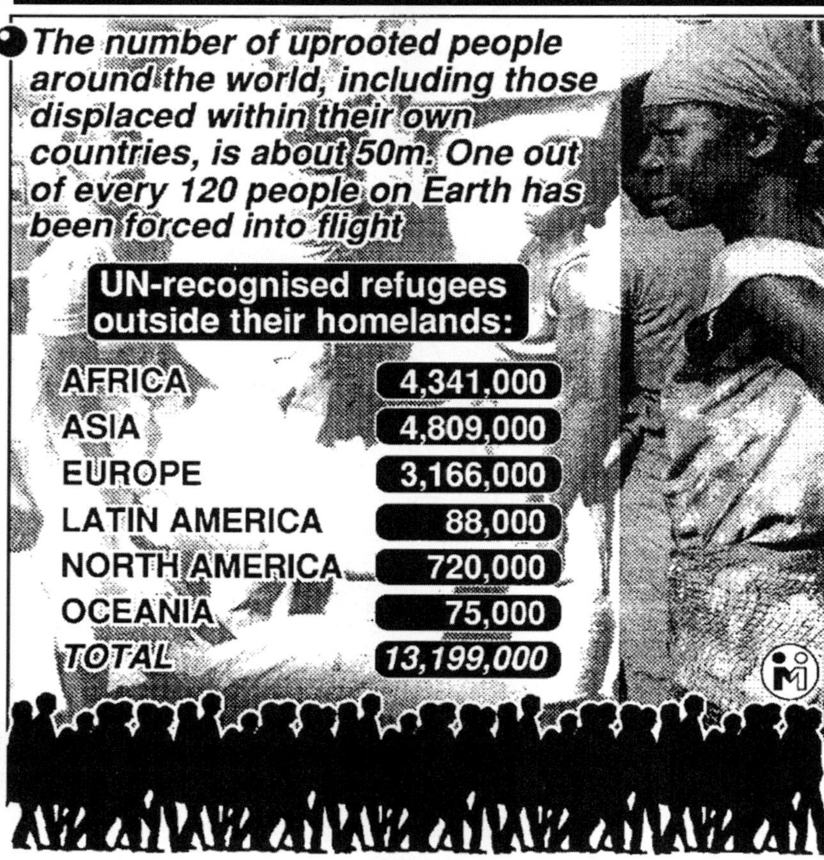

Population Revision : Summary Notes

The main idea of the Population section is....
Population change and structure vary spatially and over time. Reasons for change are complex and involve human and environmental factors.

Population structure / Demographic Transition

1. Populations can be described by **age-sex pyramids**: Pyramids can be **progressive** (expanding population); **Stationary** and/or **Regressive** (declining population).
2. Population structure of developing countries such as India are characterised by a **wide base** and a narrow top - a triangular shape indicating a high proportion of the population are young with few old people.
3. Population structure of a developed country such as Finland is characterised by a narrow base, an almost constant width and relatively broad top - indicating a small proportion of young people and a higher proportion of adults and older people.
4. The **dependency ratio** is a ratio of the economically active population to the economically inactive.
5. There are **four stages to the demographic transition** ;
   Stage **1** or "primitive" (high birth rate, high death rate, little growth);
   Stage **2** or "early expanding" (high birth rate, lowering death rate);
   Stage **3** or "late expanding" (lowering birth rate, low death rate);
   Stage **4** or "mature or advanced" (low birth and death rates, little growth).
6. Population **growth rates** were lower in the C18th and C19th, when developed countries were going through the transition, than they are today for developing countries.
7. **Malthus** suggested that populations grow at geometric rates whilst food supplies grow at arithmetic rates and therefore there will be a world food crisis. His views were conditioned by the period he lived in, when Great Britain was a largely agricultural nation.
8. The demographic transition has led to ageing populations in developed nations which places an added burden on the economically active.

Gathering population statistics

1. Population information is important to governments in order that provision for public services can be planned.
2. Methods of gathering population data include **census**, **registration** and **sampling**.
3. A **census** (people count) is the most important method of gathering population data. An **enumerator** distributes census forms to every household once every ten years - usually in the first year of each decade e.g. 2001, 2011, etc
4. **Problems** with gathering population data (especially in developing countries) include the high costs involved, a lack of literacy, the size of some countries (area/population) remoteness & poor communications / infrastructure, suspicion, internal strife/conflict (e.g. Kosovo, Algeria)

Population Change / Fertility and Mortality

1. **Accelerating population growth** is a relatively recent phenomenon. World population was about 1 billion in 1820 and will rise to over 6 billion by 2000.
2. Population change depends upon the balance between **inputs** (births, immigration) and **outputs** (deaths, emigration)
3. Population growth or decline has **three** components -
   birth rates number of babies born in a year for every 1,000 people
   death rates number of deaths in a year for every 1,000 people
   migration movement of people involving a change of residence of a substantial duration.
4. The current **developed** countries experienced rapid population growth during the industrial revolution, when death rates fell and life expectancy began to rise.
5. Since 1945 the **developing** countries have experienced dramatic growth rates as infant mortality has fallen but improvements in life expectancy have not always been accompanied by a rise in living standards.
6. **Fertility ratios** are calculated by dividing the number of children under 3 by the number of women between the ages of 15 and 44 years (around 1.8 for Europe and 6.3 for Africa)
7. **Infant mortality rates** are often a good indicator of the quality of health services. They are expressed as the number of infants under 1 year old who die in a year, out of 1,000 people in the country's population.
8. In developed countries a wide range of factors has influenced the decline of birth rates, including; later age of marriage; increased family planning (including the use of birth control methods) and higher economic and social status of women.
9. Improved medical facilities, campaigns against infectious diseases and availability of clean water have all lowered death rates.
10. In developed countries the main causes of death are degenerative diseases (**endogenic**) whilst in developing countries **exogenic** causes (environmental) are more common.
11. In general, wealthier countries (the North) have **higher life expectancies** but some relatively poor countries have succeeded in raising life expectancies to high levels by devoting a large proportion of their limited resources to improving health, e.g. Tanzania, China.
12. There are two main types of migration - **international and internal migration**.
13. **Emigration** means departure from and **immigration** means the entry into a country, to change permanent residence.

Population Revision : Unit style assessments

1a. Study figure **98**.
Describe the problems which can arise from falling birth rates in developed countries such as Finland and suggest **one solution** which such countries may have found for problems relating to falling birth rates. (5)

1b. Describe the advantages which a fall in birth and death rates can bring to a developing country such as Bangladesh. (5)

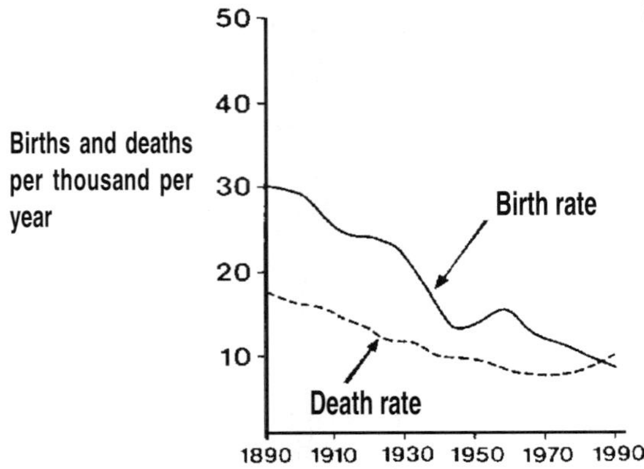

Fig.98

2a. GMT With reference to the **demographic transition model** and the **population pyramid** (figure **99**), explain how the age structure of a developing country might gradually be transformed into the structure of a developed country. (5)

2b. What effects might these changes have on provision of health care and social services ? (5)

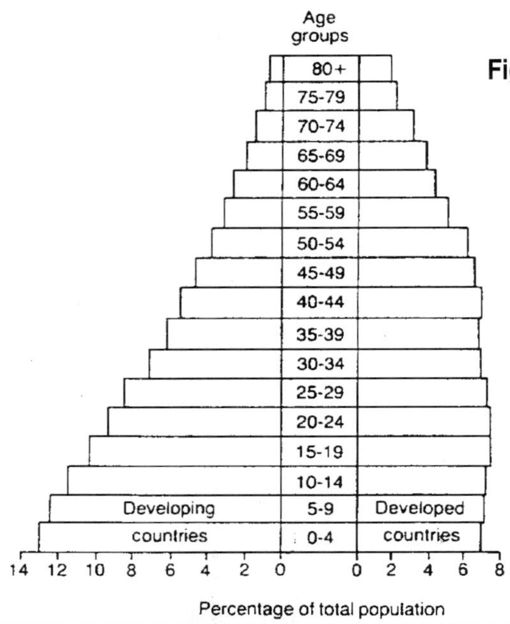

Fig.99

Population Revision : Exam style assessments

1. Briefly explain, with the help of examples, the differences between **migration** and **circulation**. (4)

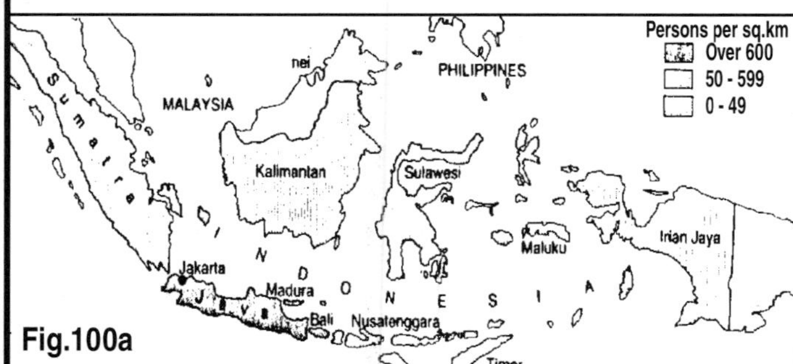

Fig.100a

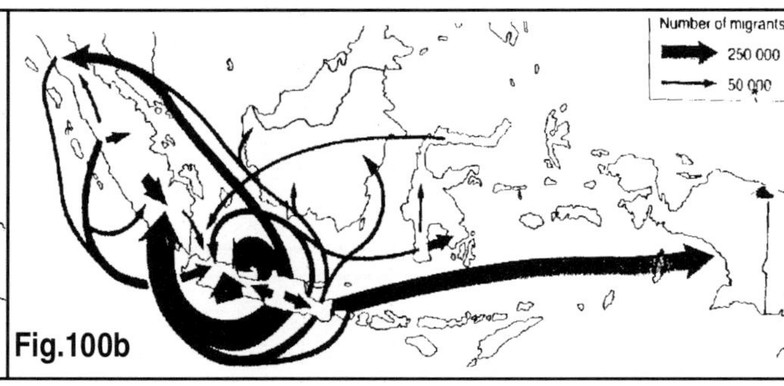

Fig.100b

2. With reference to figures **100a and 100b**, describe and explain the patterns of migration in Indonesia. (6)

3. Comparison table between Voluntary and Forced migration

Fig.100c

Type of Migration	Push factors	Pull factors	Attitude of host (receiving) country
Voluntary	Moderately important	Very important	Enthusiastic welcome
Forced	Very important	Moderately important	Less enthusiastic

With reference to the above comparison table (figure **100c**), and using two named examples of migration you have studied, compare the different attitudes which might be encountered. (6)

7. Rural Geography

The main idea of the Rural Geography section is....
Rural populations are involved in a variety of agricultural systems. These systems, associated with landscapes and settlements are subject to change.

What do you need to know ?

Students should have a knowledge and understanding of -

A Agricultural systems
- systems under different population densities, technologies, levels of commercialism and physical opportunities
- one case study location for each of shifting cultivation, e.g. Amazonia, intensive peasant farming, e.g. Ganges Valley and extensive commercial farming, e.g. East Anglia
- analysis of landuse data and crop yields in map, diagrammatic or tabular form
- analysis of farm survey results

B Rural landscapes
- landscapes including field and infrastructural patterns associated with the agricultural systems listed above
- annotation and analysis of field sketches of rural landscapes

C Rural change
- changes to the systems and landscapes above, shifting cultivation (e.g. impact of deforestation), intensive farming (e.g. the green revolution) and extensive commercial farming (e.g. the impact of government and European Union (EU) policy such as diversification of activities and crops)
- reasons for, and implications of these changes

Agricultural systems, rural landscape and rural change

The Farming System

Fig.101

Farming may be treated as a system which involved **inputs**, **processes** and **outputs** - see figure **101. The level of profit or loss depends upon the balance between inputs and outputs.**

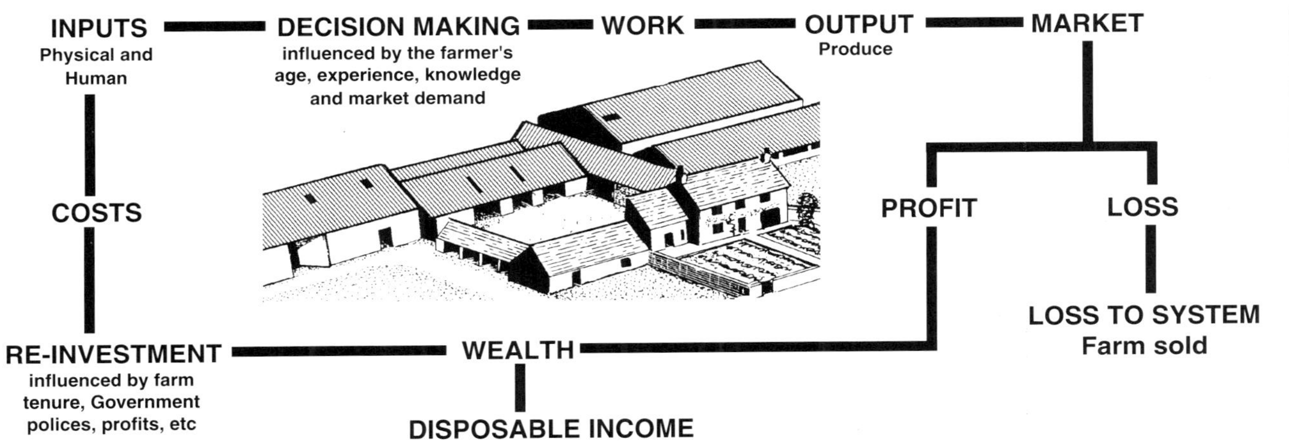

Physical inputs
Altitude
Temperate
Precipitation
Wind
Slope
Aspect
Soils

Human inputs
Transport
Markets
Capital
Technology
Government policies
Farm size
Inheritance
Tenure of farm

Processes within the system
Sowing
ploughing
breeding
milking
harvesting
fattening
etc.

Outputs
Livestock
crops
fodder crops
slurry (dung)
eggs
milk
etc.

Evolution of Farming Systems

Innovation in farming has increased in the last 50 years. Experts recognise that as any society develops, its farming systems evolve as shown in figure **102**.

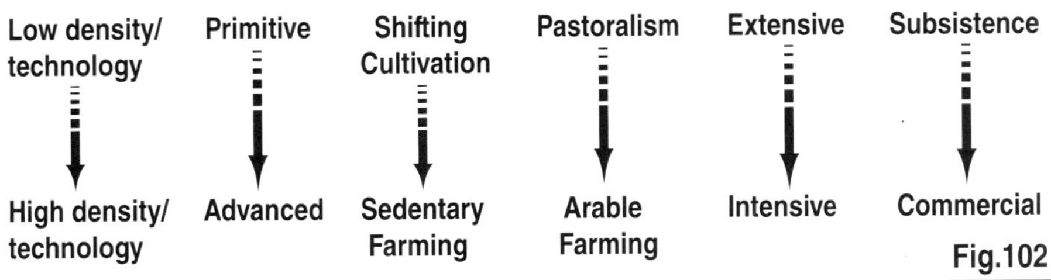

Fig.102

Major developments in farming have been
- **Pastoral to Arable** animals to crops
- **HYV** high yielding varieties (cereal crops)
- **Irrigation & fertiliser systems**
- **GM foods**, potentially, could change farming dramatically

Extensive and intensive agricultural systems

Fig.103

Figure 103 shows the relationships between land, labour and capital in **four different farming systems**. Contrasts in productivity per worker can be drawn between **Extensive** and **Intensive** farming.

Extensive farming normally involves relatively large-scale farming with a large area of land and a low output per hectare.

Intensive farming normally involves input of large amounts of labour, capital, machinery to obtain the greatest output or yield from the small area farmed.

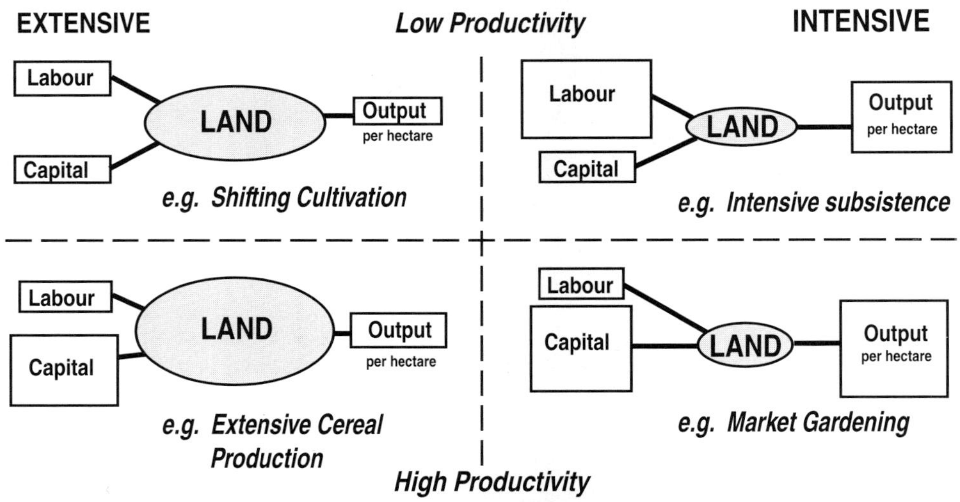

Subsistence and commercial agricultural systems

Subsistence agriculture is primarily concerned with **survival.** The farmer produces only enough food for him/herself and family. There is usually no surplus involved. Many subsistence farmers attempt to ward off failed harvests by growing a wide variety of crops - a **polycultural system** of agriculture then develops. Subsistence farmers have difficulties in increasing their output because they lack the land, technology or experience to do so. Positive feedback in this system can result in hunger and even mass famine.

Commercial agriculture is primarily concerned with generating a **profit**. In this system, farm units are usually large and the farmer utilises a great deal of technology in order to ensure efficiency and high productivity. Most commercial agriculture is supported by government subsidies and contributes a large share of a nation's wealth.

Fig.104

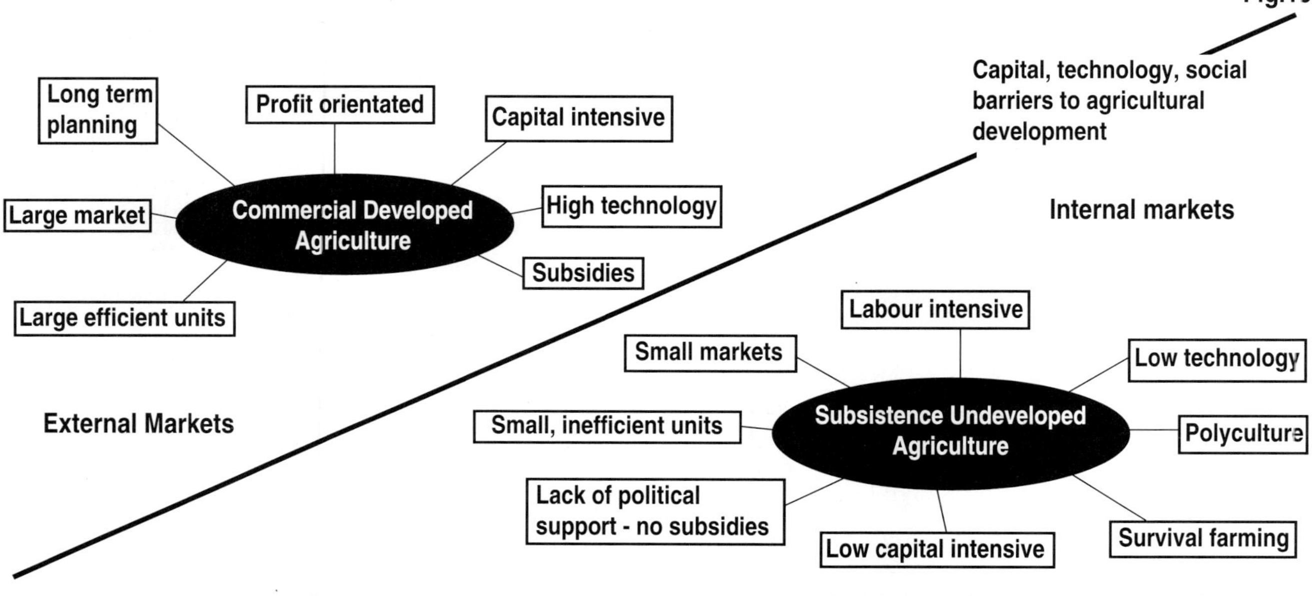

Useful terms in Rural Geography

- **Arable Farming** — growing **crops (normally** requires fertile, well-drained land)
- **Pastoral Farming** — rearing / fattening **livestock** e.g. sheep and cattle (beef and dairy)
- **Mixed Farming** — growing **crops** and rearing / fattening livestock
- **Shifting Cultivation** — where farmers move from place to place, cultivating different areas (may return after **fallowing**)
- **Fallow** — allowing land to rest from crops or livestock use
- **Sedentary Farming** — farming which takes place on the same piece of land year after year (may involve **crop rotation**)
- **Commercial Farming** — normally large-scale, i.e. to make profit (cash crops)
- **Subsistence Farming** — producing enough for one's own needs, survival farming
- **Extensive Farming** — normally on a relatively large-scale with a large area of land (output is low per hectare)
- **Intensive Farming** — normally involves input of large amounts of labour, capital and machinery to obtain the greatest output yield from the small area of land

Contrasting agricultural systems - three main ones to know...........

Shifting Cultivation

- **Extensive** with **low** technology, e.g. Amazon Indians such as the Boro Indians.
- **Small amounts of labour and capital** but a very **large area of land** is needed (to allow **fallowing**)
- **Output** per hectare is **low**.
- Only supports a **low population density** at a **subsistence** level
- If population increases the fallow period decreases; the crop yield decreases and shifting cultivation becomes unable to support the growing population; can lead to soil erosion.

Extensive Commercial Farming

- For example, **Grain production**
- Extensive **but with high technology and high output per worker,** e.g. North American **wheat** farming
- **Small input of labour but large input of capital (for machinery, fertiliser, etc.)**
- **Large amounts of land used which results in low output per hectare**
- **The large area of land** and relatively low output per hectare corresponds with a **low population** density and **scattered settlement.**
- **Labour (employment) requirements are low.**

Intensive Peasant Farming

- For example, **traditional rice cultivation in India**
- **Labour intensive** (large workforce) but **limited capital (basic tools only)**
- Uses a **small area of land** (5-10 hectares)
- Combination of **high labour input over small areas** results in a **moderate/high output per hectare**
- The high input of labour and the relatively high output per hectare can support a **high population density** (at **subsistence** level).
- If **mechanisation** is introduced, **unemployment** can result.

Case Study 1 - Shifting Cultivation (Slash and Burn) - the Boro Indians, Amazon Basin, Brazil.......

Fig.105

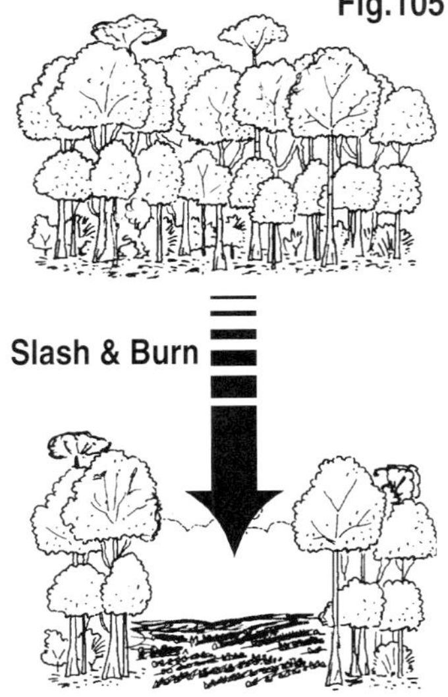

Methods....

- **Forest is cleared** with machetes
- **Tree stumps are burned** - the ash fertilises the soil
- **Crops are planted** - e.g. maize, peppers, tobacco, manioc (crops which require most nutrients first, less demanding on soil, e.g. manioc planted later) & fruit trees (seeds encourage regeneration)
- **Clearings are occupied by communities** (3-6 families) in large buildings (called malocas). These are dispersed through the forest (1,000 hectares are needed to support one person) - crops are grown in cultivated gardens known as **chagras**
- **As soil deteriorates** (nutrients taken up by plants / heavy rain causes **leaching**) - after about 10 years the clearing is abandoned
- **The clearing is left to regenerate** (restore soil fertility) by fallowing
- **Boro Indians move** (shift) to a new area and clear more forest by slash and burn methods. **Process starts again**

NB A large area is needed as up to 35 years fallowing is required for soils in clearings to regenerate fully. If the fallow period is reduced (e.g. to support a growing population) the soils do not recover and soon become infertile.

Deforestation of Rainforest areas

Fig.106

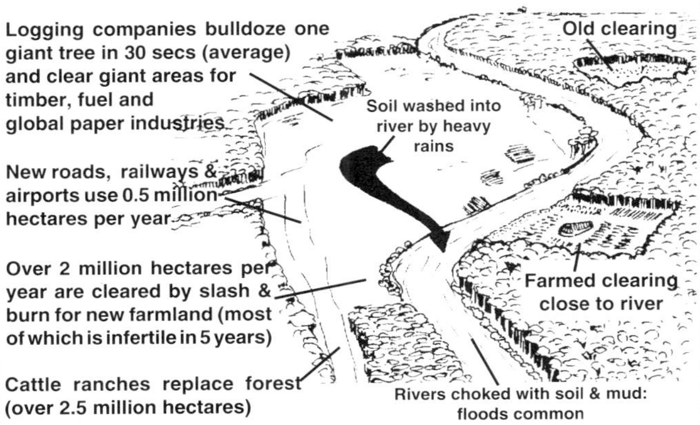

Changes in the Region

Primitive, shifting cultivation relates well to the environment, affecting only small areas and allowing forests to regenerate. However, **deforestation** (clearing forest on a large scale) for **ranching** (beef cattle), **mining**, **settlement** etc., has forced **indigenous Indians into reservations** and contact with western culture may bring disease (population **decline**) or depopulation to the cities. Where population density increases, shifting cultivation must give way to **sedentary farming** using fertilisers and crop rotation to maintain soil fertility.

In Colombia, **National Parks** have been set up to protect the forest and allow Indians to live in the traditional way (shifting cultivation). They are also encouraged to tap **rubber trees** and gather nuts, (not harmful to the forest).

World cereals map

Fig.107

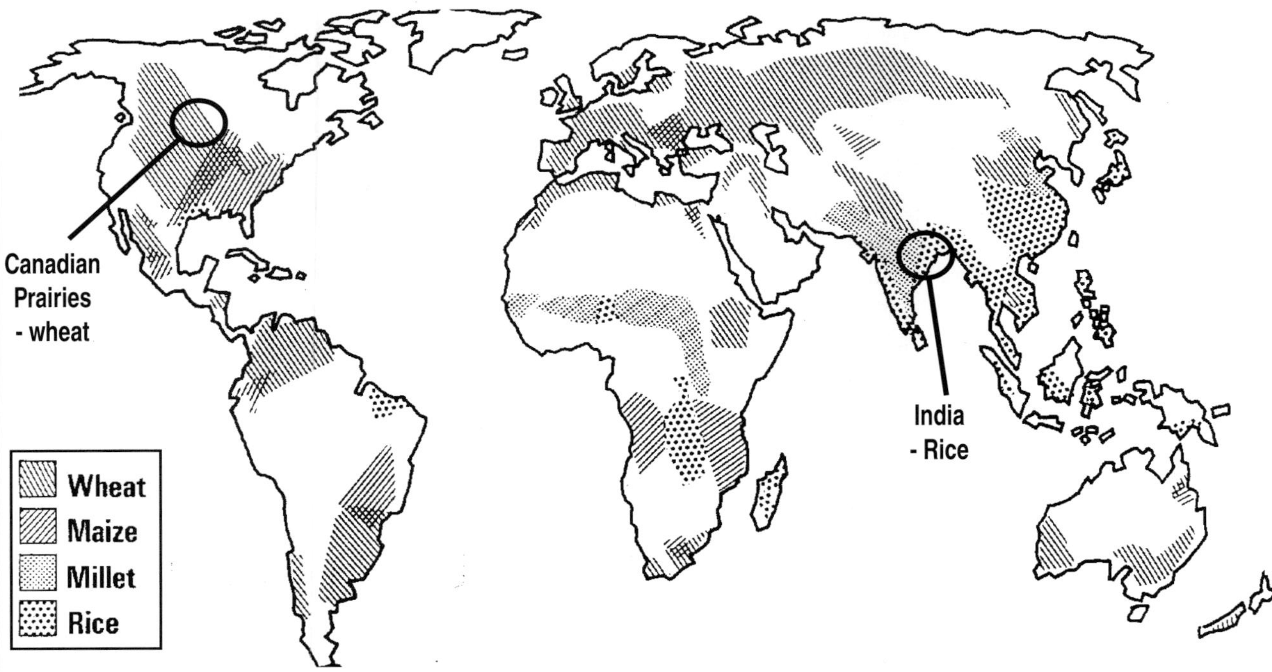

Case Study 2 - Extensive Commercial Farming - Grain production in North America, e.g. Canadian Prairies

• Climate
- adequate growing season (despite a short summer)
- warm, sunny summer - ripens wheat
- precipitation falls in growing season (when needed)
- severe winter frost breaks up soil (kills bacteria)
- warm Chinook wind melts snow early

• Relief
- vast area of flat, fertile land available (excellent for extensive commercial farming and use of large-scale machinery, transport etc.

• Potential Problems
- occasional droughts
- heavy hail storms ruin crops
- ploughed land forms monotonous landscape - with lack of shelter - prone to erosion
- remoteness and isolation

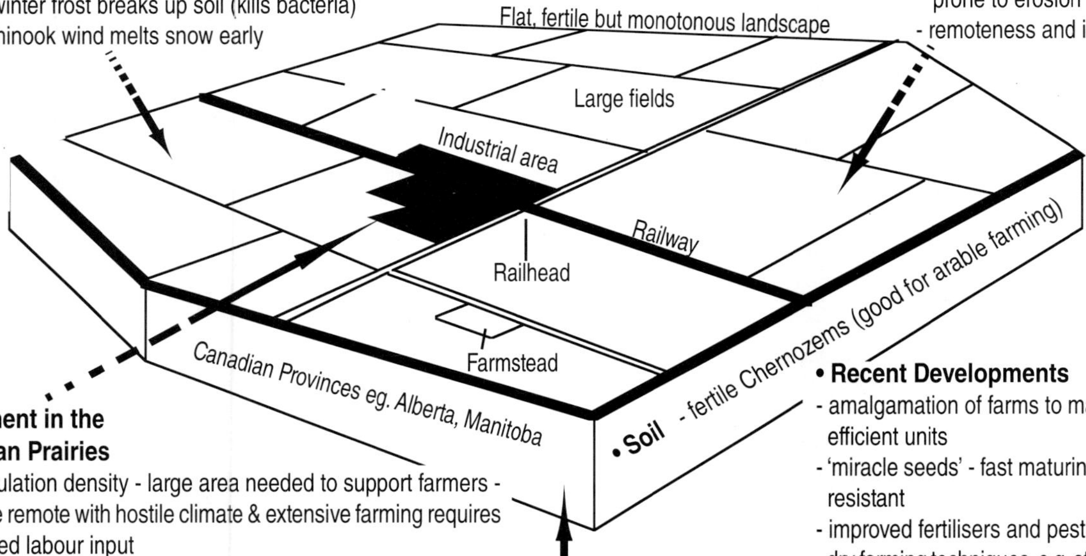

Fig.108

• Settlement in the Canadian Prairies
- Low population density - large area needed to support farmers - areas are remote with hostile climate & extensive farming requires only limited labour input
- Historical development, i.e. original settlers - each allocated 65 hectares were dispersed but with a relatively uniform population distribution/settlement pattern - farms in linear arrangement along roads/railways
- More accessible sites with better communications developed as service centres
- An hierarchy of settlements evolved - (low. middle and high order)
  - High order (most accessible locations, e.g. at road junctions or railheads, greater potential for growth (markets for produce)
  - Low and Middle order occur more frequently but in less accessible locations

• Recent Developments
- amalgamation of farms to make larger, more efficient units
- 'miracle seeds' - fast maturing & drought/frost resistant
- improved fertilisers and pesticides
- dry farming techniques, e.g. strip farming, deep planting, fallowing, irrigation, etc. all used
- very large fields with more efficient use of machinery

• Other considerations which influence farm decisions
- **Economic influences** - farmer's financial assets (investment in machinery etc., or sharing with other farmers in a co-operative), profitability of various crops
- **Political influences** - Government grants, subsidies for particular farming activities ? Quotas which restrict production ? Trade agreements for export ?
- **Social influences** - land tenure ? (owner or tenant farmer?)

Case Study 3 - Traditional Intensive Peasant Farming - Rice Cultivation in India

Fig.109

India's main industry **is agriculture, producing over 165 million tonnes of cereals, mainly rice. 70% of the population are subsistence farmers.**

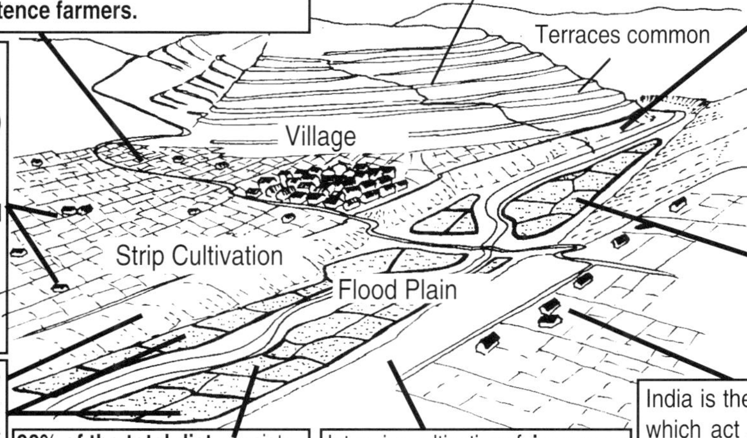

Typical intensive subsistence farms are very small (1-5 hectares) and often consist of strips of land in a dispersed pattern of land tenure. Each strip is cultivated intensively with double-cropping wherever possible

Main crops produced are subsistence crops with rice being by far the most important of all cereals grown. Other crops include wheat, barley, peas

90% of the total diet consists of rice - the staple food - some of the crop may be paid to the landlord as rent

Intensive cultivation of **rice** means maximum use of land with neither fallow nor wasted space in deltas, flood plains or on terraces.

Environment for rice......
- Minimum of 10^0C needed to germinate seedlings
- 100 days growing season
- Heavy precipitation
- Fertile silts, alluvium or lava soils
- Constant attention, weeding etc

'Paddy Fields' (rice fields) are surrounded by 'bunds' (earth walls) to keep in water. High input of labour (planting, weeding, harvesting) needed.

India is the "**land of a million villages**" which act as market centres for a busy countryside (with up to 2000 people living in one square kilometre of land in some areas) - very high population density.

- **Wet Rice cultivation -** depends on seasonal rainfall where floods on rivers such as the Ganges in turn provide fertile alluvial soils

- **Methods**

- small banks (called bunds) built around fields to retain water
- fields flooded and land ploughed by hand or water buffalo
- rice seed sown in nursery plots
- seedlings transplanted to fields (water level is maintained until plants reach maturity)
- fields then drained - allows crops to ripen
- crop is harvested using a sickle

- **Maintaining soil fertility**

- when river floods, silt provides nutrients
- rice stubble ploughed into field - provides organic material
- algae floats on water - provides nitrogen
- manure is also added

- **Dry Rice cultivation -** is used where rainfall is low or unreliable - requires irrigation to grow crops - rice is grown in wet season and drought-resistant wheat in the dry season

- **Recent changes in the farming methods**

- **Mechanisation** to improve efficiency
- **Irrigation** - allows double-cropping
- **use of Biogas** plants to produce fertiliser and fuel
- **use of Insecticides** and **Herbicides** to protect crops
- Introduction of **H.Y.V. (High yield variety)** crops of rice and wheat - they grow more quickly giving double-cropping and greater output

N.B. New methods are expensive and tend to benefit the richer farmer (mechanisation may cause unemployment).

- **Rural settlement in India**

- Intensive farming can support a high population density with nucleation in villages. Some settlement is dispersed through rural areas - linear pattern beside roads
- People may be segregated by the caste system (further divides rich and poor)
- Increased profits from the Green Revolution (see below) & government help and aid
- Changes in the landscape - fields amalgamated (more efficient farms) and new roads, schools and electricity supply, etc., all targeted to raise living standards (schools provide education which further encourages the green revolution)

The Green Revolution - a brief summary

The term **Green Revolution** generally refers to the application of modern, western-type farming techniques in countries of the South, e.g. India. An evaluation of the Green Revolution in India recognises both successes and failures as listed below......

Success of the Green Revolution

- **Crop yields** have doubled (in rice and wheat)
- **Double-cropping** has been achieved.
- A **wider diet** is now available through rice, maize and wheat.
- Some farmers are now able to afford tractors, seeds and fertiliser and have a **higher standard of living**.
- The need for fertilisers has led to demand for **new industries** & **employment**.
- **Road improvements** in some areas.
- **More irrigated land** area.

Conclusion *- an economic and production success - has lessened the threat of famine in some areas but at something of a political and environmental cost.*

Failures within the Green Revolution

- **HYV seeds** need heavy use of fertiliser and pesticides. These have increased costs and led to **pollution of water supplies** in some areas.
- **Extra irrigation** is not always possible.
- **HYV crops** are not always drought-resistant and unsuited to water-logged conditions.
- Farmers cannot always afford tractors, seeds, fertilisers and have become relatively **poorer.**
- **Debt** problems have risen due to borrowing to afford tractors, etc.
- **Mechanisation** has increased unemployment in many areas.
- **Some HYV crops** are unpalatable (have poor taste).

Rural Geography Revision : Summary Notes

The main idea of the Rural Geography section is....
Rural populations are involved in a variety of agricultural systems. These systems, associated with landscapes and settlements, are subject to change.

Rural Geography

1. A working definition of **rural** might be less densely populated parts of the landscape showing signs of present or recent agricultural activity.
2. The major land use of rural areas is **agriculture**.
3. The location of different types of agriculture are a result of a combination of physical, economic and human (cultural) factors.
4. **Physical or environmental factors** such as sunlight, temperature, effective precipitation, slopes, aspect, soils and altitude influence the viability of farming. The actual choice of method used or crops grown is also related to the society engaged in farming.
5. McCarty and Lindberg suggest that there is an optimum or ideal location for each type of agriculture which is mainly based on **physical factors**.
6. **Cereals** are grown over half of the farmed land surface. They have a nutritious food content and are easy to grow, harvest, store and transport.
7. **Livestock** farming dominates just under half the farmed land surface, in areas climatically unsuitable for cereal cultivation.

Farming systems

1. Farming like many other aspects of geography can be viewed as a **system** with inputs, processes and outputs.
2. Physical, economic and human factors form the **inputs** to the system.
3. Farming systems may be **classified** according to whether they are **arable or pastoral**, **shifting or sedentary**, **subsistence or commercial**, **intensive or extensive**.
4. **Arable** farming is concerned with growing crops and tends to occupy the best quality, flattest land.
5. **Pastoral** farming or livestock rearing is normally carried out in less favourable areas (i.e. areas which are too dry or too wet for arable farming).
6. **Mixed** farming involves both crops and livestock and is more commonly practised in developed economies.
7. **Shifting cultivation** involves movement from one area to another. This form of agriculture is found in areas where the soil is poor and there is low population density. Technology used is of a low level and primitive in design.
8. **Sedentary farming** is established in one place. Sedentary farmers often use crop rotation and fertilisers in order to maintain the quality of their land.
9. **Subsistence agriculture** produces only enough food for the farmer's family without a surplus. This is also regarded as survival farming, and farmers are often unable to increase their crop yields because they lack the land or appropriate technology to increase production.

10. **Commercial farming** is concerned with making a profit. Much commercial farming is on a large scale and supported by high level technology and production methods. Maximum efficiency is often best achieved through producing one crop (**monoculture**) or rearing one type of animal.

12. **Extensive agriculture** is carried out on a large scale utilising large areas of land.
13. **Intensive agriculture** involves a concentration of resources on the land farmed. Large amounts of labour and/or capital are used per unit of land.

Distribution of the main farming types.

1. **Shifting cultivation** is largely limited to areas of tropical rainforest which tend to be isolated and inaccessible. This type of agriculture is also known as **slash and burn** and examples are found in the Amazon Basin & Indonesia.
2. **Intensive subsistence farming** is restricted to South East Asia and is concerned with the cultivation of rice - the **staple food** of the region. Farms are small and fragmented but productivity is high with 2 crops possible per year in some areas.
3. **Extensive cereal production** involves low productivity per hectare but the lack of labour required means that per worker, productivity is relatively high. Examples are found in the North American Prairies, the Steppes of Eastern Europe-Central Asia,some parts of Europe and Australia.
4. **Intensive commercial agriculture** covers a wide variety of types of farming including market gardening, dairying and fruit farming often found in belts surrounding settlements. A large input of capital and labour results in a high productivity per hectare and farm worker. Examples are found in most areas of the world especially in Europe, eastern USA, South Africa, Australia and New Zealand.
5. There is a tendency for all farming systems to become **more intensive**, and for nomadism and shifting cultivation to change to **sedentary cultivation**.
6. **Subsistence farming** can only change to commercial agriculture if there are adequate inputs of technology and money.

The Green Revolution

1. **High Yielding Varieties (HYV)** of cereal crops have doubled the output of wheat and rice since 1965.
2. **The Green Revolution** has had both advantages and disadvantages for developing countries.
3. Despite increasing global food production, a **poor global food distribution system** leaves millions hungry.

Rural Geography Revision : Unit style assessments

1a. Describe the main features and environmental impact of **Shifting Cultivation**. (5)

1b. With reference to the **Amazon Basin,** or another area of shifting cultivation, describe and explain the population density and settlement pattern which have developed. (5)

2a. Using data from figure **110**, describe and suggest reasons for the changes which have taken place. (4)

Figure **110** **Agriculture in S.E. Asia**	1965	1975	1995
Percentage of land irrigated by wells	37	75	85
Fertiliser applied per hectare	24	325	450
Area of HYV wheat (hectares)	24	225,000	455,000
Wheat yield (kilogrammes per hectare)	1,650	4,000	5,100

2b. **GMT** Make a simple sketch of the photograph (figure **111**).

Annotate the sketch to identify and explain the main farming activities taking place. (5)

2c. Briefly suggest how the farming landscape might change with the introduction of the Green Revolution. (4)

Figure **111**

Rural Geography Revision : Exam style assessments

1. Use figure 112 and any additional information to explain how **intensive peasant farming** achieves a much higher output per hectare and can support a higher population density than Shifting Cultivation. (5)

Fig.112

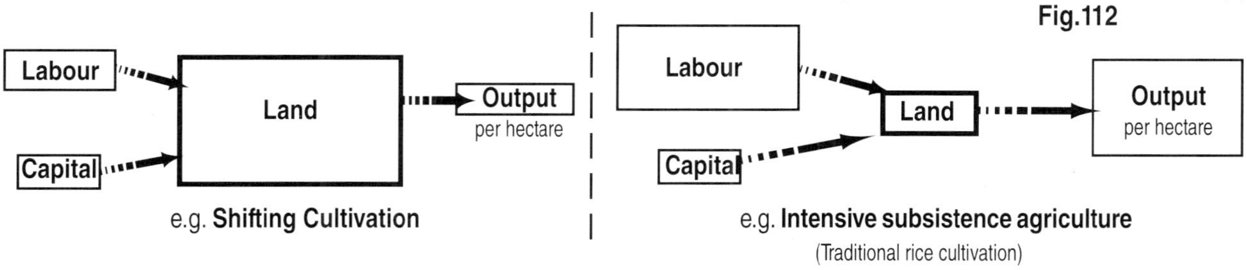

2. **GMT** Comment on the results shown in figure **113** - a **farm survey in Southern England** (5)

Fig.113	**1970**	**1995**
Average field size	**2.5 has**	**4.5 has**
Number of Beef Cattle	**1200**	**500**
Area under 'Set Aside' schemes	**--**	**1000 has**
Area of land leased for Recreational Use	**--**	**500has**

3. Explain the effect of the following changes on **two** different agricultural systems - (5)

- Introducing a fertiliser subsidy for **intensive peasant farmers**
- Shortening the fallow period in an area of **shifting cultivation**
- Overuse of artificial fertiliser at the expense of crop rotation in a **commercial farming system**

8. Industrial Geography

What do you need to know ?

Students should have a knowledge and understanding of -

A Industrial systems

- classification of industry - primary, secondary, tertiary and quaternary
- location factors such as inputs, outputs, linkages, technology, chance factors, national and international economic, political and environmental considerations
- interaction of these factors to explain industrial locations over time
- historical changes in industrial location, e.g. water, power, coalfield, footloose, coastal locations

B Industrial landscapes

- the diversity of industrial landscapes and environmental consequences brought about by industrial activity, including comparisons between old and new industrial landscapes
- use of maps to describe and explain industrial locations and landscapes

C Industrial change

- reasons for and implications of industrial change - including changes in raw material supply, transport and communication changes, employment changes, impact of Government and EU decisions, free market and currency change implications, etc.

The main idea of the Industrial Geography section is....
Areas of industrial concentration contain a range of manufacturing and other economic activities. These concentrations develop and change spatially over time.

Industrial Systems

Industry can be described as any economic activity and, because it is such an all-encompassing term, it is usual to classify industrial activity into **four main** categories -

- **Primary Industry** where **raw materials** are **extracted** from the earth e.g. mining, forestry, fishing.
- **Secondary Industry** where raw materials are transformed (**processing** or **manufacturing**) into **consumable products** e.g. shipbuilding, electronics.
- **Tertiary Industry** where a **service** is provided for customers or consumers e.g. retailing, professional services, tourism.
- **Quaternary Industry** includes **research** and **development** (Universities), the media, etc. Where the main outputs are **information** and **expertise** (often transmitted electronically)

Note. Industry in a given area often **evolves** from mainly primary and secondary initially to a later focus on tertiary (thus demonstrating the main industrial process of c**hange through time and location**).

Note . The proportion of employment in each sector or category of industry has changed markedly in the last 200 years, in developed countries, employment composition can be used as a measure of the level of development of a country. Most experts now recognise the following stages or phases in the industrial development of a country :

Fig.114

i	ii	iii	iv	v	vi
Agrarian Society —	Industrial Revolution —	Industrialisation & Development —	Late Industrial —	Post-Industrial —	?

At the same time as the relative importance of the different sectors of industry has changed, the way of analysing industry has also undergone something of a major change. Industry can be considered as a **system** in much the same way as agriculture. Experts now recognise that industries, especially those in the secondary, tertiary and quaternary sectors, consist of inputs, processes and outputs (fig.**115**). (Profits can be made through processing and used to pay for interest on borrowed capital, raw materials, rents, energy consumed, wages and future development & expansion).

The Industrial System **Fig.115**

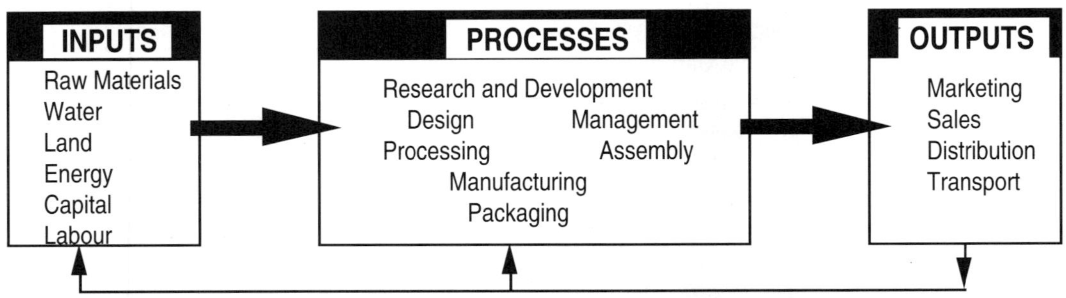

Location Factors for industry

The location of any industry can be influenced by a complex variety of inter-connecting physical or human factors.

An industrial landscape

Fig.116

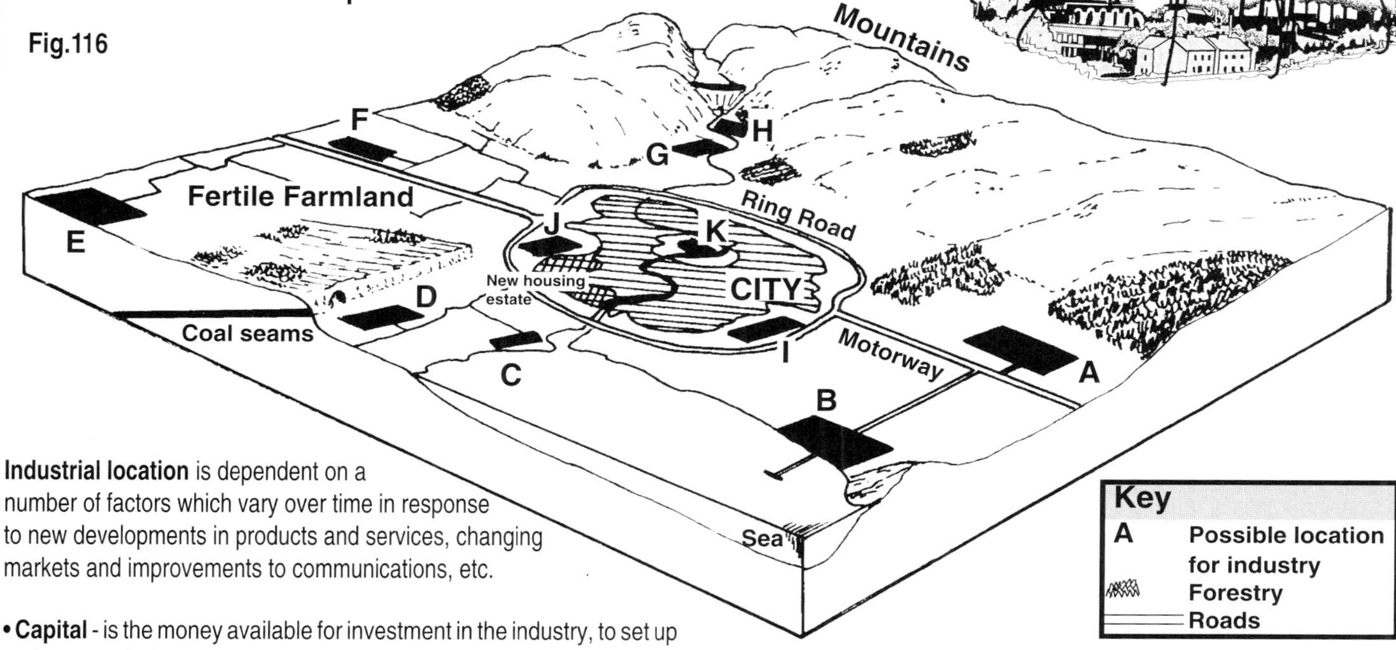

Industrial location is dependent on a number of factors which vary over time in response to new developments in products and services, changing markets and improvements to communications, etc.

- **Capital** - is the money available for investment in the industry, to set up and run new industries.

- **Raw Materials** - many industries locate as close as possible to supplies of raw materials which they use most, e.g. a cement works is usually located in close proximity to a limestone quarry. This location saves money on transport costs, especially where the raw material is heavy and bulky to transport.

- **Communications** - good communication and transport links are essential factors influencing the location of industry. The movements of people, goods and ideas along natural and artificial routeways, utilising roads, railways, air and sea routes and various telecommunication links play a vital part in the successful operation of many industries.

- **Site** - the actual land the industry is built upon is also an important consideration. Ideally it should be cheap, flat with adequate room for expansion and close to good communication links.

- **Markets** - places where goods and services are sold. Many industries supply goods and services for sale in large urban areas. By locating near to or within a large city, a large market is provided and transport costs reduced.

- **Labour and Skills** - every industry needs people (their technical and organisational skills) as workers. The larger the required labour force, the more likely that location is close to a large urban area.

- **Power** - all industries require power of some sort. Industries which require large amounts of power, e.g. aluminium smelting or petro-chemical refining may locate close to a power station or even build their own. Industries which can locate almost anywhere there is a power supply are known as *footloose industries*.

- **Government Policy** - governments - UK and EU, usually try to encourage industries to locate in less developed areas - where unemployment is high - using a selection of incentives such as grants, pre-built factories, training schemes, Objective 1 funding in deprived areas, etc.

- **Climate** - some climates are too extreme for certain industries to locate in. Other *environmental* considerations which influence the location of industry include the laws on pollution of land and water within certain areas, and the amount of greenery in the surrounding area. For example modern electronics industries require dust-free, greenfield areas in which to manufacture silicon products.

- **Inertia** - because it is always extremely expensive for industries to relocate elsewhere, many old industries have tended to stay in the locality where they were first established. This is called industrial inertia.

- **Agglomeration** - some industries attract others to locate beside them. Such a collection of industries is known as an agglomeration.

- **Product or Service Life Cycle** - a product or service usually goes through various stages in its life-cycle (Infancy-Youth-Maturity-Old Age) which can influence its location.

Industries can also be classified according to their particular type of location (Fig.116). Some locations are better suited to some industries than others, e.g. Site **A** is a *greenfield site*. Site **B** is a *tidewater site*. Both have pleasant locations with cheap flat land available. Large industries may be attracted to locate in these areas even although they lie some way from the city and will attract fewer visiting customers. Site **K** is a city centre location where land is very expensive and transport of products difficult due to congestion. However site K has access to many thousands of city centre workers, shoppers and visitors.

The factors influencing the location of industry are not all of equal importance. They may vary in different places and at different times. But wherever industry is located it requires a good **infrastructure** - buildings, power & water and good communications networks.

Industrial Landscapes - some hints on the use of maps

Questions may focus on industrial location and landscape.

- **Early Industry (pre late 18th.C)** — Mills etc. close to rivers (**weirs**) for **water** power.
- **19th Century Industry** — Often close to city centre/C.B.D. and mixed with housing - cramped environment with tall buildings - may be near rivers or beside **railways** and **canals** (important for **transport**.)

Primary Industry — May show mines, quarries, shafts and old waste tips/derelict land.

Secondary Industry — Factories usually shown by abbreviation **Wks** (Works).

Fig.117

① **'Brown earth gap' site** - close to city centre and canals/railways reflecting 19th.Century transport links

② **Old run down buildings and outdated facilities** - Old industrial complexes with 19th.Century equipment and buildings usually in close proximity to housing, schools, shops, churches etc.

③ **Poor communications links** - poor infrastructural links - narrow streets, congested roads, traffic lights, lack of parking space for workers' cars and delivery vehicles

④ **Jumble of buildings and land-uses in a small area** - wasteground and buildings cramped together with evidence of environmental pollution

- **Late 20th Century Industry**

Light Industry — e.g. Electronics or biomedical plants
Usually on the **outskirts** of towns (not too close to housing), areas of **flat** land with room for expansion, good **access** to main roads/motorways. Ordered, spacious, planned layout (often in industrial **estates**) - linked to electricity supply.

Heavy Industry — e.g. Iron and steel. oil refining
Normally in **coastal** locations, deep water (access for ore carriers, tankers) often on 'cheap', reclaimed marsh beside the coast.

Fig.118

① **'Greenfield' site** - in countryside surrounded by clean environment, little noise or air pollution - located on urban outskirts, on rural-urban fringe

② **New buildings and facilities** - modern industrial complexes with 21st.century equipment and buildings usually in well-planned technology or science parks

③ **Excellent communications** - good infrastructural links - close to motorways, airports, ferries for import and export

④ **High amenity residential areas** nearby provide workforce with high quality environment for living & working

Industrial Change Case Study One : South Wales

Fig.119 Map of South Wales Coalfield

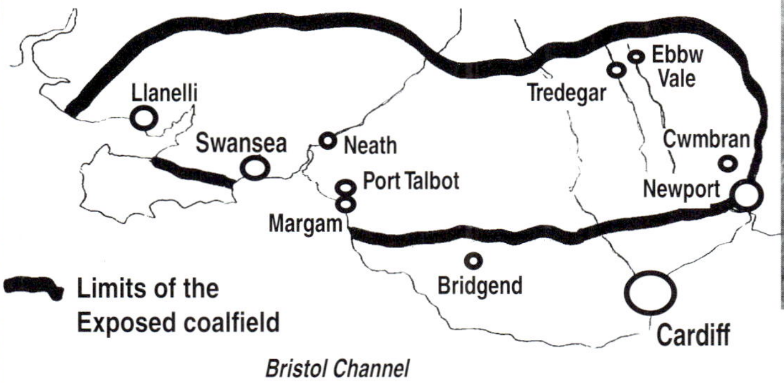

Fig.120 Aerial photo of Ebbw Vale

- **Reasons for early industrial growth - (19th.Century)**
  - Abundant local supplies of raw materials (coal + iron ore) in Welsh valleys - easy to extract. Led to the growth of major iron and steel industry with access to coast/ports - large market for products in the British Empire.
  - Traditional mining and metal working skills of workforce (figure 119).

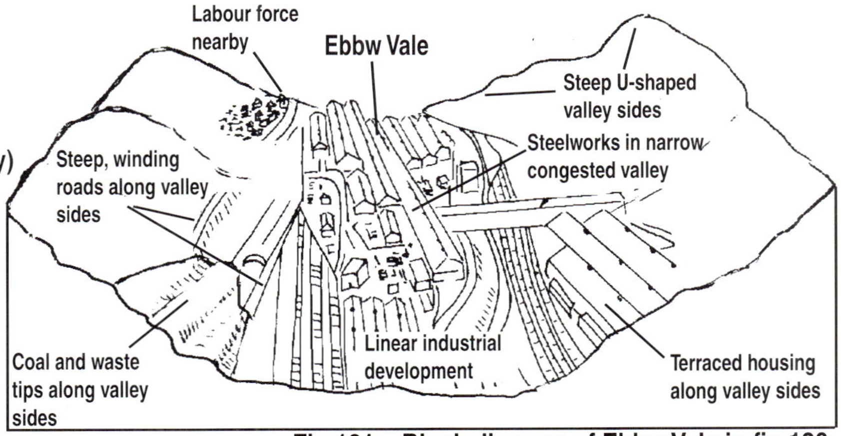

Fig.121 Block diagram of Ebbw Vale in fig.120

- **Reasons for/results of industrial decline - (Early 20th.Century) - figs 120/121**
  - local supplies of raw materials began to run out and coal seams too thin for mechanisation - led to mine closures
  - foreign competition (cheaper imported raw materials) e.g. from Poland, U.S.A
  - increased transport costs for inland iron and steel works led to closures
  - Social problems as mines/factories close included major **unemployment**
  - people moved away to look for jobs (**depopulation**)
  - break up of communities and families as a result
  - 'Ghost towns' as a result of closures
  - Economic problems caused by unemployment including loss of wages
  - reduced purchasing power
  - shops & services lose trade, leading to shop closures and lack of new investment
  - Environmental problems arising from closures - including many derelict buildings and disused mineworkings
  - Other environmental features of the abandoned industrial landscape included polluted rivers and abandoned open-cast mine workings
  - Eyesores destroy landscape quality and are often dangerous to the public

- **Recent Industrial Growth**
  - **Traditional Industry - e.g. Iron and Steel**
    - Two major Iron and Steel works remain open (Newport and Port Talbot) in coastal locations (access to cheaper, imported raw materials).
    - Processes are automated (more efficient but creates unemployment).
    - Works are **integrated** i.e. all processes from iron making to finished steel production take place on one site.
  - **New Industries**
    - Government **investment** to reduce unemployment/depopulation i.e. **industrial estates** with **purpose-built** factories,
    - **Rate and Rent free sites**
    - **Grants** for machinery, financial incentives for new jobs created.
    - **Training schemes** for all new jobs and workers
    - **Good access to markets, e.g.** M4 Motorway to London (Severn Bridge)
    - Also **tourist potential** of old mines (museum, trips underground, landscaping, etc)

    Note New Industries e.g. Electronics have arrived but unemployment remains high and many new jobs are monotonous 'screwdriver jobs'.

European Industry 3 principal areas with contrasting opportunities.

- **Eurocore** (figure **122)**
  A circular area with 350km radius centred on Brussels (includes Belgium, Luxembourg, Netherlands, N.France., N.Germany and S.E.England). Favoured for development for various reasons:
  - High population density (Consumer spending power is high)
  - Highly skilled labour force
  - Abundant natural resources e.g. oil, coal, iron ore
  - Close to political decision- making (Brussels)
  - Prime agricultural land
  - Excellent communications infrastructure - access to markets/airports, motorways, River Rhine, railways and the Channel Tunnel.

- **The Hot Banana** (figure **123**)
  Manchester - Milan Axis - A narrow belt stretching from N.Italy to NW England with similar advantages to the Eurocore.

- **Peripheral Regions** (figure **123**)
  The Euro-Periphery e.g. Mezzogiorno (S.Italy), Ireland, Portugal, the Highlands of Scotland, etc.
  Remote areas of the E.U.
  Lack of development due to -
  - Low economic potential
  - Isolation and poor communications systems
  - Low population density (mainly rural areas)
  - Distance from main markets
  - Lack of resources and financial investment

  Note - many of these areas have high unemployment

Principal Industrial Areas of Europe

Fig.122

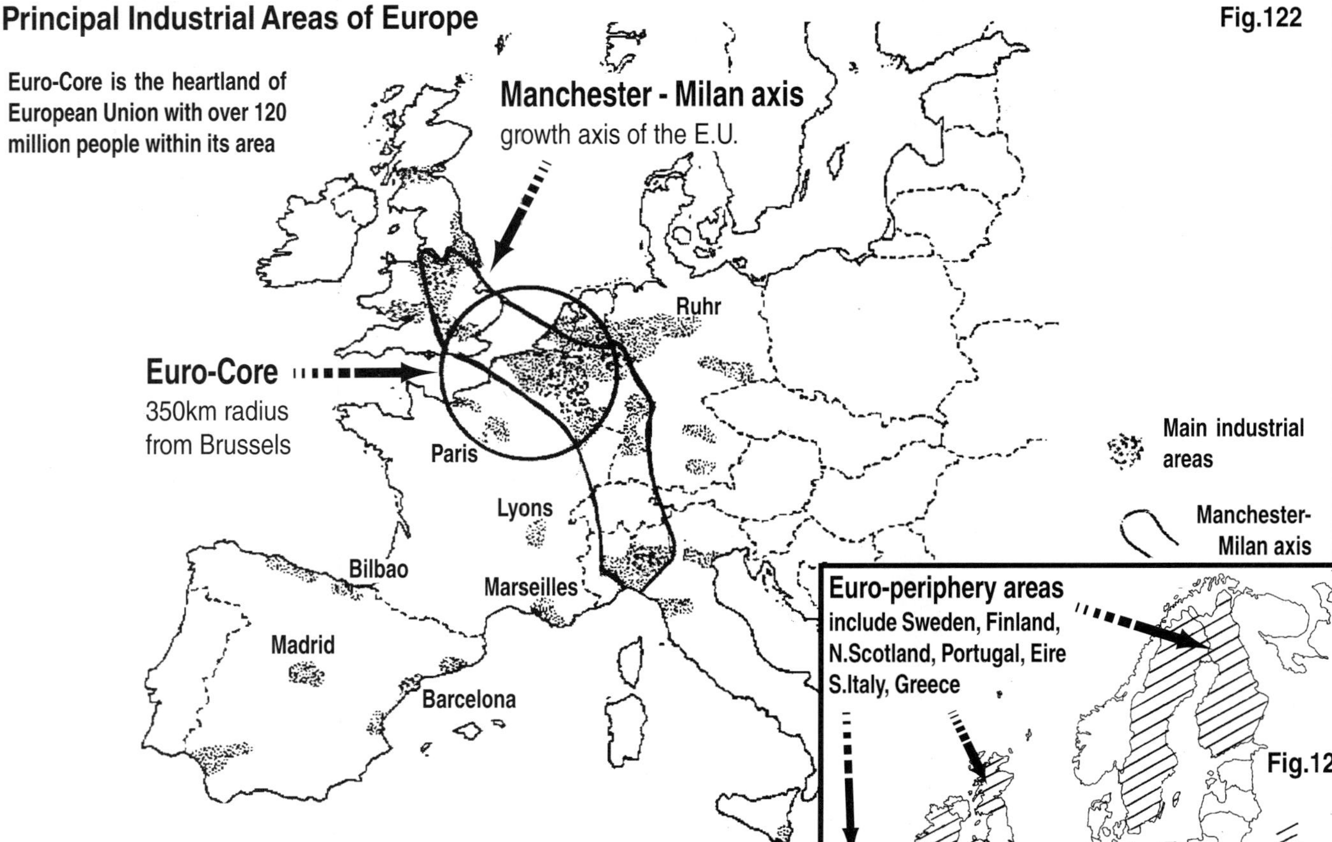

Fig.123

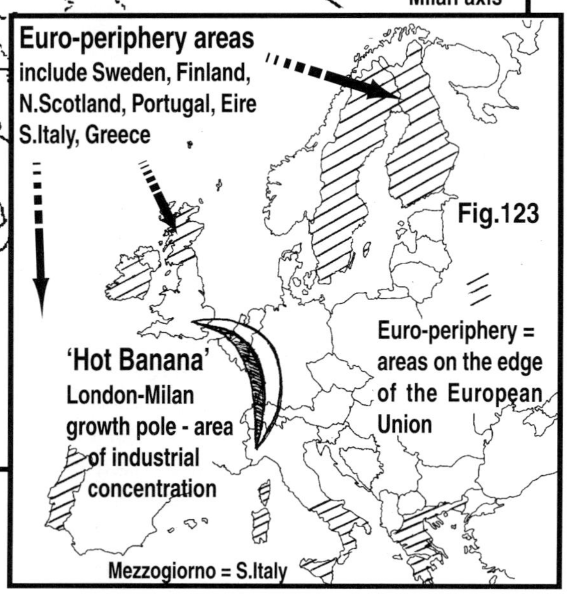

European Case Studies

Fig.124 Ruhr location

• Eurocore - Industrial Change in the Ruhr Region (Germany)

Europe's most important industrial region - located about 200km from the mouth of the Rhine - see figure **124.**

- **Early Development** - In 19th.Century coal, iron and steel industries based on local supplies of raw materials (coal and iron ore exposed at the surface - easier/cheaper to mine)
- **Mid 20th.Century -** As surface raw materials were used up, mining had to go deeper into concealed coalfields with increasing costs and mechanisation leading to unemployment, depopulation. Also coal faced competition from other fuels e.g. Oil and Gas - the Ruhr lies 200km from the North Sea (increased costs for imports)
- **Late 20th.Century -** Mining Areas have been rehabilitated with landscaping and rebuilding in derelict areas (strict controls on waste disposal). New industrial estates and leisure estates.
  New Steel Works have been constructed at **break of bulk** locations i.e. where imported raw materials are unloaded from barges on the Rhine (reduces transport costs)
  Major Cities e.g. Dortmund have developed service (office based) industries as manufacturing has declined.
  A general move from heavy to light industry, using Government Grants (also less pollution)
  Improved communications to help market products throughout the E.U. etc.

Note **Diversification** into new industries has helped the Ruhr region, but unemployment remains high and German reunification has created a surplus of unskilled workers.

European Case Studies

A Peripheral Area - North West Scotland - figure 125

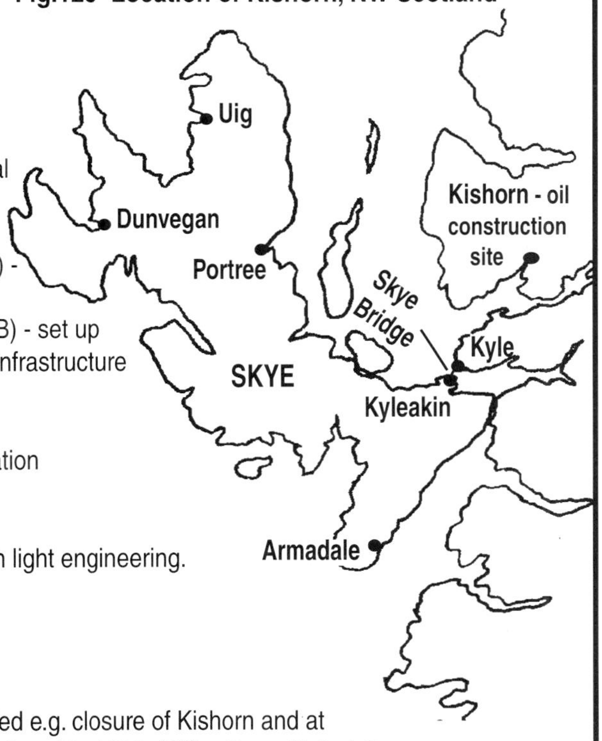

Fig.125 Location of Kishorn, NW Scotland

25% of Scotland's area but only 3% of the population - mountainous with very poor communications. Infertile soils, hostile climate and a major lack of industrial investment.

- **Early Development** (**Pre 1965**) - **Traditional industries** (mainly Primary) - crofting, fishing, weaving, whisky and limited tourism.
- **1965 - 1980** - The **Highlands and Islands Development Board** (H.I.D.B) - set up to increase employment opportunities / prevent depopulation / improve infrastructure (Roads, power supply, telecommunications, etc)

Main areas of focus -
- **Major Projects** e.g. Dounreay Nuclear Power Station
  Corpach (Fort William) Pulp and Paper Mill
  Kishorn Oil-Rig Construction Site
- **Industrial Estates** e.g. Longman (Inverness) with light engineering.
- **Expansion of Forestry**
- **Fish Farming** Development
- **Tourism / Recreation** e.g. Aviemore/Cairngorms

Note. Some success was achieved but unfortunately some schemes failed e.g. closure of Kishorn and at Fort William the Pulp Mill was closed. Aluminium in Kinlochleven closed in 1999. (Difficulties with isolation and foreign competition, etc)

- **1980 - Present day** Future Areas for Development & Expansion include -
  - **Tourism** e.g. skiing, (Aonach Mor) & Timeshare Developments (eg. Dalfaber, Aviemore)
  - **Hi-Tech Aquaculture** (in more exposed areas) + 'New fish' e.g. Halibut.
  - **Oil Exploration** (Western Isles. West of Scotland, Shetland)
  - **Use of Telecommunications** e.g. Call Centres (Inverness), Fax machines, Internet for home based computer-related tasks (overcomes problems of remoteness) - the 'Thatched Computer' etc.
  - **Biomedical Industries** (Inverness medical, etc.)

Industrial Geography Revision : Summary Notes

The main idea of the Industrial Geography section is....
Areas of industrial concentration contain a range of manufacturing and other economic activities. These concentrations develop and change spatially over time.

Industrial Systems

1. **Industry** is **work carried out for economic gain** and forms the economic base upon which any country's standard of living depends.
2. There are **4 main types of industry.**
3. **Primary industries** are those which are extractive, removing raw materials from the land or sea.
3. **Secondary industries** are those which include manufacturing, processing or assembly activities where raw materials or components are transformed into consumable products.
4. **Tertiary industries** are concerned with providing a service and include transport, medical, retailing, commercial and other services
5. **Quaternary industries** are office and information based activities and include universities, research and development, media and political policy units.
6. Industries can be considered as **systems** since there are **inputs** (such as raw materials, energy and capital), **processes** (welding, assembly) and **outputs** (products, effluent).
7. The **industrial development** of any country or area can be recognised as a series of phases from agrarian-based industry to the post-industrial phase of industrial development.
8. **Fourastie** (1964) suggested that as mechanisation and technology develops primary industry declines in importance as secondary industry expands. Automation increases the importance of tertiary industries at the expense of secondary industry etc.

Industrial Landscapes

1. **Europe can be viewed as an industrial landscape** with a wide variation in both the nature and distribution of sectors of industrial development.
2. The type and level of industrial development directly influences the **employment structure and standard of living** in any industrial landscape.
3. The **Euro-core** is regarded as the **industrial heartland** of the European Union and is located within a radius of 350km from Brussels.
4. **The Euro-periphery** is regarded as the outer-fringe of the European Union and can be defined as the area with less than 25% of the maximum economic potential.
5. There have been many attempts at **redirecting new industrial development** to the Euro-periphery in order to improve economic prosperity, employment and infrastructure.
6. Within the Euro-periphery there are many **varied industrial land scapes.**
7. **Large scale state intervention programmes** such as that of the **Mezzogiorno** have had both advantages and disadvantages for these peripheral areas. Advantages include infrastructural improvements, the development of growth poles and large scale investment programmes. Disadvantages include the overdependence on monotechnic development, relatively few large scale labour intensive or consumer goods industries and overconcentration of investment in a few growth poles.
8. **Rapidly diversifying industrial landscapes**, e.g. those found in areas of Spain and Portugal, create industrial conflicts between secondary and tertiary industries in areas of manufacturing and tourism.
9. Transition within the Euro-core is also common. Older smokestack areas (e.g. Ruhr, Sambre-Meuse) are experiencing major industrial change which has economic, social & environmental consequences.
10. Areas of new industrial growth are located around the Euro-core fringe, in urban greenbelts and in the ski or sunbelts, e.g. Bavaria, Greater Paris, Jura or Alpine areas.
11. Traditional retailing industries are also relocating to greenfield sites, to out of town retail parks or shopping centres.
12. Deglomeration is also a feature of new industrial developments where industrial plants are being developed in rural areas, around airports or in eastern bloc countries.

Industrial Location

1. The factors which influence the location of all sectors or types of industry can be classified as **Physical** and **Human/Economic.**
2. **Physical location factors** include those of raw materials, energy supply, site, climate, water supply, etc.
3. **Human or Economic location factors** include those of transport, labour, technology, capital, Government intervention and inertia.
4. Few contemporary industrial locations are tied to raw material locations. **Ports and coastal locations** have become the most important raw material locations.
5. The freeing of location tied to energy supplies through the cheap transport of electricity over long distances has encouraged the growth of **Footloose industries**.
6. Good **communications and transport links** exert a powerful influence on location of industry today. Break of bulk points are important as transport location factors but add to handling costs.
7. The supply and level of skill of the **labour force** is a major factor in the location of industry . This can lead to a differentiation of location within an industry where research & development is carried out in specialised locations (e.g. in proximity to universities) and production is carried out in proximity to major markets.
8. The implementation of **technological advance** increases production but at a substantial cost in terms of increased unemployment for manual workers.
9. Today industries have forsaken land ownership in favour of lease hold arrangements which have helped release **capital for relocation and research & development**.
10. Industrial location is often due to continuing **inertia** where locational reasons that were important in the past are often not obvious today, or the potential loss of investment in plant, machinery and skill would be too great to contemplate.
11. Products evolve through a **life-cycle** from research & development, to production, to market saturation and eventually to obsolescence.
12. **Industrial linkages** influence location of industry through differentiation of individual company design and production in different areas and through agglomeration principles.
13. **Industrial parks or estates** are the most innovative and influential change in location in the last 50 years and offer many advantages to companies.
14. Governments pursue **intervention policies** (which include the creation of Development areas, Enterprise Zones and procurement e.g. defence orders) in an effort to redirect industrial activity to locations lacking industrial development or those of high unemployment.

Industrial Geography Revision : Unit style assessments

1. **Refer to Map Extract 926/111 - Sheffield** - answer **two parts** from **(a), (b)** or **(c)**

(a) Study the industrial complex in squares **4286** and **4287**. Describe features of the old industrial landscape in this area and explain locational factors which would have encouraged industrial growth. (5)

and

(b) With reference to this area, or any other old (traditional) industrial region you have studied, comment on the problems that colliery closure might cause, and outline measures that could be used to encourage industrial regeneration. (5)

or

(c) Study the map extract and identify a potential location for a modern industrial estate or a science park. Support your choice with map and other evidence. (5)

Total = 10 marks

2. Refer to figures **117** and **118** on page **63**.

GMT

(a) Make a simple sketch of each photo (figs. 117 & 118). Annotate both photos to clearly show the differences in the two industrial landscapes shown. (5)

(b) Study reference table - figure 126 below.

Reference Table - Employment Survey Results (1998) **Fig.126**

Country	**% Employed in Primary Industry**	**% Employed in Secondary Industry**	**% Employed in Tertiary Industry**	**% Employed in Quaternary Industry**
Germany	**7**	**43**	**33**	**17**
UK	**4**	**39**	**39**	**18**
France	**12**	**38**	**36**	**14**
Portugal	**29**	**30**	**33**	**8**

i. Describe the similarities and differences in **employment patterns** as shown in the table above.

ii. If **Portugal** continues to develop, how would you expect the employment pattern to change over the next 20 years ? (5)

Industrial Geography Revision : Exam style assessments

1. Refer to Map Extract 926/111 - **Sheffield**

Industries are often classified under the following headings - primary, secondary, tertiary and quaternary. List the industries found in squares **4587 4089** and **4286** under these headings, explaining how you have reached your decisions. (5)

2. With reference to the **trends s**hown in the table below - figure **127,** describe and explain the possible future implications for many of the industries found in the map area. (5)

GMT

UK Employment Structure 1951 to 1999 **Fig.127**

	1951	1991	1999
Primary	6%	5%	4%
Secondary	59%	48%	39%
Tertiary	31%	34%	36%
Quaternary	4%	13%	18%

3. With reference to a named **industrial concentration in the European Union** which you have studied -

Explain how, as industry has evolved, **human** and **economic** factors have become more important than **physical** factors. (5)

9. Urban Geography - Core & Application

The main idea of the Urban Geography section is....
Urban settlements provide a range of employment, services and residential opportunities which may be located in different parts of the settlement.

What do you need to know ?

Students should have a knowledge and understanding of -

A Urban systems

- urban systems as dynamic entities, including location, site, historical and cultural contexts, growth and functions, site and situation of case study city; and identification of settlement sites on maps

B Functions and structures

- characteristics of and interaction between urban zones - commercial, industrial, residential functions and landscapes and identification of urban zones on maps
- analysis of landuse maps, transects and survey data
- annotation and analysis of field sketches of urban landscapes

C Urban change

- process of change, reasons for and implications of change within large urban concentrations, e.g. changes in industry and industrial location housing (especially in Inner-City redevelopment schemes), traffic management, Central Business District (CBD) - pedestrianisation and impact of out-of-town shopping centres) and linkages between these changes

Urban Core and Urban Change & Management Application - important note for students

The **Urban Core** and **Application** sections have been integrated as there is considerable overlap in content. However, if only the **Core** is being studied, materials relating to the Developing World may be ignored, i.e. just focus on pages **69 to 75**.

Urban Definitions

- **Conurbation** - several towns merging together e.g. Glasgow, Dumbarton & Paisley; Birmingham & Coventry
- **Megalopolis** - densely populated region with several major cities e.g. **Boswash** (Washington, Boston, New York, etc.)
- **Primate City** - single dominant city in a country e.g. London (UK), Lima (Peru)
- **Million City** - city withover I million people e.g. Munich (Germany)
- **Megacity** - city with over 5 million people e.g. Shanghai (China)

Urbanisation processes

Experts recognise that throughout the previous 200 years of urban development, within the developed countries, there has been a cycle of urban development

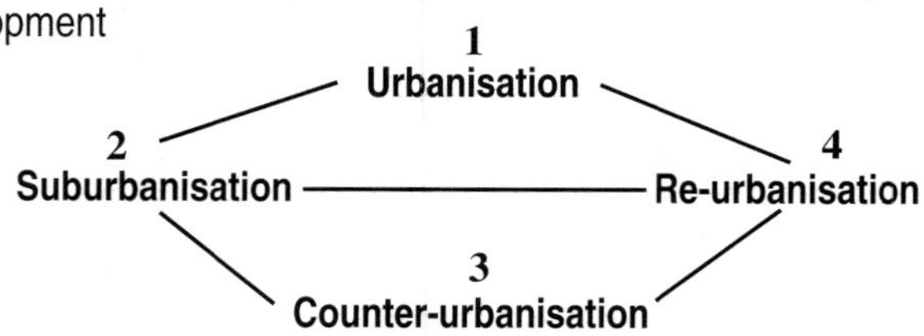

Urbanisation is the process of becoming an urban-based society. It involves rural to urban migration in combination with a rapid natural increase in population. **Suburbanisation** is the decentralisation of industry and people to the urban periphery. **Counter-urbanisation** is the movement of industry and people to small settlements outwith the urban area.
Re-urbanisation is the movement of industry and people **back into urban** areas left abandoned as a result of industrial closure or suburbanisation. Urbanisation is at its height in **developing countries** and the cause of much misery..........

Rural settlement patterns

This normally refers to settlements which are smaller than towns and are agricultural in nature. The study of rural settlement involves the analysis of the **morphology** (form or shape) of settlement. It is possible to recognise several distinct types as follows :

Dispersed settlement. Rural settlements may be scattered such as crofting townships or hamlets in the Scottish borders.

Nucleated settlement. Often located at route junctions or for economic reasons.

Linear settlement. Physical conditions often stimulate the growth of linear settlements, e.g. along narrow valleys or coastal strips. This type of setlement can also be found strung out along lines of communication, e.g. canals, railways and roads.

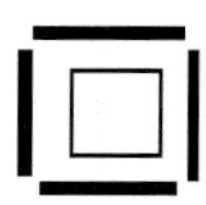

Green or ring settlements. Villages built around a central green or common.

Planned settlements. During the Agrarian revolution many planned agricultural settlements were built to house the excess population from the land. Today exurban villages are often planned carefully.

Urban Settlement Patterns

Fig.128

Urban settlements also display a variety of patterns on the landscape. The main patterns which can be identified are:-

1. Medieval Zone or Core

- Villages which expanded into towns during the Middle Ages may have an irregular pattern of narrow, closely-spaced streets in their central areas. This reflected the unplanned nature of expansion and lack of space within the common defensive walls.

THE OLD TOWN, EDINBURGH

Common features of such layouts are Market Squares, Castles or Palaces, many Churches and Town Walls, e.g. Edinburgh's Old Town

2. 19th. Century Zone

- The areas of towns which developed at the time of the Industrial expansion in the 19th. Century usually have a regular pattern of evenly spaced streets crossing each other at right angles. This is known as a grid-iron pattern. Here factories and houses were built in close proximity.

GOVANHILL

Common features of such layouts are railways, terraced housing, factories and a dense, regular road network, e.g. Govanhill, Glasgow.

3. 20th Century Zone

- During the 20th.Century, most towns expanded first of all outwards along main roads. Large areas of housing built between the 1st and 2nd World Wars, however, have a geometric street layout with crescents, semi-circular and radiating streets and cul-de-sacs (dead-end streets)

MUIRHOUSE, EDINBURGH

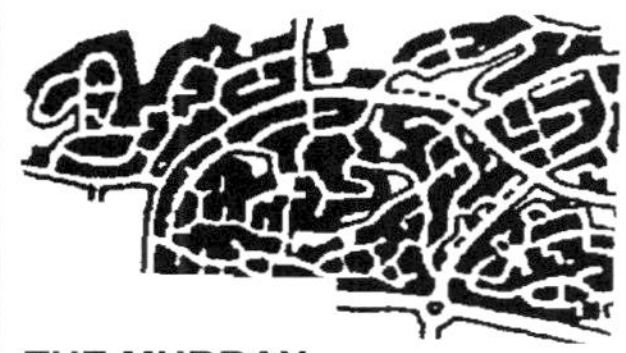

THE MURRAY

Housing areas built since the 2nd.World War tend to have less regular, gradually curving streets and numerous cul-de-sacs, e.g. The Murray, East Kilbride.

4. Industrial Zone

- Industrial zones can often be identified on O.S. maps because the built-up areas are larger than housing blocks, and the streets are not so closely or regularly spaced. Some industrial areas, especially older ones, have branch railway lines leading into them.

CRAIGNEUK

Large Urban-Industrial Zones are associated with large Steel-making, Shipbuilding, Engineering or Chemical factories, e.g. Craigneuk, Glasgow.

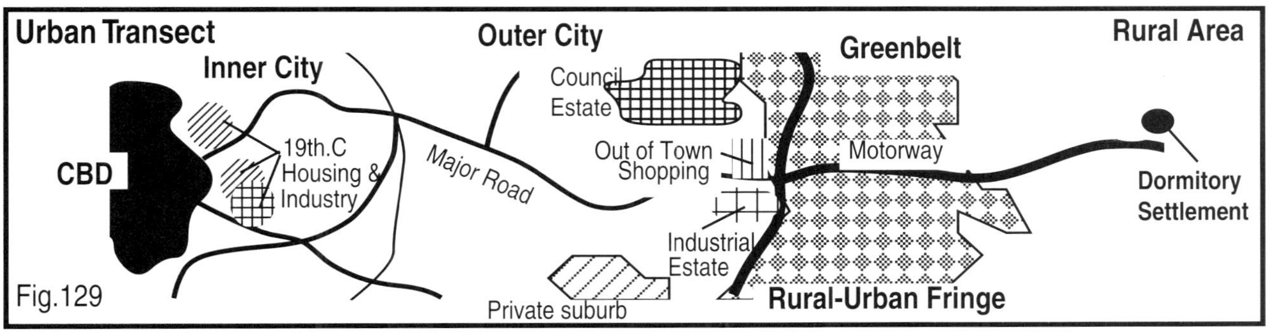

Fig.129

Urban Zones

- **CBD (Central Business District)** - normally near the geographical centre of a town/city. Look for - public buildings e.g. T.H. (Town Hall), Cath (Cathedral), Churches, Mus (Museum); transport terminals e.g. Bus Station, Railway Station & focus of main roads.
- **19th Century Low-Cost Housing** - in the Inner City area surrounding the C.B.D. usually a rectangular street pattern with terraced houses and lack of open space - may be close to old industrial areas such as docks, railyards, works, etc.
- **19th Century Industry** (Old Industrial Areas) - usually close to the C.B.D and also near housing - may be beside a river with railways and canals for transport. Look for Wks (Works/Factory) and also map evidence of industrial waste (tips, etc.).
- **20th Century High Cost Housing** - On the outskirts away from industry. Streets are often curved with Cul-de-sacs. Open space/ parkland with recreational areas e.g. Golf courses. Large scale maps may show detached or semi-detached houses with gardens.
- **20th Century Council Housing** (normally in Large Estates) - May also be on the outskirts with the cul-de-sacs, etc. but more regular housing - short terraced flats (lack of individual gardens common).
- **Recent (Late 20th Century) Industrial Areas** - may be shown as industrial estates - usually on the outskirts - close to main roads / motorways for transport - more regular, spacious layout than 19th Century areas. (cleaner environment, accessible to housing (Workers) but not too close). Other developments include giant out-of-town shopping complexes, e.g. the Gyle (Edinburgh).
- **Greenbelts** - on the **Rural-Urban Fringe** or edge - used by planners to control urban sprawl into surrounding rural landscapes. Often greenbelts are characterised by golf courses, country parks, airports and market gardens. Criss-crossed by motorways and rail links.
- **Dormitory or satellite settlements** - expansion of small rural settlements with good communication links (e.g. proximity to motorway or rail links) as commuter-satellite settlements - few services available for commuter population but otherwise high quality of living available. Examples are Linlithgow (West Lothian), Kemnay (Aberdeen), Fortrose (Inverness).

Settlement Function - Shopping, Services and Settlements

The importance of a settlement is equated with the following:-

- The **range and number of functions or services** within a settlement
- The **size of a settlement** - its area and population
- The **sphere of influence** of a settlement.

Settlements provide services to those who live and work in them. The larger the settlement, the more services it usually provides. Fig.**130** is a generalised **hierarchy** of settlements based on service provision. Important to the study of services are the terms **Threshold** - the minimum number of customers needed for a service to be profitable and **Range** of a service - the distance people are willing to travel to obtain that service. **Low order services** are those which have a small threshold and range of service. People use them frequently and they are numerous. They are found in villages, towns and cities and tend to be dispersed throughout the settlement, e.g. a newsagents. **Middle Order services** have a moderate threshold and have moderate range, in that people may be willing to travel some distance to obtain them. They are found only in towns and cities and are often located in large shopping centres and in the town centre, e.g. shoe shops. **High Order services** have very large thresholds and range of services. Normally only found in town centres and cities, they tend to be centrally located because they require large customer flows to be profitable, e.g. department stores. The **Sphere of Influence** of a settlement can be defined as the area served by it. The size of the sphere of influence depends on the size, importance and functions of the settlement and its surroundings, the transport facilities available and the level of competition from rival settlements (Fig.**131**).

Fig.130 Hierarchy of settlement - the relationship between size, importance & functions

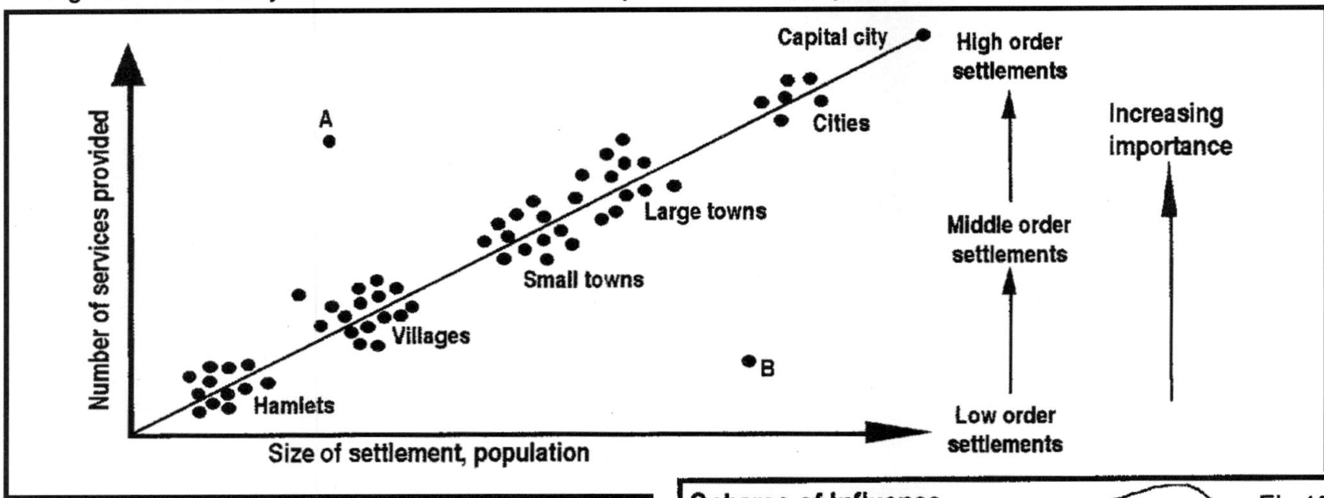

People who live in rural settlements generally rely on towns to provide all but everyday basic services. The hamlet or village are said to be within the sphere of influence of a town because people are served by that town for middle and high order services. Towns and cities compete for the custom of people living within their surroundings (or hinterland). Various factors are important when people decide which larger settlement they will use, e.g.

- **Distance and ease of transport**
- **Type and variety of services** provided
- **Local environment** - some settlements may be more attractive or 'friendly' to shop in than others
- **Personal contact or choice** - relatives, easier parking or better customer service may influence people to shop in a settlement which is not necessarily closer to home.

Spheres of Influence Fig.131

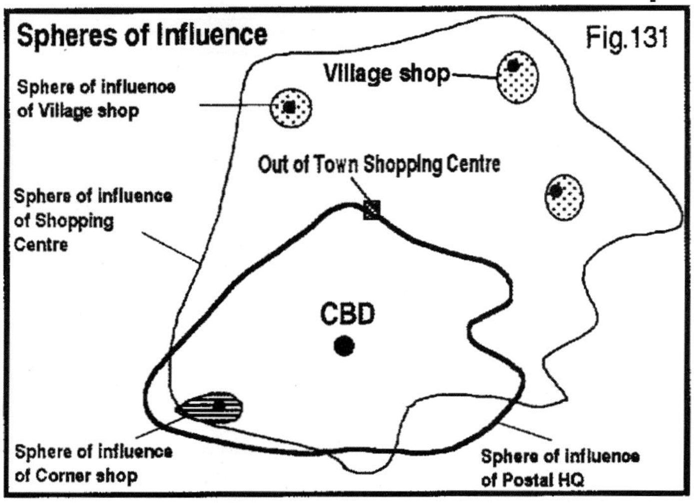

Retailing locations in an urban area - Retailing and shopping distribution patterns across a settlement

Fig.132

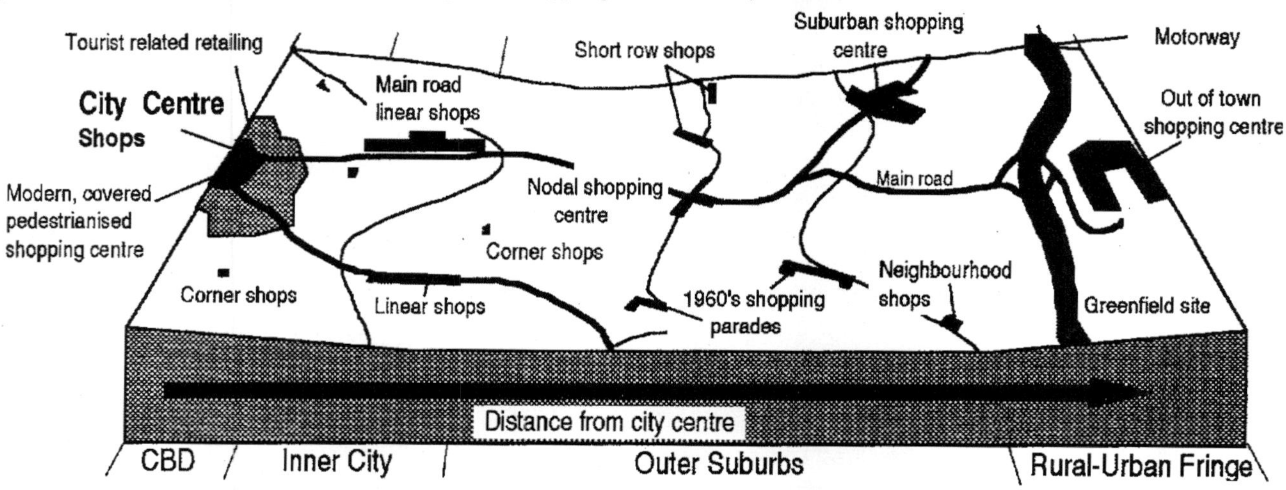

Models of Urban Growth in the Developed World

Fig.133

Concentric Zone Model

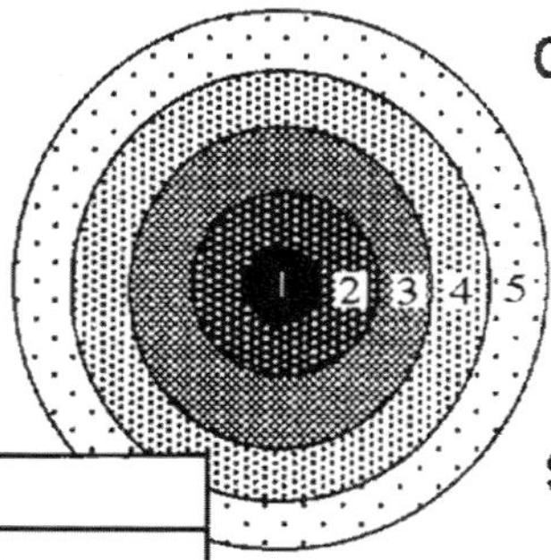

KEY

1 CBD
2 Light manufactur
3 Low class resid.
4 Medium class res
5 High class resid.
6 Heavy manufact.
7 Outlying BD.
8 Resid. suburb
9 Industrial suburb
10 Commuter zone

Sector Model

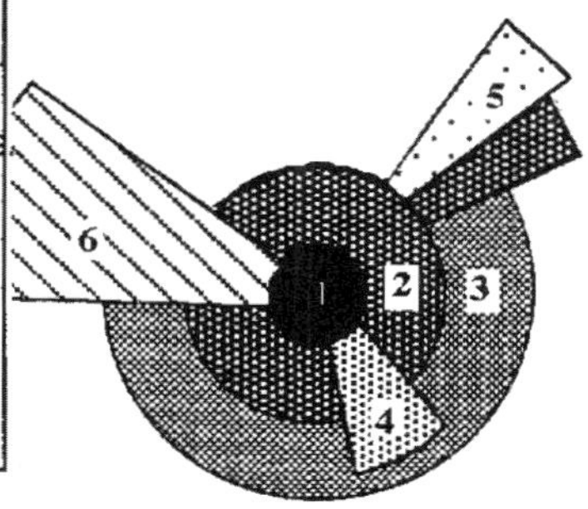

Multiple Nuclei Model

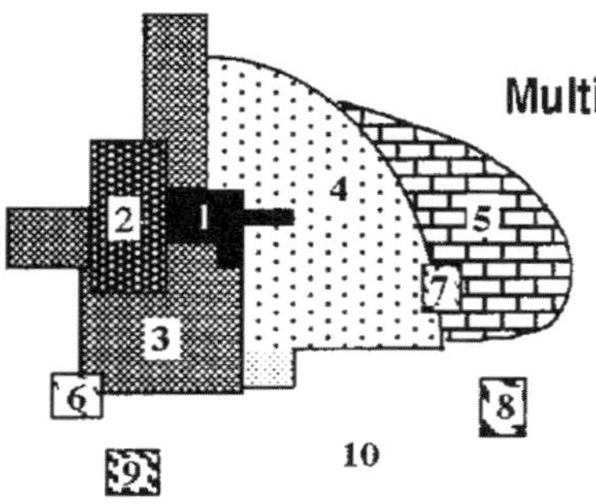

British City Model

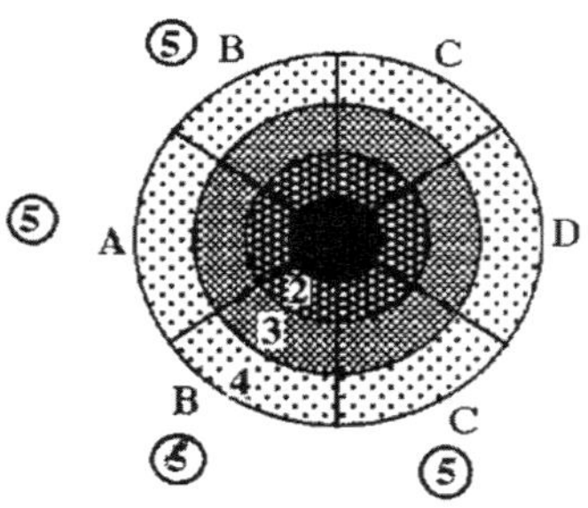

1 - CBD
2 - Transitional zone
3 - Pre-1918 housing
4 - Post-1918 housing
5 - Commuter zone
A - Middle class sector
B - Lower middle class
C - Working class sector
D - Industry and lowest working class sector

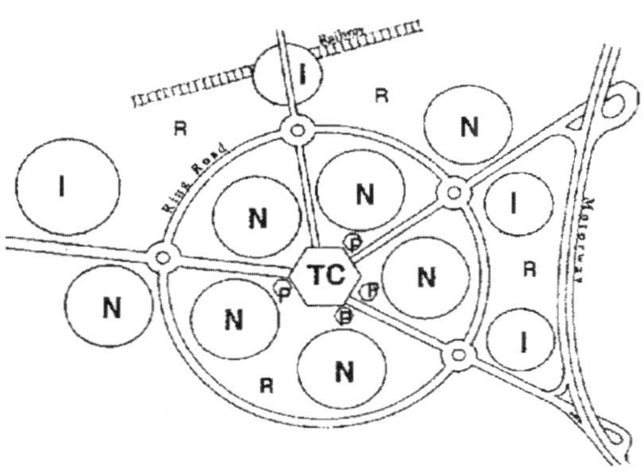

New Town Model

KEY

TC Town Centre
I Industrial Estates
R Recreational Areas
P Parking Areas
N Neighbourhoods (Housing areas)

As settlements have grown both in population and area during this century, their urban form and pattern has become complex. There are many different **land uses** found in settlements. The larger the settlement, the greater the number and variety of land uses there are within its boundaries. Land uses - the ways in which land is used - can include the following categories -

- **Commercial** - shops and offices
- **Industrial** - factories, workshops, docks, estates
- **Residential** - housing areas of different quality
- **Recreational** - parks, sports & leisure facilities, etc.
- **Transport** - roads, railways, airports, etc.
- **Wasteland** - derelict and cleared land.

Older settlements have generally **evolved** - in other words they have grown and developed over time, adapting to change. This usually takes hundreds of years and the pattern of land use in older settlements is often very complex. In contrast **New Towns** are carefully planned with a clear pattern of land use more easily identifiable.
The different types of land use listed above are often found in certain parts of a settlement. For example, commercial land use is usually associated with the centre of a settlement. This land use zone is referred to as the CBD (Central Business District).
It is possible to distinguish patterns or zones of land use within settlements especially in larger towns and cities. These patterns reflect the development or evolution of the settlement over time.
The distribution of land use can often be explained by referring to one or more of the following **Models of Urban Land Use** (figure **133**). Each land use model contains four main zones -

- **CBD**
- **Inner City**
- **Residential Areas**
- **Industrial Zones**

There have been several major attempts to systematically study urban spatial patterns and variations in their structure. The growth of some cities may closely follow one of the patterns outlined below.

· Concentric Model
Where a Town /City grows **outwards** in a series of concentric land use rings with more recent developments on the outskirts.

· Sector Model
Where a Town / City grows outwards in **wedges** (sectors) of the same land use - usually along lines of **communication.**

· Multiple Nuclei Model
In a large town / city where growth takes place around more than one centre (**Nucleus**).

· British City Model - (Mann 1960s)
Based around the development of larger British cities such as Glasgow, Birmingham and Manchester and takes the Concentric and Sector models as its basis.

· British New Town Model
Developed since the end of World War 2 in the late 1940s when the British Government planned wholescale development of urban areas. Different from the other models since the pattern of land use has been specifically planned for - where for example, there have been deliberate attempts to separate industry and housing areas, where the CBD is centralised for access from all areas of the settlement.

Land Use Changes With Distance From City Centres

- **CBD** - mainly shops (comparison e.g. jewellers, clothes, etc.) and offices which benefit most from the accessibility of the city centre. According to **bid-rent theory** shops, etc. will gain the greatest profit from being in the C.B.D. and can afford the **high rents/land prices**.
- **Outer City** - away from the CBD, as land prices fall and more space is available, industry and housing become more common. Shops are mainly **convenience** i.e. **low** order shops e.g. grocers serving the local community.
- **Note** Land Values tend to be highest in the CBD and they decrease with distance from the centre. Minor land value peaks may occur at more accessible locations, i.e. main road intersections (roundabouts etc.).

CBDs in Developed World Cities - Problems and Solutions

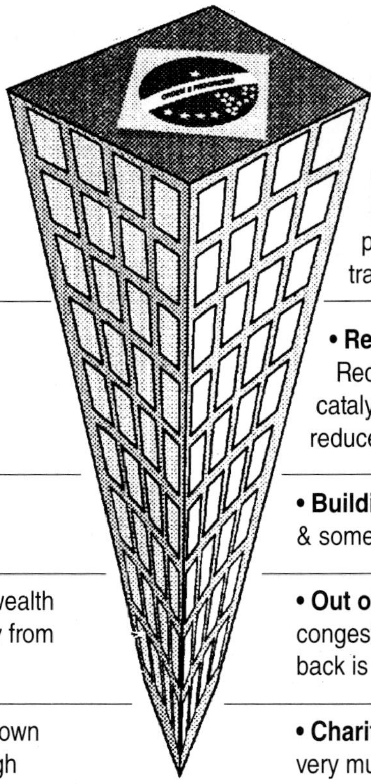

Problems	Solutions
• **Traffic Congestion** caused by increased car ownership (& commuting), narrow streets and radiating pattern of main roads (converge on CBD) as well as increased number of shoppers, etc.	• **Pedestrian Precincts and Shopping Malls** separate shoppers from traffic, one-way streets, parking meters, multi-storey car parks, bus lanes, ring roads, flexi-time for workers, traffic lights and roundabouts, improved public transport systems, park and ride, cycle routes....all used to improve traffic problems in CBDs in Britain.
• **Pollution** - caused by high transport density and industrial effluents emitted into atmosphere.	• **Reduce car use** - by improving public transport. Reduce car pollution with unleaded petrols and use of catalytic converters. Emissions from industry can be reduced by using gas filters, etc.
• **High Land Prices - Rents - Rates** - force some businesses to close or move out to suburbs.	• **Buildings are tall** - to maximise use of expensive land & some companies/shops relocate on cheaper sites.
• **1960 - 1970s Shopping Congestion** (increased wealth and leisure time) - but recently trade is moving away from CBD to out of town shopping malls or complexes.	• **Out of Town Shopping Trends** - these relieve congestion but attract trade away from the CBD - fight back is now on with CBD 'malls'
• **Homelessness** - an increasing CBD problem of 'down and outs' begging on busy streets and sleeping rough (skippering) in doorways, etc.	• **Charity and sheltered accommodation schemes** - but very much stop gap solutions - better long term Government plans needed to deal with homelessness.

Inner City Changes - Redevelopment

Normally this refers to the area surrounding the CBD, sometimes referred to as the **zone of transition** or the **twilight zone**.

Inner City Problems	Changes / Solutions*
• **Housing** - slum conditions, e.g. Birmingham, Glasgow (old tenements), overcrowded & unhygienic, poor state of repair and lack of services (schools, recreation, shops etc.).	• **Redevelopment** - demolition of slums and replacement with modern flats (bathrooms etc.) at lower overall housing density - excess population moved out (called overspill) to new towns and outer city housing estates. More recently - programme of **renovation** of remaining slum areas (renewing of old houses - rewiring, replumbing, modernisation and improved structures, etc.).
• **Industry** - declining narrow range of traditional industries (due to foreign competition, lack of demand, new technology and techniques, etc.). Problems of unemployment affecting social and environmental quality of areas.	• **New industrial estates** - with greater diversification and government incentives deployed to attract new businesses, e.g. **enterprise zones** (Clydebank, Docklands (London)) - purpose built factories and industrial units (rent/rate free), grants for machinery, training schemes, etc.

* **Early redevelopment schemes** concentrated on High-Rise Flats which, when surrounded with open space, reduced overall population density but redevelopment broke up families and communities. New shopping centres were far from housing areas. Structure and appearance of flats has quickly deteriorated with vandalism, etc. Renovation is cheaper, retains community spirit and local corner shops survive. For example, successful renovation schemes include Glasgow's East End. Unsuccessful redevelopment schemes with high-rise flats include the Gorbals area of Glasgow.

Contrasting urban landscapes

Residential land uses form the largest user of space within any urban area and can be classified according to location, age, bid rent, and tenure (fig.134).
In general, the youngest housing tends to be located towards the Rural-urban Fringe. Experts recognise that housing is subject to filtering (fig.135) as occupiers tend to move up the housing market, leaving in their wake deteriorating housing. In recent times, many areas of the Inner City have been **gentrified** and new life breathed into old urban areas but there is still much to be done to improve the residential environment of many inner cities (fig.136). The largest sector of housing is located within the suburbs which have grown rapidly this century with the development of transport networks.

Pattern of Residential environments in a UK city **Fig.134**

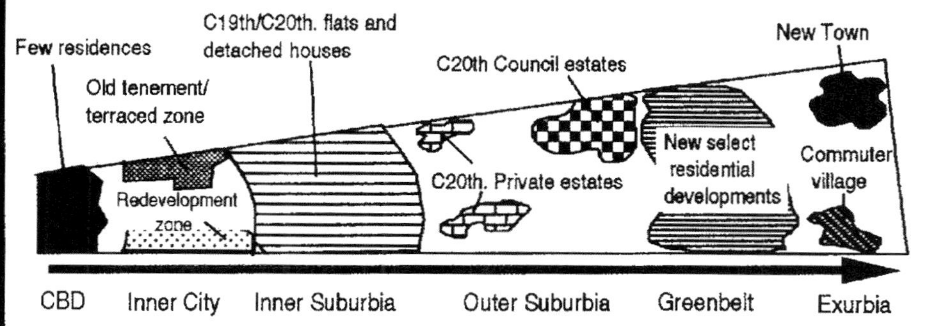

Filtering and Gentrification processes **Fig.135**

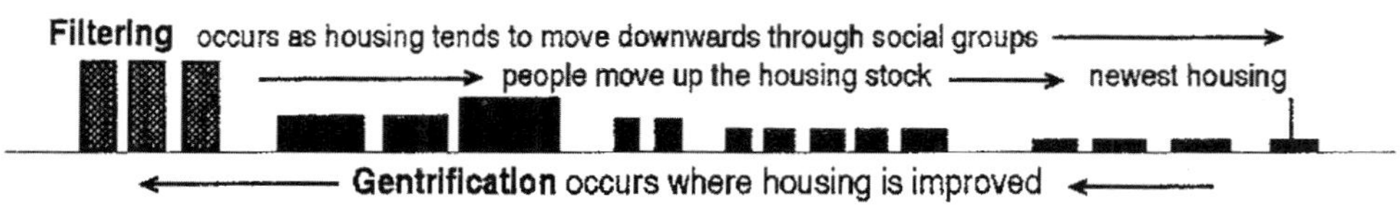

Fig.137
Outer Suburbia - Barnton, Edinburgh - large expensive detached houses with big gardens front and back

Contrasting Residential areas

Fig.136 An **Inner City 19th.Century** residential area in **Leith**

Fig.138
Muirhouse, Edinburgh
20th.Century Council Housing Estate with high-rise, low-rise and terraced housing

Conflict on the Periphery (outskirts and rural-urban fringe) of developed cities, e.g. London

The uncontrolled expansion of towns and cities (**urban sprawl**) have led to introduction of **Green Belt** policy i.e. cities such as London were surrounded by a Green Belt area where future building developments are severely restricted and countryside is protected.
However conflict may arise between various potential land users i.e. transport (M25 around London, Channel Tunnel Rail Link), Industrial Estates on Green field sites, Recreation e.g. Golf courses, agriculture, housing and conservation, Out-of-town Shopping Centres, etc.
Note. Green Belt Policy would support conservation/agriculture, but economic development would encourage industry/transport. Farmers may sell land at high prices to housing developers (for commuter/dormitory settlements) or for recreational use (Country parks/Golf courses). Development may be limited by planning controls and various 'green' buffers as shown in figure 139 below.

Green Belts
Fig.139

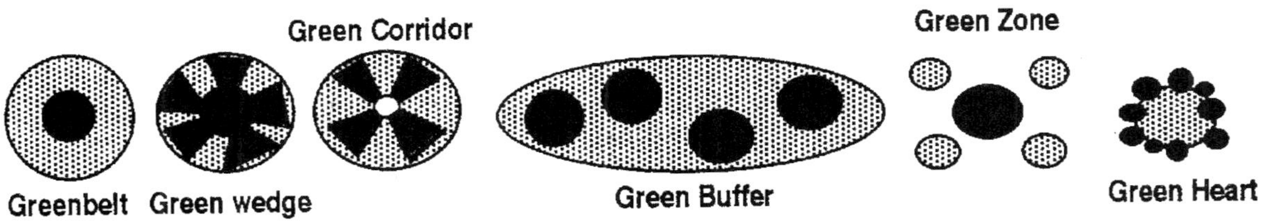

There are almost 2,000 million hectares of greenbelt land in the UK. **Greenbelts** are land protected from development by Acts of Parliament (**1938** Green Belt & **1947** Town and Country Planning Acts). Development includes housing and industrial proposals. Greenbelts are located around almost all of the large urban areas in England & Wales and around Edinburgh and Glasgow in Scotland. Around London alone there are plans for over 25 new towns (and 50 other expanded communities). Conservationists and developers seem set for further confrontation over land reserved for wildlife, forestry , farming and recreation.

Case Study of a Developed World City - Birmingham

• Location and Background

Birmingham is close to the geographical centre of England and Wales (with good access to London, NW England, S.Wales, etc.) The area is undulating, low-lying land - good for construction of canals & railways in 19th.Century and, more recently, major motorway networks (M6, M40). Birmingham was close to raw material supplies (e.g. coal & iron ore) and metal using industries expanded during the industrial revolution (19th.Century) and continued to boom in the early 20th.Century.
Since the end of World War Two (1945) Birmingham has faced a range of problems: - CBD reconstruction, inner city housing, traffic congestion, major industrial decline, foreign competition, competition from SE England and modern industries, social conflicts, etc.

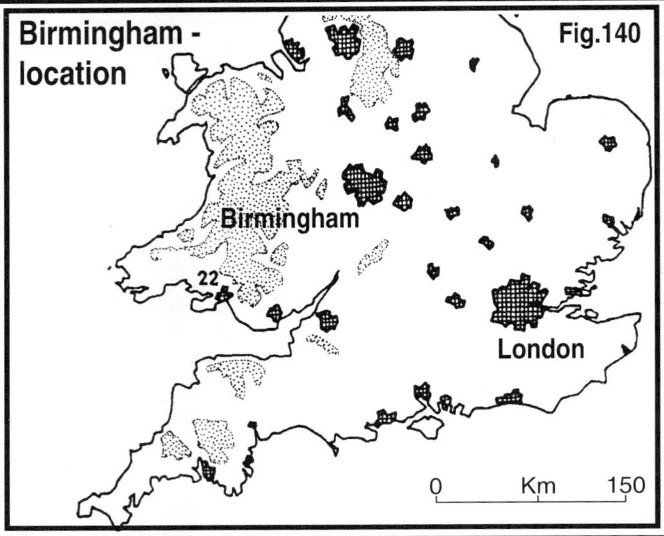

• Birmingham - problems and solutions

Fig.141

Problems	Solutions
• C.B.D Bomb damage in World War Two destroyed many city centre buildings, major problems of building dereliction and modern problems of traffic congestion (see below)	**• Reconstruction** With a variety of land uses - offices (e.g. Rotunda), Pedestrian Shopping Centres (e.g. Bull Ring), gardens, transport terminals (Bus and Railway Stations - e.g. New Street) & Inner Ring Road to increase traffic flow. **Note.** Buildings are tall to maximise use of expensive land.
• Housing / Population By 1950 the Inner-City area surrounding the C.B.D consisted of overcrowded slums with poor living conditions (100,000 living in slums; 81,000 without baths; 35,000 with shared toilets) Housing was mixed with industry/pollution (lack of open space, environmental pollution from smokestack industries, etc.).	• Two Redevelopment plans 1961 and 1974 5 Comprehensive Development Areas (**C.D.A**s) e.g. Ladywood, were identified - **In 1961** - mainly **demolition** with construction of **new flats** at a lower density (flats with modern comforts - baths, toilets etc., but lacked community spirit, and services were remote from houses) Excess population (overspill) was moved to new towns e.g. Telford and outer city housing estates. **In 1974** - mainly **Renovation** of remaining slums (retained community spirit and local services e.g. corner shops)

Before

After

Problems	Solutions
• Traffic congestion Narrow streets; radial pattern of main roads converging on the C.B.D. ; out dated trams, inefficient public trans port system ; increased car ownership and shopping density; lack of parking space.	**• Traffic congestion** one-way streets; ring roads to remove 'through traffic' ; improved public transport - bus lanes, electrified railways ; roundabouts and flyovers to improve traffic flow ; multistorey car parks; pedestrian precincts.
• Industrial Decline / Employment Overspecialisation in metal-using industry (including motor vehicles) - lack of demand, high costs, foreign competition e.g. Japanese Motorbikes, failure to modernise, poor industrial relations (strikes, etc.) - Factory closures e.g. (B.S.A.) & major unemployment problems.	**• Industrial Diversification** Expansion of new industry e.g. insurance, tourism, etc. (Tertiary sector). Government incentives - new industrial estates (separated from housing) with purpose-built factories (rate/rent free), grants for machinery, training schemes and excellent access to markets - MI to London, M6 to Manchester etc.
• Social Conflict Immigrants were encouraged to the area during the 1950's - with plenty of unskilled jobs (mixed races - Indians, Pakistanis, West Indians - conflict, tension, discrimination, riots) - recent unemployment amongst local population has caused increased resentment. Also increased poverty and crime problems.	**• Integration of Immigrants** Into local communities (Schools, etc.) Community Policing with multi-racial police force. Training Schemes to help unemployed. **Note.** The above attempts have improved the situation but unemployment remains high and racial tension remains in some areas.

Fig.142

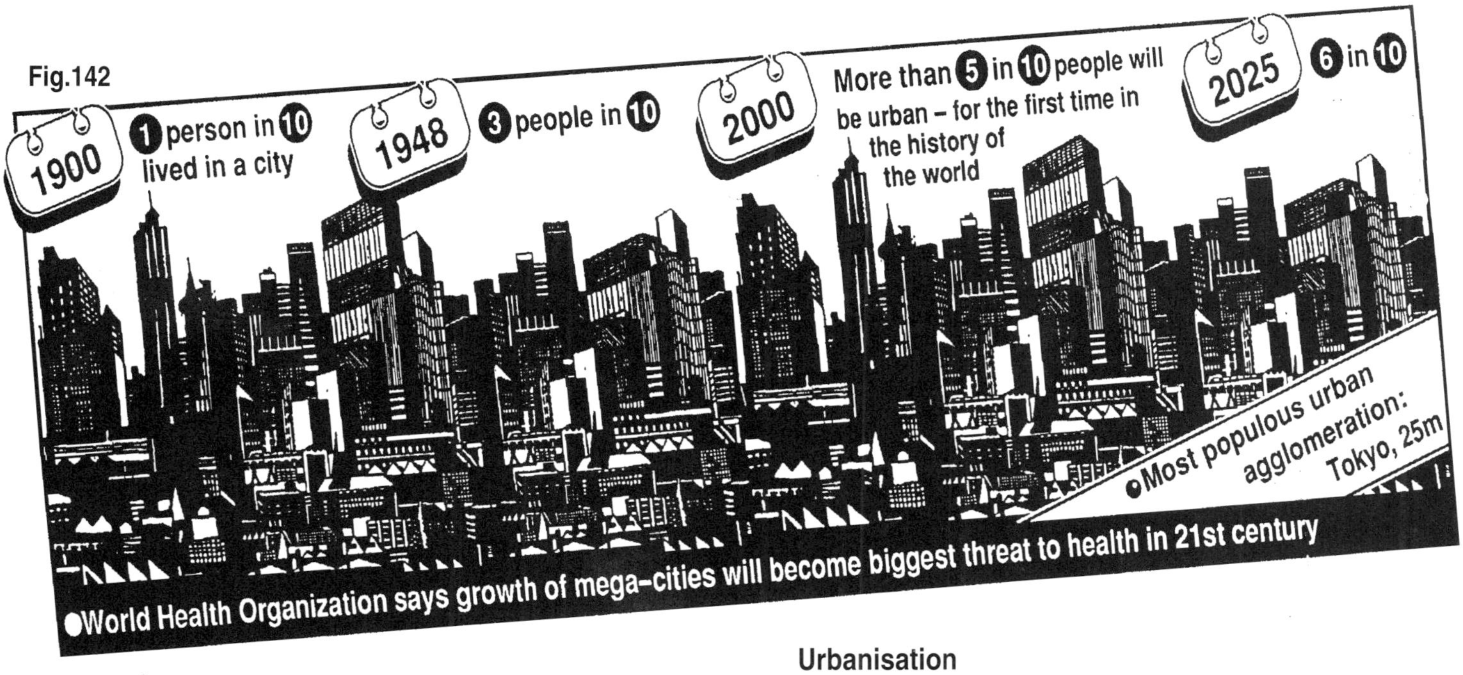

Fig.143

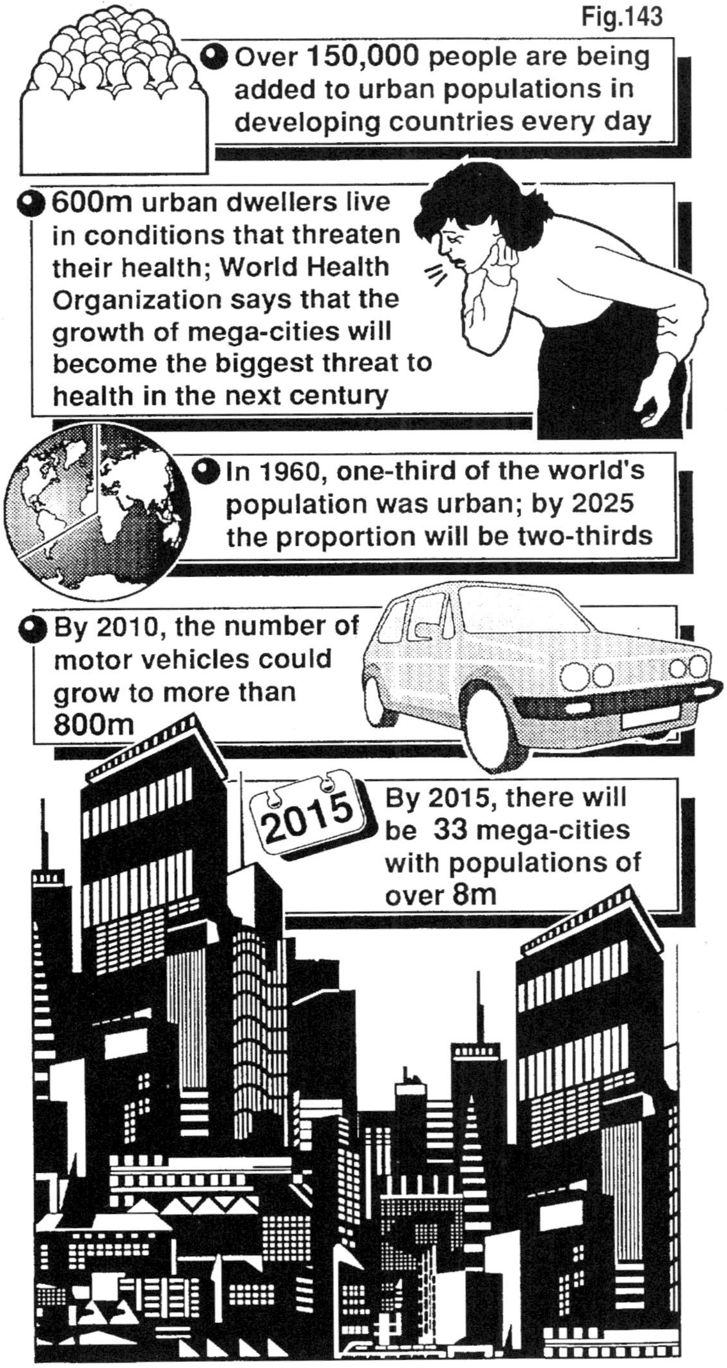

Urbanisation

For the first time in the history of planet, humans are becoming urban animals - with more people living in towns and cities than in villages. Over 50% of the population of Earth lives in urban settlements - and the proportion is growing. As cities consume over 75% of the Earth's resources and create most of its pollution, what we do or don't do with our cities is vital not only for citizens but for the planet too. The trends are all urban (see figures **142** and **143**).

Contrasts in urbanisation processes are marked between the **North** (Developed countries) and the **South** (Developing countries).

- **Developed Countries or the North**
  Very rapid growth in urban areas during the 19th.Century coincided with the Industrial Revolution - workers migrated to cities to find jobs in expanding industry.
  In 20th.Century population in developed world cities has stabilised or begun to decline e.g. London (planning against urban sprawl - redevelopment/overspill/greenbelt policy & rural preference- counter-urbanisation / commuting to work) - people moving to "exurbs" (rural area, beyond the city periphery) - Dormitory settlements in countryside.

- **Developing Countries or the South**
  Prior to Mid 20th.Century, majority of population lived in rural areas and worked in agriculture. Increased industrial development/ modernisation post 1950 has caused massive urban growth (Rural-urban migration & high birth-rate)

- **Changing Distribution of Major Cities**
  Up to 1950 (and even 1970) most major cities were in Developed countries e.g. London, New York, Paris etc.
  Rapid expansion in developing world e.g. Mexico City (23m) Sao Paulo (24m). Combined with stabilisation / decline in developed countries.

Despite the lure of bright lights in the coming decades most of the world's poor will be urban, living under conditions often worse than those of the rural poor.

Urbanisation in Developing Countries - lure and reality of Megacities

Fig.144

Key to simplified model of land use in a Megacity in the South

- CBD
- 1 - Inner City Low income
- 2 - Upper Middle Income Housing
- 3 - Spontaneous Housing Zone

Megacity in a developing country

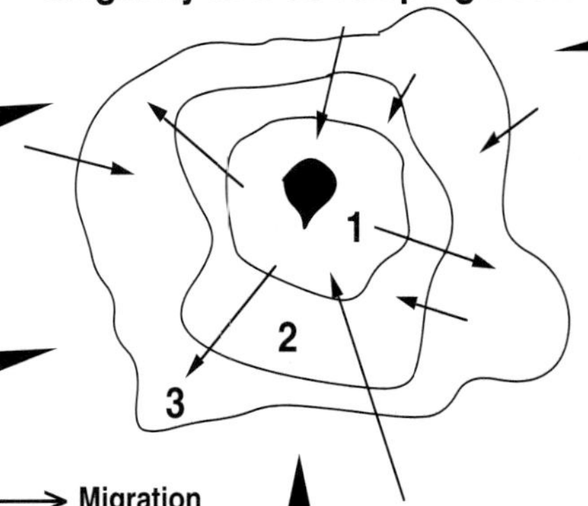

→ Migration

Synonyms for spontaneous settlements around the world

Shanty Towns	Bustees
Favelas	Slums
Bidonvilles	Barriadas

Advantages of Spontaneous Settlements

- provide homes for rural migrants
- cheap homes for poor people
- easy to build
- large pool of labour available
- community spirit develops in otherwise large Megacity

Characteristics of Spontaneous settlements

- on a variety of sites - steep, wet, wasteland, rubbish tips - usually illegal
- high population density
- makeshift shacks
- lack of basic services
- epidemic disease & poor health
- poor communications
- high unemployment
- social services non-existent

Characteristics of inhabitants of Spontaneous Settlements

- in dire poverty
- unemployed, often unskilled
- landless or homeless
- male at first then large family arrives

Disadvantages of Spontaneous Settlements

- built on illegal sites
- unhealthy living conditions
- unsafe houses
- urban eyesores
- high unemployment levels within resident population
- Often centres of crime, vice etc
- centres of mass poverty

Fig.145

Distribution of Towns / Cities in Developing Countries e.g. Peru

May relate to **colonisation** e.g. towns / cities along coast for trade. More recent development is close to communications (main roads and railways). Towns in more isolated locations usually serve as regional administrative/service centres.

Rural Push Factors

- Famine
- Malnutrition
- Natural Disasters
- Desertification
- Disease and ill-health
- Poverty & homelessness
- Unemployment
- Low living standards
- Lack of land

Urban Pull Factors (perceived)

- Food supplies available
- Entertainment
- Improved services
- Improved housing
- Better and more jobs
- Medical care
- Wealth
- Education and training
- Improved living conditions

Note.... migrants and refugees move into large cities perceiving there to be a wide range of urban advantages over rural poverty & problems. Sadly the urban reality is often a quality of life lower than that of the rural hinterland left behind, e.g. Calcutta, India (fig.**147**).

Pattern of growth within Developing World Cities - see figure 145

The C.B.D is often surrounded by an old area of housing and industry- old slum housing may be inhabited by temporary migrants. Around this zone is an area of middle and high income housing (may be separated in some cities) (former colonial residences). On the outskirts (sometimes on illegal sites) and outside the city boundaries are squatter settlements (Shanty Towns - see figure **144**) mainly occupied by semi-permanent migrants. Shanties may be on old rubbish tips or dangerous, steep ground (avoided by conventional housing.)

Model of a City in a Developing Country

Fig.146

- CBD
- Elite Residential
- Maturity Zone
- In Situ Accretion
- Spontaneous Settlement Zone

Calcutta - an urban apocalypse ?

Typifying the current urbanisation process led by the developing countries at the end of the 20th.century is Calcutta, India. The exponential urban growth experienced by cities such as Calcutta is the result of a complex combination of factors which include ; **Rural Push** factors(famine, debt, poverty, drought, civil war, etc.) ; **Urban Pull** factors (perceived advantages including employment, housing, food, education, entertainment, medical care, etc.) and **Urban Improvement** schemes which increase the perceived attraction of megacities. The high rate of urbanisation in Calcutta is due to a lack of economic development rather than the results of it..........

Fig.147

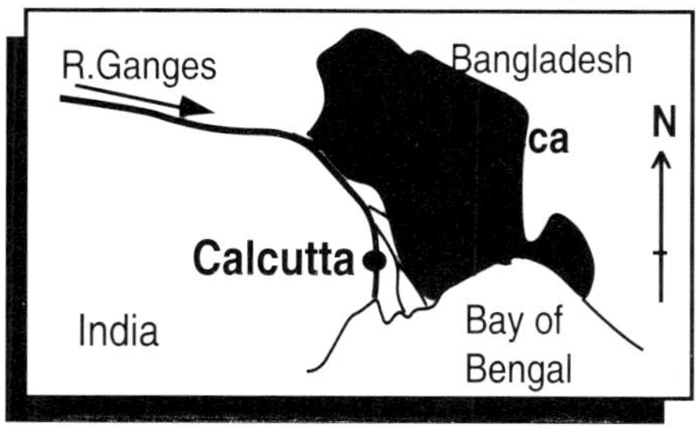

Growth and Development of Calcutta

Founded by the East India Company in 1892 and situated 160 km from the sea on a distributary of the mighty Ganges - the Hooghly River. Capital of India 1773-1911. Major industrial and commercial centre handling over 30% of India's trade. The largest tea exporting centre in the world. Industry based on agricultural products from Calcutta's hinterland, including jute (fibres), tea, cotton, silk, rice, sugar-refining, paper-manufacture and engineering. Two large urban areas have developed divided by the R.Hooghly - Calcutta (east) and Howrah (west).
Industrial expansion occurred rapidly in the late 1800s, occupying suburban locations - jute on east bank of the Hooghly and engineering on west bank in Howrah. Today an 80km urban sprawl along both river banks is India's major urban magnet.

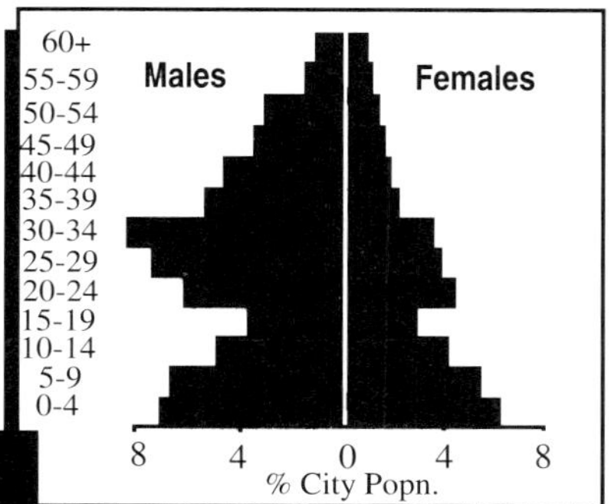

Site of Calcutta

Major site disadvantges apply to Calcutta. The city lies 160 km from the Bay of Bengal, on a levee above malarial marshes. The River Hooghly is slowly silting up and the city regularly floods during the spring (with snow-melt in the Himalayas) and the summer monsoon rains. Associated cyclones batter the area between June and November and there is now no room for urban expansion. Calcutta is "blessed" by the Hindu Goddess Khali (Goddess of Destruction) !

Calcutta

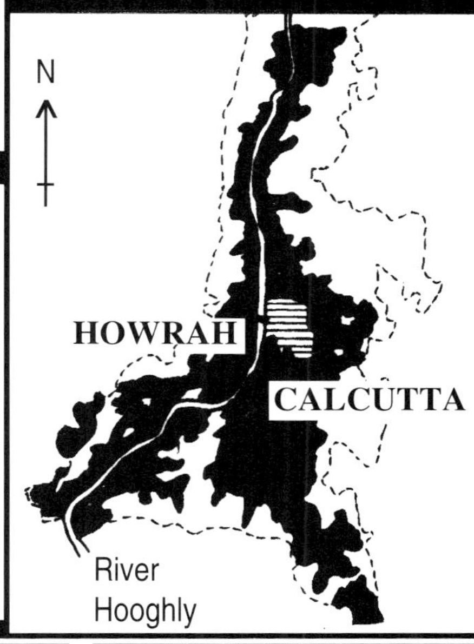

The twin-cities of Calcutta and Howrah are divided by the R.Hooghly and linked by only four bridges. Both have a high urban density of population (825 people/km2 compared with New York 395 people/km2). In contrast with cities such as London or Paris in which rapid urban sprawl was encouraged by improvements in mass public transport, Calcutta has seen increasing densities as it remains encircled by marshland..

Key ⬬ **Urban area**
⊖ **CBD**

Calcutta is home to over 15 million people - approx. 6 million of whom live in massive bustees (or Spontaneous settlements) surrounding the city. Official estimates state that over 250,000 people are currently "pavement dwellers" and 90% of the population earn less than £5 per week. Only 2% live in private housing. 35% of all families have less than one-third of a room to live in. 61% of all houses have no toilet and 78% have no water. This is a city of paradox - where very rich and very poor live side by side. Some of India's major industries located here creating enormous wealth whilst millions are unemployed, live in dire poverty and are forced to defecate in the street.....

350 rural migrants each day are estimated to move into Calcutta in search of a better way of life, employment or to escape debt, famine or religious intolerance. As the population pyramid for Calcutta (above) illustrates, the influx causes an imbalance in the population structure since many migrants are young males, often married with the intention of obtaining work and sending home their pay whilst their wives and families farm small subsistence plots. Most migrants are homeless and eventually move into one of Calcutta's many bustees, half of which lie on the eastern edges of the city. Official city reports classify 65% of bustees as a danger to public health and centres for the spread of Cholera.
Other major urban problems include the rising unemployment in the jute industry (foreign competition from oil-based fibres), lack of money for public services, deteriorating educational provision, continuing transport chaos and food shortages. Calcutta has been described as a **Miseropolis** - yet rural migrants still perceive life there as better........

Urban Geography Revision : Summary Notes

The main idea of the Urban Geography section is....
Urban settlements provide a range of employment, services and residential opportunities which may be located in different parts of the settlement.

Settlement

1. A **settlement** is any place in which people live more or less permanently.
2. **Present-day settlements** nearly all result from a **legacy** of environmental, social and economic change.
3. **Rural Settlements** take a variety of forms :
   - **Linear** - often dictated by routeways or topography
   - **Nucleated** - usually centrally-placed in an agricultural area.
   - **Dispersed** -often influenced by distribution of fertile land or communications routes.
   - **Isolated** - often in areas of extreme physical difficulty.
   - **Ring** - associated with pastoralism
   - **Planned** - associated with agrarian reform or overspill from urban regeneration.
4. **Rural** settlements can be classified into isolated buildings, hamlets, villages, small market towns.
5. Rural settlement patterns are influenced by population density, the type of rural economy and topography.
6. The **site of a settlement** is the exact spot on the landscape on which it is constructed.
7. The **situation of a settlement** is its relative position within an area.
8. **Urbanisation** is the process of becoming an urban-based society.
9. **Suburbanisation** is associated with the C20th. expansion of urban areas into surrounding countryside and is the growth of residential areas on the outskirts of a settlement.
10. **Counter-urbansiation** is the reversal of rural-depopulation ; the relocation of people and industry from urban areas to rural areas.
11. Urbanisation is preceding at a **faster rate** in **developing** countries today.
12. **Urban growth** was related to **industrialisation** in developed countries and has taken up to 300 years.
13. Urban growth is a younger phenomenon in developing countries and is often associated with **rural problems**.
14. A **conurbation** is a grouping of urban areas.
15. A **primate city** develops in developing countries where few urban centres are required.

Urban structure

1. The distribution of **distinct land use zones** can be traced in time, height and distance from sites of central importance within a settlement.
2. **Competition** between urban land uses results in a pattern related to bid rent analysis.
3. **Bid-rent** is related to functions which will derive the most benefit from a particular location within an urban area.
4. The **bid-rent pattern** is usually - retail, wholesale, manufacturing, residential.
5. Bid-rent analysis reveals other high-peaks at **nodal points** on ring roads, motorway intersections, etc.strong lines of communications and contrasts in land quality.
6. **Models of urban structure** include -
   - the **Concentric Model** (Burgess - 1925)
   - the **Sector Model** (Hoyt - 1939)
   - the **Multiple Nuclei Model** (Harris-Ullman - 1945)
   - **British City Model** (Mann - 1965)

8. The **Concentric Model** is based on a uniform landscape providing equal easy access in all directions from the C.B.D. It is based on bid-rent patterns from the C.B.D..
9. The **Sector Model** is best related to settlements in which there are strong lines of communications and contrasts in land quality.
9. The **Multiple Nuclei Model** is better suited to large urban areas with more than one recognised centre.
10. The **Central Business District** or prime site lies at the heart of the urban transport network and can be identified by the highest bid-rents, lack of space for expansion, high degree of congestion, dense road network and low night-time population density.
11. Major retailing remains clustered within the C.B.D but the develop ment of **Out of Town Shopping Centres** poses something of a threat to the retailing dominance of the C.B.D.
12. Industry is relocating to the **urban periphery** to industrial parks and estates.
13. **Residential land uses** are the largest urban land users and residential areas can be classified into -
    - **inner city "twilight" zones**
    - **inner suburbia**
    - **outer suburbia**
    - **exurbia**
14. **Suburbs** grew outwards as communications systems (first rail then roads) developed.
15. **Inner City residential areas** are the subject of Urban Regeneration and Comprehensive Redevelopment schemes as a partnership between public and private authorities, e.g. GEAR (Glasgow) and LDDC (London).
16. **Filtering** is the deterioration of housing as housing moves downwards through socio-economic groups.
17. **Gentrification** is the reversal of filtering where housing is rehabilitated with a concomitant rise in property value.
18. **Greenbelts** and **New Towns** are an attempt to limit urban sprawl and create new, planned, self-contained settlements housing overspill population and relocated industry.
19. **Exurban** residential development is located within rural areas and is the result of counter-urbanisation and/or the growth of commuterism. Dormitory settlements are dependent on good communication links.

Urbanisation in developing countries

1. The **rate of urbanisation** is prolific in developing countries.
2. Large **urban areas in developing countries** do not develop zoned structures as they have **poor transport** .
3. Urban areas of developing countries in transect have -
   - **a western-style C.B.D.** (often mixed together with a crowded inner city of poor people)
   - **affluent inner suburbs**
   - **a large outer area** of relatively high density slum or spontaneous colonies.
4. The **upper socio-economic groups** are usually concentrated near to a central communications spine.
5. The **communications spine** is also the zone of industry.
6. C.B.D., industry and high status residential land uses tend to expand in the **same direction**.
7. Urban areas mostly grow at their margins through the **gradual stabilisation of spontaneous settlements.**

Urban Core Geography Revision : Unit style assessments

1. **Refer to Map Extract 926/111 - Sheffield**

   (a) The photographs - **figures 148, 149** and **150** were taken in different parts of **Sheffield**.

Fig.148

Fig.149

Fig.150

Look at the photos and match them with the appropriate grid squares (choosing from **3590 3488** and **3587**) and **land use zones** (choose from CBD, Inner City and 20th.Century housing). (4)

   (b) Explain in detail the evidence you used to reach your conclusions in 1(a). (6)

2. Study figures **148 to 150** which show differing urban landscapes of **Sheffield**.

GMT

   (a) Make a simple fieldsketch of **two** of these photos.
   Annotate the fieldsketches to show the main features of each urban landscape. (6)

   (b) Describe at least **two urban problems** of areas such as those in 2(a) and **attempted solutions**. (4)

Urban Core Geography Revision : Exam style assessments

1. Refer to Map Extract **926/111** - **Sheffield**

   Describe and explain how you would expect land prices to change along the line of Northing **87** from **340870** to **410870**. (5)

2. Study the plan of the **Meadowhall Leisure Shopping Development** (fig.151) and its map location (squares **3990** and **3991**.)

   Describe in detail the advantages of this **location** and explain why this site would have been preferred to other sites closer to the C.B.D. (5)

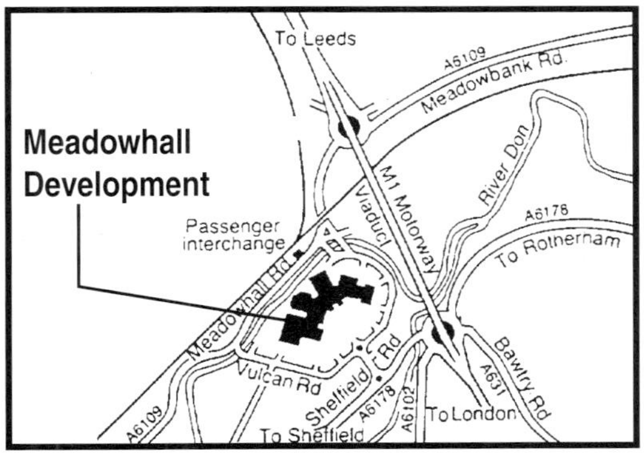

Fig.151

3. Study figure **152** which shows land use changes along a transect from the CBD of a city.

GMT

   "Land use changes greatly as you move from the city centre outwards to the edge of the city."

   Describe and analyse figure 150.
   Does the evidence support this statement ? (5)

Fig.152

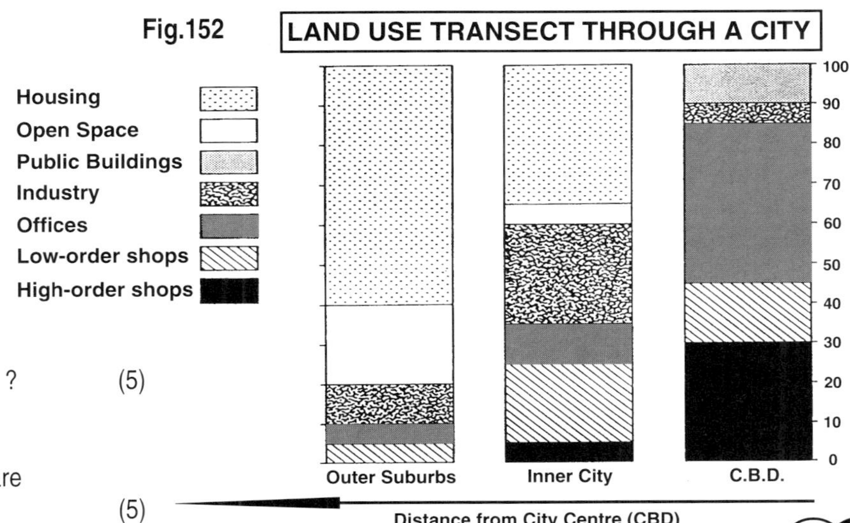

4. For a major city you have studied, describe the range of functions and activities which are to be found in the Central Business District. (5)

Urban Application Geography Revision : Unit style assessments

1. **Refer to figure 153 - % Urban Population per selected country.**

Fig.153

Country	Urban % of Total Popn.	Country	Urban % of Total Popn.	Country	Urban % of Total Popn.
USA	79	Saudi Arabia	21	Indonesia	26
Mexico	68	UK	75	Australia	84
Brazil	71	Sweden	81	New Zealand	76
Argentina	80	Norway	61	Turkey	25
Sudan	9	USSR	72	Italy	71
Lybia	49	China	21	Canada	77
Mozambique	11	Japan	85	Thailand	11
Chad	19	India	23	Albania	34

(a) Give a full definition of **urbanisation**, **Megacity, counter-urbanisation** and **re-urbanisation** (6)

(b) Briefly account for the high degree of urbanisation (over 75%) in **one** selected country in figure **153**. (4)

(c) Briefly account for the low degree of urbanisation (less than 30%) in **one** selected country in figure **153**. (4)

Refer to figure **154** - the Urban Explosion

(d) Describe and account for the urban explosion illustrated in figure **154**. (6)

Total = 20 marks

Urban Explosion **Fig.154**

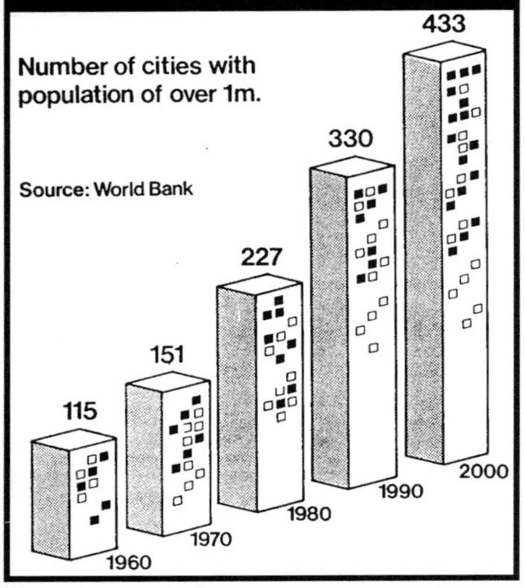

Urban Application Geography Revision : Exam style assessments

1. Despite being at different stages of urban evolution, both developed and developing world cities have serious problems with **poor quality housing** and **traffic congestion**.

With reference to **named cities** from the developed and developing world :

(a) Describe the **housing difficulties** and assess the effectiveness of **attempted solutions**. (9)

(b) Analyse the main **causes of traffic congestion** and evaluate the success of **traffic management policies**. (9)

(c) Study figure **155**

Factors relating to shopping location **Fig.155**

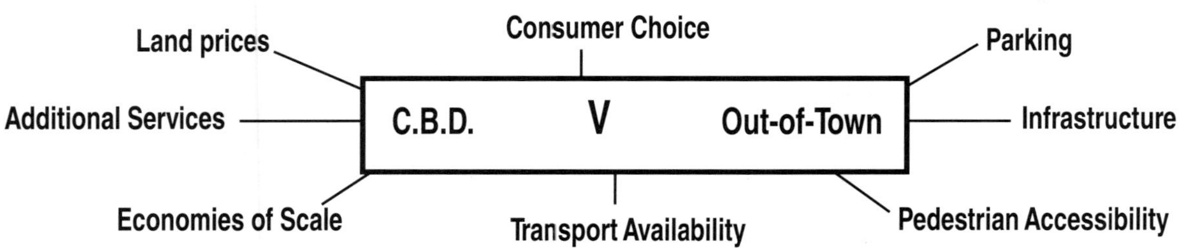

Assess the **advantages** and **disadvantages** of locating a shopping centre in the **C.B.D.** compared with an **out-of-town** location. (7)

Total = 25 marks

Terminology – test yourself on the Human Core !

Try this test - and don't look back at any of the Human Core sections - do this exercise to judge for yourself how well your revision is going for Higher Geography !

What to do This is a **terminology test.** Complete the **definitions** of each of these important/**key terms**. A few have been completed for you. Good luck !

Population

Demography - the study of population
Population Pyramid
Birth Rate
Death Rate
Mortality
Census - a count of the number of people
Enumerator
Demographic Transition
Natural increase
Dependency Ratio
Infant Mortality
Life Expectancy
Fertility Ratio
Immigration
Emigration
Migration
Causes of migration
Migration - push/pull factors
Migration - major problems
Endogenic diseases
Exogenic diseases
Eugenics
Genetic Modification
Population structure
Malthus

Rural Geography

Rural
Arable farming - crop farming
Pastoral farming
Mixed farming
HYV
Extensive agriculture
Intensive agriculture
Commercial agriculture
Subsistence agriculture
Shifting Cultivation
Sedentary agriculture
Crop yield - crop output per hectare
Farming system
Farm inputs
Farm processes
Farm outputs
Fallow
Polyculture
Cereals - grains e.g. rice, maize, wheat, rye
Wet rice
Dry rice
Irrigation
Biogas
Green Revolution
Monoculture - one crop farming
Staple food

Industrial Geography

Primary Industry
Secondary Industry
Tertiary Industry - service industries e.g. shops
Quaternary Industry
Agrarian society - society based on farming
Industrial Revolution
Industrialisation period
Late industrial period
Post-Industrial society
Industrial system
Industrial inputs
Industrial processes
Industrial outputs
Location factors
Capital - money available for investment
Site
Markets
Infrastructure
Inertia
Agglomeration
Product Life Cycle
Labour - workforce
Greenfield site
Tidewater site
Brown Earth Gap site
C19th. industrial landscape
Late C20th.industrial landscape
Industrial estate
Light industry
Heavy industry
Smokestack industry
Sunrise industry
Integrated steelworks
Incentives & grants
EuroCore
Hot Banana
Europeriphery
Diversification
The Ruhr Valley
NW Scotland
Mezzogiorno
Deglomeration
Footloose industries
Enterprise Zones
Objective One
Automation - use of robotics in industry
State Intervention schemes
Science Parks
Economic, social and environmental consequences of industrial decline and industrial development

Urban Core Geography

Conurbation
Megalopolis
Primate City - single dominant city, e.g. Lima
Megacity
Urban morphology
Dispersed settlement
Nucleated settlement
Linear settlement
Urbanisation - urban-based society
Suburbanisation
Re-urbanisation
Counter-urbanisation
Urban zones - CBD - Central Business District
C19th.Low-cost housing
C19th.Industry
C20th. High-cost housing
C20th. Council housing
Recent Industrial areas
Greenbelts
Rural-Urban Fringe
Dormitory (satellite) settlement
Urban functions
Range of service
Service Threshold
Hinterland
Sphere of Influence
Low, middle & high order services
Out of Town Shopping Developments
Urban Models - Concentric Zone
Sector Theory Model
Multiple-Nuclei Model
New Town Model
Bid-rent theory
CBD problems & solutions
Inner City Redevelopment schemes
Inner City Renovation schemes
Filtering
Gentrification - improvements in housing
Urban sprawl
Case Study UK - Birmingham

Urban Application Geography

Birmingham - urban problems & solutions
Rate of urbanisation - fastest in The South
Problems of global urbanisation
City in a Developing Country - model
Spontaneous settlements
Rural push factors
Urban pull factors
Urbanisation problems
Calcutta - urban apocalypse
Urban solutions

10. River Basin Management Application

The main idea of the River Basin Management application is....
Within river basins, water control projects are undertaken for a variety of reasons and on a range of scales. These projects are examples of human interference with systems, especially hydrological systems. The changes often have both beneficial and adverse consequences.

What do you need to know ?

Students should have a knowledge and understanding of -

A Areas of study from either **Africa** or **North America** including the detailed study of **one** river basin
B The general distribution and scales of river basins and river basin water control projects within either Africa or North America.
C The physical characteristics of the selected river basin - climate, structure and rock type, landforms, vegetation and soils.
D The hydrological cycle as applied to the selected river basin before and after the control project(s) - inputs, transfers, outputs.
E The socioeconomic, political and technological conditions of the selected river basin (and, where appropriate, adjacent areas) and the need and potential for water resource management.
F The influence of discharge, geology, landforms, soils and human factors on the selection and development of sites for storage, transfer and use of water in the basin and surrounding areas.
G The social, economic, political and environmental benefits and adverse consequences of water control projects on the selected basin and, where appropriate, adjacent areas.

Distribution of River Basins and Water Control Projects in Africa

Fig.156

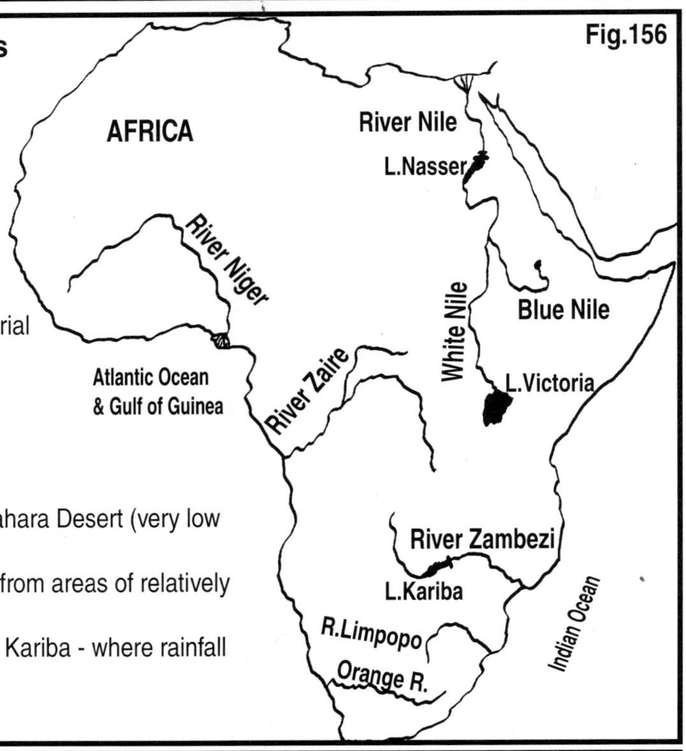

River Basins
Absence in North Africa (Sahara desert) apart from the **Nile** which drains north from Lake Victoria (White Nile) and the Ethiopian Highlands (Blue Nile).
Several major systems flow South and West to the Atlantic and the Gulf of Guinea (Rivers Niger and Zaire). These are fed by generally higher rainfall areas (sometimes seasonal) in the Equatorial and Savannah areas).
The Zambezi is the major river flowing east to the Indian Ocean - it drains the upland areas of Zambia and Zimbabwe.

Water Control Projects
General absence of schemes in the interior regions such as the Sahara Desert (very low rainfall).
However, important schemes e.g. the Nile and Niger provide water from areas of relatively high rainfall to supply arid regions e.g. Egypt.
Schemes also for H.E.P., Irrigation and flood control e.g. Zambesi - Kariba - where rainfall is unreliable.

Distribution of River Basins and Water Control Projects in North America

Fig.157

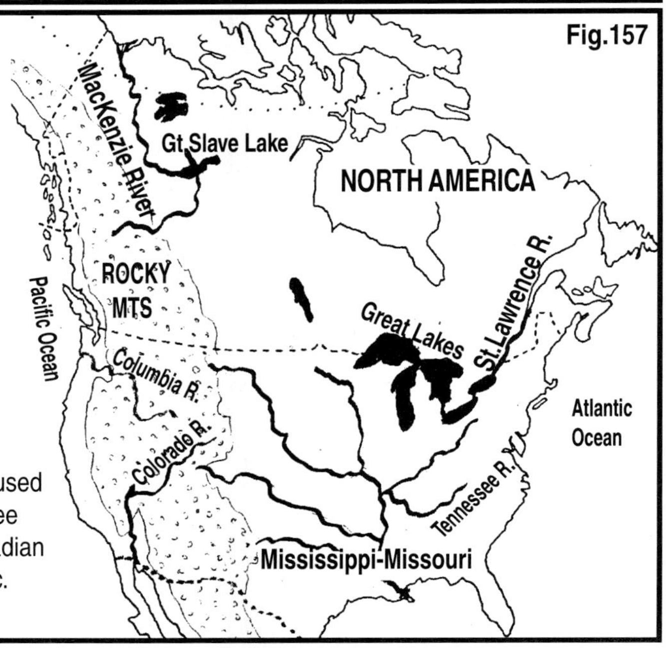

River Basins
The Mackenzie River flows north to the Arctic Ocean from the Great Slave Lake and fed by **spring snow melt**.
The Rocky Mountains form a major watershed with the Columbia and Colorado rivers draining west to the Pacific Ocean and the Mississippi/Missouri system flowing south and east to the Gulf of Mexico. The Tennessee river joins the Mississippi system flowing from the Appalachian mountains in Eastern USA. The St. Lawrence flows east from the Great Lakes into the Atlantic Ocean.

Water Control Projects
These are concentrated in the Western USA e.g. Colorado Basin in California where problems of flooding and water shortages were caused by variable river flow. Other important schemes include the Tennessee Valley (T.V.A.) in the Appalachians and the St.Lawrence on the Canadian border. These were needed to improve navigation, provide H.E.P., etc.

What creates a need for River Basin Management ? (refer to figure 158 - Lesotho's water export drive)

Physical Factors include

- **Unreliable climate / Rainfall** with variations in river flow and seasonal flooding or water shortages
- **Desert** climate with high evaporation rates and a lack of water for crops, etc.
- **Soil erosion** (caused by "flash floods") and lack of vegetation where silting in rivers has reduced water flow

Social / Economic Factors include

- Shortages of water **for domestic use (as population increases)**
- **Need for reliable** supply of water for crops (**irrigation**) & industry
- **Generation of H.E.P.** for industry and urban areas

Lesotho's water export drive

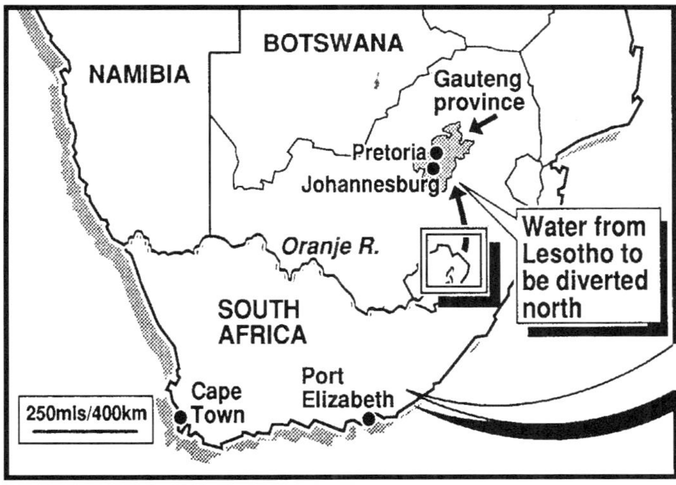

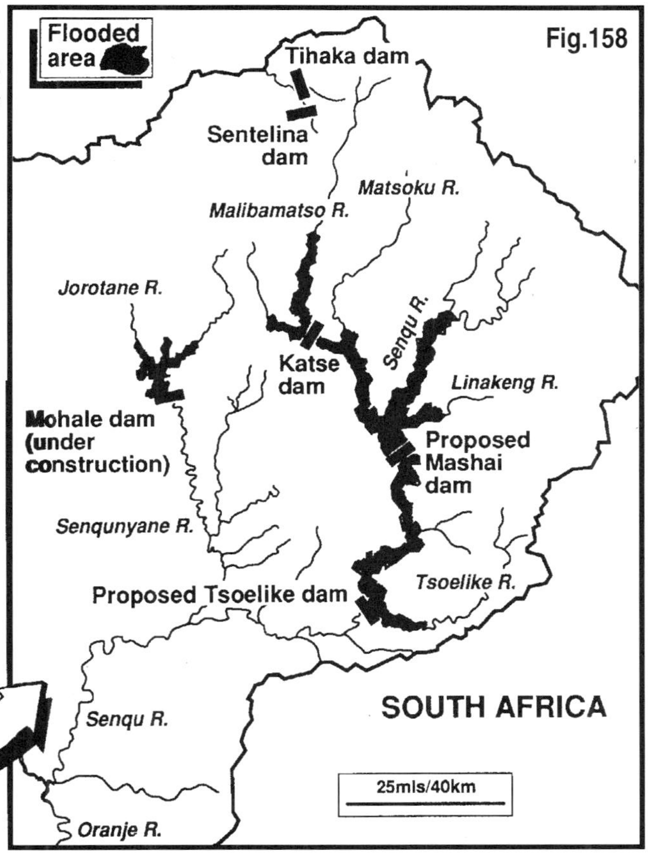

Fig.158

- **Evaporation** is a major problem in southern Africa - more water evaporates from Lake Kariba in one year than is consumed in Zimbabwe in the same period
- **Irrigation** accounts for almost two-thirds of water use in the region
- **At current population growth rates**, dry regions - particularly Botswana and South Africa - will experience chronic water shortage within 25 years

Selection of sites for Water Control Projects

Fig.159

To be successful, the following requirements are important -

For Dam construction -

- **Stable, solid foundation** - free from subsidence and / or potential earthquake damage
- **Narrow valley** which reduces the size of the dam (means lower costs) and a smaller surface area of reservoir (means less evaporation)
- **Deep valley** - larger volume of water
- **Water supply** from surrounding catchment area (precipitation and snowmelt)
- **Impermeable rock** to reduce water loss by seepage

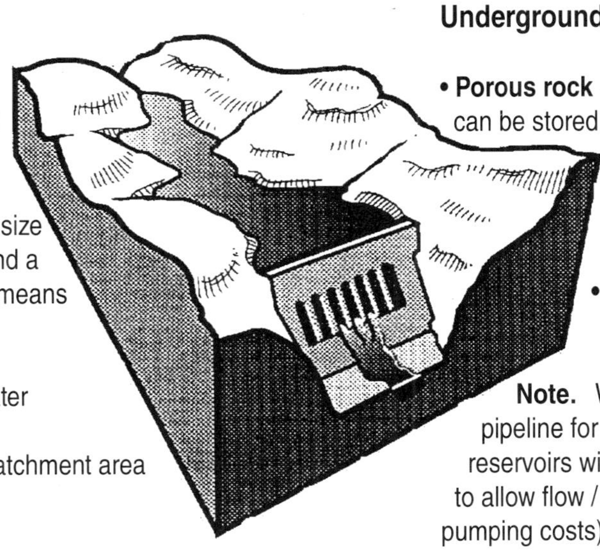

Underground Storage schemes -

- **Porous rock** - e.g. sandstone, as an **aquifer** (water can be stored in rock pore spaces below surface).
- **Consistent water table** to supply wells
- **Lack of pollution** affecting **ground water**

Note. Water may need to be transferred by pipeline for hundreds of kilometres. Ideally reservoirs will be located in mountainous areas to allow flow / transfer by the force of gravity (reduces pumping costs) - this also helps generation of H.E.P.

Benefits and Adverse Consequences of Water Control Projects

Many of these are common to all schemes. Some specific examples are given to relate points to North America or Africa. Points can usually be divided under headings, i.e. **environmental, social, economic** and **political**.

Benefits (advantages) of of Water Control projects

Social

- **Fresh water supply all year round** leads to increased food output and supports population growth, e.g. in Californian Urban areas (L.A, etc)
- **Fresh clean water supply** leads to a reduced risk of disease such as cholera, etc.
- **Opportunities for Tourism & Recreation** creates greater employment, e.g. on Lake Meade (Colorado River)
- **Provides H.E.P.** for remote isolated communities

Economic

- Dams provide H.E.P. leading to **industrial expansion and greater employment**, e.g. California
- Increased water supply provides **irrigation** for double cropping with increased output/yields, e.g. Egypt
- **Control of water flow** improves navigation, e.g. on the Tennessee River

Political

- Exploitation of Water Resources **can aid** co-operation between countries / states e.g. **Colorado - US states with Mexico**
- Costs may be shared **between countries and states**

Environmental

- Reservoir provides more fresh water and can **improve sanitation and drinking water supplies** e.g. Nile Basin
- Large lake or reservoir may **enhance scenery** and provide **recreational opportunities**, e.g Lake Nasser
- **Flood control**
- Consistent, more even **seasonal water flow**

Note
The **Hydrological Cycle** in a given river basin will be **modified** by a major water control project.
The downward flow of water to the sea or lake may be severely restricted, e.g. in the Colorado River Basin the river now barely reaches the Gulf of California as water is diverted to irrigation schemes upstream.
Large reservoirs will affect rates of evaporation and can affect the micro-climate of a region.
Ground-water storage schemes and the level of the water table may be adversely affected by extensive use of wells and boreholes for water extraction.

Adverse consequences (Disadvantages) of Water Control projects

Social

- Reservoirs and irrigation channels may increase risk of water-related **diseases** e.g. Bilharzia, Malaria (Egypt - R.Nile)
- People forced to **abandon settlements** which are flooded by reservoirs, e.g. Aswan Dam, R.Nile

Economic

- **Dams are very expensive** and beyond the economies of most Developing Countries who must **rely on foreign aid** leading to international **debt**
- **More fertiliser** is needed which increases agricultural costs
- Reservoirs may severely disrupt **communications**

Political

- Regions downstream must depend on the co-operation of 'partners' upstream for **water supply and control** e.g. Mexico suffers from inconsistent flow to irrigation projects supplied by the Colorado River
- **Pollution** moving downstream across borders, e.g. USA to Mexico along the Colorado River

Environmental

- **Risk of Pollution**
- **Dams prevent fresh Alluvial Soil** from reaching and renewing in the flood plain
- **Soil Erosion** e.g. Egypt (R.Nile) silting of reservoirs behind the dam e.g. Lake Powell, US
- **Threat to wildlife** and important sites e.g. Rainbow Arch (Colorado) and various archaeological sites along the River Nile
- **Changes in Micro-Climates** caused by large reservoirs

Effectiveness of a Water Control Project

The Colorado River Basin (figure 160)

The construction of a series of major dams e.g. the **Hoover** and **Glen Canyon** has largely controlled water supply and flooding. Water is widely used for irrigation, increasing crop production, and H.E.P. has encouraged industrial development. The increased water supply has helped support the huge population growth in South West USA.

However, although flooding has been reduced, in exceptional years e.g. the 'El Nino' floods of 1983 the dams are unable to prevent devastation. The dams also trap sediment which reduces reservoir capacity and must be dredged. The lower reaches of the river no longer carries fresh water through Mexico to the Gulf of California and Mexican farmers have problems with irrigation due to the high water salinity. The Colorado Delta, once home to a variety of wildlife (birds, jaguars and porpoises etc) is now a wasteland.

Fig.160

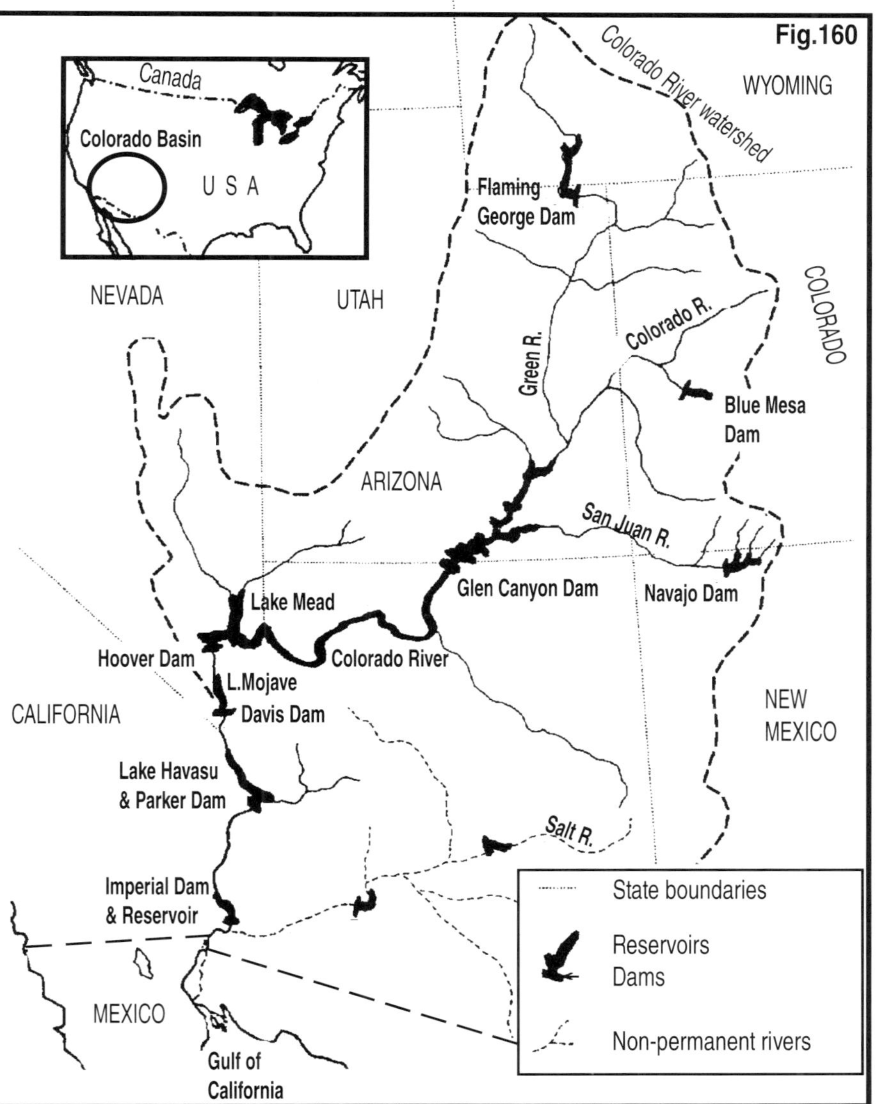

Model of the Stages in Water Resource Development

Fig.161

Stage One	Stage Two	Stage Three		Stage Four
Hydraulic engineering through small-scale projects	Integrated water resources management & multi-purpose river basin development	Transfer of water into over-developed basins. Water demand management begins to be considered.	Environmental backlash as the long-term adverse and sometimes irreversible effects of earlier projects begin to be recognised and understood	Co-ordinated management of water and land resources within a basin.

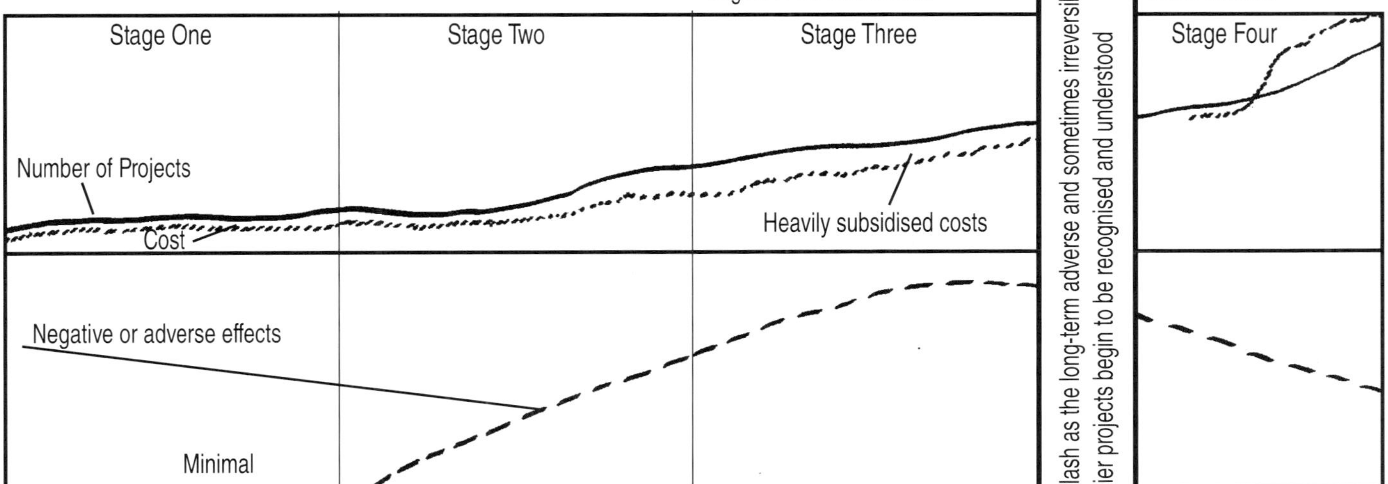

Stage One	Stage Two	Stage Three	Stage Four
Major rivers virtually unregulated	Increasing regulation involving storage development, inter-basin connections, artificial recharge of groundwater.	Maximum attainable level of stream-flow regulation in most major river systems. Further development only possible through increasing efficiency.	Water availability is accepted as a regional constraint. Self-reliance and appropriate technology are promoted.
Community approach	Engineering approach. Development led.	Technological approach - problem led.	Engineering approaches used.

River Basin Management Revision : Summary Notes

The main idea of the River Basin Management section is....
Within river basins, water control projects are undertaken for a variety of reasons and on a range of scales. These projects are examples of human interference with systems, especially hydrological systems. The changes often have both beneficial and adverse consequences.

Distribution of River Basins and Water Control Projects

1. In **Africa,** major absence in North Africa apart from the **Nile** Several major systems in West (**Niger** & **Zaire**) and South (**Zambezi**).
2. In **North America**, the MacKenzie River flows north into the Arctic Ocean (fed by snow melt); The Rocky Mountains provide a major watershed with the **Colorado** & **Columbia River** systems flowing westwards into the Pacific Ocean; the major **Mississippi-Missouri** system flows southwards into the Gulf of Mexico; the **St.Lawrence** system flows NE into the Atlantic.
3. **Water control projects** include -
   in Africa
   - **Nile/Aswan/Nasser** project in Egypt
   - **Zambezi-Kariba** project for H.E.P., irrigation and flood control

   in North America
   - **TVA** (Tennessee Valley Authority) project
   - **Colorado Basin** project in California
   - **St.Lawrence** project - all to provide H.E.P., flood control improve navigation, etc.

What creates the need for Water Basin Management ?

1. **Physical factors** include -
   - **unreliable climate**
   - **wide variations** in rainfall patterns
   - **desert climate** with high evaporation
   - **soil erosion problems** & resultant silting of rivers
2. **Social / Economic factors** include -
   - **shortages of water** for domestic use
   - **population increase**
   - **need for reliable water supplies** for crop irrigation and industry
   - need for water power for **H.E.P. generation** for industry and urban uses

Selection of sites for Water Control Projects

1. **Dam construction -**
   - **stable solid foundation**
   - **lack of subsidence** and earthquake threat
   - **narrow valleys** reduces costs in building and smaller surface area
   - **deep valleys** for larger volume of water
   - **consistent water supply** from catchment area
   - **impermeable rock**
2. **Underground storage schemes -**
   - **porous rock** needed for water storage in rock pore spaces
   - **consistent water table**
   - **lack of pollution**

Benefits of Water Control projects

1. **Social -**
   - **fresh water supply all year round**
   - **fresh clean water supply** means less threat from water-related disease
   - **greater opportunities for tourism & recreation**
   - **provision of H.E.P.**
2. **Economic -**
   - **H.E.P.** production stimulates industrial expansion and greater employment
   - **irrigation water for crops** increases crop yields
   - control of water flow improves **navigation**
3. **Political**
   - increased **co-operation** between countries and states
   - **shared costs** between countries and states
4. **Environmental -**
   - **improved sanitation and drinking water**
   - **enhancement of scenery**
   - **greater recreational opportunities**
   - **flood control**
   - **more even** seasonal water flow

Adverse consequences of Water Control projects

5. **Social -**
   - reservoirs & irrigation channels increase risk of water-related **diseases**
   - **abandoned settlements** along areas flooded by reservoirs
6. **Economic -**
   - **dams are very expensive**
   - **increased international debt**
   - **increased international dependency**
   - **more fertiliser** required
   - reservoirs disrupt **communications**
7. **Political -**
   - problems of water supply and control **downstream**
   - **pollution downstream**
8. **Environmental -**
   - dam prevents fresh **alluvial soil** renewing the flood plain
   - **soil erosion** and silting of reservoirs
   - **threats to wildlife**
   - **changes in micro-climates** caused by large reservoirs
9. **Hydrological Cycle** can be interrupted and disturbed in a given water control project, e.g. downstream flow to the sea or lakes can be restricted; reservoirs can affect rates of evaporation/micro-climates; water-table levels can be depleted, etc.

River Basin Management Revision : Unit style assessments

1. **Refer to figure 162** - a flow diagram relating to stages in the development of a river basin to supply water for irrigation and domestic use.

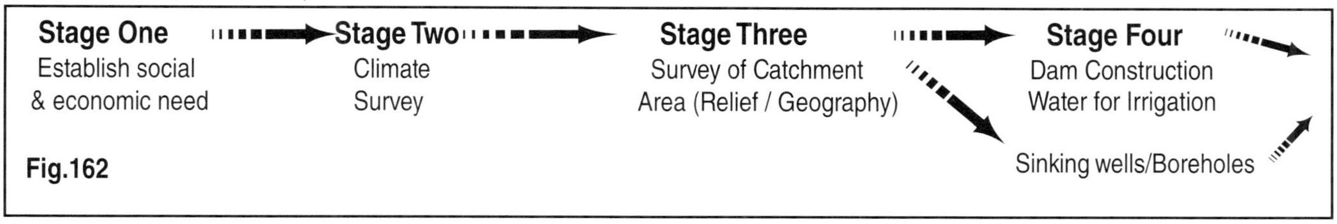

Fig.162

(a) Describe and explain the importance of each stage in the development, and compare **the two** different methods of obtaining water. (10)

(b) With reference to a river basin in either Africa or North America, outline the additional social, economic and environmental benefits which dam construction would provide and discuss any potential harmful effects on the environment. (10)

Total = 20 marks

River Basin Management Revision : Exam style assessments

1. **Refer to figures 163 and 164 -** a map and table which show variations of river flow on the Colorado River at different stages of water control.

The Colorado River Basin

Fig.163

Flow \ Year	Pre 1935	1935 - 63	Post 1963
Max. Flow	98,000	32,000	17,000
Min. Flow	2,000	4,000	4,000
Average Flow	31,000	15,000	10,000

(Units of flow - cubic feet/second)

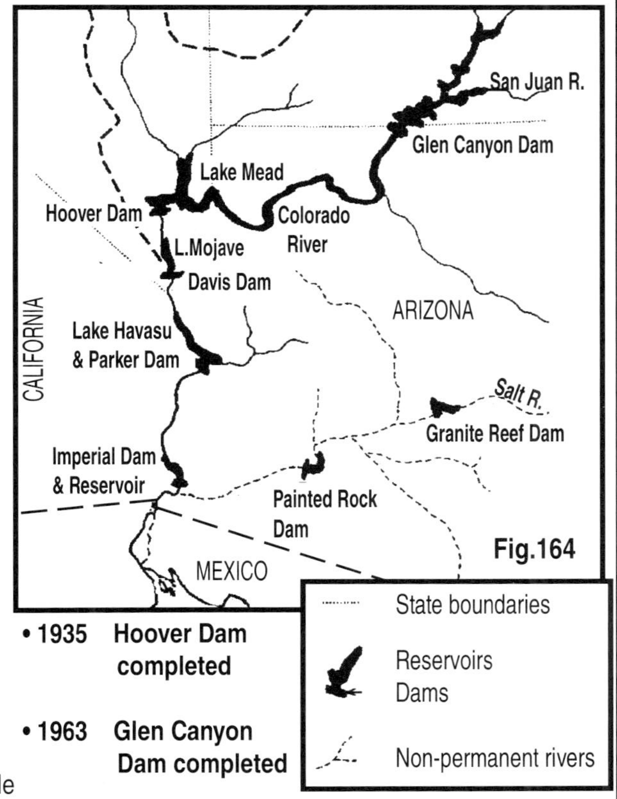

Fig.164

• **1935 Hoover Dam completed**

• **1963 Glen Canyon Dam completed**

(a) Describe and explain the variations and changes in river flow before, during and after the completion of the Hoover and Glen Canyon Dams in 1935 and 1963. (6)

(b) Describe the environmental advantages and disadvantages of controlling river flow in this manner. (6)

(c) Explain how the construction of a major dam, together with with subsequent changes in river flow, can affect the local hydrological cycle. (4)

(d) Study figure **165** showing some potential benefits and possible adverse consequences of water control projects....

Fig.165

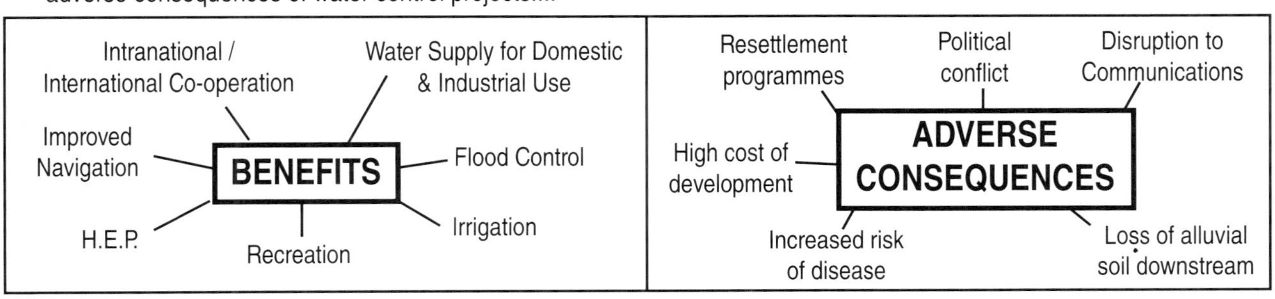

With reference to figure **165** and using specific examples from a named river basin in Africa or North America, describe and explain the social and political benefits and adverse consequences of water control projects. (9) Total = 25 marks

11. Rural Land Resources
Application

The main idea of the Rural Land Resources application section is....
Rural land resources are the product of the interaction of a wide range of physical factors modified by human activity. The resultant rural landscapes offer a variety of physical, economic and social opportunities.

What do you need to know ?

Students should have a knowledge and understanding of -

A The characteristics of glaciated upland, scarp and vale (Jurassic Limestone and Chalk) and upland limestone landscapes; the formation of the physical features associated with these landscapes should be dealt with in detail particularly in relation to land use.

B The factors involved in the evolution of these landscapes - structure, rock type, geology, major geomorphological processes, climate pattern, soils, human factors related to changing land use and settlement.

C The inter-related economical nd social opportunities which the land resource base provides - agriculture (including the impact of UK and EU policies), recreation and tourism, mineral exploitation, industry and water storage.

D main areas of study - United Kingdom

Characteristics of landscapes covered in the Rural Land Resources Application

Fig.156

Both the **Lithosphere** (Core section) and **Rural Land Resources** (Application section) require an understanding of three different landscape types -

- **Glaciated uplands** - pages 29 to 31
- **Upland Limestone** - pages 32 to 33
- **Scarp and Vale scenery** - pages 34 to 35
  (**Lithosphere summary** - page 36)

Pass Higher Geography covers the revision of these three landscapes in detail and as a reminder , you should review these sections now before going into the Rural Land Resources application.

Note. The Lithosphere also requires knowledge of weathering and slope formation. Rural Land Resources includes detailed understanding of **Rural Land Management,** i.e. conservation bodies / methods, conflicts over land use, rural management schemes, National Parks, etc.

Managing the Countryside

Why is Conservation needed ?

Britain has many areas of unique and beautiful scenery - see fig.157. The expansion of towns and cities (Urban Sprawl) has threatened rural areas.
Increased leisure time and recreation with improved access e.g. new roads (A9) have greatly increased the numbers of visitors, thus threatening the environment through people pressure.

Fig.157

Who runs what ?

- **In England and Wales** - two main organisations are involved -
  - **English Nature** - designate **Nature Reserves** and **S.S.S.I.'s** (Sites of Special Scientific Interest) (these SSSIs mainly relate to protecting wildlife (Flora and fauna) and geological sites (e.g. rock formations).
  - **Countryside Commission** - they designate and run **National Park** areas i.e. large areas of spectacular scenery, e.g. The Lake District (the role of the Countryside Commission is conservation of scenery and environment)

- **In Scotland** - there is one body involved -
  - **Scottish Natural Heritage** (**S.N.H.**) is responsible for conservation of landscape and wildlife etc.

Note. Other organisations i.e. The Forestry Commission, The National Trust, the R.S.P.B. and Local Authorities (which organise Country Parks) also make a large contribution to conservation and provide facilities and amenities for active (walking, orienteering, cycling) and passive (picnics, car touring, painting) recreation.

Rural Management Policies

Basic discussion point first - what is the difference between Conservation and Preservation approaches to Rural land Management ?

- **Preservation** involves moth-balling of the landscape - where very little change is considered.
- **Conservation** involves more of a working approach to the landscape based on local decision making and consultation.

Several schemes have been introduced - these have had an impact on the rural environment.
The schemes outlined below have 3 principal purposes:-

- To **conserve rural habitats**
- To encourage **development** in remote rural areas.
- To reduce **overproduction of farm produce**

Schemes include the following -

E.S.A.s (Environmentally Sensitive Areas)

Areas of **scenic and/or wildlife** importance e.g. coastal machair in the Uists. Farmers receive **grants** to encourage farming methods which conserve the environment e.g. use N**atural fertilisers** such as seaweed and harvest in a manner which protects threatened bird species.

L.F.A.s (Less Favoured Areas)

Isolated regions e.g. Western Isles with the problems of **rural depopulation and/or unemployment**. **Grants** and **loans** given to support farming and encourage new developments e.g. tourism.

F.D.G.s (Farm Diversification Grants)

Grants given to increase the range of rural land uses and to reduce overproduction of wheat, etc.. **Financial help** for alternative land uses, e.g. golf courses, tourist developments, etc.

Production Quotas

Limits are set by the **E.U.** (C.A.P. - Common Agricultural Policy) on the output of farm produce e.g. milk from dairy farms - the aim is to reduce overproduction (e.g. milk lakes).

Set Aside Schemes

Financed by the **E.U.** (C.A.P.). Farmers receive **annual payments** to leave areas of **arable land unused** for 5-year periods. The aim is to reduce overproduction of wheat etc. (grain mountains).

National Parks (Lake District, Snowdonia, Dartmoor, etc.)

Origin

Eleven Parks were **designated** in **1949** to '**protect**' the countryside from urban sprawl and increased visitor access (then thought unnecessary in Scotland - so much 'wildscape'). Figure 158 is a map of the National Parks of England and Wales.

Main functions -

- To **conserve and enhance** the natural beauty of the countryside
- To encourage **the** provision of **recreational facilities and amenities**

Note. This **dual role** may lead to **conflict** between recreation and conservation.

Benefits

National Parks help to -

- **Preserve** the beauty of the landscape
- Protect **wildlife**
- **Conserve** the traditional rural lifestyle and buildings (old barns, dry-stone walls, etc.)
- **Restrict** major industrial and Military developments which might destroy the landscape.

National Parks of England & Wales

Fig.158

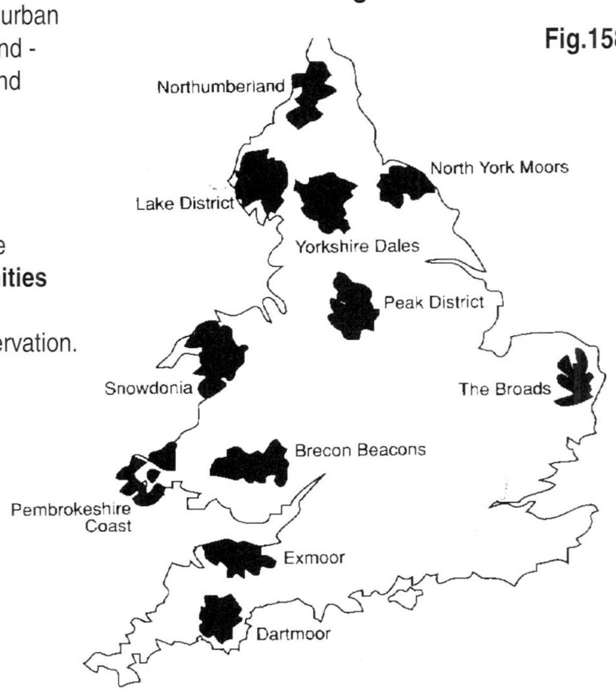

Problems in National Parks

Fig.159 Off-roaders conflict with walkers in the Lake District

- **Improved Access** (New Roads) encourages more visitors which in turn present a greater environmental threat (less peace and quiet)
- **New facilities may** have a detrimental visual effect on the scenery
- **Car Parks, Picnic Sites,** etc. act as nodes or '**honey pots** - attracting large numbers of visitors (this encourages litter, soil erosion and disturbs wildlife)
- **Conflicts** occur between users of parks (visitors, walkers, bikers, off-roaders, etc.) and between users and owners of land areas due to increased people pressure.
- Some popular areas are now subject to non-advertising in Park brochure and information for protection reasons, e.g. Tarn Hows in the Lake District

Note. The creation of a National Park emphasises its scenic attraction which, in turn, acts as a magnet to visitors.

Problems of Land Ownership in National Parks

National Parks may include a wide variety of **land owners** e.g. National Trust, Forestry Commission, Water Authorities, Ministry of Defence, Private Owners, etc.

- The range of ownership makes it hard for the National Park Authority to restrict new Developments.
- Some owners e.g. **M.O.D.** may have particular influence and can claim that new buildings etc. (which destroy the environment) are in the national interest.
- The National Park Authority only owns limited amounts of land.
- The National Park Authority have limited control over private owners.

Development in Rural Areas - the attractions of Glaciated Upland Landscapes for Development Case Study areas - The Lake District, Snowdonia, Cairngorms

Tourism

Scenery is varied and beautiful - mountains, lakes, forest, rivers, waterfalls and glaciated features i.e. corries, aretes, tarns, U-shaped valleys with ribbon lakes and rocky cliffs (truncated spurs) with scree and varied wildlife (Golden Eagle, Deer etc.).
This **environment is** good for **active recreation,** e.g. mountaineering, rock climbing, water skiing, wind surfing, pony trekking, ski-ing etc. The landscape is also good for **passive recreation**, e.g. sight-seeing, picnicking, birdwatching, etc.
Also the **rural farming landscape** - stone-built farmhouses, dry-stone walls etc. and peace and quiet contrast with urban areas (the home of many visitors).
Tourism is catered for with hotels, bed and breakfast, cafes, visitor centres, museums, craft shops, boat trips, etc.

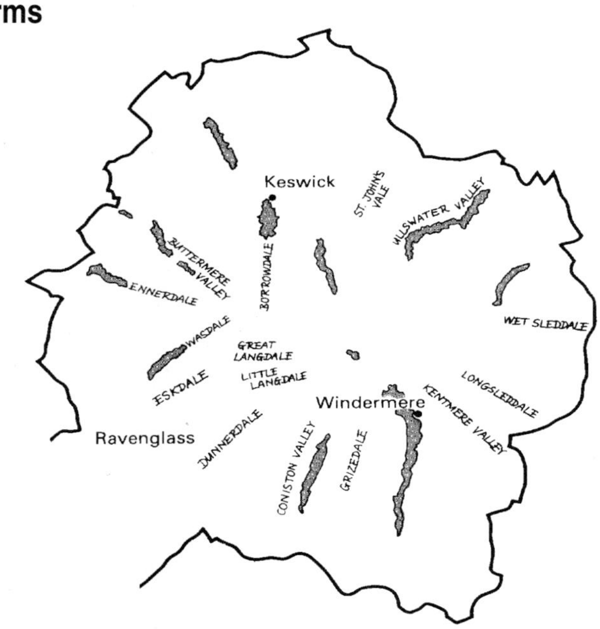

Fig.160 The Lake District - Physical base map

Water Supply - Hydro Electric Power

The high rainfall and steep-sided U-shaped valleys with impermeable rock are ideal for building dams and making reservoirs for water storage, e.g. Thirlmere in the Lake District - in Snowdonia H.E.P. is generated e.g. Dinorwic

Forestry

Sheltered, well-drained valley sides with a reasonable depth of soil are ideal for forestry, e.g. Ennerdale in the Lake District.
Land is too steep, rocky and infertile for farming (apart from Hill Sheep).
Forestry helps to reduce soil erosion and may, encourage tourism (Nature trails, picnic sites, etc)

Mining and Quarrying

Common in both the Lake District and Snowdonia also Limestone Quarries in the Yorkshire Dales.
Strong environmental objections and conflicts with tourism associated with mining and quarrying.

Physical attractions of Glaciated Upland Landscapes
The Lake District

The Lake District has a wide variety of landscape for a small area of the UK. This is partly explained by the underlying geology, most of which is between 400 and 570 million years old (fig.**161**). None of the rocks are younger than 200 million years old except the glacial and alluvial deposits. The various geological upheavals of the area include quiet sedimentary environments of the Cambrian and Silurian periods, major volcanic eruptions, tropical seas, the Caledonian and Alpine Orogenies with their huge earthquakes and twenty different glaciations. Where there are sediments, the landscape is lower and rounder (see figure **162**). The resistant volcanic rocks give rise to dramatic, craggy, jagged peaks such as the Langdale Pikes. The lower undulating plateau and valley landscape of the Windermere area is associated with the softer Silurian sedimentary rocks such as shale and sandstone.

Fig.161 The Lake District - Geology map

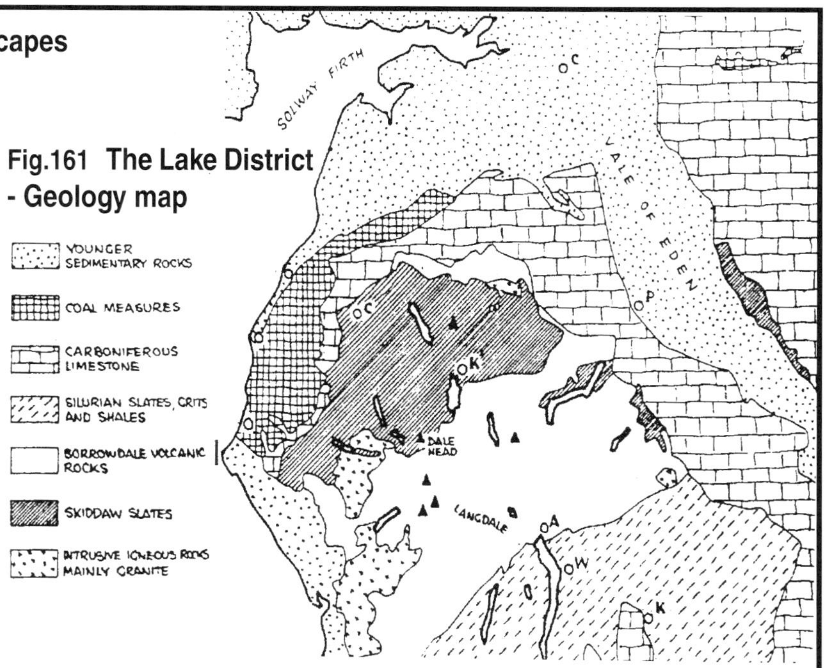

The Lake District - Structure and relief

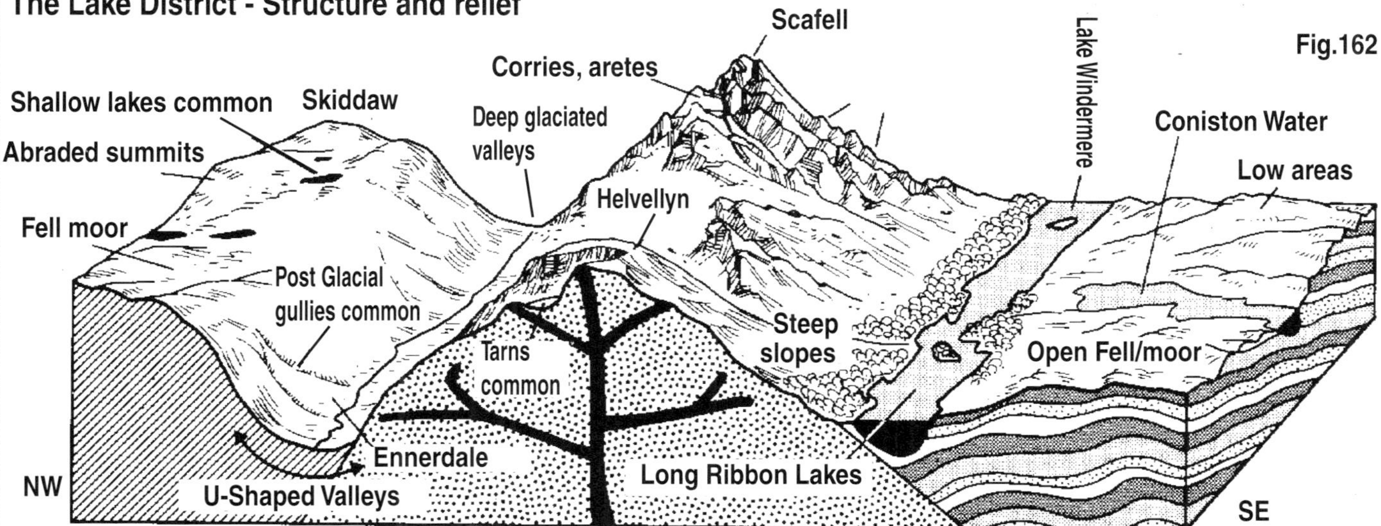

Fig.162

Skiddaw Slates - old hard metamorphic rocks with veins of minerals (copper, lead, etc.). Higher area of abraded summits with open moorland common.

Borrowdale Volcanics - with some granites. A series of lava layers with softer fine-grained tuffs (ashes) compose this central Lake District area. This area is one of classic rugged, frost-shattered summits, e.g. Helvellyn. Differential erosion in the Pleistocene by glaciations has formed many glaciated features. There are deep U-shaped valleys with long ribbon lakes, e.g. Lake Windermere.

Sediments - softer beds of sedimentary rocks - shales, sandstones, grits etc.have been folded and then eroded by ice. The result is a low landscape of abraded (smoothed) hills, gentle slops and shallow lakes - e.g. the Coniston area.

Fig.163

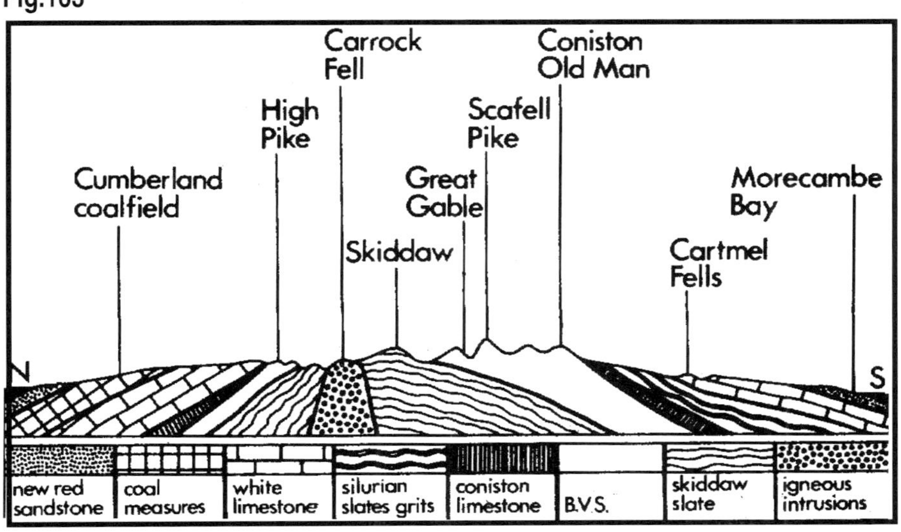

Since its formation the Lake District has been repeatedly glaciated. This has resulted in the removal of thousands of metres of the original rock surface and the development of a radial drainage pattern, emanating from the central Borrowdale Volcanic area. Much evidence of glacial and post-glacial action remains today, producing an often spectacular, beautiful landscape which in turn attracts millions of visitors annually.

The cross-section of the Lake District reveals its geological structure (figure **163**) as well as the main rock types underlying the National Park.

Restrictions on Development in Upland areas

Fig.164

(includes National Parks e.g. Lake District, Snowdonia and also other areas e.g. Cairngorms).

Most problems which restrict development are of a **physical nature.**

Relief
Steep slopes, often rocky, high and exposed - glaciated landscapes in the U.K.are often too rugged for farming, forestry and skiing on a large scale.

Drainage
Often poor, particularly in hollows and valleys - extensive marsh & bog.

Soils
Often thin, rocky and infertile - may be peaty (acidic).

Geology
Mainly hard, igneous rocks creating rugged scenery (steep rock, etc.) - impermeable, encourages poor drainage.

Climate
High precipitation (snow in winter) - low temperatures, particularly at altitude -strong winds in exposed areas.

Remoteness and inaccessibility
Made worse by hostile relief and poor communications (single track roads common).

Problems in Rural Areas caused by large numbers of tourists - and possible solutions

Fig.165

Problems	Possible solutions
1. **Congestion** on roads - cars, buses, caravans, motor-caravans	Encourage **minibuses** and/or **public service buses**, **one-way system** on narrow roads, **restrict entry** for private cars.
2. **Erosion** of footpaths by walkers	**Pave tracks and paths** and **improve drainage**.
3. **Cars parked** on verges along narrow roads	Provide extensive **free car parks**.
4. **Buildings spoiling** scenery	Must **blend with environment**, screen with trees.
5. **Overcrowding** at honeypot villages	**By-pass villages** to remove "through traffic".
6. **Congestion** in peak holiday periods, e.g. summer, bank holidays	Promote **off-peak holidays**.
7. **Noise pollution** and erosion caused by power boats and water-skiers	**Limit use** - encourage sailing and canoeing.
8. **Litter** problems along footpaths, beside picnic sites, etc.	**Provide bins** and / or **public education** at visitor centres, leaflets and signs. **Employ wardens** or park rangers.
9. **Abuse of farmland** - gates left open, livestock disturbed, walls destroyed, etc.	**Educate public** about the Country Code.

Case Study - an Upland Limestone area - The Yorkshire Dales National Park

Description

A **high plateau** (about 600 metres) dissected by valleys (Dales) - main activities are sheep farming, Tourism and Limestone Quarrying. Limestone features are common in the area - see pages 32 to 33 for Karst scenery section.

Opportunities (social and economic) in the area

Tourism, quarrying etc. which provides employment in remote areas and helps prevent depopulation i.e. the communities are maintained and local services (shops, schools, etc.) remain open. Tourism brings economic expansion and local prosperity i.e. more trade for hotels, shops, cafes, B and B's etc. and new opportunities i.e. farmland for camping and caravan sites, tourist trips into limestone caves, etc. Quarrying provides extra jobs in transport, etc.

Environmental conflicts arising from development

Tourism - extra visitors create overcrowding in scenic areas - litter, erosion of footpaths, dogs worrying sheep, congestion on narrow roads, destruction of limestone scenery (limestone pavements, stalactites and stalagmites, etc).

Quarrying - noise and dust pollution, quarries ruin landscape, noise may disturb wildlife, heavy lorries block narrow roads.

Possible solutions

Tourism - restrict tourist access to vulnerable sites; surface footpaths, introduce one-way systems on narrow roads; provide more car parks; picnic sites with litter bins; open visitor centres and guided walks to educate the public.

Quarrying - restrict blasting; restore and landscape old quarries and mines; divert lorries from tourist routes.

Case studies of conflict in upland areas

Forestry in Ennerdale Valley - the Lake District - a National Park - figure 166

Benefits

Provides employment and prevents depopulation. Preserves remote communities. Provides a scarce natural resource (Timber). Utilizes land unsuitable for commercial farming. Helps to reduce soil erosion on valley sides. New roads provide access to isolated areas.

Problems

Takes land which may be used by hill sheep farmers. Makes access to hills difficult. Destroys natural scenery and wildlife habitats. Creates a fire risk. At least 20 years before initial financial return. Destroys peace and quiet of remote areas.

Fig.166

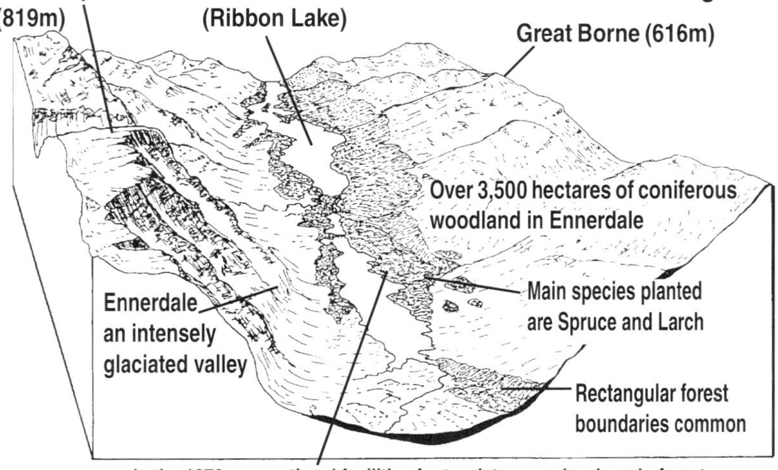

Attempts to compromise and resolve problems

Gaps separate plantations to allow access to hills and to reduce fire risk. A mixture of trees is planted to provide varied scenery and habitat. Plantations blend with relief and contour patterns. Forestry Commission provides car parks., picnic sites, nature trails to accommodate tourists.

Copper Mining in Snowdonia - a National Park

Benefits

- Local employment and influx of workers may **increase the population** and **improve local services**, shops, hotels, etc.
- **Increased prosperity** to the area and new roads etc. to access the site for copper mining.

Problems

- **Open-cast mining** destroys the scenery (an eyesore !).
- **Blasting of rock** creates noise and dust pollution - disturbs wildlife and deters tourists.
- **Heavy lorries** congest narrow roads.
- **Takes employment** from traditional occupations e.g. farming.

Attempts to resolve conflicts

- Promises to **restore landscape** after mining is complete, i.e. reafforestation and flooding pits for water sports.
- Mine buildings to **blend with environment**.
- Lorries to **avoid tourist routes** (where possible).

Expansion of skiing developments at Lurcher's Gully in the Cairngorms - Nature Reserve

Benefits
- **Local employment** and increased **prosperity** for shops, hotels, cafes, etc.
- Helps to increase **all-year tourism**.
- **Reduces congestion** on existing ski-slopes.
- **New roads provide access** for walkers, mountaineers.

Problems
- **Chairlifts** destroy the scenery.
- **Visitor pressure** increases soil erosion.
- **Fragile habitat** (rare arctic plants and animals) is threatened.
- **Destroys peace and quiet** - one of the attractions !

Attempts to resolve conflicts
- **New buildings to blend with landscape** - some will be sunk into the mountain.
- **All topsoil removed** and bagged for replacement in exact original position.
- **Paving of tracks** and paths to reduce erosion.
- All individual plants and even rocks are mapped by GPS systems so that they will be **replaced in exact original position**.
- **Employ wardens** and rangers to help protect habitats.

Rural Land Resources Revision : Summary Notes

The main idea of the Rural Land Resources application section is....
Rural land resources are the product of the interaction of a wide range of physical factors modified by human activity. The resultant rural landscapes offer a variety of physical, economic and social opportunities.

Landscape characteristics covered in Rural Land Resources

1. Covered in both the Lithosphere and Rural Land Resources sections - need to understand three different landscape types -
   - **Glaciated uplands** - e.g. Lake District, Cairngorms
   - **Upland Limestone** - e.g. Yorkshire Dales
   - **Scarp & Vale scenery** - e.g. The South Downs
2. Candidates must know the characteristic **landscape features** for each of the three types listed above - link with Lithosphere revision.
3. Rural land Resources requires detailed understanding of Rural Land **Management** - i.e. conservation bodies and methods, conflicts over land use, rural management schemes, National Parks.

Managing the Countryside

1. **Conservation** is needed in the UK because of our beautiful scenery; urban expansion into rural areas; increased leisure time and recreation; improved access via roads; visitor pressure
2. In England & Wales there are **two** main organisations involved -
   - **English Nature** - Nature Reserves and SSSIs
   - **Countryside Commission** - National Parks
3. In Scotland there is **one** major organisation involved -
   - **Scottish Natural Heritage** - (SNH) conservation work
4. Management Policies about **preservation** (moth-balling - no change in landscape) versus **conservation** (a working landscape conserved through local decision making) - these include -
   - **ESAs** (Environmentally Sensitive Areas)
   - **LFAs** (Less Favoured Areas)
   - **FDGs** (Farm Diversification Grants)
   - **Quotas** - EU limits to production
   - **Set Aside Schemes**

National Parks - Lake District, Snowdonia, Dartmoor, etc.

1. **Eleven National Parks** designated in 1949 in England & Wales to
   - **protect** the countryside from urban sprawl
   - **increase visitor access** to the countryside
2. This **dual role** can result in **conflict** between conservation and recreation

Problems in National Parks

1. Improved access increases visitor pressure which in turn causes greater environmental threats especially around **honeypots**
2. New facilities may have detrimental visual effects on scenery
3. Conflicts between users and users (e.g. walkers and bikers) and between users and owners (e.g. walkers and landowners)
4. Land ownership problems in National Parks include -
   - **wide range of ownership** can increase new development
   - **MOD** can cause problems with new building/overflying
   - **National Park Authorities** often only own limited areas
   - **Only limited control** over private owners possible

Development in Rural Areas - attractions of National Parks

1. **Tourism** - major development due to unique scenery and wild life - great for active and passive recreation; tourist related farming and economic boost to the local communities
2. **Water Supply developments (HEP)** - high rainfall and U-shaped valleys good for building dams and reservoirs (water storage)
3. **Forestry** - major plantations suited to remote and high areas
4. **Mining and Quarrying** - common e.g. Slates and Limestones

Restrictions on development in Upland Areas

1. Main problems are of a **physical nature** including
   - **relief** • **drainage** • **soils** • **geology** • **climate**
   - **remoteness and inaccessibility**

Problems caused by tourists and possible solutions

1. Main problems caused by tourists include the following -
   - **road congestion**
   - **footpath erosion**
   - **visual pollution**
   - **overcrowding**
   - **noise and litter pollution**
   - **abuse of farmland**
2. Possible solutions to the above problems include -
   - encourage alternative road use - minibuses, one-way systems
   - pave tracks and paths
   - by-pass villages
   - provide car parks
   - limit use of some areas
   - promote off-peak holidays
   - educate the public

Case Studies worth knowing about ....

1. **Lake District** as a glaciated upland National Park
2. The **Yorkshire Dales** as an upland limestone National Park
3. **Conflict** studies - Ennerdale Valley, Copper Mining in Snowdonia, Lurcher's Gully (Cairngorm Skiing expansion)

Rural Land Resources Revision : Unit style assessments

1. Refer to Map Extract **1056/01M2** - **Ingleton, Yorkshire**

a. The photographs below were taken in the area of the map extract and show typical scenic features to be found in the Yorkshire Dales National Park.
Explain in detail the formation of the main scenic features shown in figures **167 and 168** and describe what underground features one might expect to find in the cave system shown in figure **169**. (6)

Fig.167 - Thornton Force waterfall

Fig.168 - Limestone pavement near Ingleborough

Fig.169 - Entrance to White Scar Caves

b. Figure 170 shows a partly drawn sketch section between (700755) and (750755).
Copy and complete figure 170 and annotate (i) **relief features** typical of a Carboniferous limestone area (ii) **drainage features** to show clearly the boundaries between pervious and impervious rocks. (5)

Fig.170

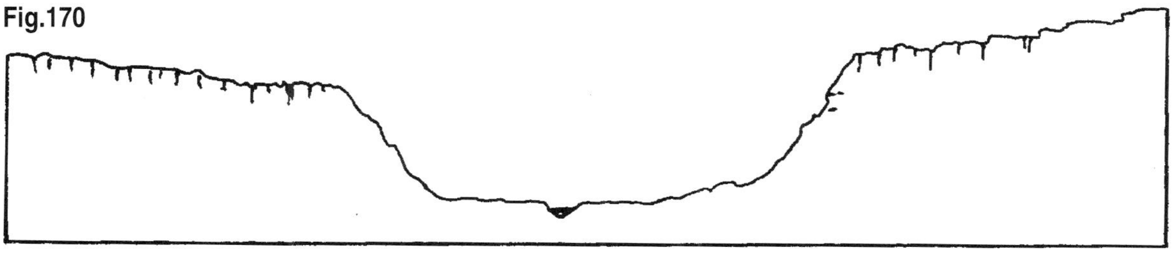

c. Area **X** on the map (fig.171) shows a variety of potentially conflicting land uses within a small area.
i. Identify at least **four** different land uses in the area (2)
ii. Explain **potential conflicts** between land uses in the area (4)
iii. Much of area **X** lies within the National Park. In what ways might this status encourage or discourage future developments ? (3)

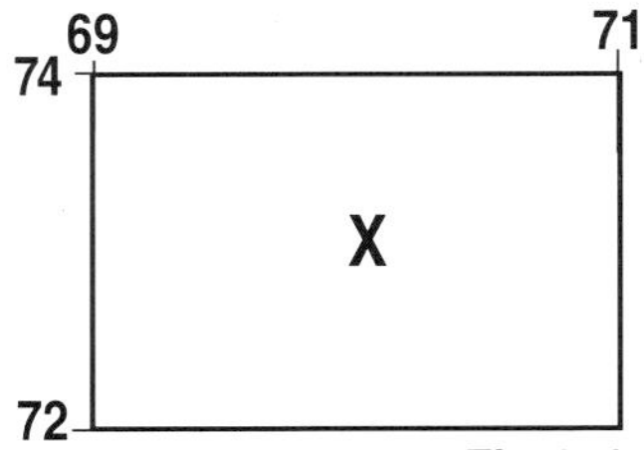

Fig.171

Total = 20 marks

2. Figure **172** is a sketch showing the relief across a **scarp and vale** area in South East England.

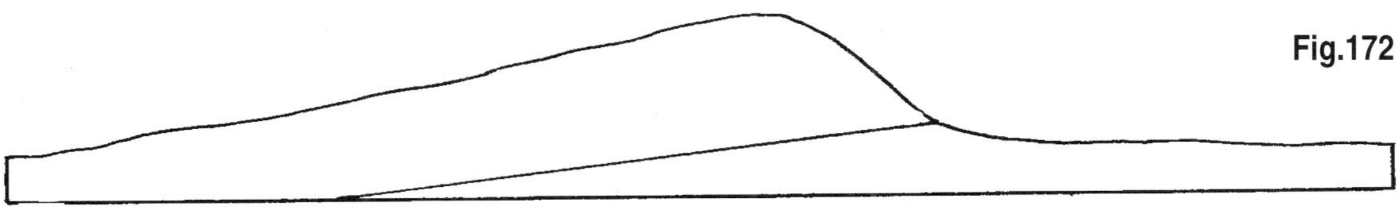

Fig.172

a. **Trace the outline of fig.172** and annotate the diagram to describe the relief and drainage. (5)
b. Explain the **drainage system** of this structure. (2)
c. Describe how the relief and drainage may have influenced the location and distribution of ancient and modern settlement in an area such as this. (4)
d. Areas of South East England have been affected by a variety of rural management schemes, e.g. Set Aside, Quotas, ESAs and SSSIs, etc. Choose **two** such schemes and, for each, outline its purpose and the impact it might have on the local environment. (5)
e. The rural landscape of South East England has experienced many changes in the last fifty years. .
Identify major changes to the rural landscape and comment on the possible environmental impact. (4)

Total = 20 marks

Rural land Resources : Exam style assessments

1. **a.** Describe the c**haracteristic features** of the landscape in a **named** part of the **U.K.** -

either a **glaciated upland** area
or an **upland limestone** area (6)

b. Explain, with the aid of diagrams, the formation of any **two** features you have described in your answer to question 1a.. (5)

c. Study figures **173** and **174**

Fig.173 Land Ownership in three National Parks			
Owner	**Dartmoor**	**Lake District**	**Peak District**
Private	**28**	**63**	**78**
Park Authority	**5**	**3**	**2**
MOD	**27**	**0**	**0**
Water Authority	**3**	**7**	**14**
Forestry Com.	**20**	**5**	**1**
National Trust	**1**	**22**	**5**
Other	**19**	**0**	**0**

Fig.174 National parks in England & Wales

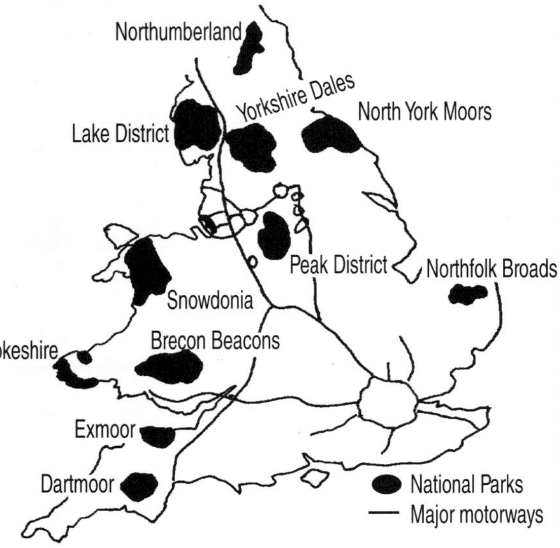

d. Comment on the **different patterns of land ownership**, and identify **potential problems** which might result from the limited ownership of the Park Authority. (5)

e. For a **National Park**, or **upland area** of your choice, identify problems caused by **increasing visitor pressure** and suggest **possible solutions** to these problems. (9)

Total = 25 marks

2. Study figure **175.**

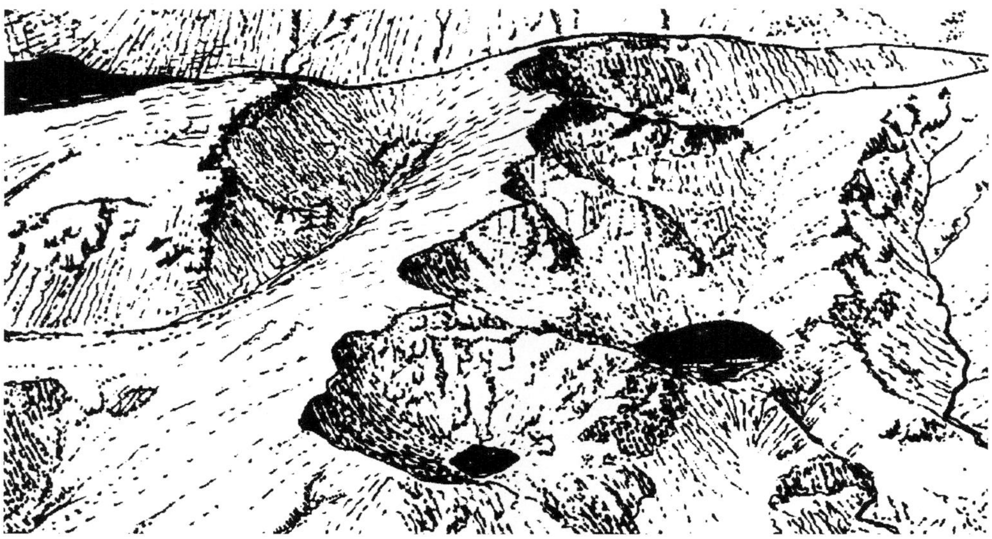

Fig.175 Upland glaciated landscape

a. Upland areas such as that of the Cairngorms contain glaciated features which are characteristic of such areas. These characteristic features make them attractive to visitors.
Describe and explain the **formation of three physical features** in the Cairngorms or in any glaciated upland area you have studied. (9)

b. Areas such as the Cairngorms have considerable **potential for economic development** and yet the prospect of such development is not always welcomed.

i. For an **upland area** of your choice describe and explain the **economic and resultant social benefits** which might result from development (8)

ii. Identify possible **sources of objection** to economic development and present arguments which might be used to support these viewpoints. (9)

Total = 25 marks

12. Rural Land Degradation
Application

The main idea of the Rural Land Degradation application section is....
Rural land resources are subject to degradation, which may be the result of natural processes, human activity or a combination of both. The decline in land productivity & other consequences of land degradation have direct social and economic consequences and have led to the development of soil conservation and land management strategies.

What do you need to know ?

Students should have a knowledge and understanding of -

A The nature and processes of soil erosion and degradation (desertification), impact of vegetation removal, soil erosion by water (sheet, rill, gully) and soil erosion by wind.

B The effects of climate and its variability on these processes, problems posed by climatic variability in North America (e.g. the Great Plains), variable movement of Inter Tropical Discontinuity (ITCZ) across Africa north of the Equator and intensity of rainfall in the tropics.

C The modification of ecosystems caused by human activity, deforestation, monoculture, overcultivation, overgrazing, inappropriate cultivation and irrigation techniques.

D The consequences of soil erosion and degradation (desertification) including physical impact on the landscape and the climate, social impact on people and economic impact on ways of life.

E Specific examples of soil conservation and land management strategies; case studies from the selected areal contexts, e.g. Magic Stones or Diguettes (Burkina Faso) and Intercropping (USA).

The Rural Land Degradation Application

This application is concerned with the decline in land productivity as a result of physical processes and human activity,.
As the world's population increases, the demand on fragile natural resources such as soil also rises because of the need to grow more food, collect and burn firewood and the need for more space. These great demands in recent years have damaged forests, grasslands and the topsoil humans depend on. Instead of using our resources in a sustainable way, we are using them up or damaging them beyond recovery. We depend on the world's soils to grow food and timber, yet we are using them so badly that they are being lost through **degradation, soil erosion and desertification.** More than 75 billion tonnes of soil are washed into the sea or swept away by the wind each year and can never be replaced.

Distribution of principal areas of degradation and desertification **Fig.176**

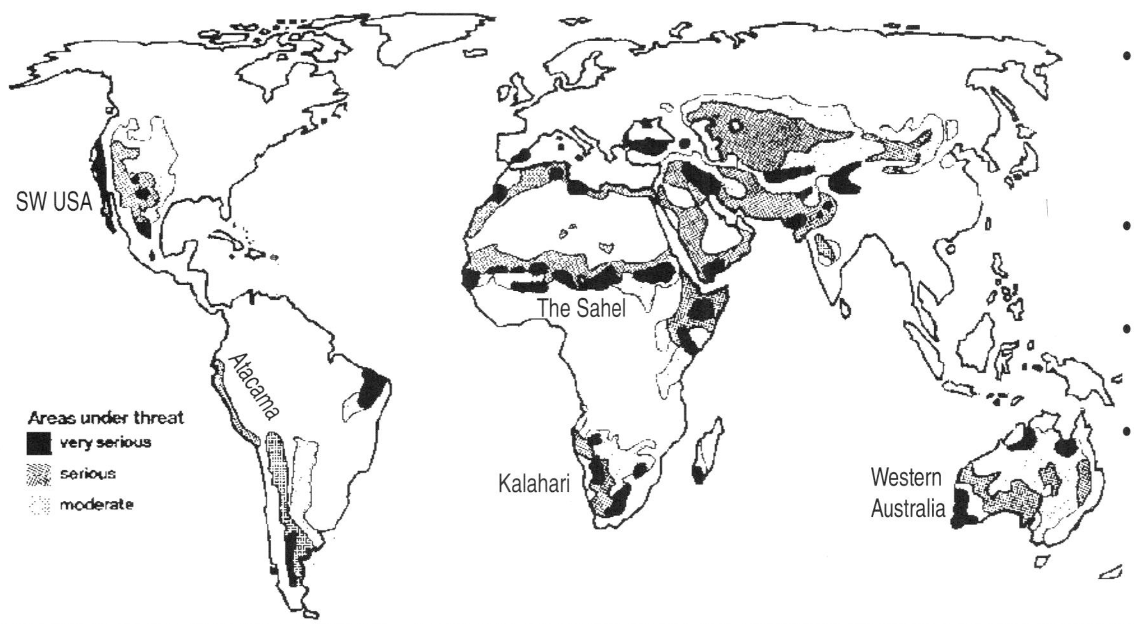

- **The UN Environment Programme (UNEP) estimates that 35% of all land is at risk from degradation**
- **6 million tonnes of land lost to desert each year.**
- **100 countries, 1 in 5 of the world's population affected**
- **Degradation affects two-thirds of nations It is a global problem**

Land degradation is most common in Tropical and Sub-Tropical areas (20˚- 30˚ North and South of the Equator) - mainly on west sides of continents , where frequent dry winds cause prolonged periods of drought, i.e. the Sahara (Sahel counties), Kalahari, central and western Australia, S.West USA and the Atacama Desert (Peru and Chile). The most valuable areas surround the deserts themselves.

Note. In Africa north of the Equator the movement of the ITCZ brings a mixture of periods of drought and heavy rainfall. In North America's Great Plains precipitation is very unpredictable with major fluctuations from year to year. The above conditions worsen the problems of degradation.

General processes and causes of degradation

These are usually related to **unreliable climate**, i.e. periods of drought with occasional heavy rain.

There are three kinds of action which commonly lead to land degradation - **physical, biological and chemical action.**
Physical **- often causes the soil to compact - where land is frequently used by humans (walking, animal hooves, heavy machinery, etc.).** This wear and tear destroys plants and leaves bare earth open to the weather and erosion. Without vegetation cover compaction of soil often prevents water from penetrating the soil and causes run-off at the surface which in turn accelarates soil erosion. Extreme physical damage is caused where quarrying and open-cast mining is found.
Biological - is concerned with the removal of vegetation cover - trees, grass, etc. More rain reaches the soil and it can be washed away much more rapidly, increasing soil erosion. In dry areas, removal of vegetation increases the effects of the wind which in turn leads to greater wind erosion of topsoil. Other biological action can result from natural causes such as plant diseases or locust or quelea bird attacks (which strip vegetation during feeding frenzies).
Chemical - occurs where farmers overuse the soil - minerals are often not replaced, the soil becomes less able to support plants, the organic content of the soil is reduced, its structure is loosened and more easily removed by rain and wind. Soil contamination can also occur through acid rainfall, the dumping of hazardous industrial waste including tips, and over-use of fertilisers and pesticides which can accumulate in the soil over time and destroy the quality and structure leading to degradation.

Human activities create physical, biological and chemical effects on the land surface. However, it is the effects of the processes of erosion by water and wind which are the major causes of land degradation throughout the world.

Natural processes of land degradation are -

Wind erosion

- **Processes** - Soil Creep (very slow movement over ground surface), **Saltation** (rolling and bouncing) and **Suspension** - (movement of fine soil (suspended in the air) - may be over long distances - important - removes fertile topsoil.
- **Causes**
  - **Climatic** - drought and high temperatures dry out the topsoil, loose dry topsoil is vulnerable to erosion by wind
  - **Relief** - flat, exposed land with a lack of shelter to break the wind
  - **Lack of vegetation** to bind the soil (may result from deforestation and overgrazing which destroy the vegetation cover). **Deforestation** also removes shelter which could protect the soil
  - **Poor farming techniques** e.g. Monoculture (drains the soil of nutrients), Ploughing more vulnerable marginal land, overuse of artificial fertilisers and use of heavy machinery (destroys soil structure through compaction)

Water erosion

- **Processes** - Rainsplash moves fine soil (helped downhill by gravity). Frequent heavy rain may remove surface topsoil (through sheet erosion) or form **rills** (channels) which may be enlarged into deep gullies. Persistent rain may cause leaching, i.e. minerals are dissolved from topsoil and washed away (reduces soil fertility).
- **Causes**
  - **Heavy rainfall** (often flash floods)
  - **Ploughing downhill** (encourages gullying)
  - **Deforestation** (removal of roots which bind the soil)
  - **Relief** (erosion greater on steep slopes)
  - **Overgrazing** (livestock destroy vegatation cover)

Water erosion **Fig.177**

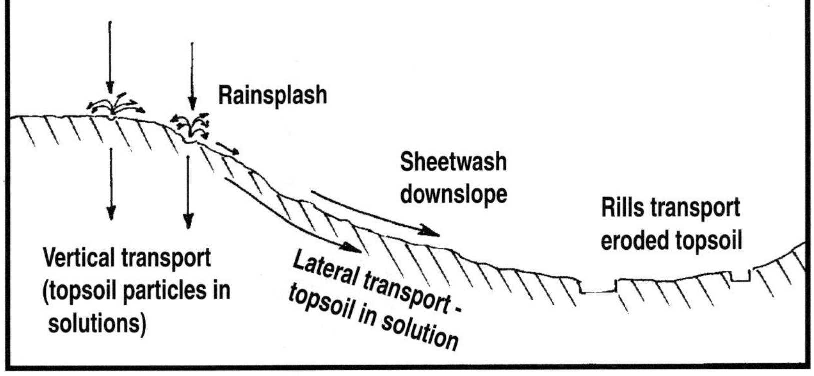

Soil erosion affected by vegatation cover **Fig.178**

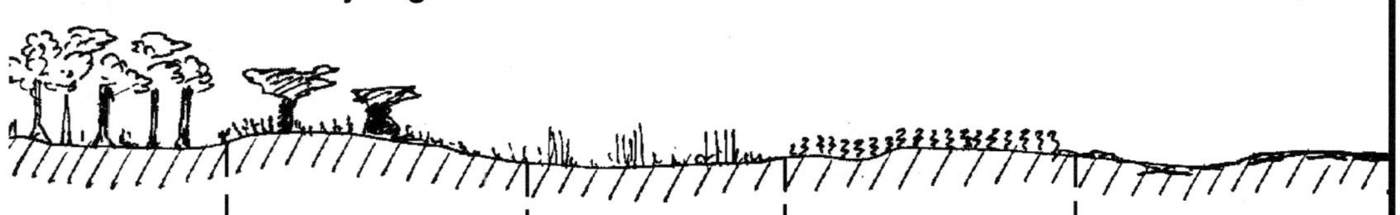

Forest	Ungrazed scrub	Grassland	Millet cropping	Bare ground
No soil lost by erosion.	No soil lost by erosion.	No soil lost by erosion.	75 tonnes of soil lost by erosion.	150 tonnes of soil lost by erosion.
0.1% rainfall lost through run-off.	0.4% rainfall lost through run-off.	2.0% rainfall lost through run-off.	27.5% rainfall lost through run-off.	52% rainfall lost through run-off.

Causes of land degradation and soil erosion

Soil erosion is a natural process. Egypt's fertile plains were created in the desert by the annual flooding of the Nile, which, as it receded, deposited the soil carried by its waters on the surrounding land. The soil had been washed down from the highlands of Ethiopia, where summer rainstorms stripped it from the hills and mountains. Under natural conditions, the rate of erosion is balanced by regeneration. But bad farming techniques greatly accelerate the process. The collapse of great ancient civilisations such as those of the Maya in Central America and the Romans was partly due to the results of massive soil erosion. Although soil erosion occurs all over the world, it is worst in the Tropics. Here, almost all the rain falls in fierce storms during the rainy season. The impact of each raindrop dislodges small soil particles, washing them into streams and eventually into the sea. Thinner soil produces poorer crops, less resistant to pests and diseases, and farmers cannot feed their families on the low yield. In the poorest and most marginal areas, families leave the land, often migrating across borders becoming environmental refugees. In the wealthier countries soil erosion can be masked by the use of fertilisers but is no less as serious. The Dustbowl problems in the mid-west of the USA was caused by overfarming of poor quality of land. There are technical solutions to reduce soil erosion but often the political will necessary to fully implement them is lacking. Figure **179** shows the major causes of soil erosion and some solutions necessary to attempt to solve the massive problems of land degradation.

Fig.179

Causes of soil erosion **Possible solutions**

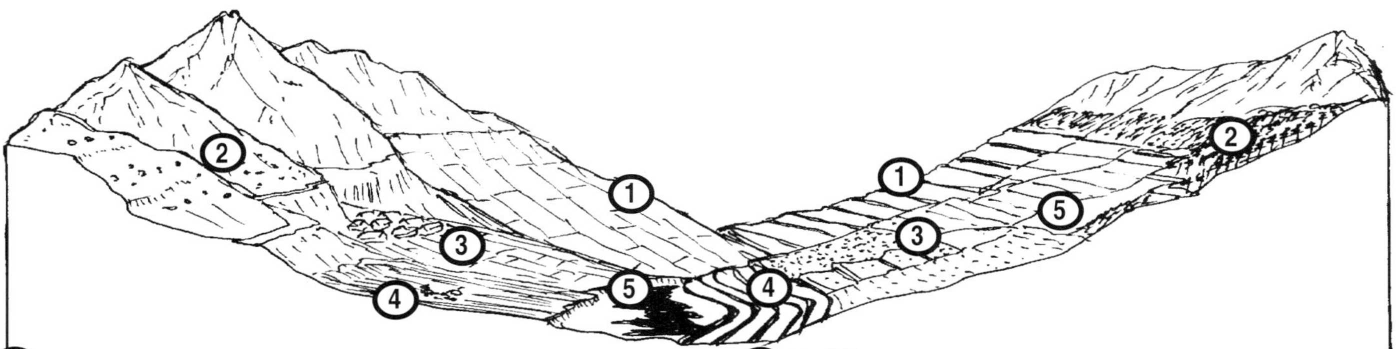

Causes of soil erosion

1. **Farming steep slopes** - lack of land due to overpopulation leads to farmers clearing forest to plant crops on very steep slopes.
2. **Overgrazing** - if vegetation is grazed down to its roots the soil is easily washed away. Too many animals for an area remove vegetation quickly and constantly, leading to erosion.
3. **Overcropping** - shortage of land leads to lack of fallowing (rested land) - nutrients needed to protect the soil are removed quickly due to planting crops too often.
4. **Bad farming techniques** - leaving a field bare, ploughing vertical furrows, removal of trees along field boundaries etc. leads to accelerated soil erosion.
5. **Result** - soil and water run down the valley ruining the fields

Possible solutions

1. **Building terraces** - across slopes holds the soil together preventing erosion and landslips.
2. **Trees and grasses planted** - on the grazing land & areas closed off to allow plant regeneration. Animals can be kept in stalls inside rather being allowed to freely graze. Manure can be collected and used either as fuel or as fertiliser.
3. **Investment for research** - into how to improve yields will allow farmers to produce more in one year and so leave land fallow the next year.
4. **Strip cultivation** - planting different crop varieties to protect each, horizontal ploughing to stop slopewash, planting trees along field boundaries to provide shelter belts and bind soils.
5. **Result** - good farmland preserved. Less migration from area.

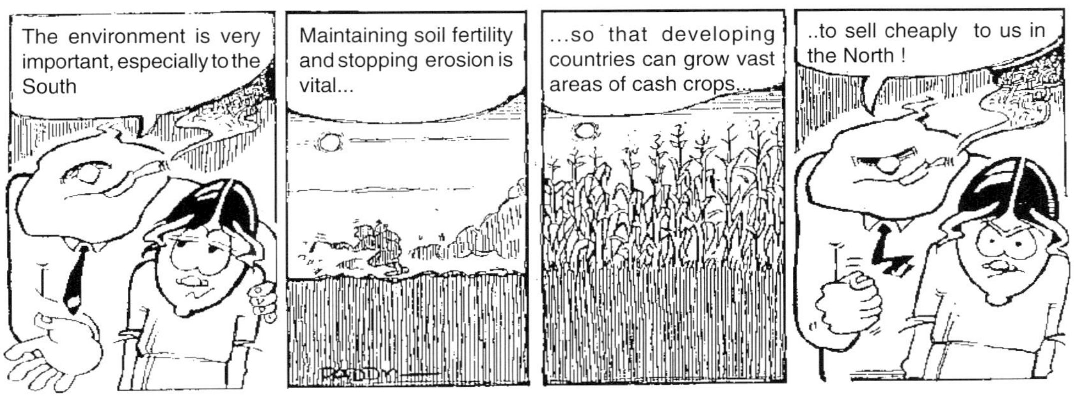

Case study areas

Each case study (two from **North America** and one from **Africa** north of the Equator) focuses on the causes and consequences of land degradation, and also identifies possible conservation strategies.

North America (USA)

Despite more than 50 years of soil conservation practice, soil erosion remains one of the USA's most serious environmental problems (figure 180). About one-third of cropland in the USA is now suffering a decline in long term productivity which will eventually reduce US exports of food. A major incidence of soil erosion is outlined below -

Fig.180

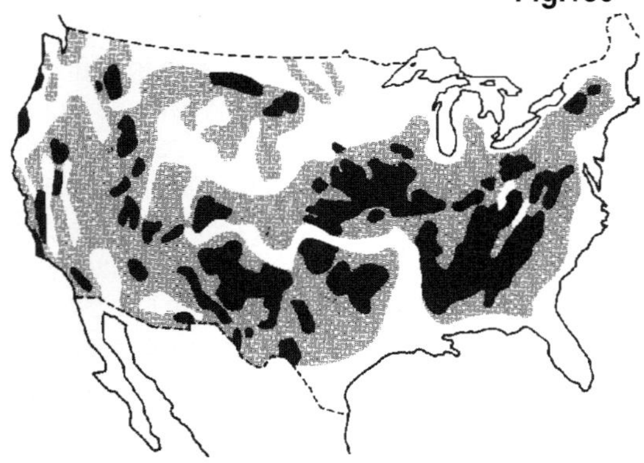

Severe - more than 75% of topsoil lost

Moderate - 25-75% of topsoil lost

The Great Plains (The Dustbowl) - (Kansas, Oklahoma, North Texas) - (Main process - degradation/erosion by wind erosion)

Physical causes of soil erosion

- **Relief** - lack of shelter, i.e. flat featureless plains
- **Climate** - prolonged drought & strong winds after several years of moist weather and problems of vicious **tornadoes**
- **Vegetation** - destruction of natural vegetation (grassland) which had anchored soils
- **Sandy soils** - often depleted of moisture

Human causes of soil erosion

- **Overcultivation** - during years with plenty of rainfall in the 1920s marginal grassland areas were ploughed to increase crop production.
- **Monoculture** - planting only wheat or cotton without use of fallowing or crop rotation to restore soil moisture/fertility.

Note. In the 1930's, when periods of drought arrived, the topsoil without moisture and humus to bind it together was easily eroded and removed by strong winds - hence the name 'Dustbowl'.

Dustbowl location Fig.181

Results

Environmental

Topsoil blown away in huge duststorms (or "black blizzards") - the remaining soil was barren and infertile - unsuitable for crop production.

Social and economic

Crop failure - lack of income for farmers - poverty - as soil became infertile, farms were abandoned with unemployment amongst farmworkers
Communities broke up and local shops, etc. were forced to close through lack of business .
The region was depopulated, with migration to find work in other states e.g. California..

Solutions

The **US Soil Conservation Service** was set up and used the following methods:-

- **Anchoring the soil** with long-rooted, drought-resistant grasses (also increase the soil's humus content)
- **Shelter Belts** planted to act as wind breaks
- **Fallowing** - to help retain moisture and restore soil fertility
- **Diversification** of agriculture - crop rotation instead of monoculture to maintain soil fertility
- **Irrigation** in drier areas to keep soil moist
- **Return marginal areas** to grass (roots anchor soil)
- **Contour Ploughing** (on sloping ground) to prevent formation of rills and gullies by rainwater)
- **Strip cultivation - different** crops planted in strips parallel to contours or perpendicular to prevailing wind - harvested at different times - helps to protect the soil

Effectiveness

Conservation methods have helped restore soil fertility and increase crop yields.
However, soil is at risk from **variable climate** (drought and occasional heavy rain).
As more land is needed for **urban expansion** and **new roads,** farmland might again be put at risk.

North America (USA) continued...

The Tennessee Valley

Main process - degradation/erosion by water

Physical causes of soil erosion and land degradation
Steeply sloping land and heavy rainfall causing sheet and gully erosion - made worse by a lack of vegetation and tree cover to bind the soil.

Human causes of soil erosion and land degradation
- Land cleared of trees (deforestation)
- Repeated planting of 'cash crops' e.g. tobacco which depleted the soil of nutrients
- Shortage of organic fertiliser
- Ploughing encouraged water erosion down the slope - land was left bare and exposed after the harvest
- As soil became infertile, farmers moved to clear new areas leading to more erosion and degradation.

Location of the Tennessee Valley Authority (TVA)

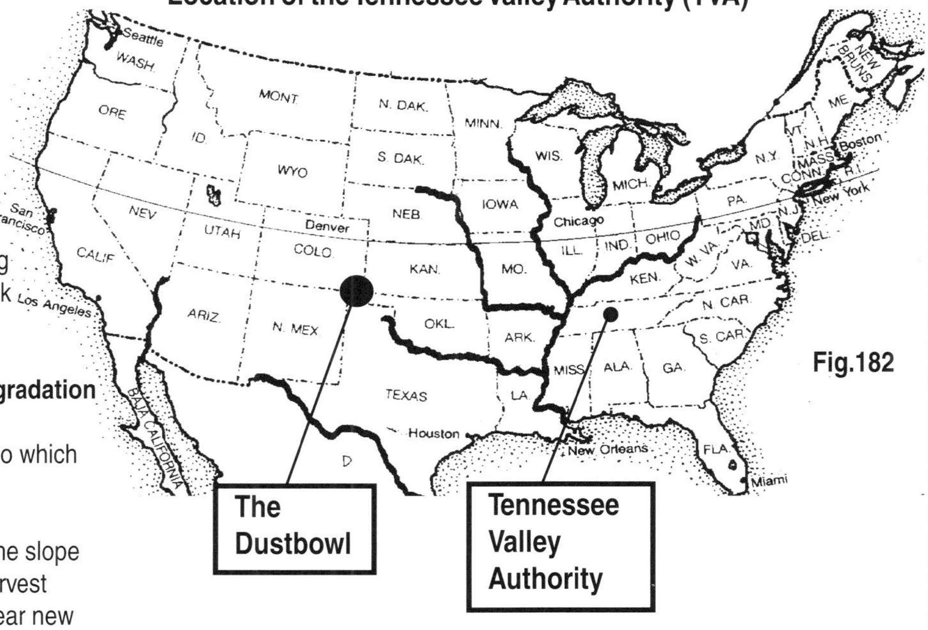

Fig.182

Tennessee Valley Authority

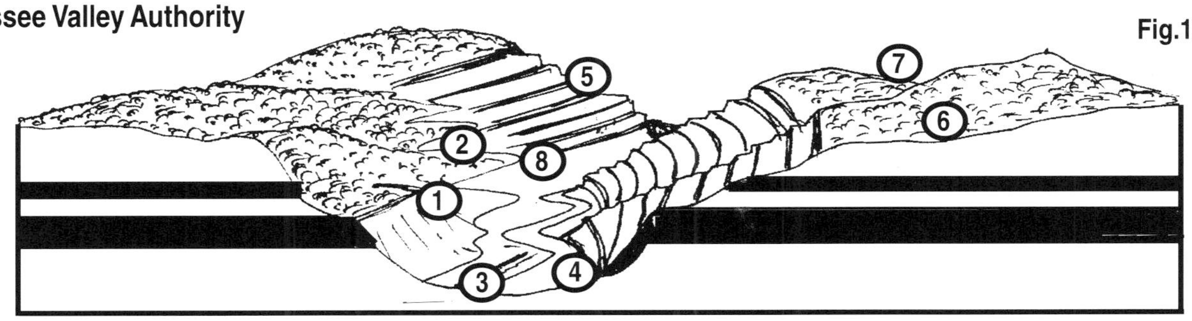

Fig.183

Results

Environmental

① Fertile topsoil on steep ground was removed by sheet erosion.
② Gullies made land difficult to plough
③ Soil was washed into rivers causing flooding and formation of swamps where malarial mosquitoes bred.
④ Scars on the landscape from local mining and quarrying
⑤ Contour mining common

Social and economic

⑥ Failure of 'cash crops' caused loss of income and widespread poverty.
⑦ Unemployment with depopulation and abandonment of some mountain villages.
⑧ The poor living conditions required large-scale Government intervention schemes (e.g. the Tennessee Valley Authority (TVA)) to relieve suffering and deprivation.

Solutions
- **In 1933 the Tennessee Valley Authority** (TVA) was set up to restore the area. Help was given to the people themselves (education, etc.), but the main focus was on the land i.e.
  - **Re-afforestation** and grassing of slopes to bind and protect the soil
  - **Contour** ploughing (across slopes) to reduce erosion by downward flow of water
  - **Terracing -** steps in the hillsides (reduce water flow)
  - **Intercropping** - planting two crops together (harvested at different times) to protect the soil
  - **Strip farming** - planting different crops in strips parallel to the contours
  - **Gully infilling** - (with fertile topsoil)
  - **Rough ploughing** - allows water to percolate downwards instead of flowing across the surface
  - **Malarial swamps were drained and** returned to their former fertile state.

Effectiveness
Overall the **TVA scheme** was very effective with land being restored and the people able to return to their communities and farmland. Crop yields improved with careful management of the soil and erosion is much less widespread than previously.

Africa - North of the Equator - Desertification problems

Fig.183

Trees cut down for fuel & shelter - roots no longer bind desert soils

Fig.184

Overused, overgrazed area around a desert oasis

Desertification - the advance of the Hot desert

"This is not just a famine we are looking at - its is severe environmental collapse. As the population has increased and the drought has continued, crop yields have fallen. People have cut down more trees to get the same size of crop yield from a larger area. Trees are used for fuel, for shelter and for fodder for animals. The soil is being stripped and the land wrecked. Animals are dying from lack of grass and others are being sold or eaten. Many people are leaving this area in search of food. This has been going on at an unprecedented rate in recent years - the people have been building a desert.."

The Guardian 22.2.91

Each year over 120,000 sq.km of land is destroyed by desertification - a gradual process in which land dies and becomes desert. It is found in every continent except Europe and daily affects the lives, economies and environment of many areas worldwide. Desertification is perhaps most severe in Africa where the countries of the Sahel Zone (see map) and Southern Africa are most at risk.

Desertification spreads like land cancer and is the result of a range of factors combining to create dead-areas often referred to as **piospheres**.

Once piospheres develop people and animals move to other areas in search of food, water and grazing for their animals. Farmland is often abandoned as patches of desertified land merge and become large areas of new desert.

It is estimated that over 30 million people in Africa are affected and many have become refugees, migrating between rural areas or towards urban areas in search of help, food and shelter. The United Nations Organisation believes it will take as much as $35billion and over 25 years to help these desertified areas. Meanwhile relief agencies such as Oxfam continue to help the people by supplying short-term aid (food, blankets, medicine, seeds, tools and money). But it is already too late for many areas affected by desertification.

Fig.185

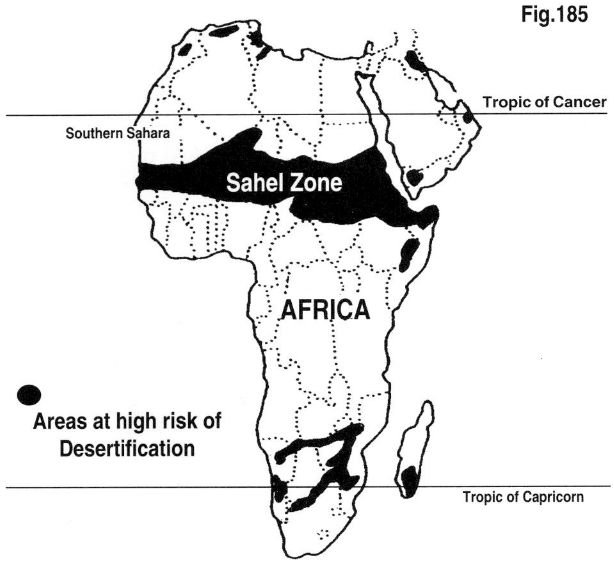

'SAHEL' means shore

Fig.186

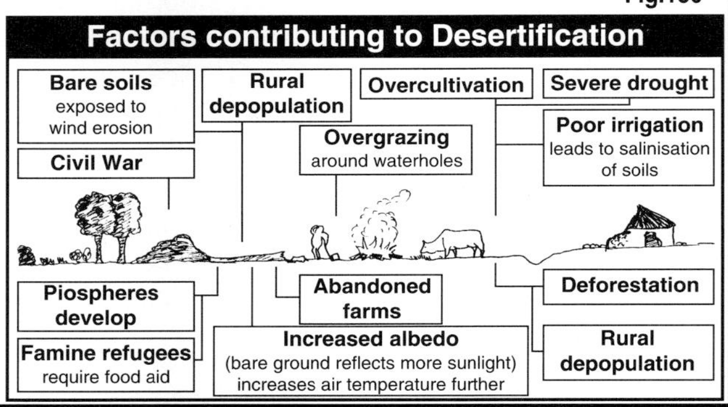

Not enough water ?

In the last two decades rainfall in Burkina Faso has dropped. But rainfall in the Sahel has always been extremely variable. It seems certain that variability has increased, causing major drought problems and adding to accelerated desertification .

Other major contributory factors to desertification include the following - **deforestation, overcultivation, overgrazing, poor irrigation, abandonment of settlements** as well as highly variable and reduced rainfall over long periods of time.

Fig.187

Rainfall in Burkina Faso

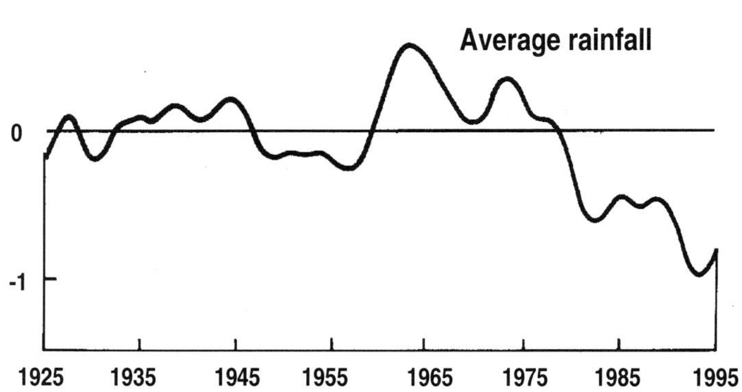

Beginning in 7000bc, the rains in the southern Sahara Desert were frequent and abundant; they replenished ground water and vast lakes and swamps in low-lying areas from the Atlantic Ocean to the Nile Basin. Today scientists are studying the change in the sub-Saharan climate to see if it can provide possible clues about the real effects of global warming.

During the wet period more than 6,000years ago the driest area of today's Sahara was inhabited by aquatic animals (shelled protozoa, crustaceans, molluscs, fish). Near the lakes lived herbivores (elephants, giraffes, rhinoceroses, antelopes) as well as carnivores (lions, crocodiles, turtles, snakes). Some humans also inhabited the area which received 30cms ppt. annually. Today the same area receives a maximum of 0.77mm ppt. annually.

Scientists have discovered evidence that around 4,500bc the climate in the Sahara began to deteriorate. An arid climate became dominant between latitudes 23 and 22 degrees North around 2,500bc. It stretched south to between 20 and 17 degrees North in 1,500bc. Today, the southern limit of the Sahara-Sahel desert region is 17 degrees North. During 16 wet centuries, the region around 23 degrees North also enjoyed winter rains and received ppt all year round. The fauna of that period and the presence of human settlements indicate that the lakes and swamps produced substantial vegetation. The rest of the Sahara was grassland. Scientists have linked core samples taken from lake and swamp beds to the work of Milutin Milankovitch to show that ice ages and the following periods of warming followed a curve of solar activity linked to astronomical factors that affect the amount of solar energy that reaches the Earth.

To date, climatic variations on the Earth have been natural. Now, humankind is intervening, warming the Earth by increasing emissions of gases such as Carbon dioxide, methane, and nitrous oxide.

The effects of human-made warming will likely occur within a few decades possibly increasing precipitation across much of the Sahara region but too late to prevent the major physical and social effects of advanced desertification.....

Physical causes of desertification
- Fall in the water table **- caused by major drought and use of wells - roots can no longer reach moisture therefore vegetation dies**
- More frequent droughts **- perhaps related to Global Warming - leaves soil vulnerable to wind erosion**
- Intermittent flash floods **cause water erosion - droughts also cause a fall in the water table**
- As vegetation dies **roots can no longer anchor the soil which in turn is easily blown away**

Human causes of dersertification
- Population growth **- a demand for more food - requires farming more marginal land**
- Increased demand **for food has shortened the fallow period - i.e. the land does not have time to recover or regenerate**
- Increased demand for firewood **- leads to deforestation**
- **Water shortages lead to the need for more wells, lowering the water table further**
- As the best land is used for cash crops**, marginal land more vulnerable to erosion is ploughed to grow food**
- **Overgrazing destroys the vegetation cover**
- **Poor irrigation** methods lead to evaporation of stagnant water leaving a salty infertile crust.

Results

Environmental

As vegetation is removed with roots no longer able to bind the soil - vulnerable to wind erosion - fertile topsoil is blown away. Land becomes infertile and barren / unproductive turning to desert (desertification). In the 1980's the Sahara was 'migrating' south at 10km per year !

Social

People forced to migrate as land becomes unproductive. Conflict over land between herdsmen and farmers. Males migrate to work in cities leaving villages with social disruption. Food shortages lead to malnutrition and famine. This can result in movement to refugee camps and abandoned villages.

Economic

As land becomes unproductive, farm income falls. Incomes are no longer able to support the population, even at subsistence level. This results in dire poverty and reliance on overseas aid.
Interest on loans to aid survival results in long-term debt.

Solutions
- **Restore vegetation cover** - increases soil's capacity to hold water and provides organic agents to bind the soil
- **Self-help projects** - plots fenced with barbed-wire to keep out grazing animals; then trees planted to provide shelter
- **Drought-resistant shrubs and grasses planted - help bind the soil**
- **Trees planted** - e.g. Acacia - roots bind soil and Acacia enriches nitrogen in soil - provides shade and this reduces evaporation leaving the soil moist (less prone to erosion)
- **Build dams** across gullies to contain erosion

Effectiveness

Some successes with anti-erosion methods (i.e. in restricting desertification) but problems remain. The continuing risk of drought through Global Warming and population growth, with an attendant demand for more farmland, will continue to pose serious threats and cause further land degradation.

Deforestation of Rainforests also leads to large scale land degradation

Every hour an estimated 14,000 hectares of tropical forest are destroyed.

Each year tropical timber worth \$8 billion is sold from South to North, destroying 25 million hectares of tropical forest. The largest exporter is Malaysia and the largest importer is Japan. Other major rainforest countries such as Brazil (Amazonia), Papua New Guinea and Indonesia are also facing serious land degradation as a result of their rainforests being 'harvested' on a gigantic scale.

Countries with Rainforest areas Fig.188

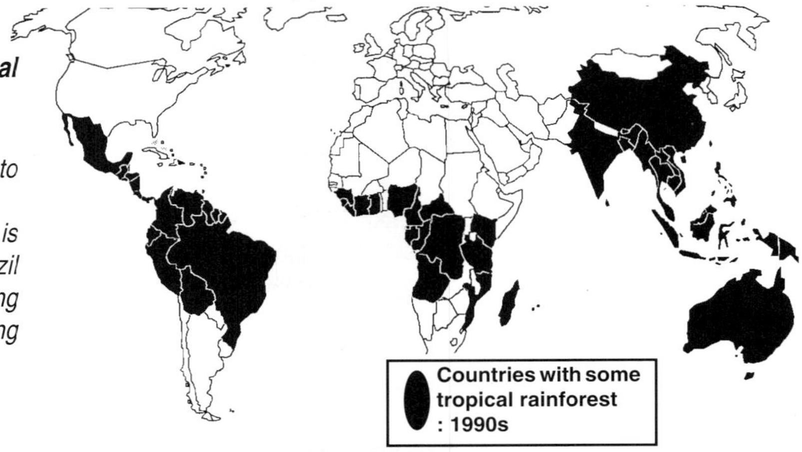

Fig.189 **DEFORESTATION IN EQUATORIAL RAINFORESTS**

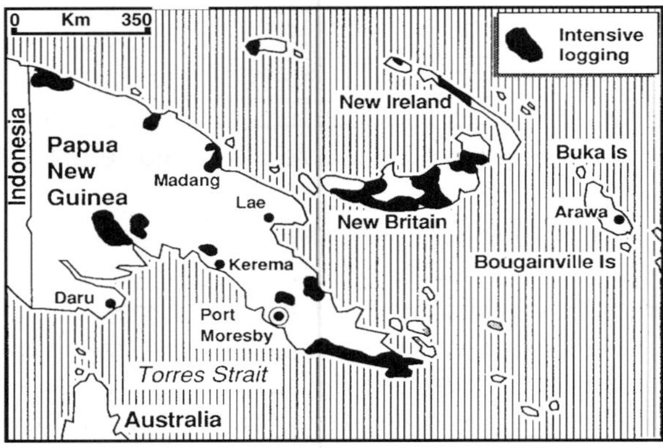

DISAPPEARING FOREST IN PAPUA NEW GUINEA

15 million hectares of lowland forest remain (worth \$100 billion).

Half already allocated for logging developments

There are many reasons for the deforestation (clearance) of rainforests. In Indonesian rainforests, the expanding population of some areas is leading to the clearance of over 1 million hectares annually to create space for farm land. Large international logging companies are also clearing rainforest (e.g. on Papua New Guinea, New Ireland and New Britain). In other rainforest areas, such as the Amazon Basin (Brazil) new industrial developments and the construction of communication routes account for an annual clearance in excess of 2 million hectares. In Central American rainforests, huge areas are firebombed then seeded with grass from the air (which grows well in the conditions and in the remaining woodash). Large scale ranches are set up to fatten cattle quickly - the meat being sold to multinational hamburger and food processing companies.

DEFORESTATION IN RAINFOREST AREAS

Logging companies bulldoze one giant tree in 30 secs (average) and clear giant areas for timber, fuel and global paper industries

New roads, railways & airports use 0.5 million hectares per year

Over 2 million hectares per year are cleared by slash & burn for new farmland (most of which is infertile in 5 years)

Cattle ranches replace forest (over 2.5 million hectares)

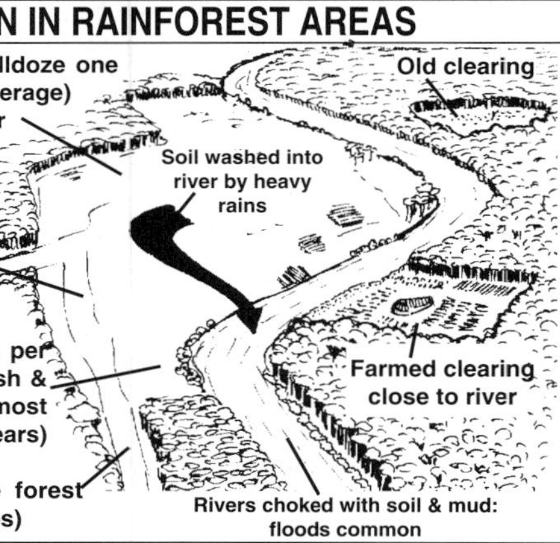

Traditional rainforest agriculture is known as "Shifting Cultivation"

Forest peoples such as the Warani clear a small patch of forest by chopping down trees and burning the trunks. Plants such as yams and cassava are grown whilst other foods are collected (berries & fruits) or hunted (monkey, fish). The soil is delicate and after 2-5 years becomes leached of its nutrient value. The group 'shift' to a new clearing and begin the farming process again. Small forest areas are affected but are 'rested' and regenerate slowly.

There is worldwide concern over the destruction of rainforests, their flora and fauna and the effect deforestation is having on the traditional inhabitants of these areas. Some of the major problems associated with deforestation on a massive scale are listed opposite. But agreeing solutions to both the deforestation and associated problems is proving almost impossible. Many developing countries view their rainforest areas as a national resource, the development of which is thought to be their best hope of alleviating many serious economic and social problems. Developed countries often blame the developing nations for the environmental and social problems associated with deforestation. Most environmentalists consider these problems so serious that they merit immediate international co-operation and understanding, worldwide agreement is required now to reduce the rate of forest destruction before they are lost.

PROBLEMS ASSOCIATED WITH DEFORESTATION OF EQUATORIAL RAINFORESTS

SOIL EROSION & FLOODING

Where the forest floor is exposed to sunlight & heavy rain, tropical storms cause severe erosion of topsoil. Much of the topsoil is washed into rivers and streams causing flooding and silting up of lakes & reservoirs. The Panama Canal is slowly silting due to deforestation.

DESERTIFICATION

Scientists believe that the deforestation of the rainforest areas is linked to worldwide problems of desertification. Removing rainforest would eventually make their climate hotter & drier, destroying the soil, making new desert.

LOSS OF WATER & OXYGEN

Over 25% of the world's fresh water is stored in rainforest areas and over 30% of the world's oxygen comes from rainforests. These would be lost through deforestation and destruction of major rainforest areas.

GLOBAL ATMOSPHERIC PROBLEMS

Deforestation would lead to a major change in the global climate. The '**greenhouse effect**' would steadily increase due to loss of the forest filter effect on CO_2. The result would be a worldwide rise in temperature (**Global Warming**), changes to climate (UK would become steadily milder and wetter, Europe drier and warmer), and the melting of the ice caps, flooding crowded coastal areas across the world, e.g. E.China, Netherlands, Bangladesh, etc.

LOSS OF FLORA & FAUNA

Deforestation leading to the major loss of thousands of species of insect and animal. Perhaps the most serious loss would be that of the forest plants. Already they supply worldwide markets with coffee, nuts, fruits, hardwood timbers, rubber and chocolate. 40% of all medicines & drugs contain substances from rainforest plants. Some more recent discoveries include a drug for combatting leukemia (blood cancer).

EFFECT ON TRADITIONAL PEOPLES

Rainforest destruction directly affects the way of life of countless traditional peoples. They are often forced to move to other areas, infected by new diseases (such as influenza, HIV, etc) and lose their traditional knowledge & skills as they gain employment in logging camps or mines. Some are killed and young people often move to large settlements for a modern way of living.

Rural Land Degradation Revision : Summary Notes

The main idea of the Rural Land Degradation application section is....

Rural land resources are subject to degradation, which may be the result of natural processes, human activity or a combination of both. The decline in land productivity and other consequences of land degradation have direct social and economic consequences and have led to the development of soil conservation and land management strategies.

Land Degradation introduction

1. Land degradation is concerned with the **decline in land productivity** as a result of physical and human activity.
2. **Land is degraded** when it can no longer be used in the same way that it previously was.
3. Land degradation **often happens naturally** through volcanic eruptions, storms, tornadoes, flash floods, etc.
4. Land degradation is also **caused by human activity** which tends to accelerate the problems associated with degradation.
5. Land degradation is very **often linked to soil deterioration** which is caused by misuse.
6. Demand on fragile natural resources such as the **topsoil** is ever increasing through the need for more food, fuelwood and the need for space in the face of a growing world population.
7. These great demands have damaged **forests, grasslands** and the **topsoil** humans depend on.
8. Humans are using fragile resources in an **unsustainable way** and using them up beyond their natural recovery.
9. More than **75 billion tonnes of topsoil** are washed or blown away each year and can never be replaced.
10. **UNEP** estimates that 35% of all land is at risk from degradation
11. **100 countries** and more than **1 in 5 people** are affected.
12. Land degradation is **most common in** the following locations
    - **Tropical** and **Sub-tropical** areas
    - Mainly on the **west side of continents** (where frequent dry winds cause prolonged periods of drought)
    - **in specific areas** such as the Sahel, Kalahari, Central & West Australia, SW USA and the Atacama Desert
13. In Africa north of the Equator, the movement of the **ITCZ** brings a mixture of periods of drought and heavy rainfall - these conditions worsen the problems of land degradation

Causes of Land Degradation

1. Land can be degraded through **physical**, **biological** and **chemical** action
2. **Physical causes** of degradation lead to the soil/land being compacted - overuse by humans (e.g.heavy machinery, walking animals hooves etc.) - the bare ground often prevents water from penetrating the soil increasing run-off and accelerating erosion. Mining & quarrying cause extreme physical damage.
3. **Biological causes** of degradation is usually concerned with the removal of vegetation cover (trees, grasses etc.). In moist areas exposed soils can be washed away by strong winds. Other biological action includes natural causes from plant diseases or locust/quelea bird attack which remove plants
4. **Chemical causes** occur where farmers overuse the soil and soil minerals are not replaced. Thus soils become less fertile, lose their structure and are more easily eroded by wind and rain. Soil contamination has similar effects (via poisoning and overuse of fertilisers & pesticides as well as the dumping of toxic waste etc.)
5. **Human activities** create physical, biological & chemical effects on the land surface and generally accelerate these effects

Natural processes in land degradation

1. Erosion by water and wind is the **main cause of land degradation**.
2. **Vegetation protects soils** from erosion.
3. The **degree of erosion** depends on the erodibility of the topsoil and the erosivity of the rainfall.
4. **Wind erosion** processes include **soil creep**, **saltation** and **suspension**.
5. The causes of wind erosion include **climate** (drought & high temperatures), **relief** (flat exposed landscapes), **lack of vegetation**, **deforestation**, **poor farming techniques**
6. **Water erosion** processes include **rainsplash**, **frequent heavy rainfall**, **sheet and slopewash**, **leaching**
7. The causes of water erosion include **heavy persistent rainfall, ploughing downhill**, **deforestation,** relief **(steep slopes)** and **overgrazing**
8. **Human acceleration** of land degradation includes **farming steep slopes**, **overgrazing, overcropping, bad farming techniques** (vertical furrowing, removal of trees along boundaries, leaving fields bare, etc.)
9. Possible solutions to problems caused by land degradation include **building terraces, planting trees and grassland, investing in research, utilising smart farming techniques** (strip cultivation and intercropping, horizontal furrowing, drainage and irrigation, planting shelterbelts etc.)

Case Studies essential in this Application

1. Students must study **two** case studies from **North America** and **one** from **Africa** north of the Equator. Information is also included in this textbook on the major problems associated with Tropical rainforests in Brazil, Indonesia and Malaysia.
2. In each case study students should focus in on the **causes** and **consequences** of land degradation and also identify the **main conservation strategies** being used.
3. Land degradation in **North America** includes study of -
    - **The Dustbowl** of the Great Plains
    - **The Tennessee Valley Authority (TVA)** area
4. In each case study students must have a detailed knowledge of the following -
    - **Physical and human causes** of degradation
    - **The environmental, social and economic results**
    - **Solutions** attempted and their **effectiveness**
5. Areas of widespread **desertification** are amongst the most serious problem areas of the planet - these include the '**Sahel**' zone of Africa (or 'coast') as well as huge areas of cleared **rainforest** (e.g. in the **Amazon Basin**, Brazil).
6. **Topsoils** are a very fragile endangered natural resource
7. Maintaining a **vegetation cover** is an effective way of preventing land degradation.
8. Topsoil can be conserved by **controlling** the movement of water and wind.
9. **Land degradation can be reduced** if population growth is reduced & sustainable development schemes are used.

Rural Land Degradation Revision : Unit style assessments

1a. With the aid of diagrams describe in detail the physical factors and processes which influence either
• soil erosion by wind **or** **• soil erosion by water** (3)

1b. For either form of erosion from question **1a** above, explain how **human activities** have worsened the problem. Refer to specific case studies. (4)

1c. Compare the **social impact of land degradation** in **North America** with the situation in either **Africa** north of the Equator or the **Amazon Basin**. (5)

1d. For areas chosen in question **1c,** outline **methods used to reduce degradation** and comment on their effectiveness in solving **social and economic problems**. (8)

Total - 20 marks

2. Study figures **190 and 191** carefully.

Fig.190

Soil Conservation: Shelter Belts, Irrigation, Contour Ploughing, Fallowing, Terracing, Reforestation

Fig.191

Causes of Land Degradation: Deforestation, Stubble burning, Overgrazing, Vertical ploughing, Monoculture, Overfarming

a. Identify **two conservation methods** which could be used to reduce degradation in **two** of the following areas -
• The Sahel **• The Dustbowl** **• The Tennessee Valley** **• the Amazon Basin** (2)

b. For each of your four chosen methods describe and explain how it helps to **conserve the soil.** (6)

c. Select **three** of the activities shown in figure **191** and describe in detail how each of these may contribute to **land degradation**. (6)

d. ***"North American countries, with their great wealth should be much more effective at controlling degradation than countries in Africa north of the Equator or the Amazon Basin."***
With reference to case study areas comment on the truth of the above statement.
Discuss methods used to control degradation, their effectiveness and limitations. (6)

Total = 20 marks

Rural Land Degradation Revision : Exam style assessments

1. Study figure **192** carefully.

a. Describe how deforestation **and** bad farming techniques can **accelerate land degradation** in rural areas. (7)

b. For any named area in **Africa** north of the Equator or **North America** or the **Amazon Basin,** describe and explain the **social and economic impact** of rural land degradation. (8)

c. For any named area describe the methods used to try to **reduce land degradation** in rural areas (5)

d. For question (**c**) above, evaluate the **effectiveness** of these methods. (5)

Total = 25 marks

Fig.192

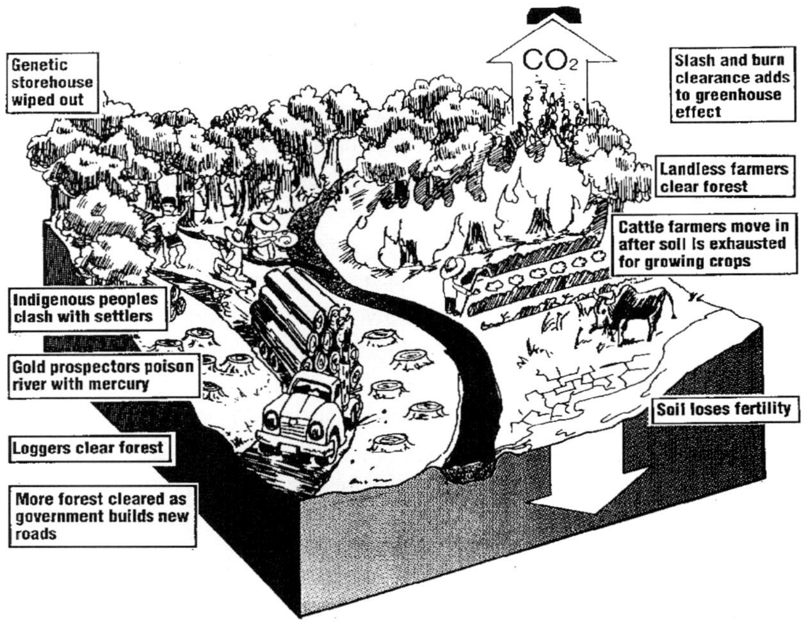

13. European Regional Inequalities
Application

The main idea of the European Regional Inequalities application section is....
Regional inequalities on a variety of scales are a feature of the contemporary world. There is a variety of physical, social and economic reasons for these spatial disparities. Within the European Union, policies are developed at national and international levels to reduce inequalities.

What do you need to know ?

Students should have a knowledge and understanding of -

A The broad EU pattern of regional inequality (the core-periphery model), based on a range of socioeconomic indicators e.g. economic growth rates, employment structure, per-capita GDP.

B Explanations for this pattern, with reference to physical, social, political and economic factors -
- * in relation to the Euro-core:
  - historical access to raw materials
  - high population density - proximity to markets
  - highly developed infrastructure
- * in relation to Euro-periphery:
  - difficult physical and climatic environment e.g. mountains, drought
  - low population density - remoteness from markets
  - high proportion of employment in agriculture.

C The spatial pattern and causes of regional inequality at a national scale within the UK and one other selected EU country (these can be identified and explained using similar indices and explanations to those listed in A and B above.

D National and EU policies and programmes and their impact on the regional inequalities identified in the two countries concerned in C above, e.g. Scottish Enterprise (UK) and Cassa per il Mezzogiorno (Italy), European Investment Bank, European Social Fund, European Regional Development Fund.

E Area of study - European Union with particular reference to two of its member states, one of which must be the United Kingdom

European Regional Inequalities

Pattern of Regional Inequality - a number of **socio-economic indicators** may be used to establish a clear pattern within the EU.
Socio-economic indicators of regional inequality include -
- **Percentage of working** population who are unemployed
- **Employment Structure** (% Primary, % Secondary, % Tertiary) or **% employed in Agriculture and Industry** - see figure **193**
- **Economic development** normally coincides with the emphasis moving from Primary to Secondary/Tertiary, etc
- **Per Capita G.D.P.** (Gross Domestic Product) - basically measures the **wealth** produced in a country in a given year per capita
- **Percentage of High Cost items** - e.g. ownership of homes, cars, etc
- **Economic Growth Rate** (% per year) - measures how fast a country's economy, (industrial output. etc.) is growing.

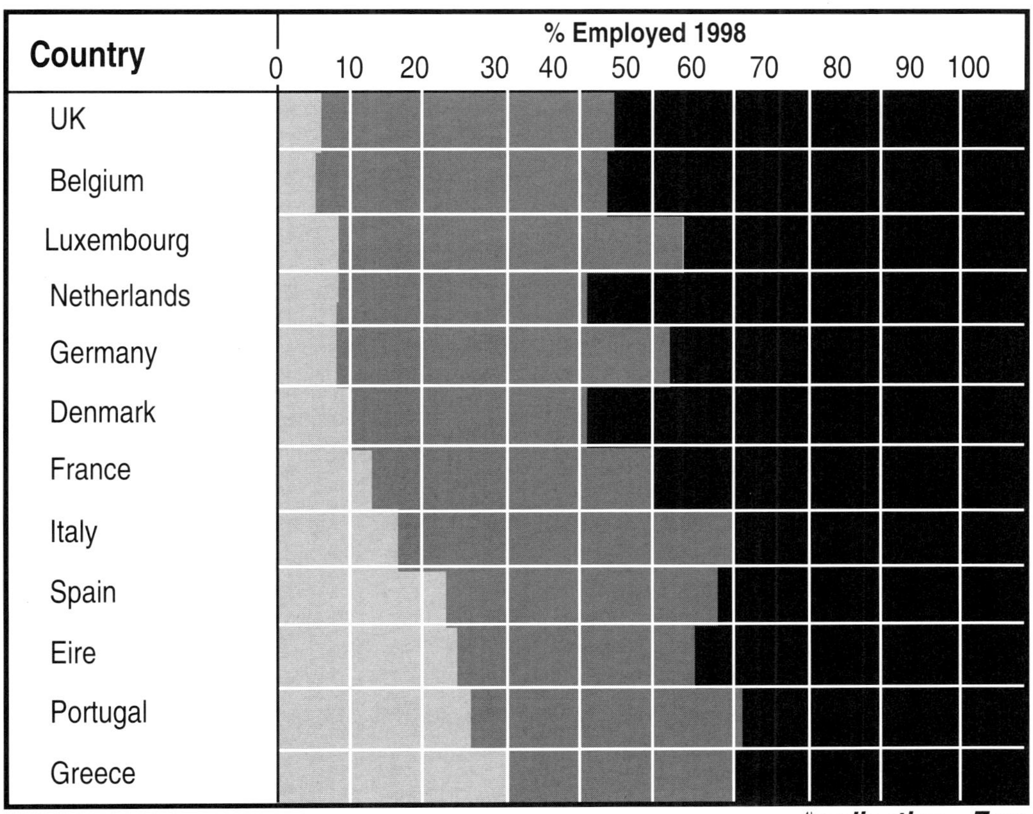

European Employment Structure **Fig.193**

KEY
- Primary Industry
- Secondary Industry
- Tertiary Industry

Note.
A combination of the above and similar indicators may be used to **assess the economic potential** of a country or region within the **E.U.**

Indicators do not tell the whole story, and are not entirely effective - a **low G.D.P.** suggests more **deprivation**, but if prices in that country are comparatively lower then the well-being of the people may be high.

A high economic growth rate may be achieved by **"streamlining"** industry i.e. greater efficiency but more unemployment.

The pattern which results from these indicators produces distinct zones within the European Union (**EU**) - see figure **194**.

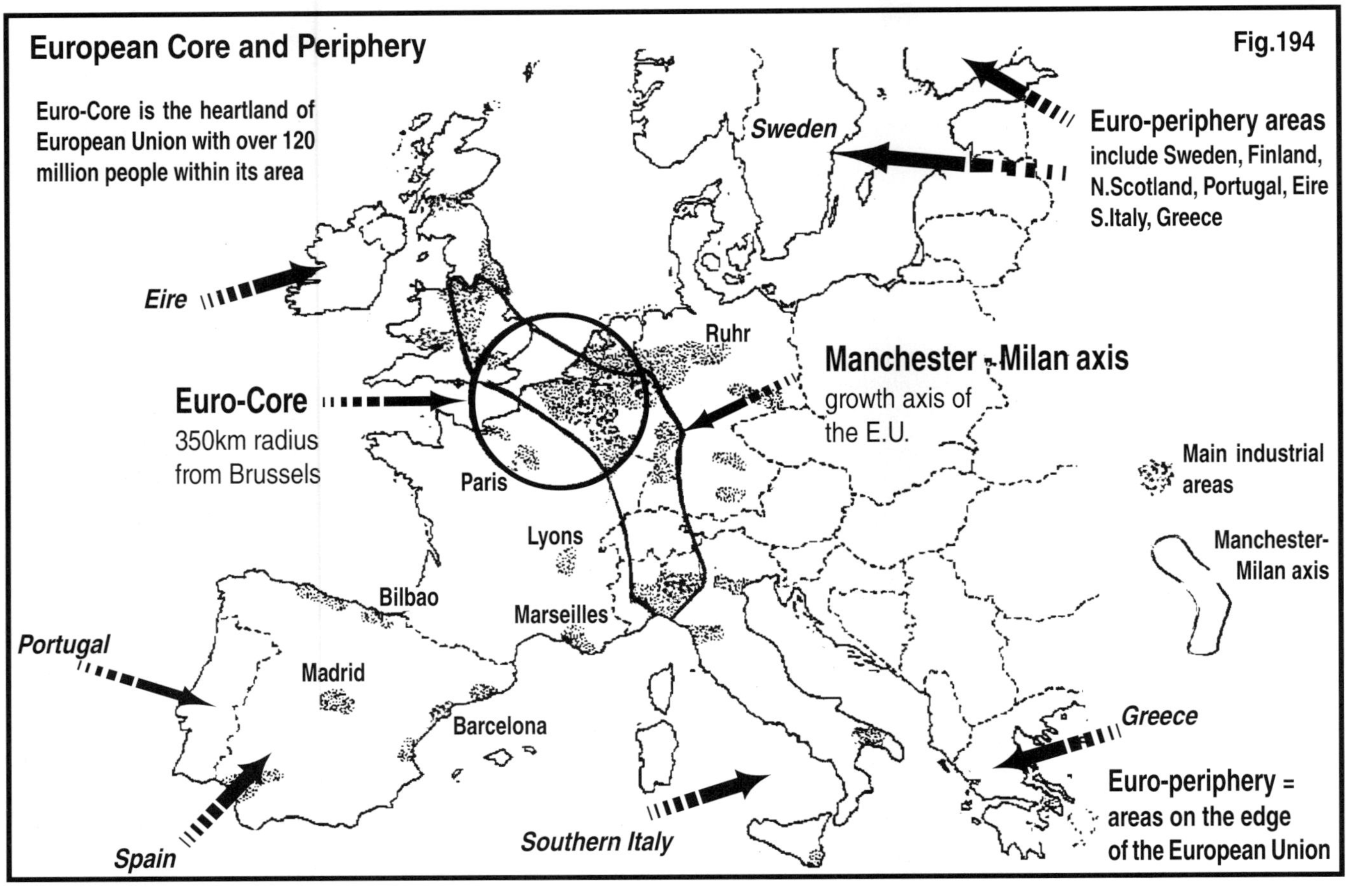

European Core and Periphery Fig.194

A The Euro-Core which has **high economic potential** (includes N. France most of Belgium and the Netherlands. N.W. Germany and South-Eastern UK). The Euro-Core is the industrial and urban heartland of the European Union. This is often defined as an area centred on Brussels with a radius of approximately 350 kilometres. The area covers the most densely populated part of Europe (often called the population heartland - 120 million people live here) as well as the Manchester-Milan industrial growth axis (see fig. 194). Many of the major decision-making economic growth centres of the European Community are located within the Euro-Core for example, London, Brussels, Paris, Bonn, Strasbourg and Luxembourg. The Euro-core also includes the main concentration of manufacturing industry producing a verylarge proportion of the EU's coal, steel, petro-chemicals, engineering, cars, textiles and foodstuffs.

B Peripheral Areas (**"The Euro-periphery'**) - relatively remote areas around the edges of the EU with **low economic potential** (includes Greece, Southern Italy, Portugal and parts of Spain, Eire and NW Scotland). These areas are the most remote within the EU and aregenerally less well developed when compared to the Euro-Core. Often handicapped by distance and dependence upon external investment to generate economic development. Despite economic growth in Eire, Southern Italy, Spain and Portugal, the Euro-Core dominates the Periphery in terms of investment, population, industrial growth and importance, decision-making and political influence.

C Intermediate Areas - regions which lie between the Core and Periphery with moderate economic potential. These include areas such as Jutland (Denmark), South East France, Wales, etc.

Factors which lead to a European Pattern of Inequality

The factors which have contributed to the formation of the unequal pattern of **European wealth and opportunity** may be divided under two main headings -

- **Physical Factors**
- **Human Factors** may be further divided into - social, political and economic factors

Physical Factors influencing European Regional Inequality

Climate

- Influence on **agricultural develop ment** i.e. temperature and rainfall and lack of growing season (gen erally shorter at higher latitudes
- **Water surplus**, e.g. in Scotland (Reservoirs and HEP), **Water short ages** (summer drought) in Greece. Southern Italy (Mezzogiorno) requires irrigation
- May influence **tourist develop ment** (temperature, sunshine, snow for winter sports)

Geographical Location

- Increases distance from markets etc .NW Scotland lies at least 300 km from major central belt markets

Fig,195 Mountain landscapes illustrate physical problems

Geology

- Influences **relief** and **drainage** - water supply
- relates to availability of **Raw Materials** & mineral deposits such as Oil, Coal, Iron-Ore which may influence Industrial development, e.g. local supplies of coal and iron-ore led to development of iron/ steel industry in Ruhr region of Germany, S.Wales, Central Scotland, N.France and the English Midlands. Also **quarrying** for building materials
- **Geological structure** - fault zones in S.Italy can lead to earthquake risk
- Influence on **soil formation** and on agriculture.

Relief and Drainage

- Mountainous areas, e.g. NW Scotland, S.Italy tend to be disadvantaged - isolation, poor communications/infrastructures
- Flatter more fertile areas eg. SE England and N.Italy encourage agricultural development
- Permeability of rocks influences water supply and surface drainage
- Major rivers e.g. the Rhine may improve transport and communications links

Human Factors influencing European Regional Inequality

Social factors

- (related to Geographical location) - **perceived isolation** from "centre" of Europe i.e. lack of motivation for development "Core" location gives an impetus for development
- Availability of level of skills/training relates to new development
- Areas of Industrial decline, e.g. NE England begins a **spiral of poverty and deprivation** - demotivates
- **Population density** (high - market for products) (low - lack of market)

Economic factors

- **Level of new investment is vital** - where there is a lack of investment - a narrow range of industries is available. Where there has been a failure to modernise, industries become uncompetitive. Foreign competition has affected the motor vehicle industry in Birmingham and caused closures. Poor infrastructure affects industrial growth Good infrastructure encourages industrial growth e.g. the 'sunrise' industries along the M4 corridor or Video Valley enjoy excellent communications
- **Investment in infrastructure** affects access to markets e.g. positive effects have been received from the Channel Tunnel throughout SE England
- The **balance** between **Industrial** (Primary, Secondary, Tertiary) and **Agricultural employment** e.g.. North & South of Italy - negative effects from poor access - e.g. NW Scotland.

Fig,196 Large urban areas are markets for industrial products and services

Political factors

- Core areas gain private investment and often prosper without Government Intervention - Peripheral areas often rely on **extra 'public money'**
- There are **variations in Government and EU support** / investment in different areas
- **Government Intervention** eg. subsidies may encourage foreign investment in declining areas such as South Wales
- **EU Objective One** funding targets specific areas for Investment/Develop ment e.g. The Highlands of Scotland
- **Absence/withdrawal of Government Support** can lead to decline and unemployment (e.g. Shipbuilding in Glasgow).

National Patterns of Inequality Two different examples are required. The **U.K.** and **Italy** are covered below.

United Kingdom

Spatial Pattern

In the U.K. a general "**North - South**" split can be identified, based on a number of **indicators** -

Fig.195

Indicator	Scotland	North of England	South East England
G.D.P. (EU average = 100)	80 - 99	80 - 99	120 - 139
Average House Price (1997 £)	60 - 65,000	55 - 60,000	> 86,000
Unemployment rate (1997 %)	7.7	9.1	7.8
Car Ownership (1997 %)	63	62	77

Note. The statistics do tend to support a "North - South" pattern but anomalies can be identified, e.g. in 1997 Scotland had a **lower** unemployment rate than South East England.

Reasons for the pattern of inequality

Physical Factors

- The "**North**" has a generally more mountainous landscape with poorer soils and a hostile climate (with high precipitation, low temperatures, etc.)
- There is therefore a lack of agricultural development
- The "North" is more isolated and remote and inaccessible
- The "**South**" is generally lower and has more fertile soils with a drier, warmer summer which is good for agricultural development
- Although the "North" had abundant natural resources e.g. coal, iron-ore, etc. in the past, most reserves are now exhausted or uneconomic to develop, e.g. coal in Central Scotland
- The "North" is a greater distance from the major markets of the Euro-Core

Human Factors
Social and Economic

- **Higher population density** in the "South" provides a larger market for industry
- More highly **developed infrastructure** in the "South" with motorways, airports, the Channel Tunnel to Europe - better access to markets
- **Greater investment in industry** - "Sunrise" industries in the "South", e.g. electronics industries near Cambridge (often called Silicon Fen) and along the M4 corridor (Video Valley)
- **Decline in the traditional heavy industries** (or sunset industries) in the "North", e.g. shipbuilding in Glasgow, iron & steel in NE England, textiles (cotton and wool) in Lancashire and Yorkshire, etc.
- Many traditional industries suffered from **poor industrial relations** with strikes and inefficient, out-dated working methods and techniques - these led to high costs of production which meant traditional products were uncompetitive and lost out very badly to cheaper foreign imports.

Results of Inequality

Social

- Factory closures in less favoured areas leading to **increased unemployment** with resultant rises in deprivation, depopulation and migration to favoured areas of the "South"
- **Increased perception** of a "North - South" divide causing resentment and social division

Economic

- Closures increase unemployment and therefore there is **less money** available to spend in shops and on services - many of which close down.
- **Decline in investment** in infrastructure
- "Wealthy" areas attract investment and experience more growth (e.g. SE England) with resultant greater division between "North" and "South"

Environmental

- As industry declines factories are often left derelict and rivers polluted. Spoil heaps (Bings) and abandoned quarries scar the landscape

UK North and South Divide

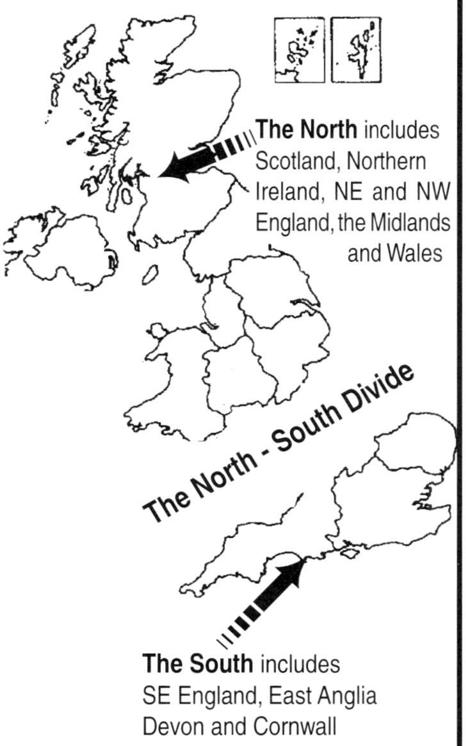

Fig.196

UK Unemployment Rate

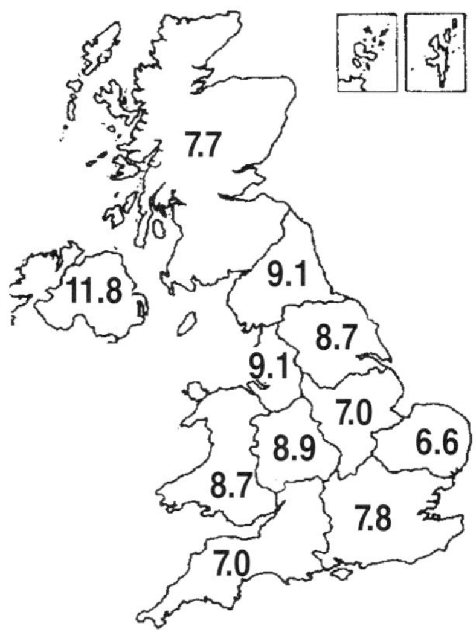

Figures show percentages of the working population unemployed in 1997.

Fig.197

UK Average House Price

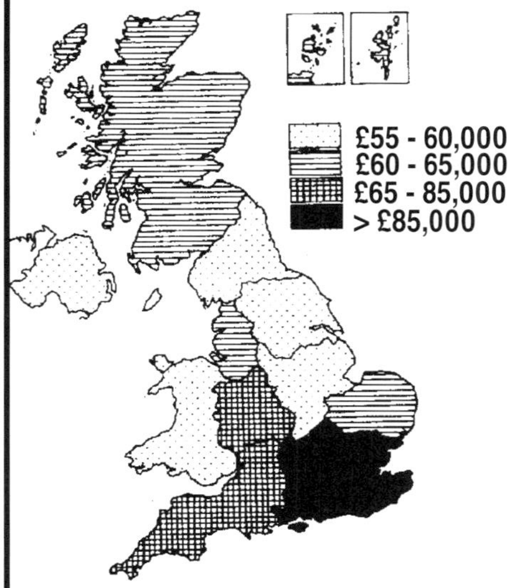

Figures show the average house prices in £ in 1997.

Fig.198

Efforts to reduce regional inequalities

Various policies and programmes have been introduced in recent years both at a National and European Union level to reduce regional inequalities.

United Kingdom

The Government has acted to overcome differences in investment, income and employment levels found in different U.K. regions. Focus has been directed towards areas with declining industry and high unemployment.

Methods include:-

Target specific areas with incentives to encourage investment

- **Assisted Areas** e.g. Central Scotland, NE England (assisted areas now encompass Development Areas and Intermediate Areas) Companies receive grants from the Government for factory construction and training schemes for labour force.
- **Regional Development Status** qualifies for grants from regional bodies e.g. W.D.A. (Welsh Development Agency) and H.I.E. (Highlands & Islands Enterprise).
- **Enterprise Zones** (EZs) e.g. Clydebank, Isle of Dogs (London), Swansea - with exemption from rents and rates, simplified planning controls, grants for technology, building and training.
- **Financial assistance** to encourage investment from overseas firms, e.g. Nissan car plant in Washington (in N.E.England)
- **Subsidies** to help specific declining industries, e.g. coal, iron and steel industries

Location or relocation of Government departments

- **Government Departments** (e.g. branches of the Civil Service such as the Inland Revenue) which employ thousands of workers have been relocated to specific areas to redress the imbalance of employment opportunity, e.g. DVLC in Swansea and M.O.D. in Glasgow

Note. The above schemes have helped to reduce unemployment in some areas, but the combination of geographical isolation and distance from markets in the Euro-Core continues to hinder investment. Improvements in infrastructure e.g. M4 / Severn Bridge to South Wales and motorway upgrading of the A74 (Glasgow to Carlisle) will improve access.

National Patterns of Inequality - Italy

Spatial Pattern In Italy a general "North - South" split is also recognisable but in contrast with the UK "the North" is wealthier than the South of Italy.

Indicator Fig.199	Lombardy "North"	Calabria "South"
Unemployment (EU average = 100)	< 51	201 - 260
G.D.P. per capita (EU average = 100)	>120	< 70
Employment Structure (%)		
Primary	8%	40%
Secondary	60%	15%
Tertiary	32%	45%

Italy - areas and employment **Fig.200**

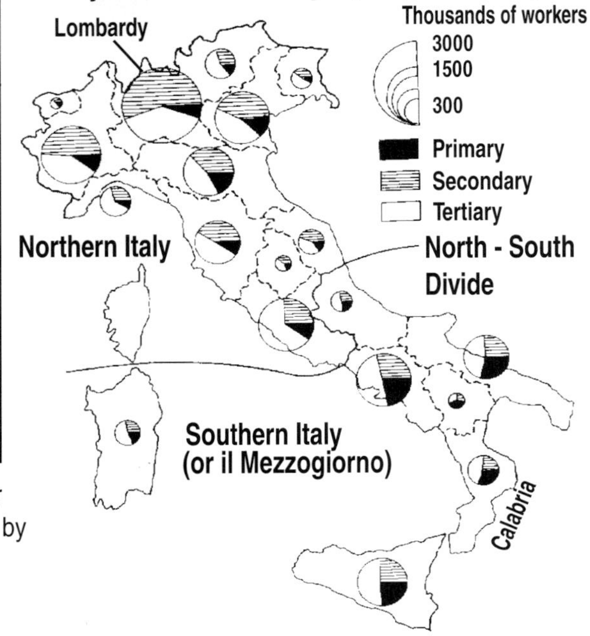

Note. The statistics indicate major differences, with the "North" having lower unemployment, higher GDP and an employment structure dominated by secondary and tertiary industry.

Reasons for the pattern of inequality

Physical factors

- "The South" (known as **il Mezzogiorno**) has a **mountainous landscape** with **thin rocky soils** and summer **droughts**
- The area **lacks natural resources**
- There is **geographical isolation** on the Euro-Periphery
- "The "North" (south of the Alps) has **flat fertile land** - the **Plain of Lombardy** has a favourable climate with warm sunny summers and adequate precipitation.
- The "North" has **abundant natural resources** (e.g. minerals for industry) and a more **accessible location**

Human factors

- The Mezzogiorno has **low population density** with a high proportion employed in agriculture
- There is a **lack of skilled labour** and **high illiteracy rates** amongst the population
- These factors have led to a **low GDP** and have resulted in **large scale emigration** (e.g. to the North and to the USA)
- There is a **lack of infrastructure** with poor access to markets leading to a lack of inward investment
- The "North" has a **high population density** with most people employed in secondary & tertiary industries.
- The "North" has a **skilled labour force** which has produced a **high GDP**
- The "North" has very **good infrastructure** (many first class motorways or autostrada) and many large wealthy cities such as Milan, Turin and Rome which provide **markets for products**.
- The "North" is **closer to the Euro-core** and falls within the Manchester-Milan growth axis, therefore will attract investment.

Results of Inequality

Social

- **Depopulation** from more isolated communities in Southern Italy
- **Social deprivation** and **poverty**
- **Migration** from the Mezzogiorno to the "North" and also overseas

Economic

- Focus of **new investment** in limited more accessible **growth areas** e.g. coastal areas in the 'South" such as Taranto
- **Less investment** in more remote, less accessible areas
- **Closure** of unprofitable factories with resultant unemployment

Environmental

- Many isolated communities are **left abandoned** with derelict buildings, etc.
- **Widespread soil erosion** on steep, overgrazed hillsides

Efforts to reduce regional inequalities

Various policies and programmes have been introduced in recent years both at a National and European Union level to reduce regional inequalities.

Italy In 1950 the Italian Government created the Cassa per il Mezzogiorno - an organisation which would attempt to develop the relatively poor South of the country.

Since the 1950s the main efforts were directed as follows -

Developments in the Mezzogiorno

Fig.201

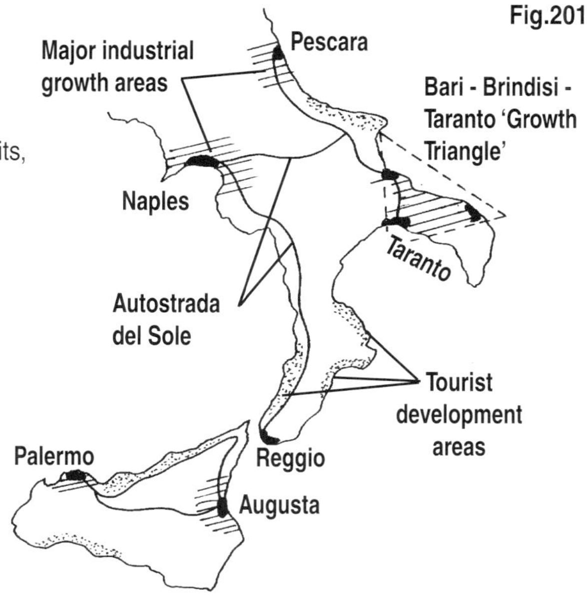

Agricultural improvements

- **Land reform** - the existing large estates (called Latifundia) were split into smaller more efficient holdings
- **More intensive farming** using irrigation gave much higher yields of citrus fruits, tomatoes, grapes etc

Industrial improvements

- **Dams and reservoirs** providing water for HEP and for irrigation of farmland
- **Government grants** - up to 85% for factories, and loans as well as tax concessions to foreign investors, were also given
- **Major industrial expansion,** e.g. steelworks at Taranto, Car manufacturing at Naples making Alfa Romeo, and Petro-chemicals brought 600,000 new jobs to the Mezzogiorno
- **Expansion of service industries** e.g. tourism - new hotels etc
- **State owned companies** had to direct 80% of their new investments to locations in Southern Italy, e.g. Fiat in Sicily

Improvements to infrastructure

- **New roads** (Autostrada), new power stations and water supplies were all heavily invested in
- **Drainage and land reclamation** schemes in areas of coastal marsh were developed
- **Improved education and training** with new schools and colleges were also introduced across the entire area

Note. Major improvements in the area have taken place with much higher agricultural output and industrial growth.

However there are **remaining problems** -

- **Shortage of skilled labour**
- New farms although more efficient remain **distant from markets** in the populous North and the Euro-core
- **Agricultural employment remains high** as modern factories employ relatively few workers
- Selected "growth" areas e.g. Taranto have developed but **less accessible areas remain stagnant**

European Union Policies and programmes

These are similar to national policies i.e. using financial incentives etc. to encourage development. The policies and programmes outlined below apply to both the U.K. and Italy

- **European Regional Development Fund (ERDF)**
- **Objective One** funding for major infrastructure projects in remote areas e.g piers, roads, causeways in the Western Isles and road tunnels and bridges in Calabria - the fund agrees to match other sources of finance - these improve access to attract further investment
- Firms are directly encouraged to **locate in disadvantaged areas** with grants and cheap loans
- **Urban projects** focus on Inner City areas e.g. Glasgow or Naples - improvements for industry, roads and the overall urban environment

- **European Social Fund (ESF)**
- Principally aimed at **boosting employment prospects**
- **Retraining** in new appropriate skills for workers e.g. unemployed from agricultural or Primary industries
- **Assistance to help workers relocate** to gain employment

- **Employment Investment Bank (EIB)**
- Main emphasis is to **boost industry** by providing loans for firms in less developed areas and for modernisation of factory buildings and improvements to infrastructure - roads, etc.

Note. European funding has helped development in areas such as the Republic of Ireland but, as the EU expands, new disadvantaged areas will require direct assistance (e.g. Greece, Poland, etc.). New funding may no longer be available to areas such as the Mezzogiorno or Scottish Highlands which currently receive financial benefits.

European Regional Inequalities Revision : Summary Notes

The main idea of the European Regional Inequalities application section is....
Regional inequalities on a variety of scales are a feature of the contemporary world. There is a variety of physical, social and economic reasons for these spatial disparities. Within the European Union, policies are developed at national and international levels to reduce inequalities.

European Regional Inequalities

1. **Inequality** can be described through the study of the physical and human factors which influence it.
2. Inequality can be described as the **unequal pattern of wealth and opportunity** within a geographical region or country.
3. **Socio-economic indicators** can be used to establish a clear pattern of inequality. These include -
   - % of working population who are **unemployed**
   - **The employment structure** of a country or area
   - **Economic Development** within an area
   - **Gross Domestic Product** per head
   - **% of high cost items owned** within an area e.g. homes
   - **Economic Growth rate** (% per year)

   A combination of indicators can be used to define the economic potential of an area or country.
4. Indicators do not tell the whole story since a low GDP may suggest more deprivation **BUT** if prices are lower in that country then the well-being of the people may be high
5. High economic growth rates can be achieved by '**streamlining**' of industry - greater efficiency but higher unemployment
6. On a Europe-wide scale these patterns of inequality reveal a regional disparity in economic potential producing three distinct zones -
   - **Euro-Core** - high economic potential zone
   - **Euro-periphery** - low economic potential
   - **Intermediate Area** - medium economic potential
7. The **Euro-Core** includes N.France, SE England, most of Belgium & the Netherlands, NW Germany - an area within a 350 km radius of Brussels. This is the most densely populated area of Europe with over 120 million people. This is the main political decision-making area of Europe as well as Europe's wealthiest and largest market place.
8. The **Euro-Periphery** contains the most isolated and remote fringes of Europe - and includes Scotland, Eire, most of Portugal and Spain, Southern Italy and Greece. Handicapped by distance and dependence on inward investment to generate economic development, these peripheral areas are dominated by the Euro-Core in terms of wealth, opportunity, population, industrial growth, decision-making and political influence.
9. The **Intermediate Areas** lie between the Euro-Core and Euro-Periphery with moderate economic potential. These areas include Wales, Jutland (Denmark) and SE France.

Factors influencing European Regional Inequality

1. **Physical factors** include the following -
   - Climate - temperature, precipitation, aspect, sunshine, etc
   - Geology - rock type, structure, soils, natural resources
   - Geographical location - distance from markets
   - Relief and drainage - mountains and lowlands, fertility and drainage, rock permeability/impermeability etc.
2. **Human influences** include -
   - **Social factors** • **Economic factors** • **Political factors**

Factors influencing European Regional Inequalities...........

3. **Social factors** include the perception of isolation of an area, proximity to the Euro-Core, availability of skills & training, population density
4. **Economic factors** include the level of investment, foreign competition, infrastructure development, balance between industrial and agricultural employment.
5. **Political factors** include public/private investment policies, variations in Government and EU support, degree of Govt. intervention, EU Objective One funding, etc.

National Patterns of European Regional Inequalities...........

1. **United Kingdom** "North - South" divide can be recognised through a study of socio-economic indicators including -
   - **GDP** - Gross Domestic Product
   - **Average House prices**
   - **Unemployment rate**
   - **Car ownership**
2. **Reasons for the "North - South" divide** include -
   - **Physical factors** - study page **111**
   - **Human factors** - study page **111**
3. **Results of regional inequality in the UK** include -
   - **Social results** - industrial decline leading to unemployment, poverty, deprivation, depopulation and migration as well as resentment and social division
   - **Economic results** - less money in economy, shops & services close, less investment in infrastructure, less growth and inward investment
   - **Environmental results** - derelict industrial sites, polluted rivers, abandoned quarries, spoil heaps etc.
4. **Methods to combat regional inequality** include -
   - Targeting specific areas with incentives to encourage investment - including Assisted Areas, Regional Development status, Enterprise Zones, direct financial assistance and subsidies, grants, loans, training, etc.
   - Location or relocation of Government departments

National Patterns of European Regional Inequalities...........

1. **Italy** - "North - South" divide can be recognised but contrasts with UK as Northern Italy is wealthier than Southern Italy
2. **Major differences** between the wealthy North - centred around the **Plain of Lombardy** and the poorer south -referred to as **il Mezzogiorno** (land of the midday sun) - with the North enjoying lower unemployment, higher GDP and more secondary & tertiary industries than the south.
3. **Major government intervention projects** - the **Cassa per il Mezzogiorno** set up in 1950 to redress the huge regional inequalities in the country - tasked to improve agriculture and industry as well as infrastructure - mainly successful with some remaining problems - see page **114**.

European Policies and programmes

1. Similar to national policies to encourage development - include
   - **European Regional Development Fund (ERDF)**
   - **European Social Fund (ESF)**
   - **European Investment Bank (EIB)**

European Regional Inequalities Revision : Unit style assessments

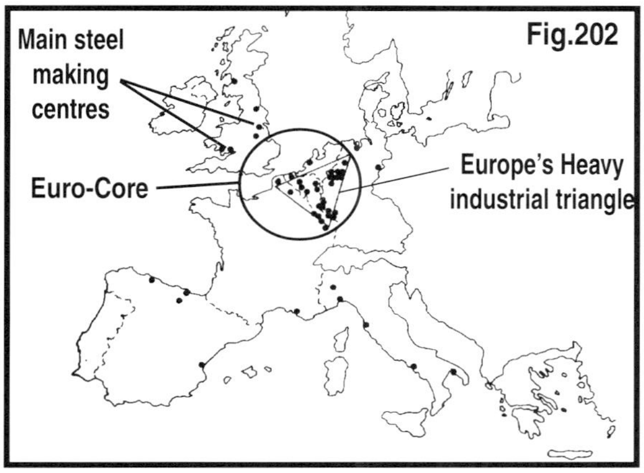

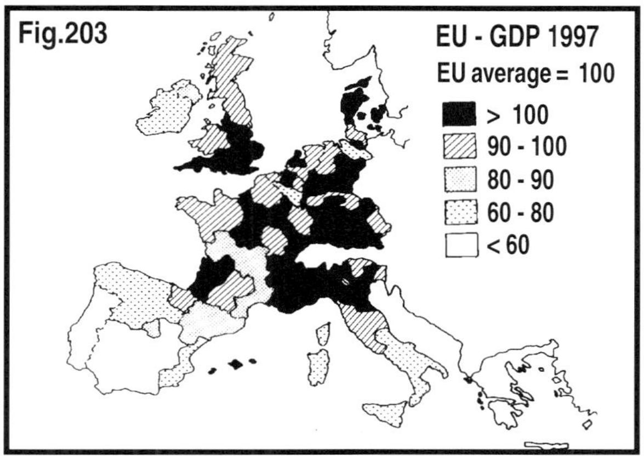

1. a. Compare figures **202 and 203**, describing the distribution of **core** and **peripheral** areas of the European Union. (6)

b. Examine figure **204** - European Core and Periphery model. Describe and explain the **physical and human factors** which have resulted in a pattern of European Regional Inequalities. (6)

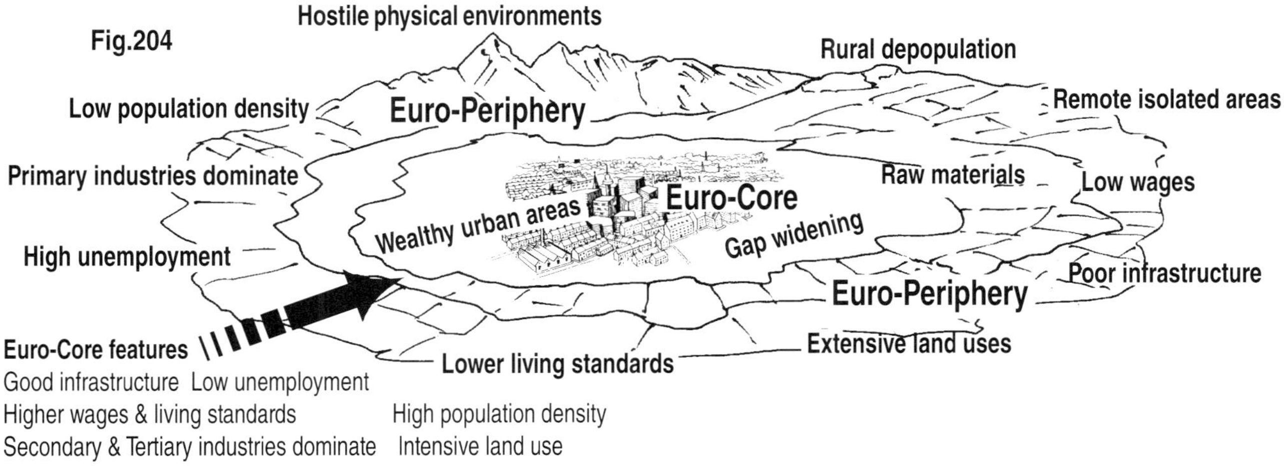

c. For any **EU country** you have studied, describe the steps taken to reduce these inequalities and comment on the effectiveness of the methods used. (8)

Total = 20 marks

European Regional Inequalities : Exam style assessments

1. Study figures **205 and 206.**

a. "The European phenomena of the **North - South** divide is a political reality and an economic fact of life"

Comment on the accuracy of this statement with reference to specific regions of Europe (7)

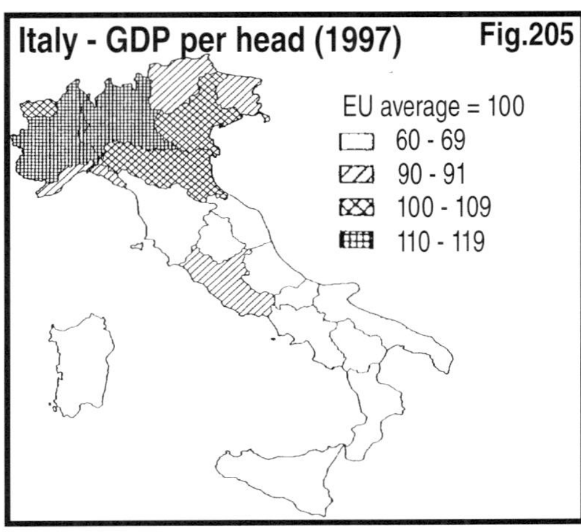

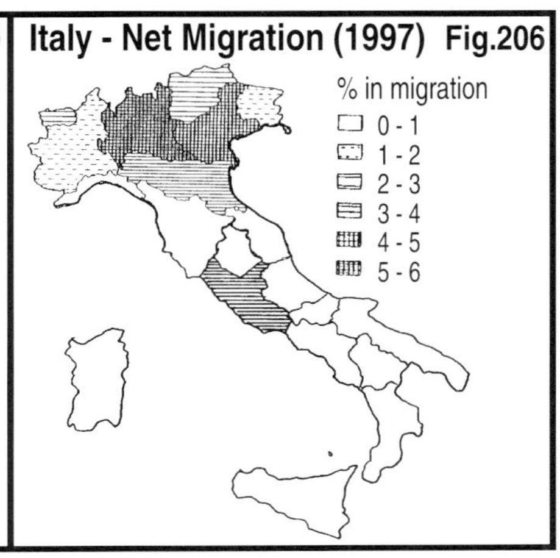

b. For Italy -

i. Describe the physical and human factors which have contributed to such regional differences

ii. Outline the social and economic problems which can arise from such differences (8)

c. For Italy, describe the steps taken by the national government and the European Union to overcome such problems and comment upon their effectiveness. (10)

Total = 25 marks

14. Development & Health
Application

The main idea of the Development & Health application section is....
Inequality of social and economic development is a major feature of the contemporary world. It exists on various scales and is measurable in several ways. Within developing countries levels of health and the incidence of disease are major indicators of levels of development. Such indicators may be explained geographically by reference to a variety of interacting processes.

What do you need to know ?

Students should have a knowledge and understanding of -

A A range of social, economic and composite **methods of measuring spatial inequality of development**, e.g. birth rate, death rate, GDP per head, physical quality of life (PQLI).

B Differences in levels of development between and within countries, for example -
- **differences between newly industrialising countries** (e.g. Pacific Rim countries) and other developing countries (e.g. Bangladesh)
- **differences within developing countries** (e.g. between south-east and north-east Brazil)
- **reasons for such differences**

C The **physical and human factors** involved in the levels of health and the incidence of disease, e.g. factors related to -
- **climate**
- **water supply**
- **wealth**
- **nutrition**
- **remoteness**

and through the study of **one water-related disease** selected from -
- **bilharzia**
- **cholera**
- **malaria**

D Strategies for improving health and the control of disease, and their impact. Strategies related to the case study disease should be used, e.g. primary health care, **immunisation programmes**.

Comparison of Countries - use of indicators measuring inequality of development

The level of development in countries may be compared using a **range of indicators**. **Gross National Product** (**G.N.P.**) per capita (head of population) is commonly used, but does not allow for the "well-being" of the people, e.g. Saudi Arabia - has very high G. N. P. but low **adult literacy** and high **infant mortality rate** (**I.M.R.**).

A more realistic comparison is obtained by using the **P.Q.L.I.** (**Physical Quality of Life Index**) which combines **Life Expectancy, Adult Literacy** (%) and **Infant Mortality Rate**.

Other indicators which may be used are:- **Diet** (**Calorie or Protein** intake); Number of **people per Doctor**; number of **Newspapers per thousand of population**; number of houses with indoor **toilets, baths** etc. Most indicators focus on levels of **Education**, **Medical** services, and **Living Standards** in a country.

What is a Developing Country ?

A "typical " **developing country** is characterised by
- **Low G.N.P.**
- **High % employed in Agriculture**
- **Low rate of Urbanisation**
- **Low levels of Industrial Development**

and a particular **Population Structure** (often high Birth Rate, high I.M.R. and relatively low Life Expectancy).

However within this pattern there are **broad variations**,
i.e. Saudi Arabia - very high G.N.P; Singapore or Taiwan - high levels of Urbanisation and Industrial development; Costa Rica - low G.N.P. but low I.M.R. and high Life Expectancy - figure 208.

Figure 207 - Big, wealthy, industrialised North can't see the South for its bulging stomach full of resources and food.....

Similarities and differences between G.N.P. and P.Q.L.I.

Many countries with a **high G.N.P.**, e.g. USA, Australia also have a **high P.Q.L.I.** - the country's wealth is used to provide high levels of education and medical services. Countries with a **low G.N.P.**, e.g. Ethiopia, Bangladesh often have a **low P.Q.L.I.** - they cannot afford an effective education and medical service.
But some countries do not follow these patterns, e.g.
- **Saudi Arabia** has a very high G.N.P. (oil rich) but a low P.Q.L.I. (relatively little is spent on education and medical services, particularly for women)
- **Costa Rica** has relatively low G.N.P. but high P.Q.L.I. (the government devotes a large amount of money to education and medical care etc).

Differences in levels of development between and within countries

Contrasts in the developing world (between developing countries)

Great **variations in Development** (G.N.P. , Life Expectancy, etc.) can be identified - for example, **Life Expectancy** ranges from 41 years in Ethiopia & Afghanistan to 74 in Singapore and Taiwan. G.N.P. per capita varies from $145 in Bangladesh to $18,000 in Kuwait - figure **210**.

The **low figures** in Ethiopia and Bangladesh result from-
- **Vicious circle of poverty** affecting countries of the South (figure **209**)
- **lack of industrial development** and wealth creation (mainly subsistence agriculture) **governments have little to spend** on medical services, education etc
- **Natural Disasters** (droughts, floods) causing crop destruction and food shortages leading to **famine and undernutrition**
- **Civil Wars** and **Government instability**
- **Endemic diseases** such as malaria
- **Poor living conditions** and **sanitation**......

The **high figures** in Singapore result from -
- **Political** and **economic stability**
- **Rapidly expanding industry** (Tiger economies)
- **Creating wealth** for the government to support development, i.e. investments made in housing, education, medical and other services such as sanitation, water supply, food supply, etc.

Kuwait gains great wealth from its **oil industry** - rich natural resources.

Classification of Development — Fig.208

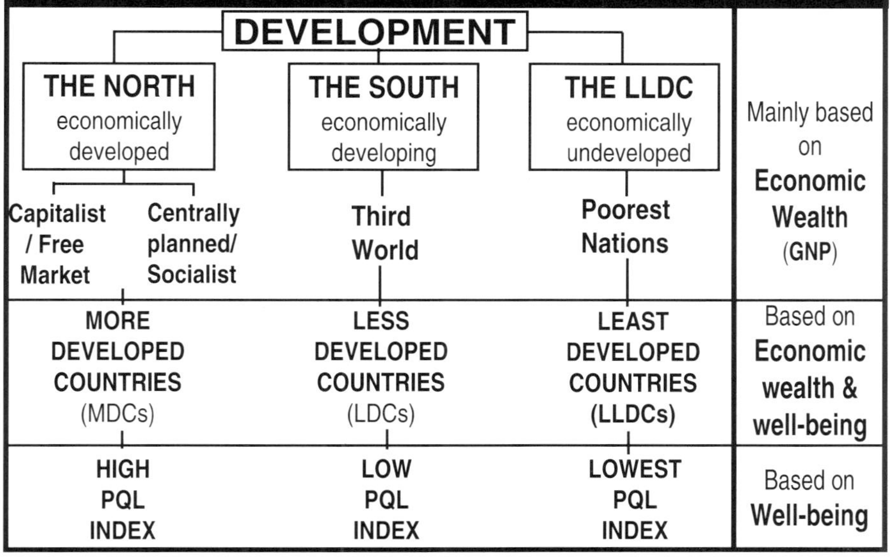

Vicious circle of Poverty — Fig.209

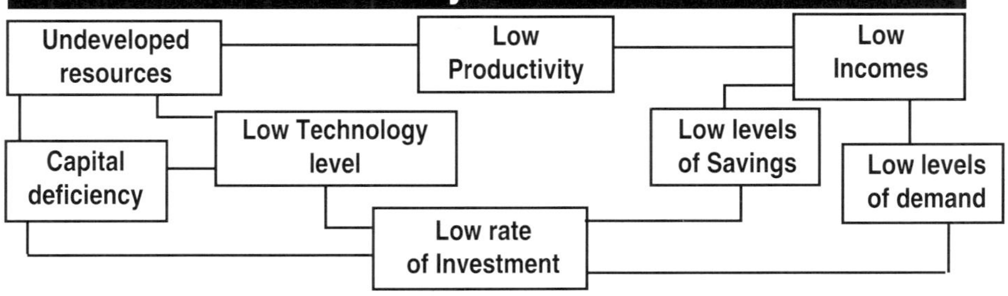

How the people fare — Fig.210

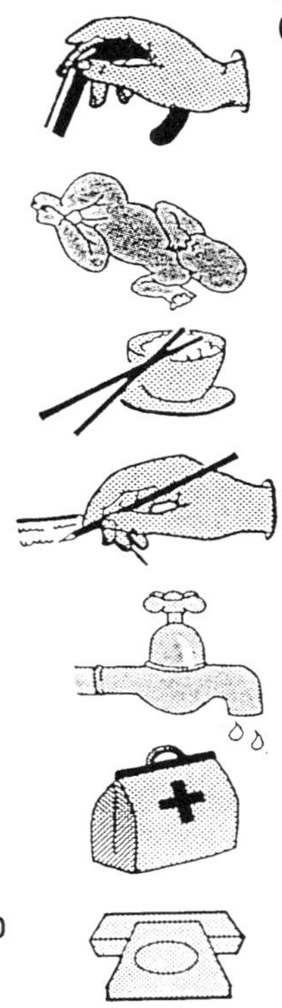

	Developing Countries	Developed Countries
Life expectancy at birth (years)	47	73
Infant mortality rate (per1,000 of pop.)	132	18
Average daily calorie intake per head	2048	3361
Adult literacy rate (%)	32	99
% of population with access to safe water	34	99
Doctors per 100,000 of pop.	11	204
Telephones per 1,000 of pop.	3	603

Variations within countries

Indicators only provide an **average** figure for the whole country - they do not identify **variations within** a country.

Human reasons for variations include - **political** (e.g. the Kurds within Iraq), **religious** (e.g. Saudi Arabia - menial status of women), **racial** (South Africa - former **apartheid** favoured white minority, and USA, more poverty amongst Negroes and Hispanics).

Physical reasons for variations include - some areas are more isolated, having a very **poor communications infrastructure** (e.g. Tibet (mountains) within China, and the Amazon Basin (rainforest) within Brazil). Some parts of larger countries, e.g. Ethiopia may be more prone to drought or disease, etc.

Fig. 211

Life Expectancy at birth

• The North - sample countries

Japan	79.6 years
Hong Kong	78.7
Sweden	78.3
Iceland	78.2
Switzerland	78.1

• The South - sample countries

Sierra Leone	39.2 years
Afghanistan	43.7
Guinea Bissau	43.8
Guinea	44.7
Uganda	44.7

Routes to Development (1)

AID Summit Fig.212

Modern thinking on the most appropriate routes to development discourages the example set in Fig.**212**. Developing nations have given serious consideration to their current predicaments and to the best way forward. Since the Second World War many of the factors used as indicators of development, such as life expectancy, have improved in developing countries. The average life expectancy in developing countries is 60 years - due mainly to improved infant mortality as a result of improvements in living standards. However most governments recognise the dire need to improve living standards in the poorest countries. A number of routes to, or strategies for, development have been attempted in various developing countries (Fig.**213**). The important factor in success or otherwise of a Development Strategy concerns the appropriateness of the plan to the individual conditions within the country concerned. Recently, small-scale, locally controlled development strategies have been favoured as opposed to large scale, externally controlled schemes.

Routes to Development (2)

Fig.213

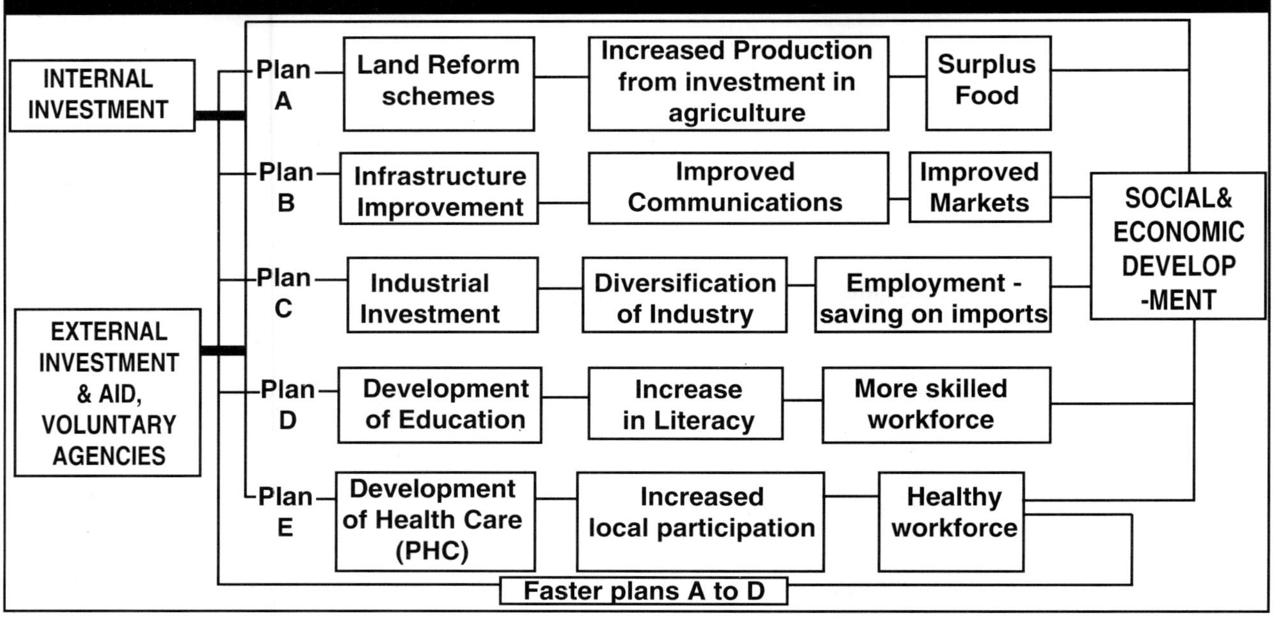

Factors involved in levels of Health and the incidence of disease

There is a **two way relationship between *development and health*** **-** one affects and influences the other...........for example...

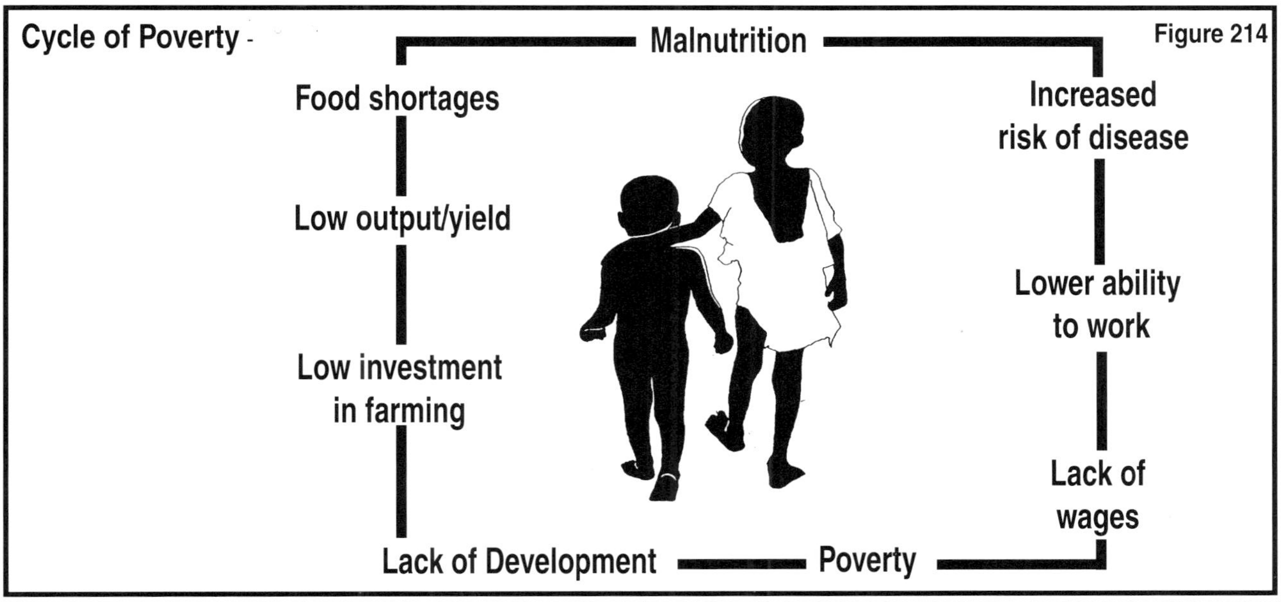

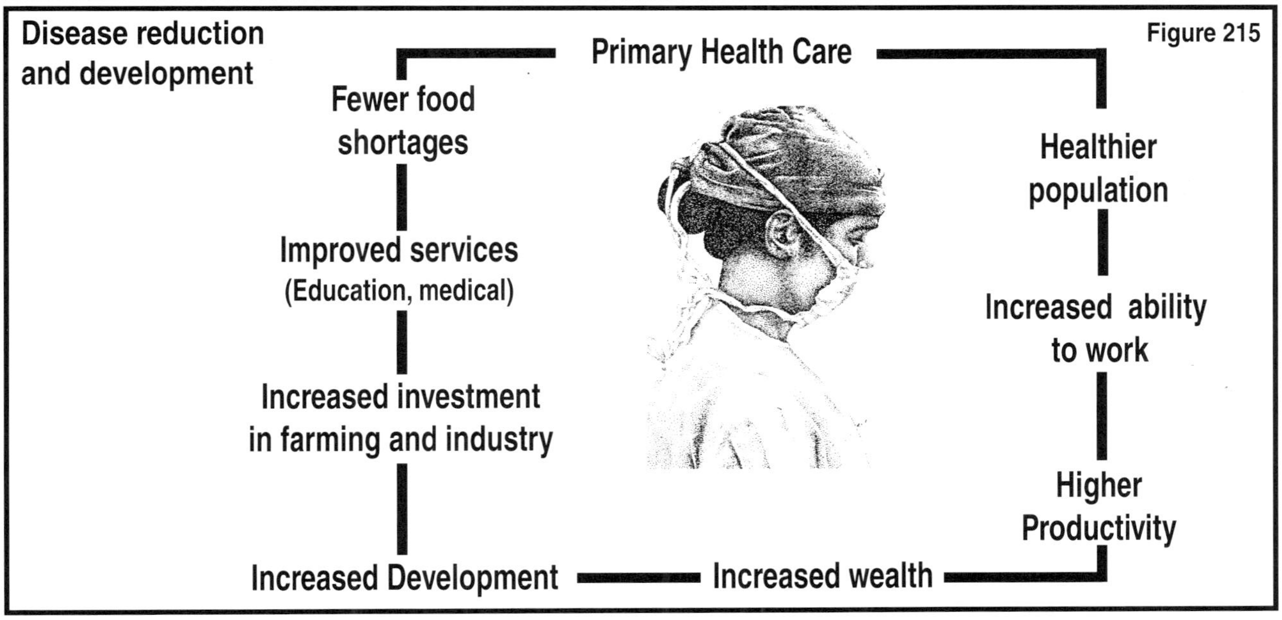

High Infant Mortality rate and Death Rate in Developing Countries e.g. Ethiopia

1. **Physical causes** include **Climate** which may cause long periods of **Drought** leading to **Crop Failure** and in turn **Famine** (Malnutrition, and undernourishment, e.g. Kwashiorkor). In addition there are **Endemic Diseases** (Malaria, Bilharzia , etc.), **Epidemic Diseases** (e.g. Cholera (due to contaminated water and food) which contribute to high I.M.R and DR. **Remoteness** (mountainous landscapes, etc.) is also a factor in high death rates of the very young and the old in countries such as Ethiopia.

2. **Human causes** include low levels of **Sanitation** and personal **Hygiene**; poor **Living Conditions** e.g. shanty towns; **Poverty** (unable to afford medicine etc.); lack of **Medical Care** (1 doctor to 50,000 people) and **Vaccinations**; lack of **Pre** and **Post Natal Care** (note the menial status of women); **Civil War**; lack of **Health Education** and **public awareness** of disease, etc.

3. **Methods of reduction** include increased **Food Supplies** which can lead to improved **Diet** (less malnutrition); **the development of a system of** Primary Health Care (PHC) which includes a **Vaccination programme,** improved **Sanitation**, **Hygiene** & **Health Education** with improved **Natal Care** (birth supervision) and basic **Drugs** & **Herbal Remedies** as well as locally trained **Health Workers** - some times called **barefoot doctors**.

4. **Effects of reduction** include **less money needed** for infant care; **Healthier Population**; **Higher Life Expectancy** ; **Larger and Healthier Workforce**; **Greater productivity** ; **Increased Development**....

Contrasts between rural and urban areas (developing countries)

Problems **greater in Rural** areas (often **remote** and **isolated**). Less **Educational or medical provision** - greater **exposure to disease** (e.g. Malaria and Bilharzia) and **contaminated water** (leading to more widespread Cholera)- greater **poverty** and **unemployment** (mainly **subsistence** farming) - greater **exposure** to **natural disasters** e.g. **drought**, **famine** leading to malnutrition (also **Civil War**).

In **Urban areas some** diseases e.g. asthma or bronchitis may be greater due to **pollution** and **high population density** spreads disease e.g. **AIDS** etc.

Water supplies, sanitation and disease

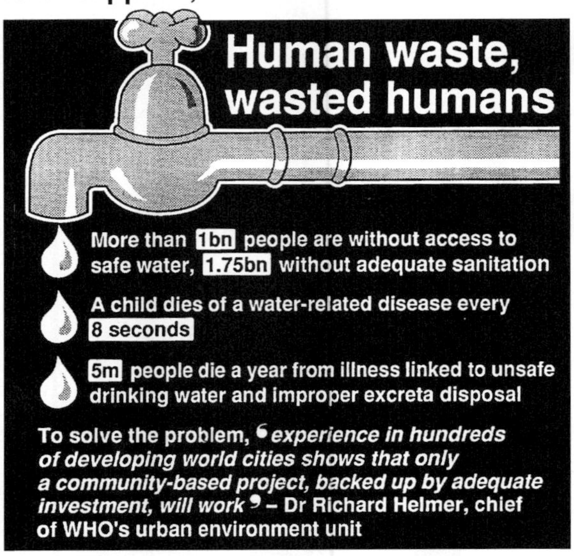

Figure 216

Figure 217 People and cattle use the water hole for drinking supplies

World Without Safe Water **Figure 218**

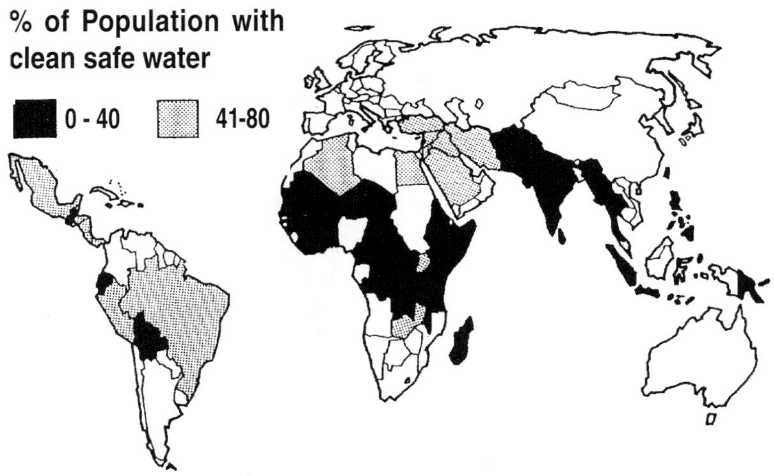

Diseases may be classified as follows -

- **Water Borne** (spread by **contaminated water**) e.g. **Cholera**
- **Water Based** (the carrier or **vector lives in water**) e.g. **Bilharzia** - spread by a water snail
- **Water Related** (the **vector breeds on water surfaces)** e.g. **Malaria**

Infection

Principal diseases related to **contaminated water** and **poor sanitation** are -

- **Cholera** water supplies are polluted with **human waste** - **bacteria** infect water supply - spread when people **drink** or **cook with** or **wash** in contaminated water - see figure **217**.
- **Bilharzia** (the vector or carrier is a snail which lives in contaminated water - worms laid by the snail enter the skin of humans washing in the water often through the foot or leg. Larvae enter the water via human waste deposited in the water - thus the water is contaminated and water based cycle of disease is continued.....

Prevention

Health Education - **public awareness** and **improvements in personal hygiene** and **sanitation** - provision of toilets and separate sewerage from water supplies. Provision of **clean or purified drinking water,** e.g. Calcutta - shanty towns - **vaccination for Cholera**.
For Bilharzia, the vector (snail) may be removed by increasing **water flow;** use of **molluscicides** and **snail-eating fish** and **health education** to protect skin and improve hygiene.

Improving health in developing countries such as Kenya

Primary Health Care (PHC) - is appropriate because of the low cost & being delivered by locals, can reach remote communities - the focus is on prevention.
Main features - Health **Education** delivered by medical aides (barefoot doctors) with basic medical training, **vaccination** and improved **sanitation**; **nutrition, herbal medicines** and **natal care** etc.
Effectiveness - has reduced disease and lowered I.M.R. but problems of scale - high population (e.g. in China); malnutrition caused by famine (e.g. in Ethiopia); remoteness (e.g. in Amazonia); suspicion (of vaccinations, drugs etc) and lack of literacy.....

Disease definitions

Endemic diseases - diseases such as **Malaria** and **Bilharzia** are diseases which are habitually present in an area because of permanent local environmental or social factors - for example **River Blindness** (or Onchocerciasis) is confined to the habitat of the female blackfly whereas **Hookworm** is found in areas where there is inadequate provision of safe water or sanitation facilities.

Epidemic diseases - diseases such as **Cholera** are defined as diseases common to a large area or group of people over a large area, spread by the direct actions of people and are not usually confined to specific geographical areas. From time to time an epidemic may spread to become a **Pandemic** - or giant epidemic affecting many millions of people over a huge area.

Disease case studies - endemic disease (1)

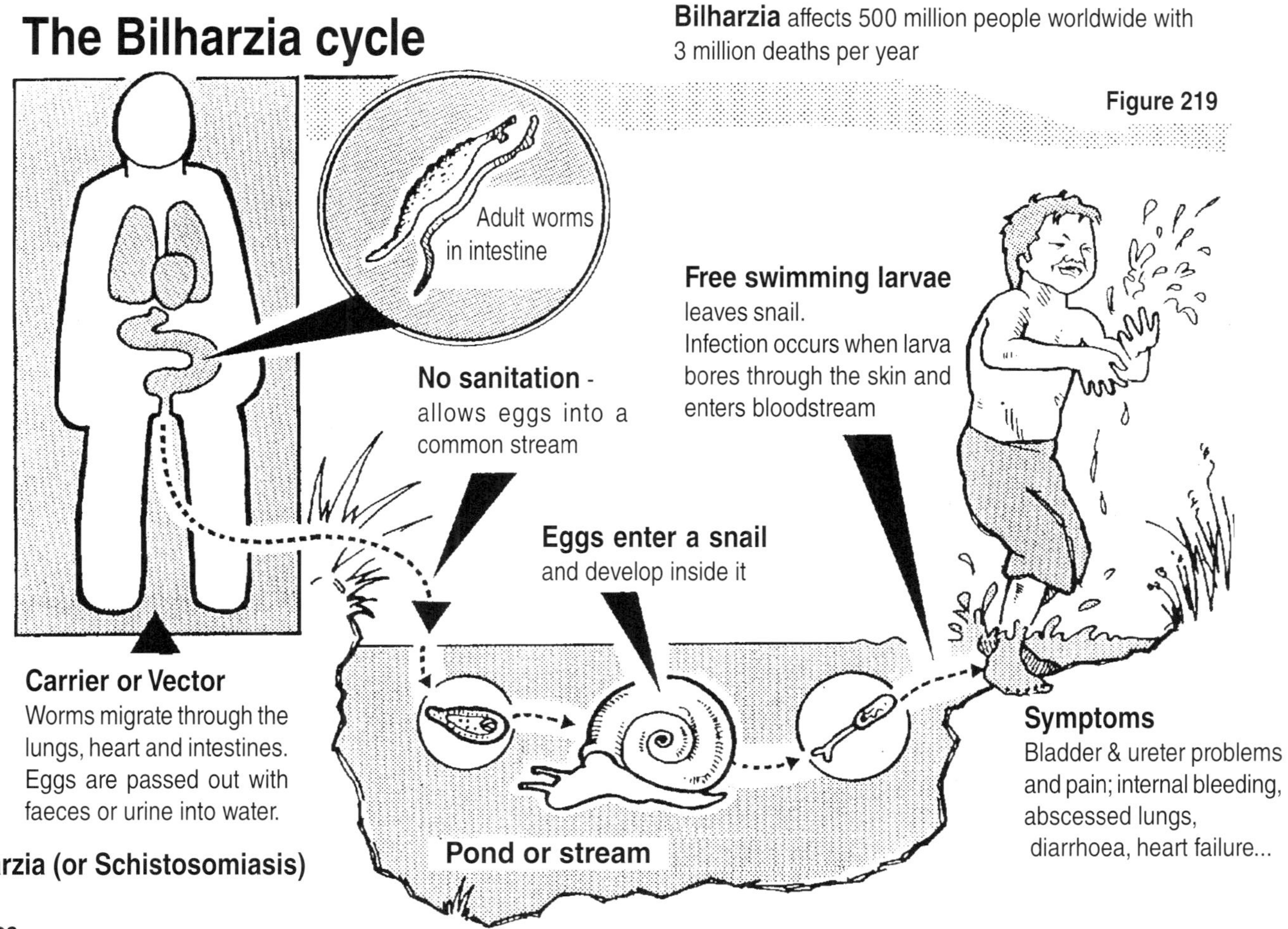

Figure 219

Bilharzia (or Schistosomiasis)

Transmission of Bilharzia/Schistosomiasis
Disease passes from faeces, urine or sick person into water-dwelling snail. Spreads in water habitat of bilharzia snail.

Causes

Physical causes
- **Tropical environments** e.g. Egypt
- **Stagnant water** infected with snails (vectors) e.g. lakes, irrigation channels, paddy fields (rice cultivation)

Human causes
- poor **Sanitation** (human waste entering water)
- **washing, swimming** etc in **contaminated water**
- **poverty**

Prevention
- increase in **water flow** to remove water snails
- use of **molluscicides** - chemicals which kill off snails (which are molluscs)
- **snail eating fish** can be introduced to water and provide food in the process
- use of **chemotherapy** and **injections** to cure infected humans
- **health education** and increased public awareness
- improved **sanitation** and **personal hygiene**

Effectiveness
- **limited by scale** because of giant problems associated with this very widespread disease
- **irrigation schemes** create new environments for snails to breed
- **illiteracy** - difficult to change habits
- **cost of molluscicides and injections**
- **easy to be re-infected**

Figure 220

Malaria - King of Diseases

Distribution of Malaria - mainly hot , wet Tropical areas (see map) including Sri Lanka, India, SE Asia, Central America, Amazon Basin, Tropical Africa

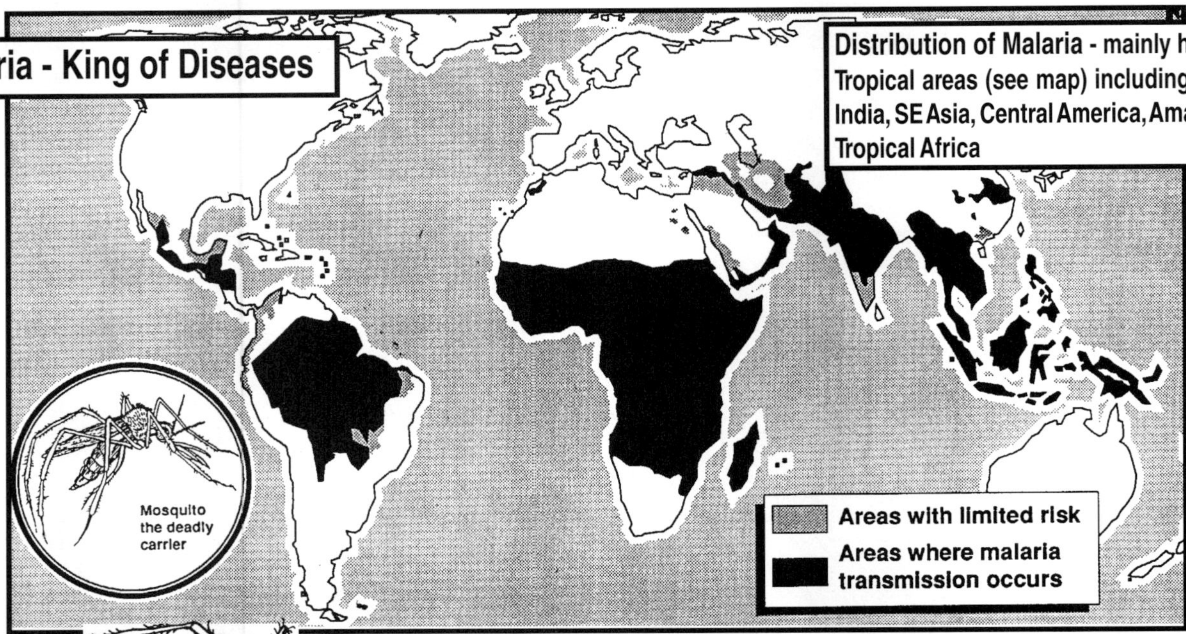

Figure 221

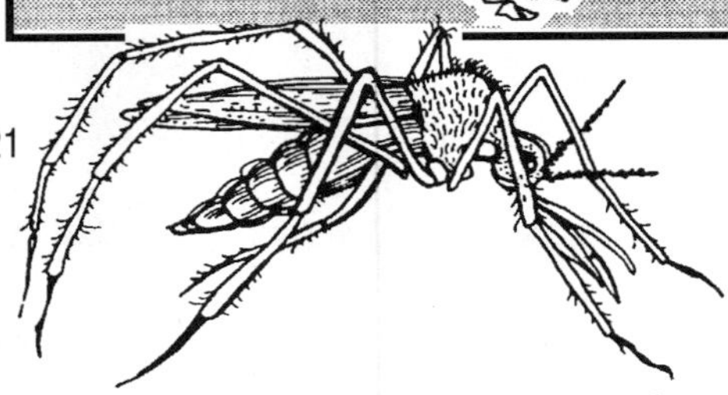

• 285 million people worldwide may be carrying the plasmodium (malaria) parasite

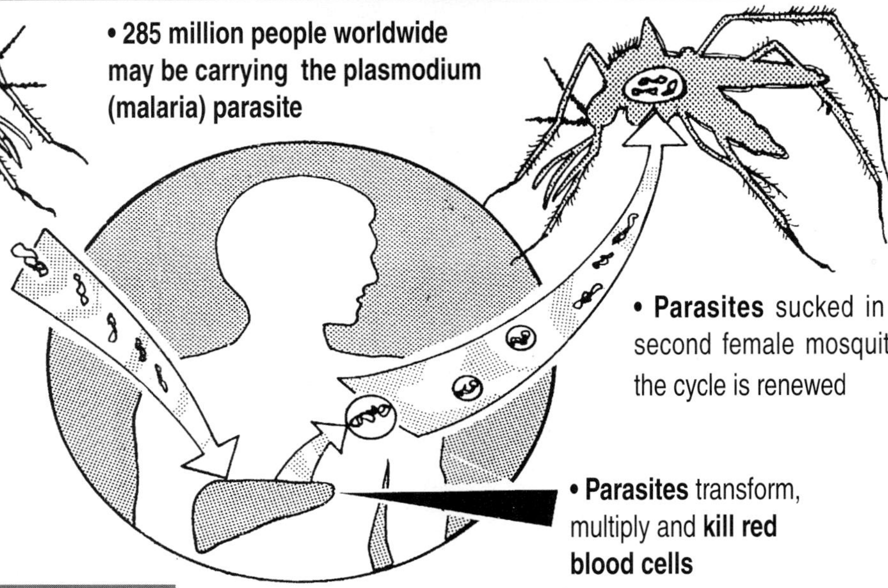

• **Parasites** transmitted by **female mosquitoes** to the human **liver**

• **Every year :** more than **1 million deaths** and **110 million new cases**

• **Main symptoms of Malaria -** plasmodium parasites invade and destroy red blood cells, lodge in liver - **symptoms** include **fevers, lethargy, coma and death**

• **Parasites** sucked in by second female mosquito - the cycle is renewed

• **Parasites** transform, multiply and **kill red blood cells**

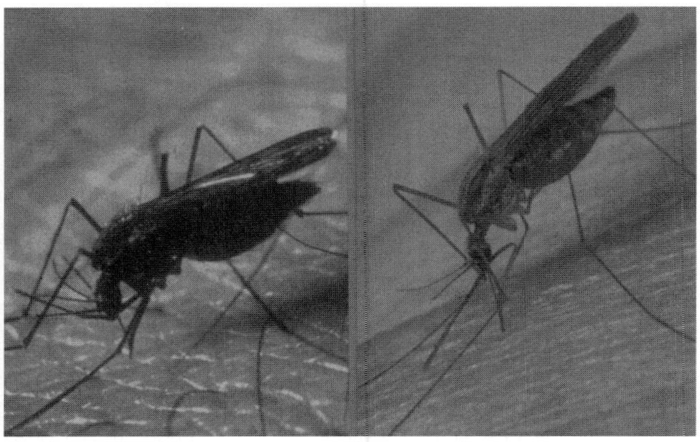

• **Malaria is one of the world's biggest killers -** two billion people are at risk from the **'King of Diseases'**

• **Treatment of Malaria** - mass drug treatment to kill parasites in humans (& destruction of mosquito/mosquito habitats)

Figure 222 - A **female mosquito** takes twice her weight in human blood to obtain proteins and nutrients for her larvae which she lays in stagnant water - these views show mosquitoes on a human finger

Causes

• Physical & Environmental	- Spread by **vector** - (**female anopheles mosquito**) passes on **parasite** (type is **plasmodium**) through 'blood meals' - requires a human blood reservoir in close proximity to habitats - **Breeds in** areas with summer temperatures **over 16^{0}C** , - Heavy **rainfall** and areas of vegetation cover / shade (under which the female digests the blood for her larvae) - Widespread **stagnant water surfaces** e.g. **swamps, irrigation channels, Paddy fields** (Indonesia) etc.
• Human	- Encouraged by **high population densities** e.g. shanty towns & **migration** (Pilgrims, Nomads and Migrant workers) - **Lack of Finance for Prevention** - e.g. drugs, insecticides etc

Prevention
- Requires initial **planning** i.e. **surveys** to locate mosquito habitats (breeding grounds) and **identification of likely human hosts (to** be treated with drugs)
- **Methods used include**
  - **Drain** mosquito habitats or breeding grounds
  - Use **insecticides** to kill mosquitoes e.g. Malathion
  - Use **nets** for **protection** against mosquitoes
  - **Spray oil** or egg white on water surfaces to **suffocate larvae** lying in stagnant water
  - Use **drugs to kill parasite** (Plasmodium) in humans - e.g. Atabrin
  - Use **genetic engineering** - produces sterile male mosquitoes

Effectiveness
- Relatively **successful** in Sri Lanka (1955) - temporary **eradication** but problems remain:- draining all breeding grounds is impractical
- Mosquitoes are **resistant** to D.D.T (also environmentally unacceptable)
- High cost of **oil** & **pollution** of water supplies if used to suffocate larvae
- Cost of **drugs is ever increasing and population often suspicious of using modern drugs anyway**
- **Immunity of parasites** to drugs - growing and serious problem

Cholera - an epidemic disease

Transmission of Cholera
- Sick person transmits disease in **faeces or vomit**
- Bacteria passes into **water** or onto **hands** or **food**
- Then drunk or eaten, **swallowed by next person**
- **New infected person** then continues the disease cycle

Symptoms
- Severe **diarrhoea**
- Major **loss of body fluids**
- Profuse **vomitting**
- Stomach and severe bowel & body **cramps**
- **Victim dehydrates to death**

Figure 223 - An open market with open sewers in Lagos, Nigeria - a likely centre of Cholera

Causes
Physical and Human
- Spread by **Bacteria** (Vibrio Cholerae - a comma shaped bacillus ❟)
- **Human Faeces** may contaminate water, soil or vegetation
- Lack of **proper toilets** and **sanitation**
- Low levels of **personal hygiene**
- Bacteria may be transported by **flies**
- Encouraged by **hot, dry weather** conditions

Distribution of Cholera
Worldwide spread - 300 million people per year affected
18 million deaths per year from Cholera

Treatment for Cholera
- Massive rehydration of victim through replacement of body fluids with weak sugar & salt solution given intravenously - usually hospital based

Prevention
- **Health education** and increasing **public awareness** of how Cholera is spread
- **Improvements in sanitation systems** and in **improved personal hygiene**
- Cooking practices to ensure all **water is boiled** before use
- Install toilets & provide clean drinking water by **chlorination** e.g. in Quito
- **Vaccination programmes for humans** (certificates for travellers to infected areas)
- **Fly control**

Effectiveness
- **Limited by high costs** (ditticult to service rapidly expanding shanty towns)
- **Lack of proper sanitation** and **clean water** supplies
- **Illiteracy** - old practices and poor hygiene difficult to overcome
- Cholera **easily spread** by migrants, etc.
- **Widespread poverty** a continuing problem

Development and Health Revision : Summary Notes

The main idea of the **Development & Health** application section is....
Inequality of social and economic development is a major feature of the contemporary world. It exists on various scales and is measurable in several ways. Within developing countries levels of health and the incidence of disease are major indicators of levels of development. Such indicators may be explained geographically by reference to a variety of interacting processes.

Development

1. **The world is divided** by levels of wealth, poverty and health with the richest 10% controlling 60% of the world's wealth - the majority of the world population is economically tied to the rich countries.
2. The poorer countries of the World are **underdeveloped** in terms of their **technological** application and **economic** organisation.
3. The **development process** is about changing economies and social organisation to reduce the gap between rich and poor nations.
4. Development concerns progress (see Gandhi) on a number of important fronts and is a combination of all of the following:-
   - **Economic** Development based on Wealth (GNP)
   - **Technological** Development - increasing the ability of machines to improve human lives.
   - **Welfare** Development - involving health, well-being and human rights.
   - The **Modernisation** of society for 21st.Century living.
5. A number of terms are used in the study of Development including the **North**, the **South**, **Third World**, **MDC**s, **LDC**s, **LLDC**s, **NIC**s, **Developed**, **Developing** and even **Poor World**, **Rich World**, **Underdeveloped**, etc.
6. There are **2** main categories of criteria used to measure development
   - **Economic indicators** based on GNP/possession-related statistics
   - **Cultural, Social and Welfare indicators** including measurements of Life Expectancy, Infant Mortality rate and Literacy among others.
7. In order to avoid the failings of one set of criteria, a number of measures can be combined into one more accurate index - the **Physical Quality of Life Index** (**PQLI**).
8. Any study of development reveals major **patterns** world-wide ; the wealthier, temperate North compared to those of the poorer, Tropical South.
9. **International Debt** and its massive burden is placing at risk many well-intentioned development programmes since some nations must repay up to 75% of their GNP simply as interest payments on loans.

"Development is progress in all ways and should be based on self-reliance : our future is in our hands and minds, we should make our determinations and seek help where appropriate for and not instead of our own efforts"
Mahatma Gandhi (1946)

Health and Development

1. **Everyone has the right to good health** but not everyone has equal access to the basic diet and medical care necessary to give them a healthy life.
2. **Good health** is more than the avoidance of disease: it amounts to the capacity to live, work and enjoy leisure to one's full potential. The aim should be not only to add years to life but to add life to the years.
3. Any **Geographical Classification of ill-health** reveals not only a wide gulf between North and South in terms of medical care, life expectancy and infant mortality but also a contrast in causes of ill-health.
4. In the main, the people in the South suffer at the expense of **exogenous** diseases which are linked to poverty, poor water and sanitation, government investment in military weaponry and urban based care.
5. People in the North suffer from **endogenous** or degenerative disease linked to lifestyle, environment and technology.
6. The countries of the South require the introduction of **Primary Health Care** schemes.
7. Without the foundation of good health (a fundamental human right), strategies toward development are likely to be ineffective. Development is inextricably linked with the promotion of good health.
8. Case studies are important in the revision of Development & Health - you should make sure that you are familiar with **Bilharzia, Malaria** and **Cholera**.

Development & Health Revision : Unit style assessments

Figure 224

In the Developed countries 90% of the population haver access to clean water and mains sanitation. In Developing countries 40% (about 1.2 billion) have access to clean water but only 25% (1.5 billion) have access to mains sanitation

Access to Safe Water (1970-1995)			Access to adequate Sanitation (1970-1995)		
Year	*Urban*	*Rural*	*Year*	*Urban*	*Rural*
1970	66%	13.2%	1970	30%	12%
1980	75%	32%	1980	54%	14%
1990	79%	43%	1990	60%	16%
1995	87%	55%	1995	79%	20%

Real progress has been made since 1970 in providing safe water and adequate sanitation. In rural areas, the percentage of people with safe water has trebled. In urban areas access to sanitation has doubled.

1. Study figure **224** - which relates to access to safe water and adequate sanitation.

a. Describe the **trends** shown in figure 224. (2)
b. Explain the differences between provision in urban and rural areas. (3)
c. In many Developing countries people are affected by diseases which relate to water contaminated with sewage. Describe in detail the causes of such diseases and outline methods used to control them. (7)
d. "The USA and Kuwait have a high G.N.P. per person therefore everyone in these countries has a high standard of living."
Discuss the accuracy of this statement, using examples to support your answer. (4)
e. Study the figures for average life expectancy in selected Developing countries.

Country	Life Expectancy (in years)
Singapore	**74**
China	**61**
Ethiopia	**42**

Explain the range of life expectancies across different developing countries. Choose countries from the table above or other examples you have studied. (4)

Total = 20 marks

Development & Health : Exam style assessments

1. **Socio-economic indicators** may be used to compare levels of development between different countries.

a. Give examples of such indicators and comment on their effectiveness (5)
b. Discuss the limitations of indicators in providing an accurate picture of living conditions **within** particular countries. Use named countries to support your answer. (5)
c. Study the figures for life expectancy in the UK and Afghanistan.

	1975	1995
UK	**72**	**78**
Afghanistan	**35**	**45**

i. Describe and explain differences between the two countries and comment on the changes between 1975 and 1995. (6)
ii. In many Developing countries Primary Health Care (P.H.C.) has been introduced. With reference to a named country, describe its purpose and main features, and explain why P.H.C. is an appropriate system of health care. (9)

Total = 25 marks

2. a. Explain what is meant by the term **development**. (3)
b. Explain the **link between development and health**. (4)

For **Cholera** or **Malaria or Bilharzia/Schistosomiasis**
c. Describe the **physical and human factors** which cause the spread of the disease (5)
d. Describe the **methods used to try to control the spread** of the disease. (8)
e. Comment on the **effectiveness of methods of controlling** the disease. (5)

Total = 25 marks

15. Summary Revision section

Revision checklist

The lists below contain a summary of all the key topics which are likely to appear in unit or exam assessments.

Tick the appropriate circle when you are sure you have learned, and understood, a particular topic.

Note. In addition to the topics listed below, students should be familiar with the **Geographical Methods and Techniques** (see page **130**).

Core Section

Physical Core

Atmosphere (see pages 9 to 16)

- O Solar energy distribution in the Earth-Atmosphere System
- O Differences in Insolation received by Tropical/Polar latitudes
- O Variations in radiation (absorbed) with latitude (Albedo effect)
- O Atmosphere circulation (basic explanation - (Fig 6, page 11))
- O Ocean circulation (basic explanation and knowledge of one ocean e.g. Atlantic)
- O Global climate changes :- O Physical Factors
  - O Human Factors
- O Air masses and the West African climate

Hydrosphere (see pages 17 to 25)

- O The Hydrological Cycle
- O The effect of Climatic Variability on Water Supply
- O Drainage basins and patterns
- O Construction and Analysis of Hydrographs
- O River processes and the effects of flowing water
- O Changes along a river valley
- O Identification of river/valley features on O.S. maps
- O Description/explanation of the formation of the following features:- O Waterfall O Meander
  - O Oxbow lake O Levee
  - O Flood Plain O River Terraces
  - O River Terraces

Lithosphere (see pages 26 to 38)

- O Processes of Weathering
- O Processes of Mass Movement
- O Glaciated Upland Landscapes - main UK areas
- O Formation of erosional features:-
  - O U-shaped valley O Roche Moutonnee
  - O Arete O Pyramidal Peak
  - O Hanging Valley O Corrie
- O Formation of depositional features:-
  - O Terminal Moraine O Drumlin
  - O Esker O Erratic (perched block)
- O Map recognition of glacial features
- O Upland limestone (Karst) landscapes - main UK areas
- O Drainage system in the Karst regions
- O The process of chemical weathering (carbonation)
- O Formation of Karst Scenery:-
  - O Limestone pavement O Stalactites & Stalagmites
  - O Caverns and gorges O Sink holes
- O Map recognition of Carboniferous limestone areas
- O Scarp and Vale scenery
  - O structure and relief
  - O drainage system
  - O map recognition

Biosphere (see pages 39 to 45)

- O Soil processes and formation
- O Soils - the influence of climate, relief and drainage
- O Soil case studies (description/explanation) - Podzol, Brown Earth & Gley soils
- O Human activities relating to soils/natural vegetation
- O Vegetation - definition of key words relating to succession
- O Case studies of plant succession - Derelict land & Sand dunes

Human Core

Population Geography (see pages 47 to 53)

- O Population terminology - B.R., DR., etc.
- O Population structure - interpretation of pyramid patterns
- O Gathering population statistics:-
  - O Methods available (census, etc.)
  - O Problems in developing countries
- O Demographic Transition:-
  - O Different stages/examples
  - O Relationship to B.R./D.R.
- O Population change:-
  - O Features influencing change (B.R., D.R., Migration)
  - O Effects of changes - Developing country
  - O Effects of changes - Developed Country
- O Migration O Terminology (different types, push and pull factors)
  - O Case Studies - Turkey to former West Germany
  - O Bosnia to Germany
  - O Rural - Urban (Calcutta).

Rural Geography (see pages 54 to 60)

- O The Farming System (Inputs, processes and outputs)
- O Characteristics of different systems (Intensive, extensive, etc.)
- O Three case studies must be known in detail (main areas, features, population density and settlement pattern)
  - O Shifting Cultivation
  - O Extensive Commercial farming
  - O Intensive Peasant farming
- O Change and impact of change in Case Study areas -
  - O Deforestation/decline in shifting cultivation
  - O Green Revolution in S.E. Asia
  - O Recent developments in commercial farming

Industrial Geography (see pages 61 to 68)

- O Definitions of types of industry (Primary, secondary, etc.)
- O The Industrial System (Inputs, processes and outputs)
- O Location Factors for industry (Physical and Human)
- O Contrasts in the features and location of old and new industrial landscapes
- O Case study of industrial change - S. Wales
  - O Reasons for early industrial growth
  - O Reasons for/results of industrial decline
  - O Recent industrial growth/changes
  - O Effectiveness of regeneration policies
- O Social, economic and environmental impact of industrial decline
- O Contrasts in development between European Core/Peripheral regions
- O Recognition of industrial areas and their characteristics on O.S. maps (Locational factors)

Urban Geography (Core + Application) (pages **69-81**)

- ○ Definitions relating to urban areas and urbanisation
- ○ Settlement patterns (in Rural and Urban areas)
- ○ Characteristics of major urban zones (C.B.D., etc.)
- ○ Services in settlements (order, threshold, location, sphere of influence, etc.)
- ○ Models of urban growth
- ○ Land use changes across developed world cities
- ○ C.B.D.s (Developed World) - Problems and Solutions
- ○ Inner city changes (Developed World)
- ○ Conflict on the Urban periphery
- ○ Case study of a Developed World City (location, growth)
- ○ Recent problems and solutions
  - ○ C.B.D.
  - ○ Housing / population
  - ○ Industrial change
  - ○ Social conflict
  - ○ Traffic congestion
- ○ Contrasts in urbanisation - developed/developing world
- ○ Growth and structure of developing world cities
- ○ Case study of a developing world city - Calcutta
  - ○ Growth and Development
  - ○ Urban problems (housing, etc.)
  - ○ Recent improvements/effectiveness

River Basin Management (see pages **83 to 88**)

- ○ The Distribution of River Basins/Water Control Projects:-
  - ○ In Africa
  - ○ In North America
- ○ Factors which create need for River Basin Management
  - ○ Physical Factors
  - ○ Social/economic Factors
- ○ Factors which influence location of Water Control Projects
  - ○ Dam construction
  - ○ Underground storage
- ○ Benefits of Water Control Projects - social, economic, political & environmental - (Case Studies in North America or Africa)
- ○ Adverse consequences of Water Control Projects
- ○ Effectiveness of Water Control Projects

Rural Land Resources (see pages **89 to 97**)

- ○ Organisations who "manage" the countryside (S.N.H. etc.)
- ○ Rural Management Policies (E.S.A.s, Set Aside, etc.)
- ○ National Parks
  - ○ functions and aims
  - ○ problems with popularity
  - ○ problems with land ownership
- ○ Developments in Rural Areas relating to Case Study areas e.g. The Lake District, Yorkshire Dales.
  - ○ Attraction of these areas for development
  - ○ Physical restrictions on development
  - ○ Social and economic opportunities
  - ○ Problems of increased tourism
  - ○ Possible "solutions" to "negative tourism"
- ○ Case Studies of conflict in upland areas
  - ○ Forestry in Ennerdale Valley
  - ○ Copper mining in Snowdonia
  - ○ Skiing developments in the Cairngorms

Rural Land Degradation (see pages **98 to 107**)

- ○ World distribution of principal areas of degradation
- ○ Processes and causes of degradation
- ○ Wind erosion
- ○ Water erosion
- ○ General causes of degradation with possible solutions
- ○ Case Study areas (for each area one must learn the causes and consequences (social, economic and environmental) of degradation, as well as conservation strategies and their effectiveness)
  - ○ North America - "The Dust Bowl" (Kansas, etc.) and the Tennessee Valley (TVA)
  - ○ Africa (North of the Equator) - The Sahel
  - ○ Amazon Basin or Rainforest

European Regional Inequalities (see pages **108-116**)

- ○ Indicators of regional inequality
- ○ European growth pattern (Core and Periphery, etc.)
- ○ Factors which lead to European Inequality:-
  - ○ Physical Factors
  - ○ Social Factors
  - ○ Economic Factors
  - ○ Political Factors
- ○ Inequality in the U.K.
  - ○ Reasons
  - ○ Results
  - ○ Efforts at reduction
- ○ Inequality in Italy
  - ○ Reasons
  - ○ Results
  - ○ Efforts at reduction
- ○ European Union Policies and programmes

Development & Health (see pages **117 to 126**)

- ○ Indicators for comparing countries development & health
- ○ G.N.P. / P.Q.L.I. - similarities and differences
- ○ Differences in Development -
  - ○ between countries
  - ○ within countries
- ○ Cycle of Poverty in developing countries
- ○ Disease reduction and development - links between
- ○ I.M.R. (causes and reduction in developing countries)
- ○ Contrasts between rural and urban areas
- ○ Water supply and disease
- ○ Primary Health Care (P.H.C.)
- ○ Disease Case Studies -
  - ○ Bilharzia
  - ○ Malaria
  - ○ Cholera

Remember in the Applications section

Students must choose **one** application from Group One - one from **River Basin Management, Rural Land Resources or Rural land Degradation** and **one** application from Group Two - one from **Urban Change & its Management, European Regional Inequalities or Development & Health**.

Summary list of Geographical Methods and Techniques (GMT)

The G.M.T.s are addressed through the **Core assessments**.
The list below identifies the questions which cover each G.M.T.
(**U** signifies **Unit Style Assessments** and **E** - **Exam Style Assessments**).

			Page	Question
Atmosphere	-	Interpretation of climatic maps etc.	16	1 (U)
	-	Construction/analysis of climatic graphs	16	1,2 (E)
Hydrosphere	-	Construction/analysis of hydrographs	**25**	**5 (U)**
	-	Presentation/interpretation of river flow data	**25**	**1 (E)**
Lithosphere	-	Identification/labelling of landscape features	**38**	**1, 3 (E)**
	-	Construction/interpretation of cross-sections	**37**	**3 (U)**
Biosphere	-	Analysis of soil profiles and soil survey data	**45**	**1 (U), 3 (E)**
	-	Interpretation/explanation of vegetation data	**45**	**2 (E)**
Population	-	Interpretation of population data	**53**	**2 (E)**
	-	Interpretation of migration flow diagrams	**53**	**1 (E)**
Rural Geography	-	Analysis of land use data	**60**	**2 (U)**
	-	Analysis of farm survey results	**60**	**2 (E)**
	-	Annotation/analysis of field sketches/photographs	**60**	**2 (U)**
Industrial Geography	-	Annotation/analysis of field sketches/photographs	**68**	**2 (U)**
	-	Analysis of industrial/employment survey results	**68**	**2(E)**
Urban Geography	-	Analysis of land use maps etc.	**80**	**3 (E)**
	-	Annotation/analysis of field sketches and photographs of urban landscapes.	**80**	**2 (U)**

Assessments

- Practice assessment questions are a vital part of any revision programme.
- Sample questions are found at the end of each section in this revision book.
- **Unit** style assessments are each worth **10 marks** for the **Core** and **20 marks** for the **Applications.**
- **Exam** style assessments are worth between **4** and **6** marks for the **Core** and **25 marks** for the **Applications**.

Revision cards

Make yourself **Revision Cards** such as the ones below and overleaf as a quick reference guide for all aspects of NQ Higher Geography. These are a great way to pep up your revision and make it more interesting for you to do, learn from and carry about with you as you prepare to ***PASS Higher Geography !*** Cut the revision cards out once you have made your own........

Swallow Hole (or Sinkhole) - cross-section

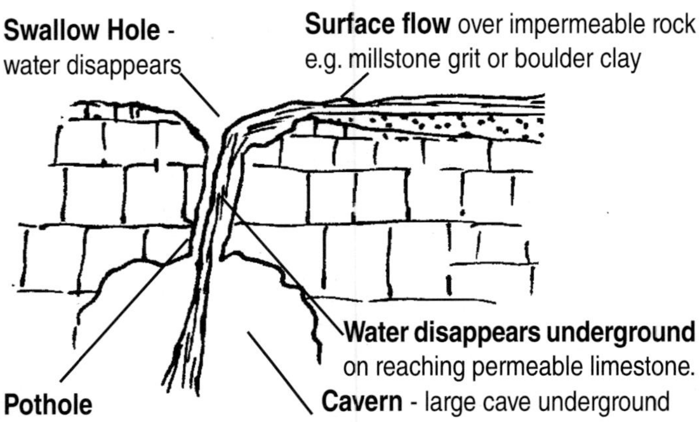

Cave features in Limestone

Calcium Bicarbonate may convert back into $CaCO_3$ when it drips from a cave ceiling over a long period. This 'reformed' limestone produces..........

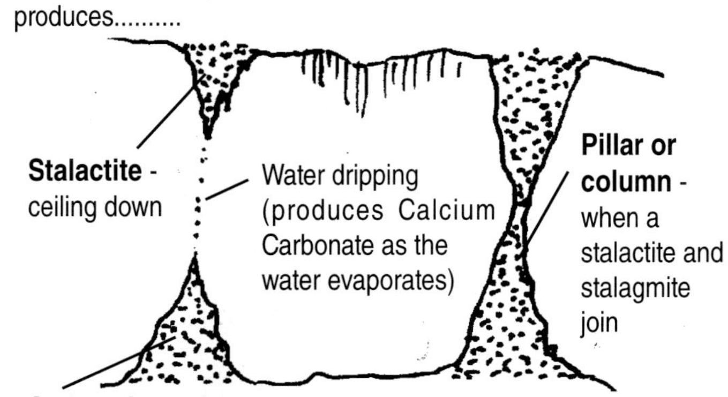

Stream Hydrographs

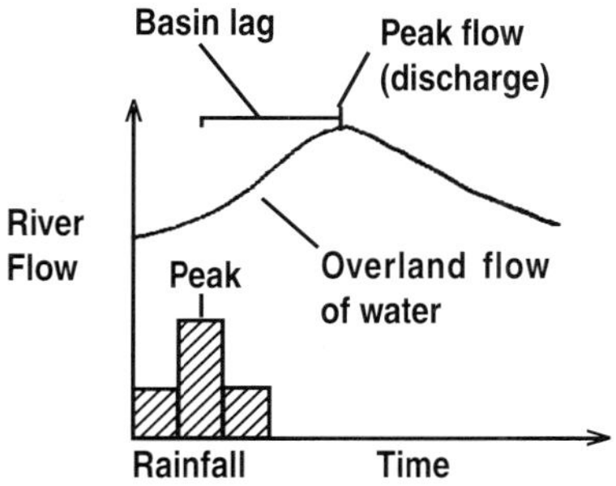

(a) Vegetated area

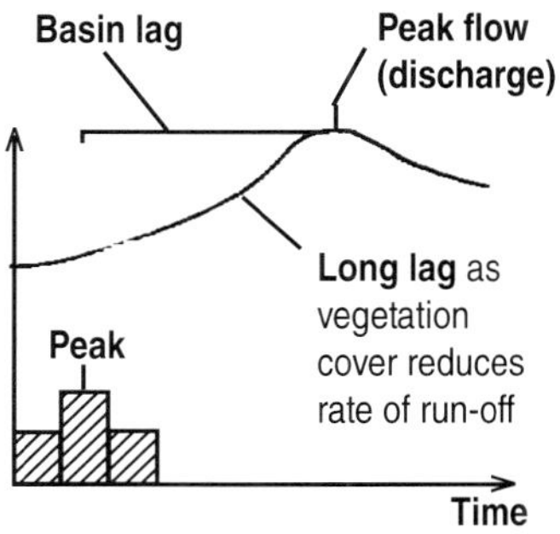

(b) Barren Area (sparse veg.)

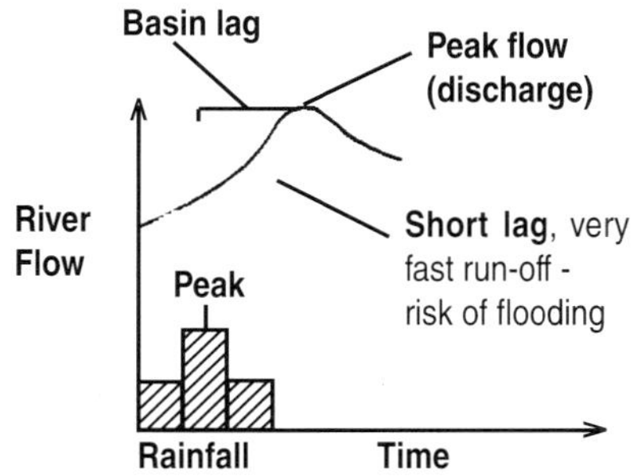

Basin lag = the time it takes for rainfall to reach the main river

Formation of River Features
Meanders

(a) A river begins to twist as differences in water depth cause variations in water flow

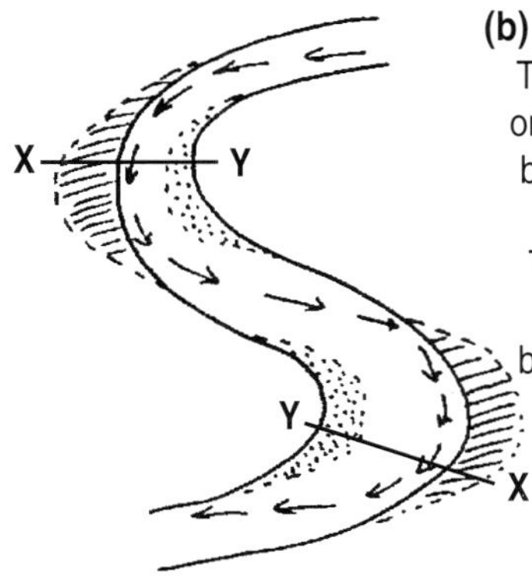

(b) The water flows more quickly on the concave outside of the bend causing erosion to take place at **X**. The water flows more slowly on the convex inside of the bend causing deposition at **Y**. Slowly the meander becomes more accentuated (sharper).

(c) Cross-section through bend **X - Y**

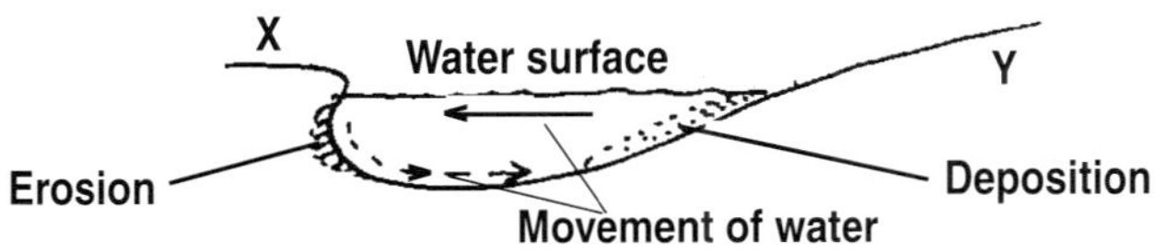

Ox-bow lakes

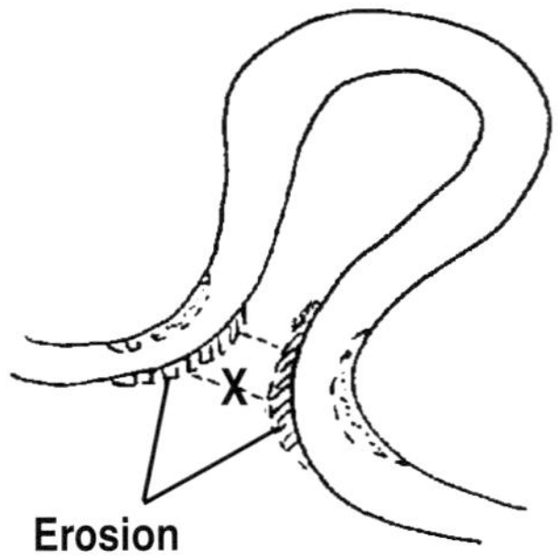

1. As erosion takes place on concave banks of a meander, a sudden **flood** may cause the river to break through at **X**.

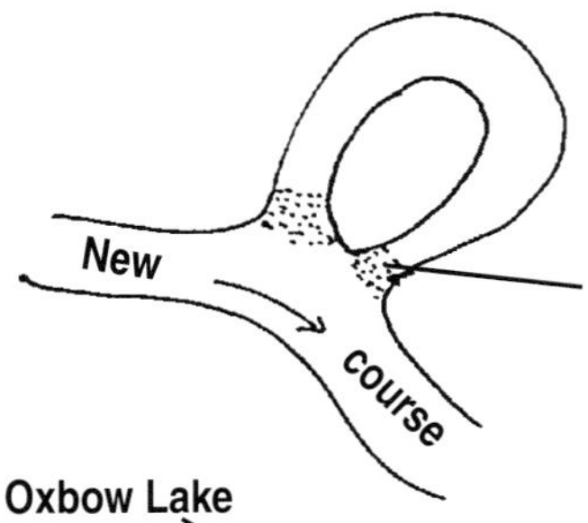

2. As the river begins to follow a new course, the meander is slowly 'cut-off' by **deposition**.

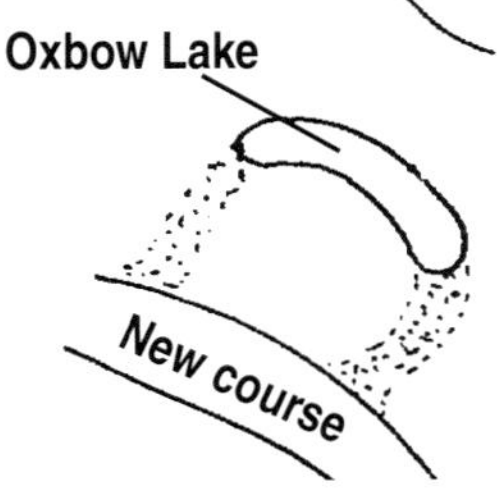

3. Eventually the old course is completely sealed off. The **Oxbow Lake** is left as a remnant of the former course.

Levees - cross sections

(a) During **spate** or **flood** - river overflows its banks - water flows slowly over the banks causing **deposition** at **X**.

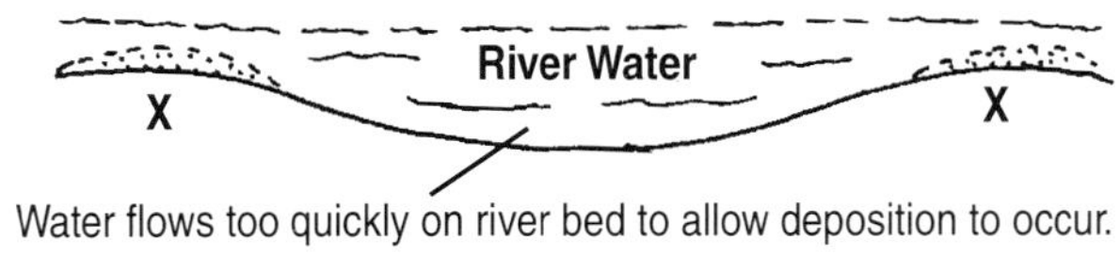

(b) Normal river flow (not in flood)

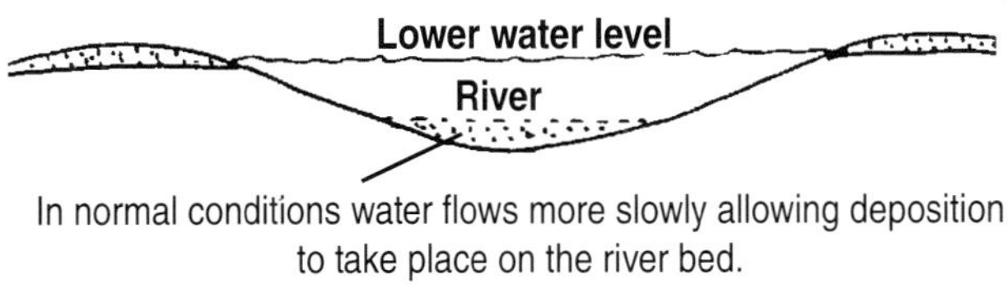

(c) Further flooding

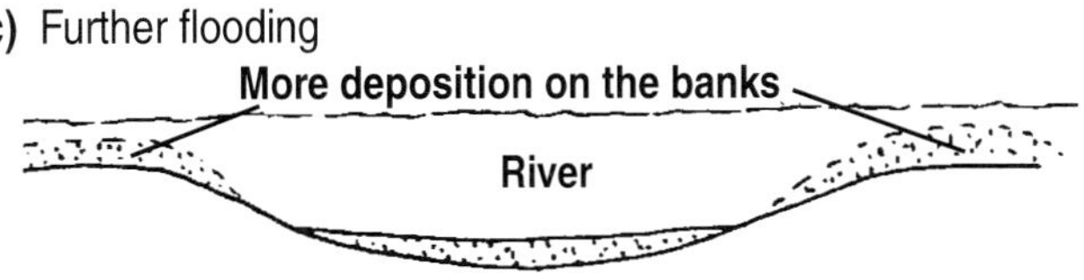

(d) After repeated flooding

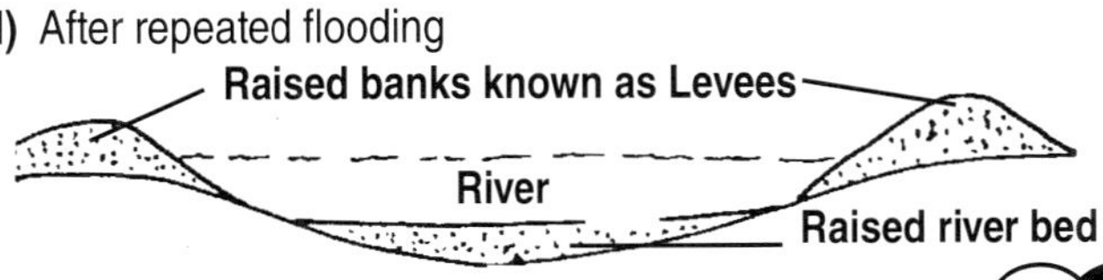

Flood Plain

(a) The valley is widened by **lateral erosion** as meanders migrate downstream.
(b) **Deposition** on the convex banks of meanders slowly fills up the valley floor.
(c) During **flooding** the river overflows and deposits fine mud across the valley floor - forming a flat flood plain.

Cross - section

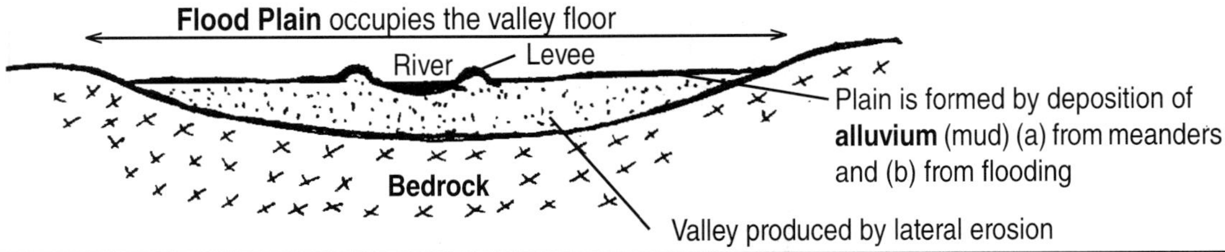

River Terraces

May be formed after a river is **rejuvenated** (given new life) e.g. if the land is uplifted (e.g. after **isostatic readjustment***) a river will have increased energy to erode downwards. As downhill erosion proceeds quickly the former flood plain is left as a **river terrace**. If uplift takes place in stages, then a series of terraces are formed.

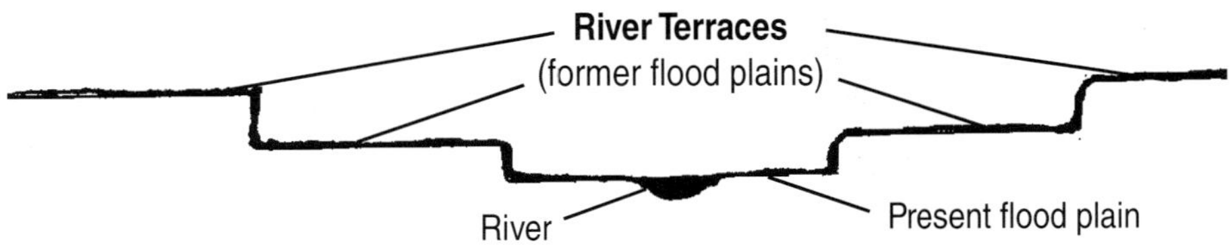

Isostatic readjustment - when the land rose as the weight of ice was removed (melted) at the end of the Ice Age

Waterfalls

Waterfalls are often formed when a layer of hard rock (more resistant to erosion) lies across a river's course. The soft rock on the downstream side is more quickly eroded than the hard rock. Beneath the waterfall the force of rapidly descending water produces a plunge pool.

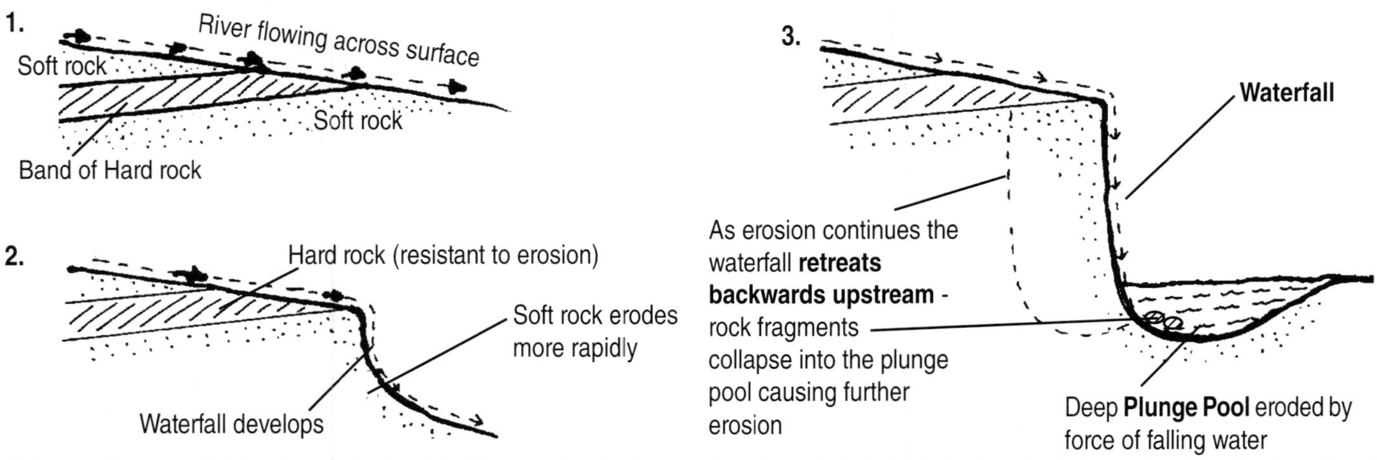

Revision cards for various Lithosphere processes -

Pyramidal Peak

- when 3 or 4 glaciers erode backwards to a central point (similar to an arete)

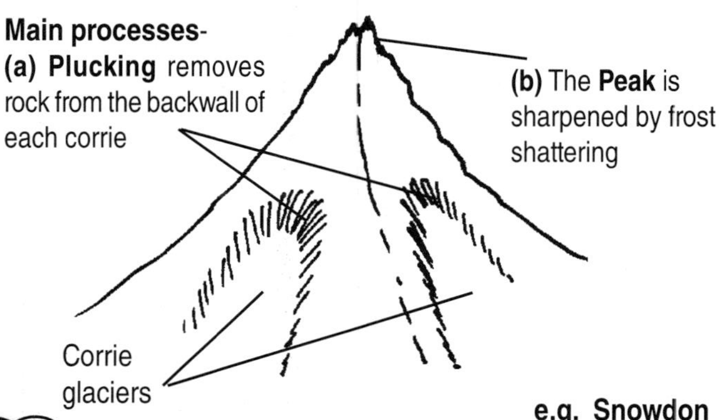

Arete

formed by two glaciers retreating backwards (often between two corries)

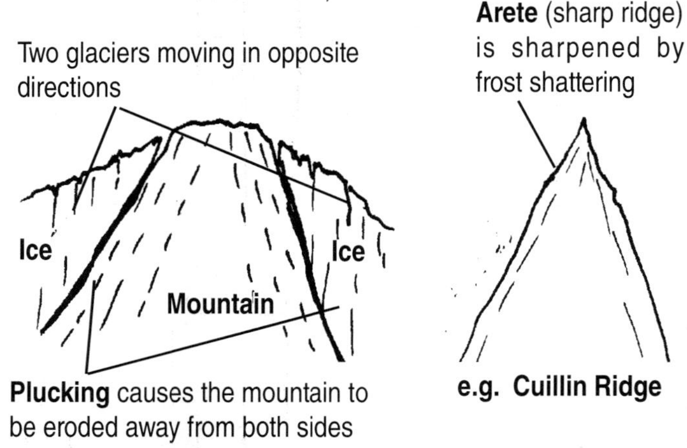

Corrie formation - cross section

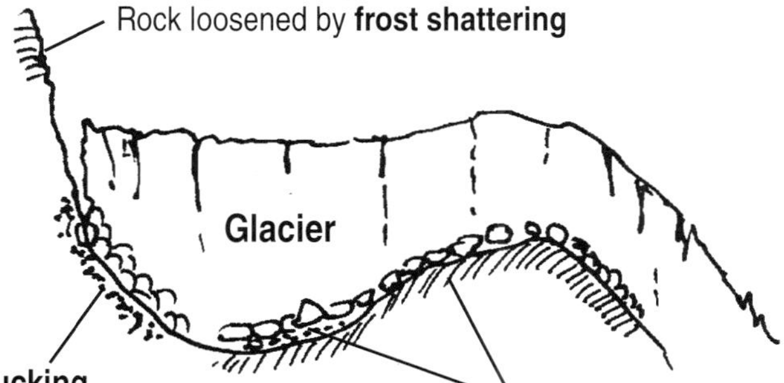

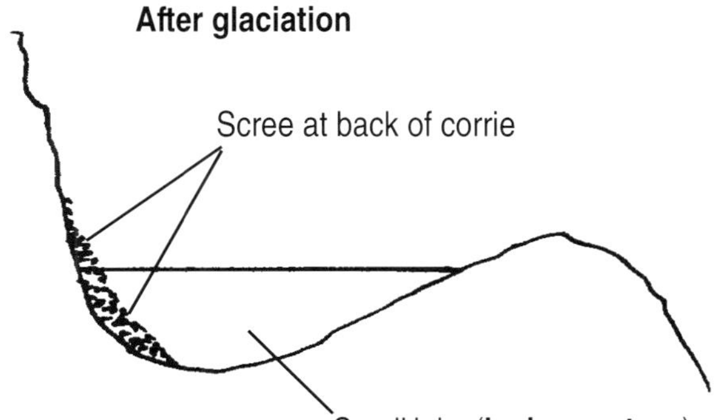

Roche Moutonnee

Smooth side of rock is produced by **abrasion**(i.e. rock is ground away by rocks embedded in the ice)

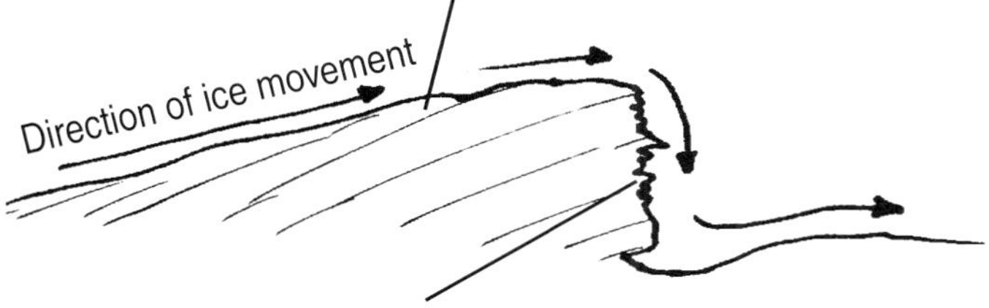

Rocks are **plucked** from the '**leeward**' side of the rock producing an irregular surface

Hanging valley and Alluvial Fan

Formation - the depth of ice is much greater in the main valley - as a result the glacier erodes to a much lower level - leaving the tributary glacier 'hanging' up above.

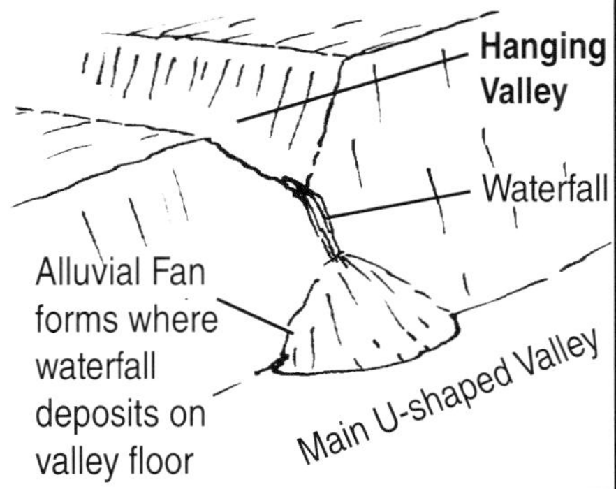

Terminal Moraine

forms at the glacier snout when the ice, stationary for a long period, produces a long ridge which marks the edge of the ice and is composed of unsorted, angular rock fragments abraded and carried along by the glacier.

1.

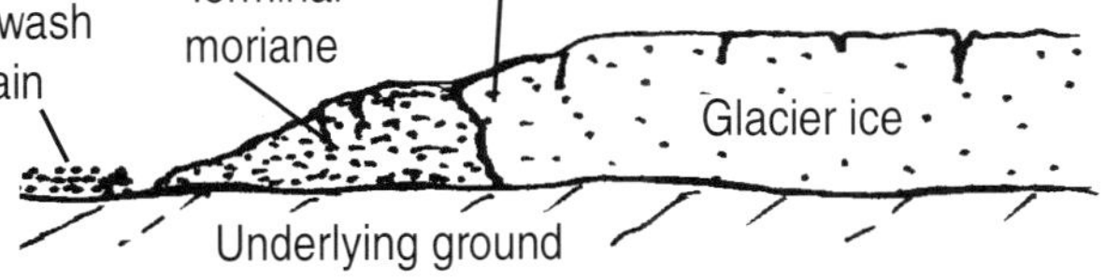

2. After glaciation

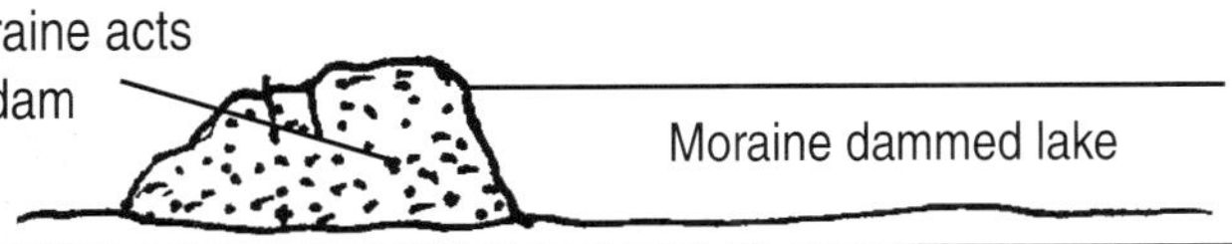

Glacial Erratic (perched block)

A large block of rock transported by the glacier and later deposited in a different location when the ice melts

1.

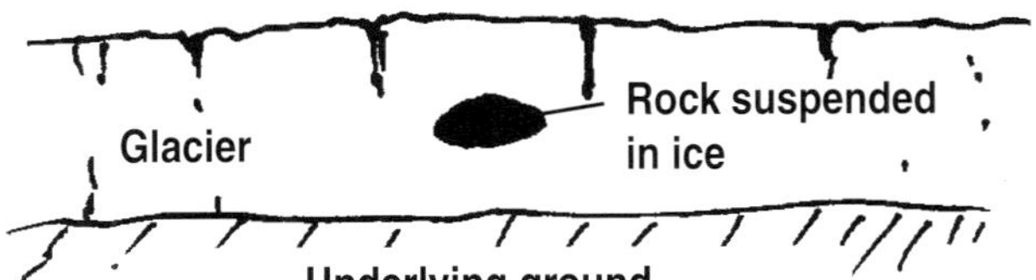

2.

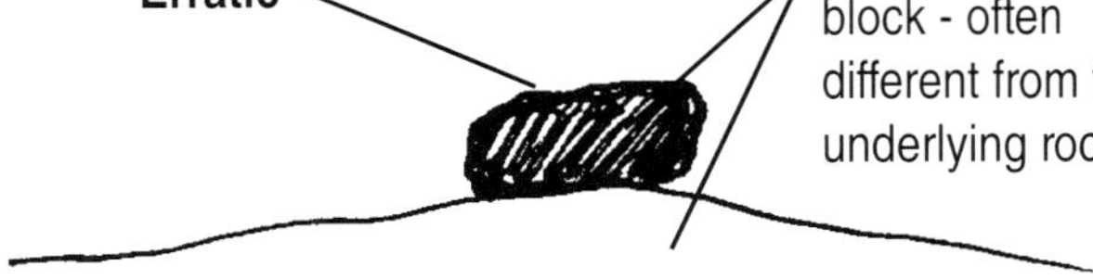

Drumlins

Oval shaped hills - formed and deposited under a moving ice sheet - consist of **unsorted ground moraine** (boulder clays) abraded by the ice. The shape of drumlins is determined by the moving ice, i.e. they are elongated in the direction of the ice movement.

Aerial view

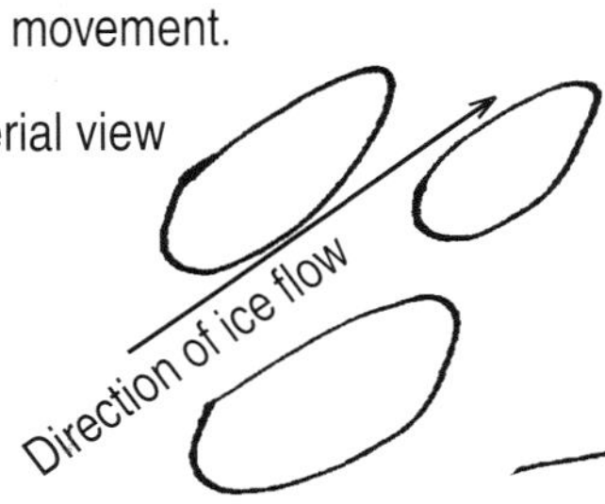

Side view

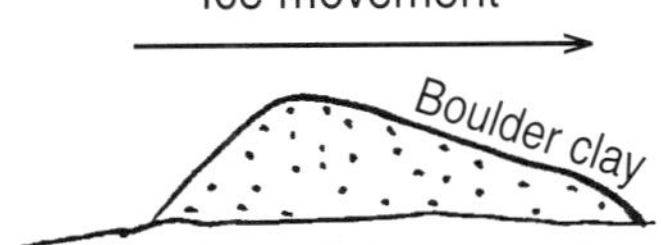

Make your own Revision Cards for --------

- **Limestone pavement**
- **Rockfalls**
- **Landslides & Mudflows**
- **Soil Creep**
- **Soil formation**
- **the Atmosphere**
- **Solar Radiation**
- **Atmospheric Circulation**
- **ITCZ**
- **Courses of a river**
- **Weathering**
- **Glaciated Upland scenery**
- **Glaciokarst scenery**
- **Scarp & vale scenery**
- **Podzols, Brown Earths**
- **Psammoseres**
- **Population structure**
- **Migration**
- **Agricultural systems**
- **Industrial location factors**
- **Models of urban structure**
- **Megacity model**

use pages *134 & 135 ....*

16. Index

Make your own Revision Cards - use the following boxes below and on page 135 to start you off

Formation of a Limestone Pavement

Rockfalls

Landslides and Mudflows

Soil creep

Soil formation - Pedocal and Pedalfer

Soil Profiles - Podsol and Brown Earth soils

The Atmosphere

Solar Radiation system

Atmospheric Circulation

ITCZ

Ocean Currents

Weathering